Shojo Beat

Tail of the Moon

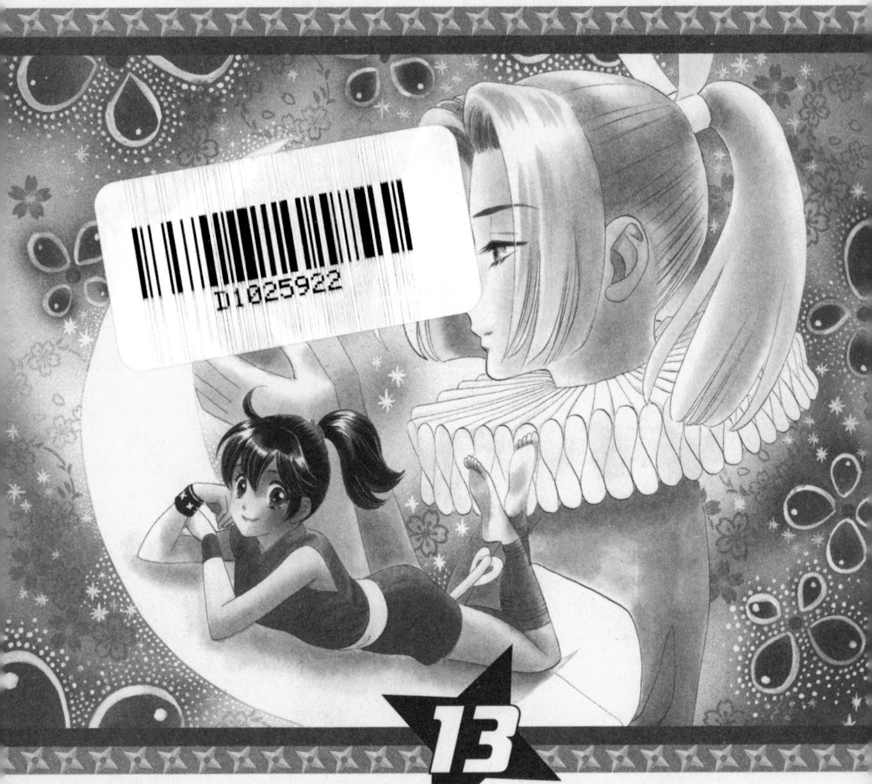

13

Story & Art by

Rinko Ueda

Volume 13

CONTENTS

Story Thus Far...

It is the Era of the Warring States. With the success of preventing Oda Nobunaga's attack on Iga, Usagi finally becomes a qualified ninja. At long last, she is able to marry Hanzo. But on the night of the wedding, Nobunaga's army attacks the village! After leading Usagi and Mamezo to a hiding place in the forest, Hanzo heads back to face the army on his own. A few days later, Usagi returns to the village and is shocked to find Iga destroyed. She also hears that Hanzo is dead.

One year later, Usagi is working under Tokugawa Ieyasu. Yukimaru, who has returned from the West, takes Usagi with him to Iga for an investigation. But as they get closer to Iga, Usagi's health begins to deteriorate. She has been unable to accept the truth of what happened in Iga. With the warm support of Yukimaru and the others, however, Usagi is finally able to gather the strength to carry on.

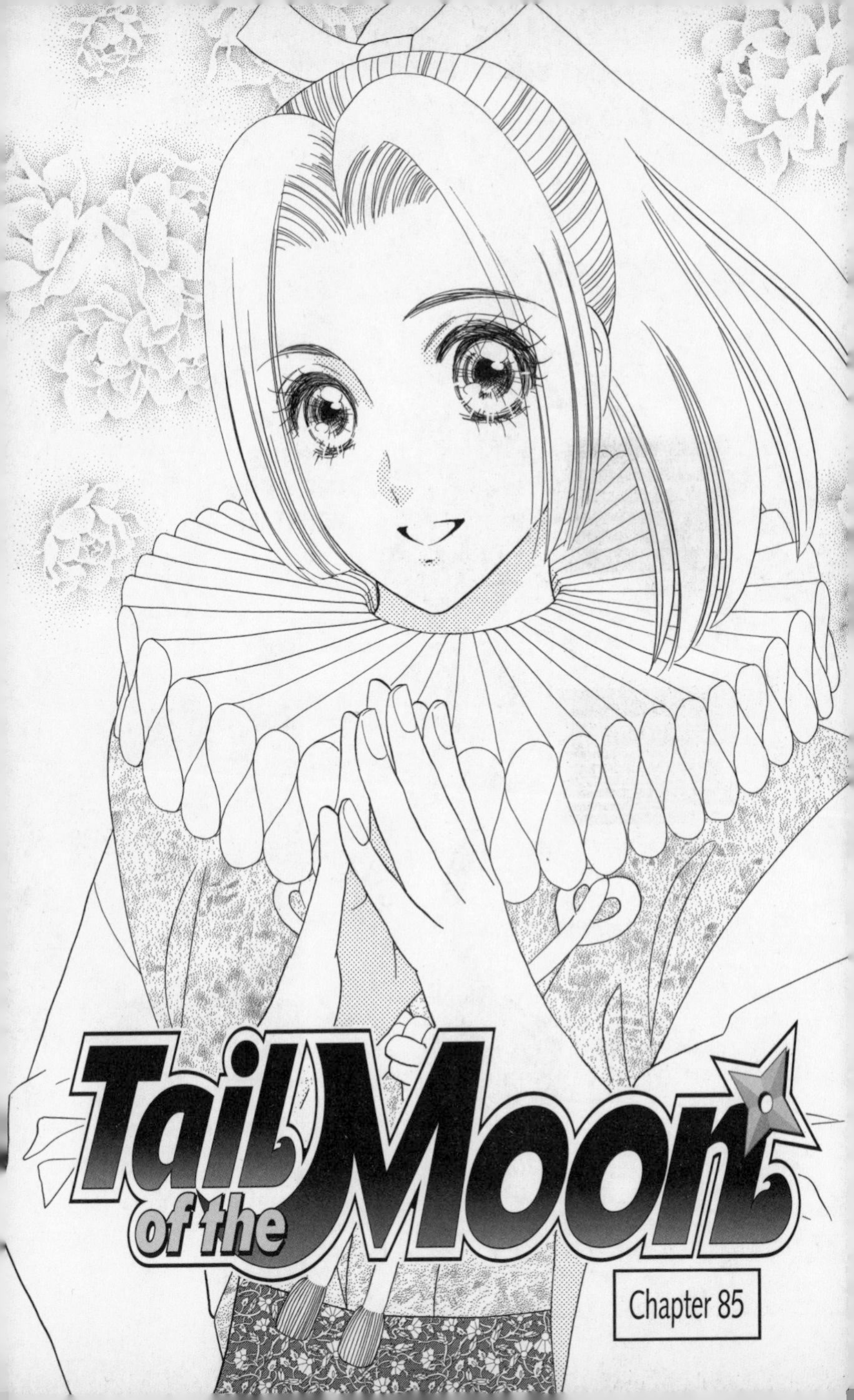
Tail of the Moon
Chapter 85

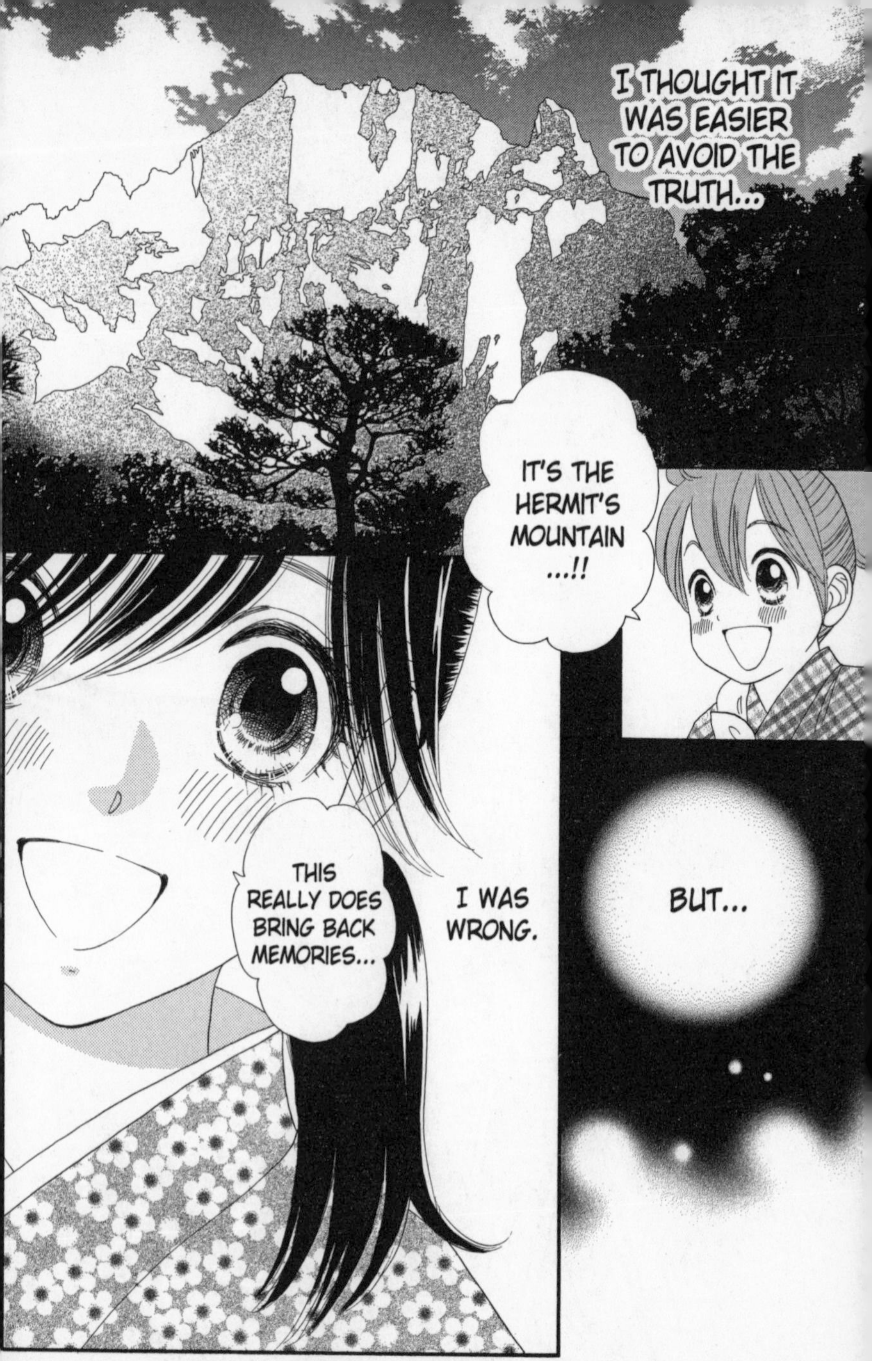
I THOUGHT IT WAS EASIER TO AVOID THE TRUTH...
IT'S THE HERMIT'S MOUNTAIN ...!!
BUT...
I WAS WRONG.
THIS REALLY DOES BRING BACK MEMORIES...

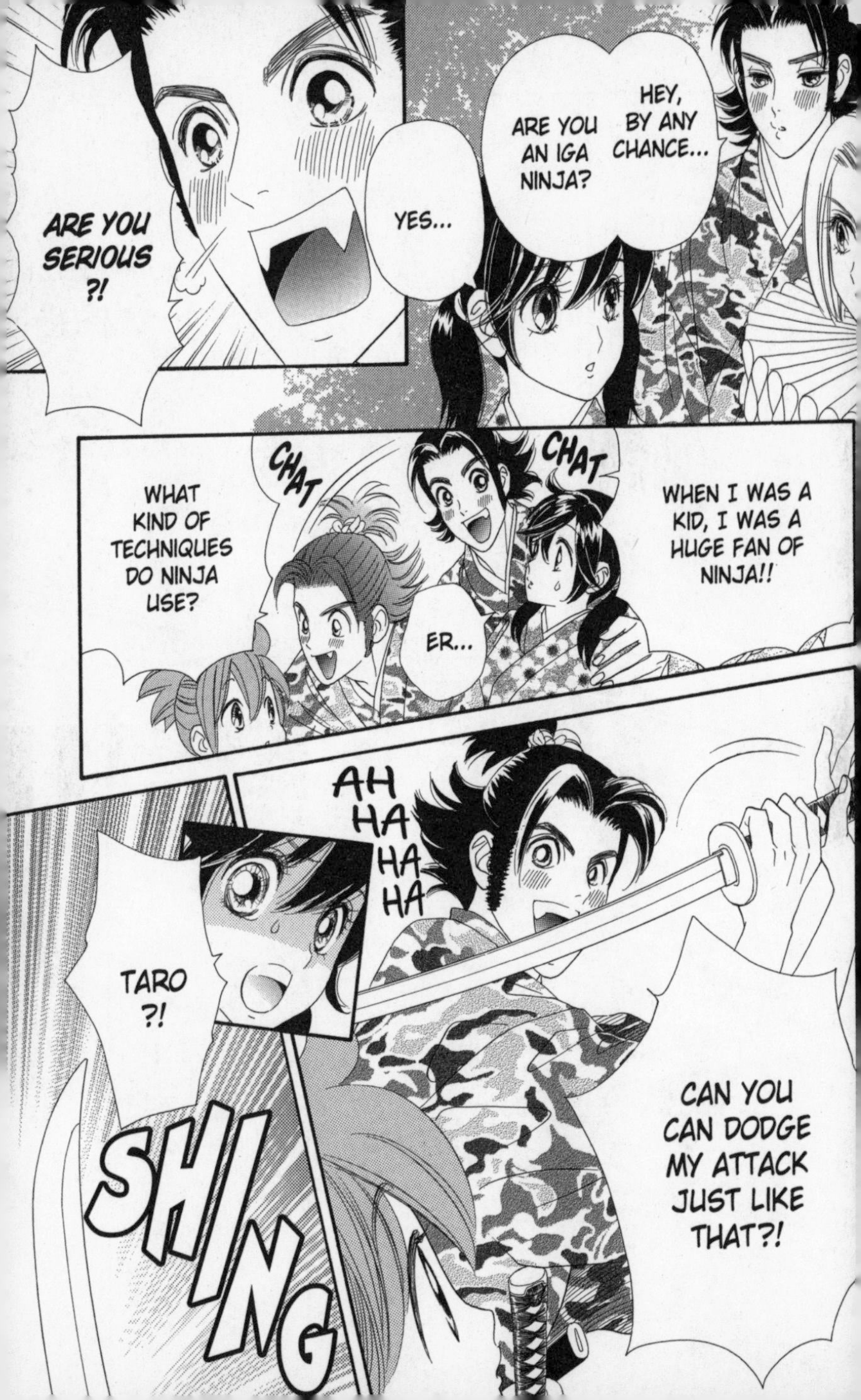

HEY, BY ANY CHANCE...
ARE YOU AN IGA NINJA?
YES...
ARE YOU SERIOUS ?!
CHAT
WHEN I WAS A KID, I WAS A HUGE FAN OF NINJA!!
CHAT
WHAT KIND OF TECHNIQUES DO NINJA USE?
ER...
AH HA HA HA
CAN YOU CAN DODGE MY ATTACK JUST LIKE THAT?!
TARO ?!
SHING

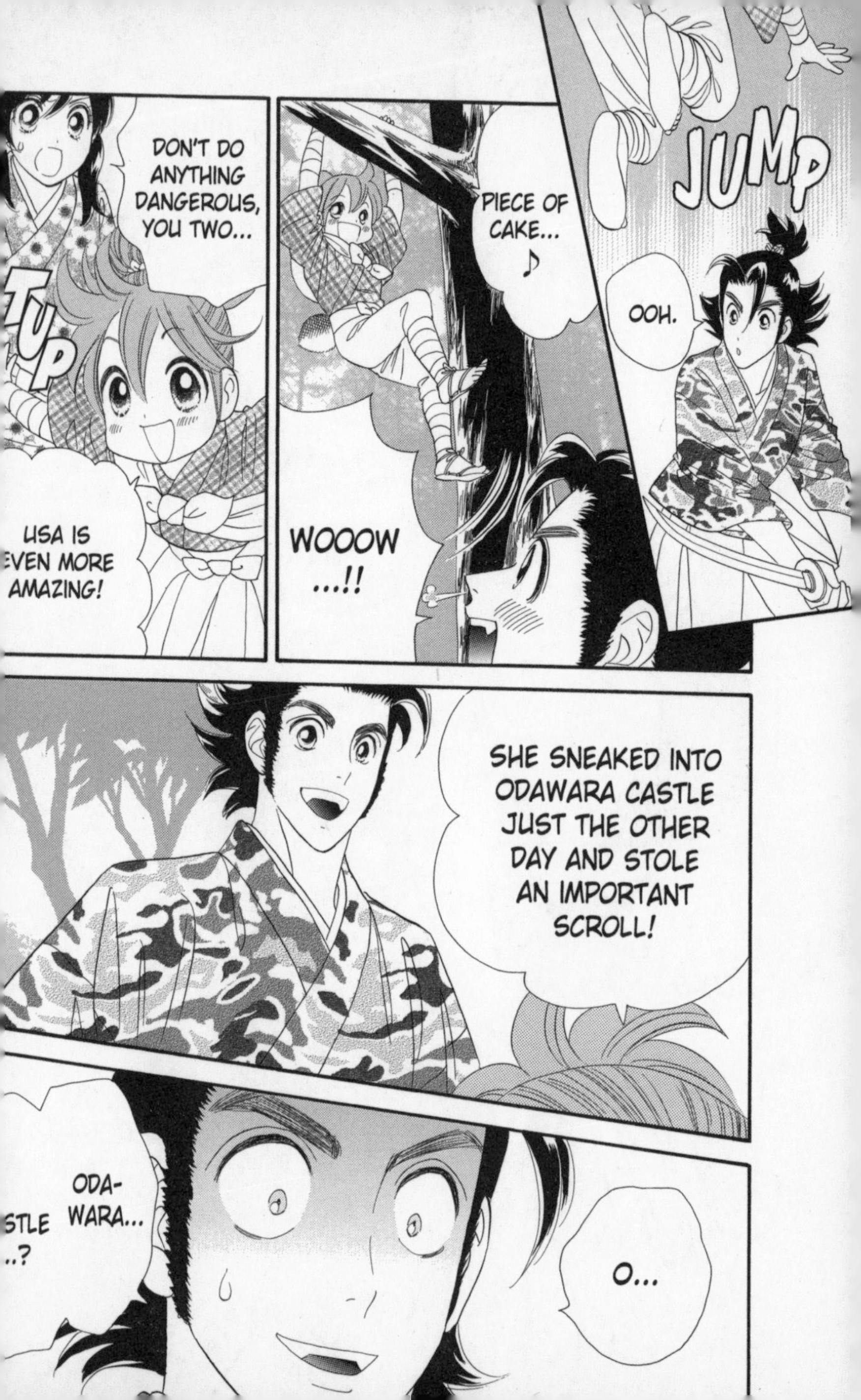
JUMP
OOH.
PIECE OF CAKE... ♪
WOOOW ...!!
DON'T DO ANYTHING DANGEROUS, YOU TWO...
TUP
USA IS EVEN MORE AMAZING!
SHE SNEAKED INTO ODAWARA CASTLE JUST THE OTHER DAY AND STOLE AN IMPORTANT SCROLL!
O...
ODA-WARA...
STLE ..?

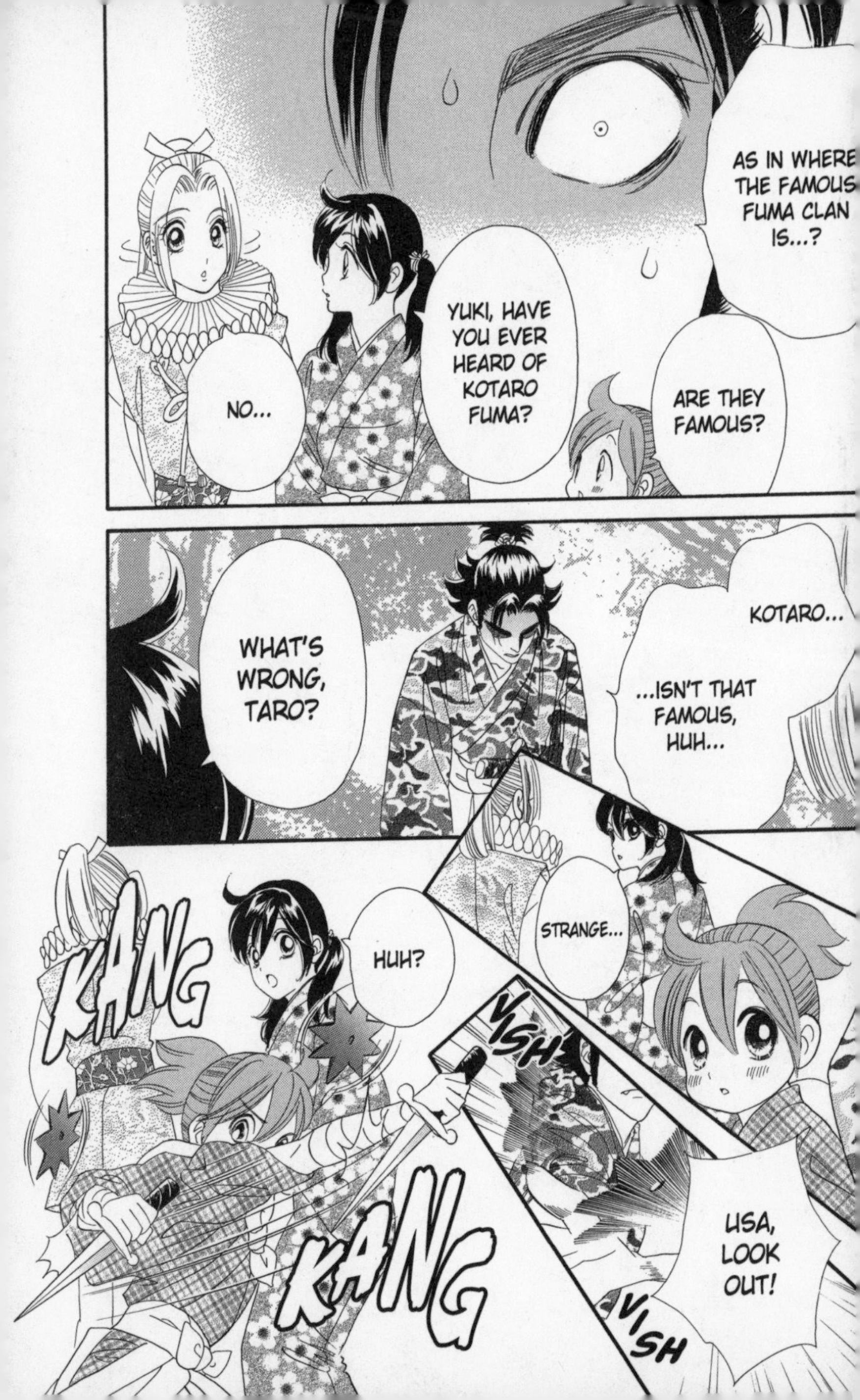
AS IN WHERE THE FAMOUS FUMA CLAN IS...?
ARE THEY FAMOUS?
YUKI, HAVE YOU EVER HEARD OF KOTARO FUMA?
NO...
KOTARO...
...ISN'T THAT FAMOUS, HUH...
WHAT'S WRONG, TARO?
STRANGE...
VISH
USA, LOOK OUT!
VISH
HUH?
KANG
KANG

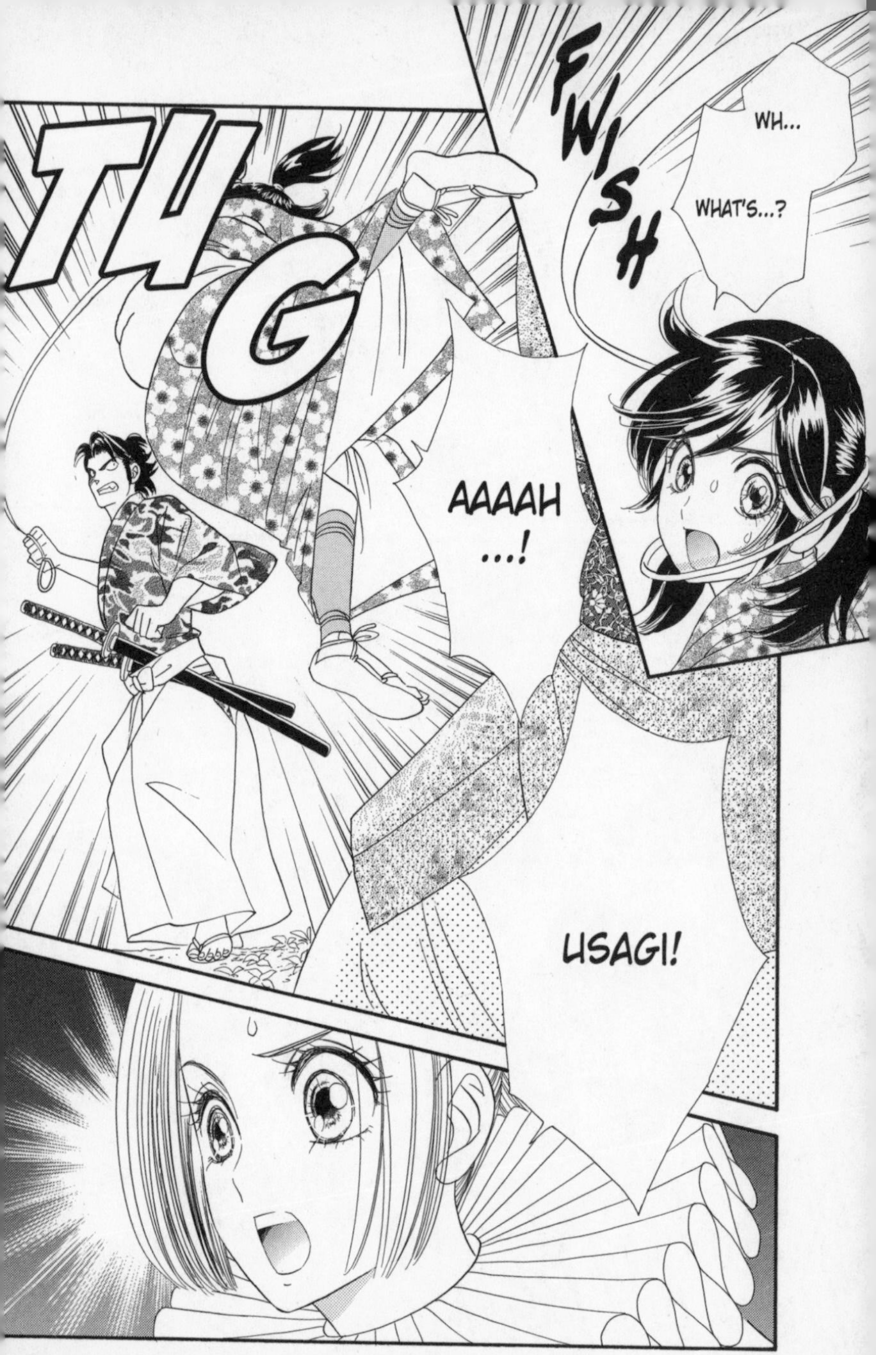
FWISH
WH...
WHAT'S...?
THG
AAAAH ...!
USAGI!

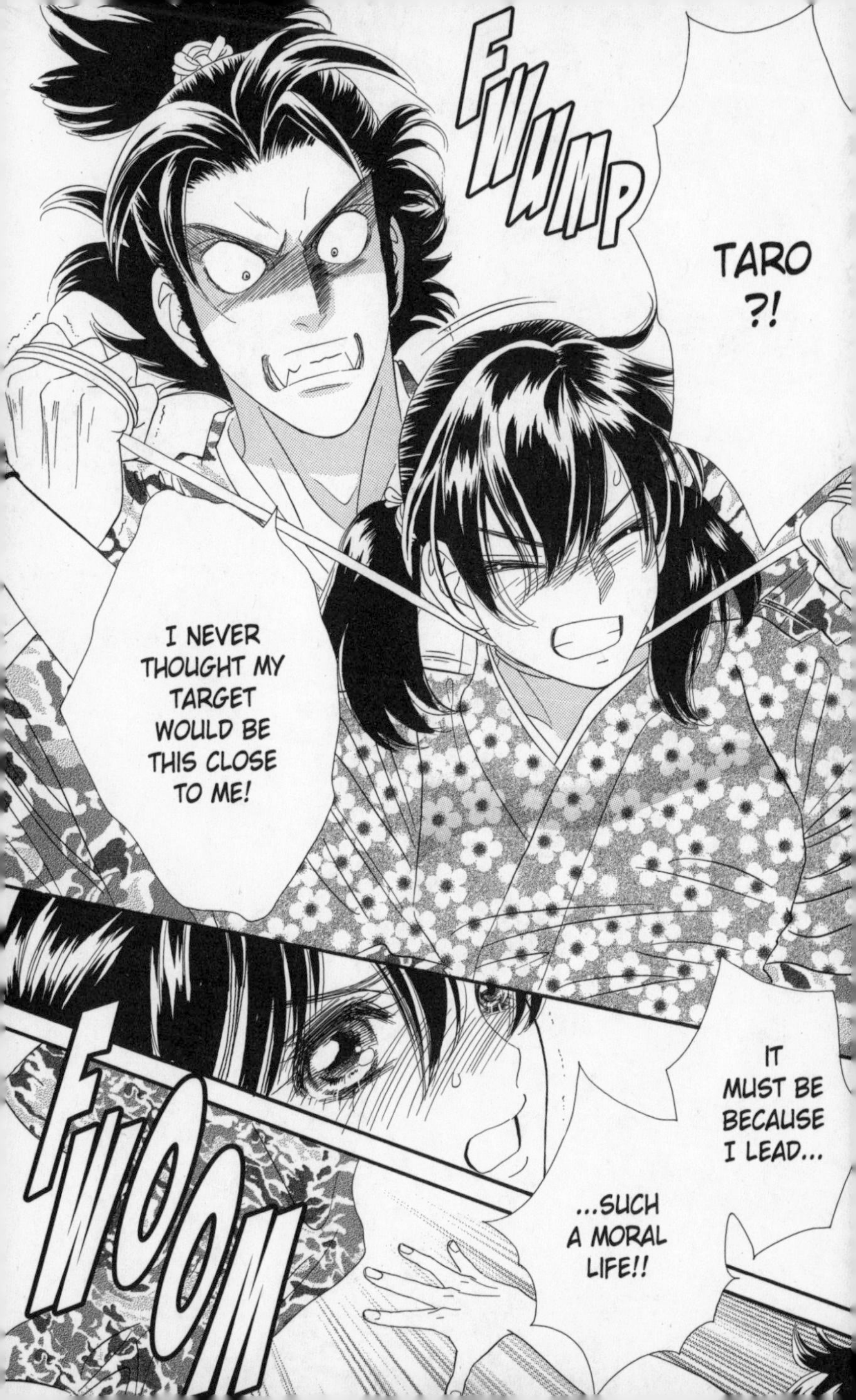
TARO ?!
FWUMP
I NEVER THOUGHT MY TARGET WOULD BE THIS CLOSE TO ME!
IT MUST BE BECAUSE I LEAD...
...SUCH A MORAL LIFE!!
FROOM

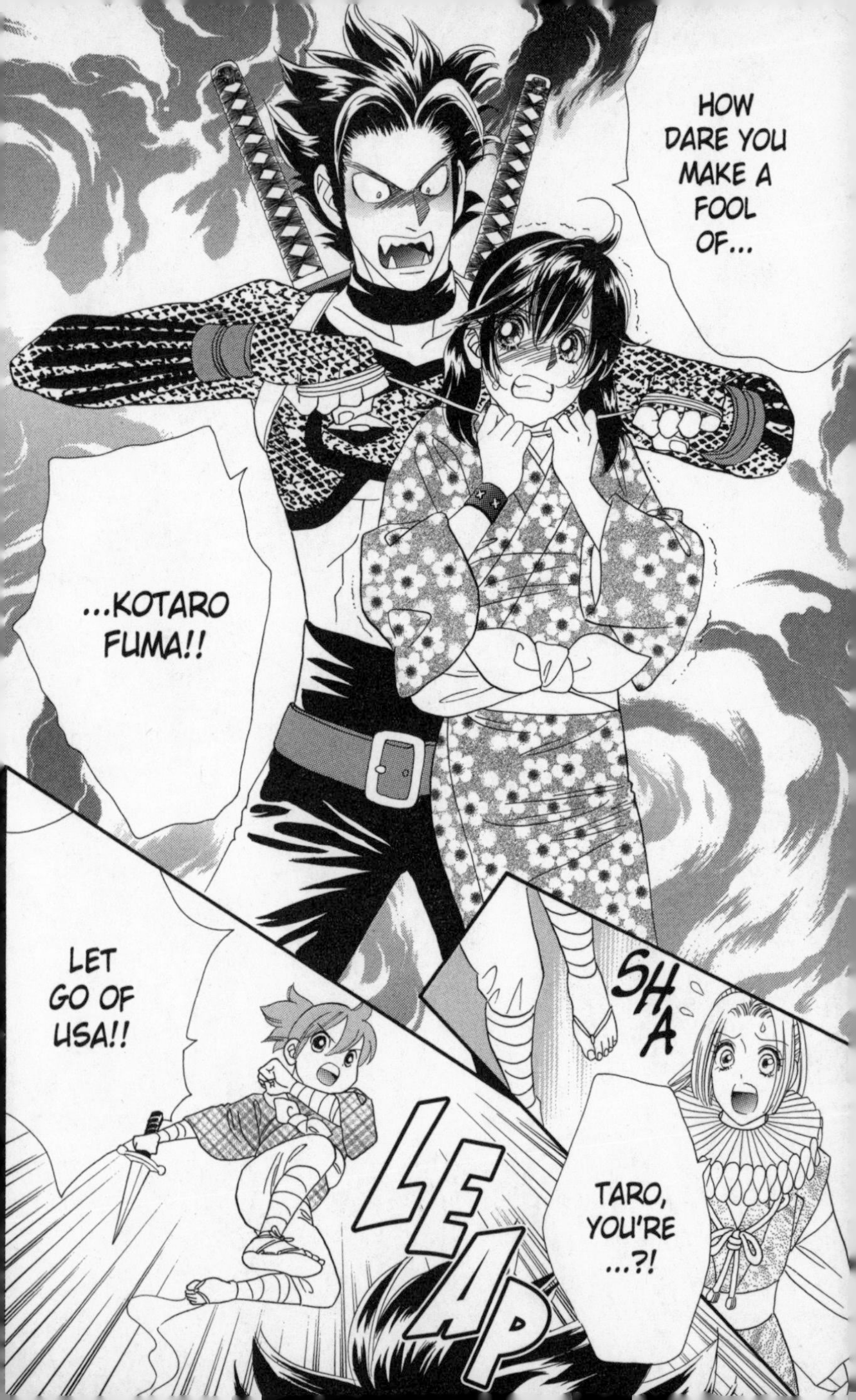
HOW DARE YOU MAKE A FOOL OF...
...KOTARO FUMA!!
SHA
TARO, YOU'RE ...?!
LET GO OF USA!!
LEAP

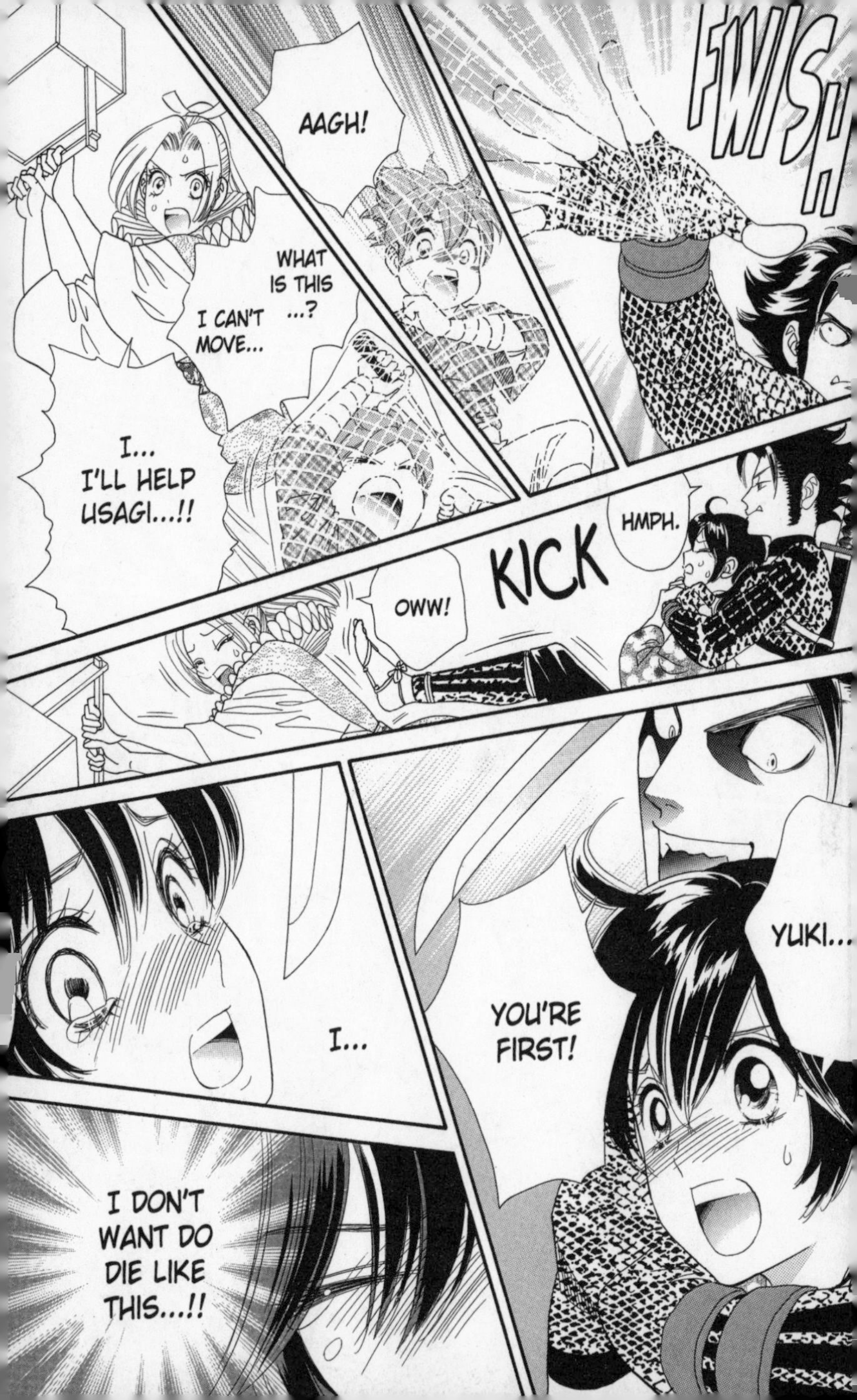
FWISH
AAGH!
WHAT IS THIS ...?
I CAN'T MOVE...
I... I'LL HELP USAGI...!!
HMPH.
KICK
OWW!
YUKI...
YOU'RE FIRST!
I...
I DON'T WANT DO DIE LIKE THIS...!!

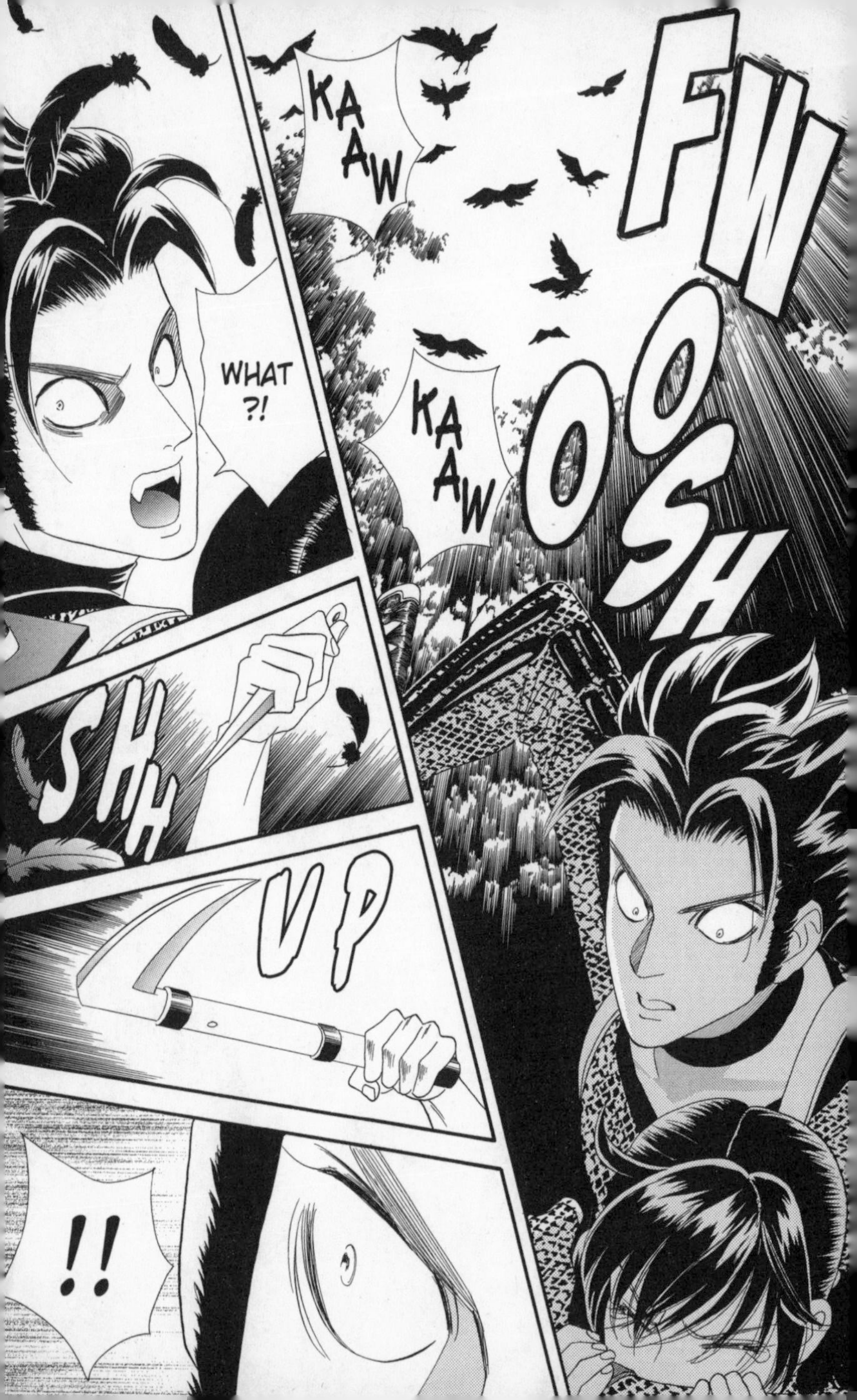
FWOOSH
KAAW
KAAW
WHAT ?!
SHH
VUP
!!

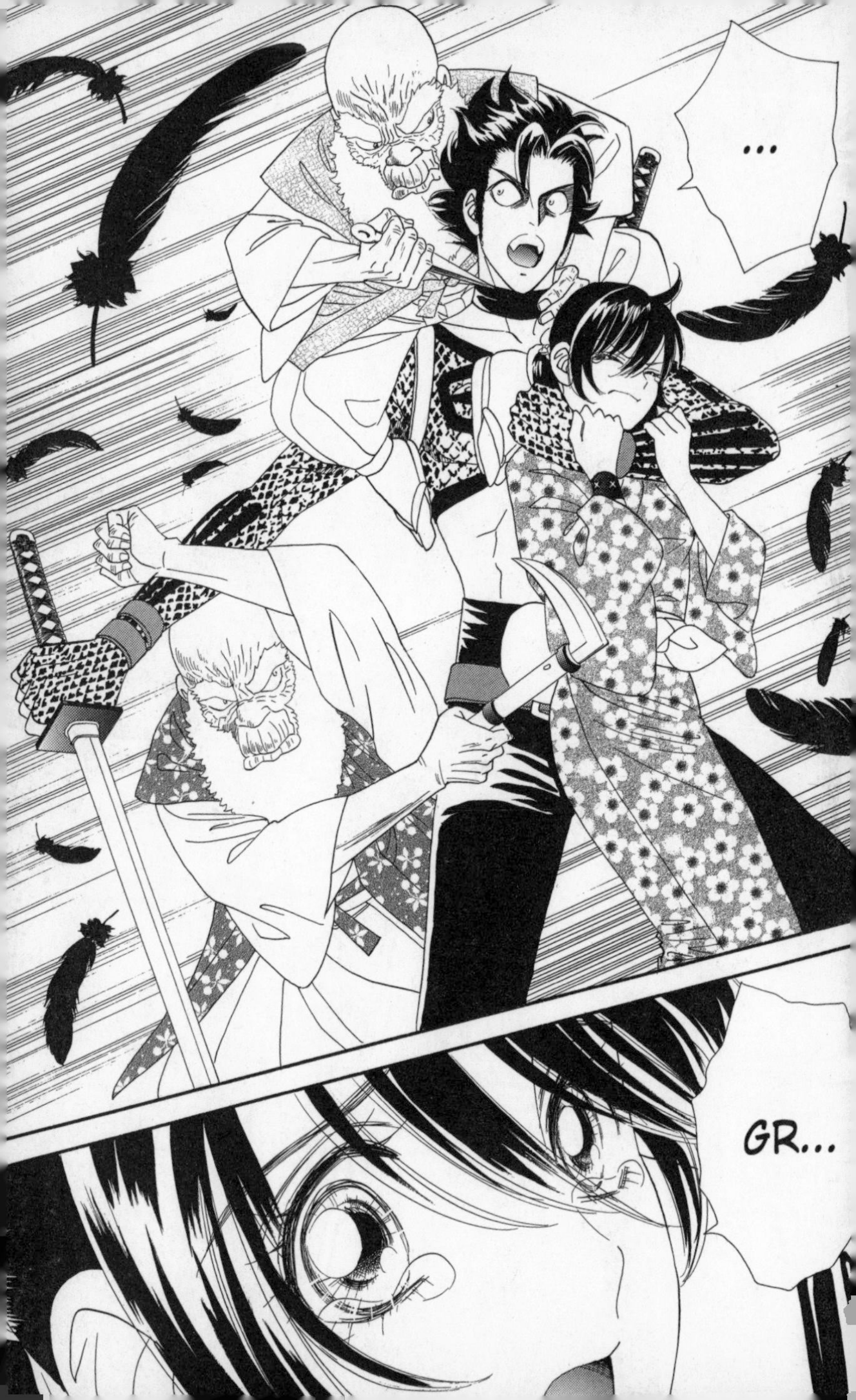
...
GR...

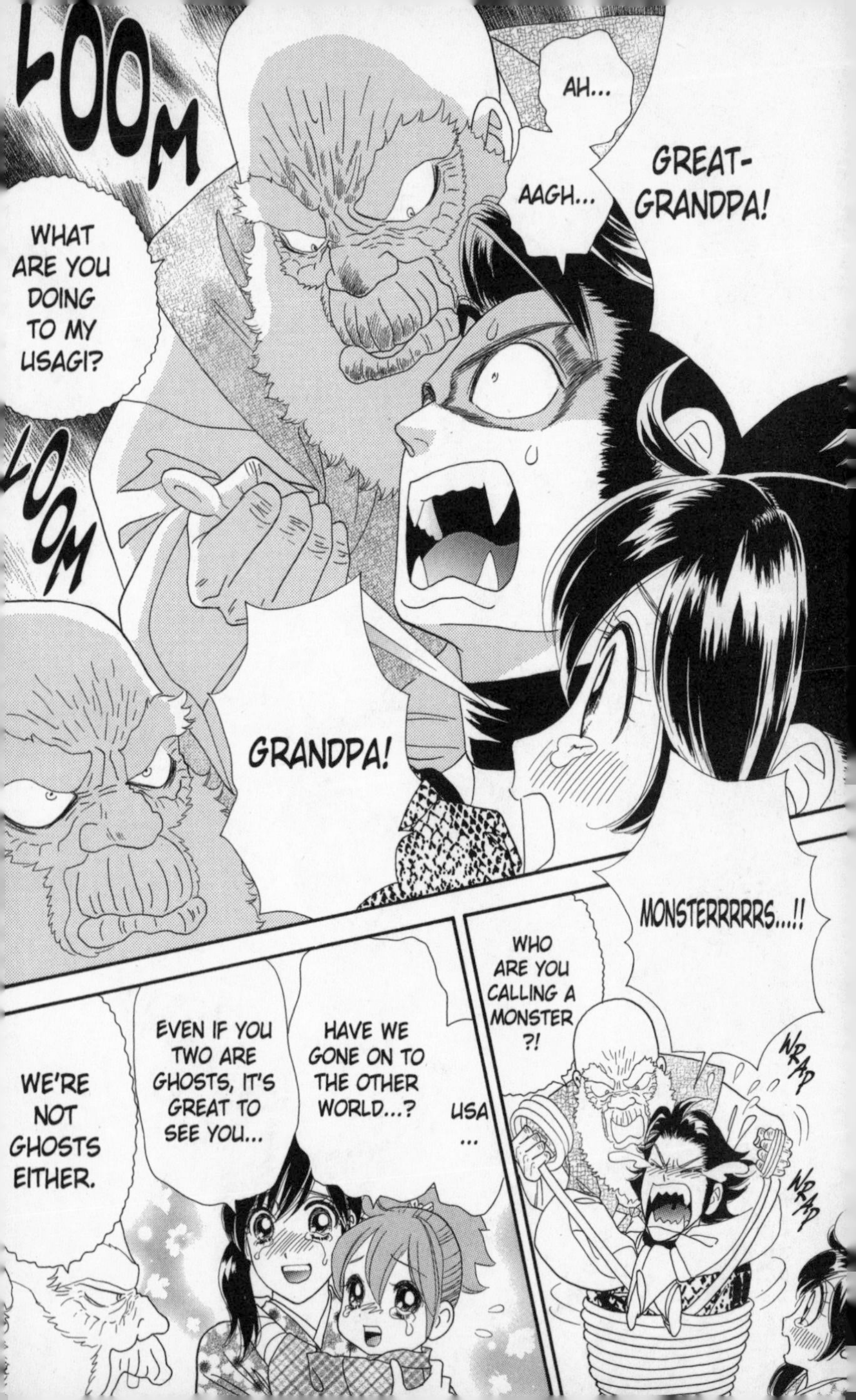
AH...
GREAT-GRANDPA!
AAGH...
LOOM
WHAT ARE YOU DOING TO MY USAGI?
LOOM
GRANDPA!
MONSTERRRRS...!!
WHO ARE YOU CALLING A MONSTER?!
WRAP
WRAP
USA...
HAVE WE GONE ON TO THE OTHER WORLD...?
EVEN IF YOU TWO ARE GHOSTS, IT'S GREAT TO SEE YOU...
WE'RE NOT GHOSTS EITHER.

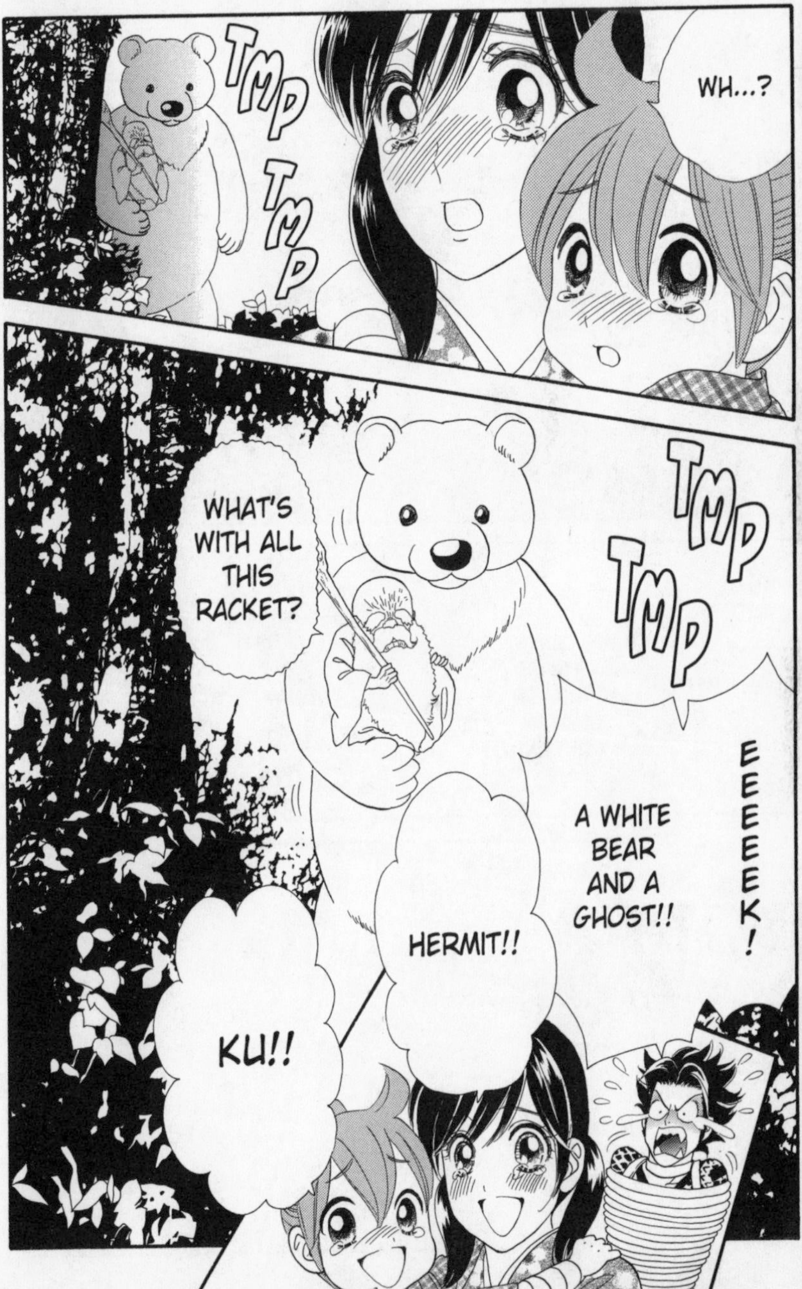
WH...?
TMP TMP
TMP TMP
WHAT'S WITH ALL THIS RACKET?
EEEEEK!
A WHITE BEAR AND A GHOST!!
HERMIT!!
KU!!

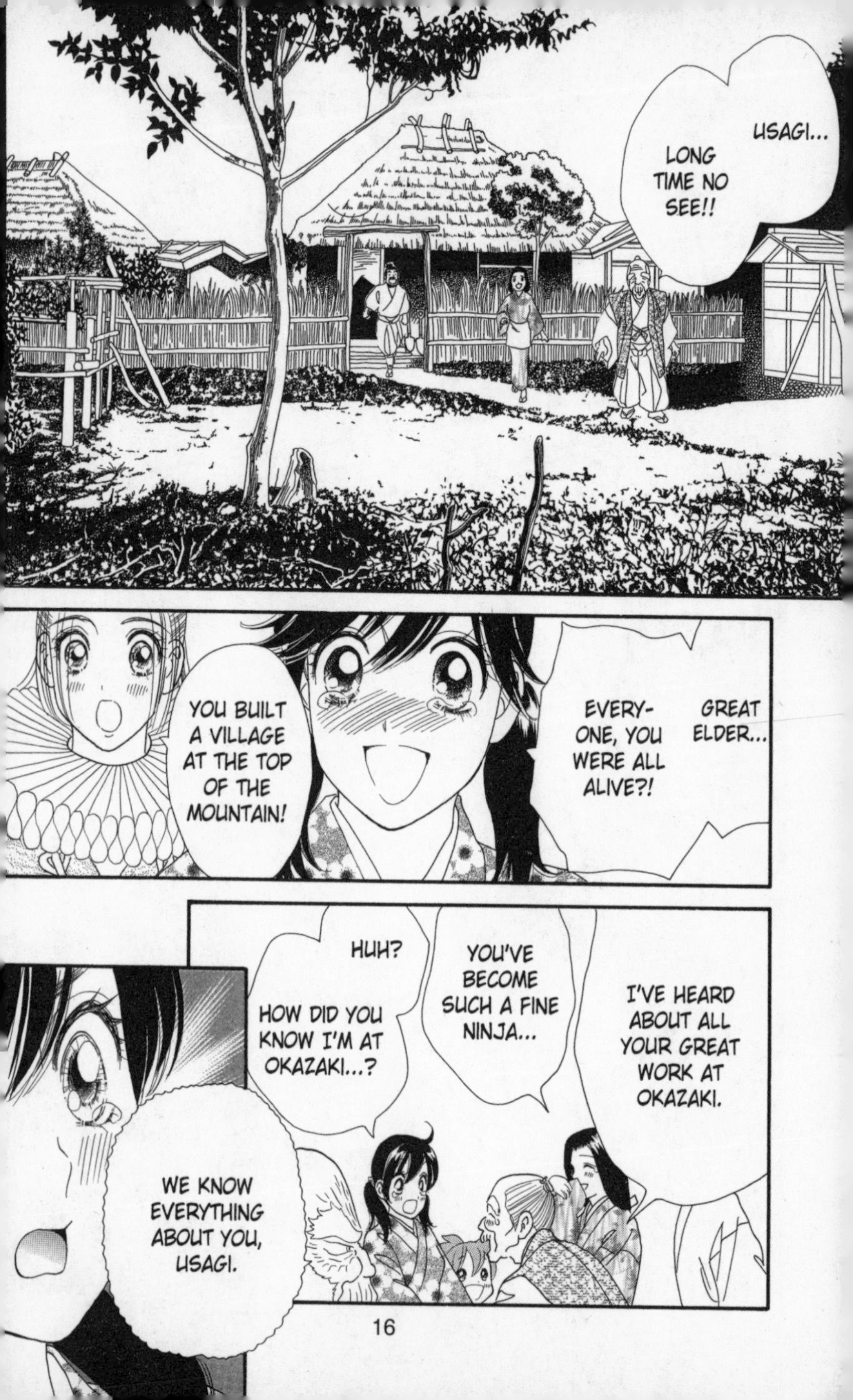
USAGI...
LONG TIME NO SEE!!
GREAT ELDER...
EVERY-ONE, YOU WERE ALL ALIVE?!
YOU BUILT A VILLAGE AT THE TOP OF THE MOUNTAIN!
I'VE HEARD ABOUT ALL YOUR GREAT WORK AT OKAZAKI.
YOU'VE BECOME SUCH A FINE NINJA...
HUH?
HOW DID YOU KNOW I'M AT OKAZAKI...?
WE KNOW EVERYTHING ABOUT YOU, USAGI.

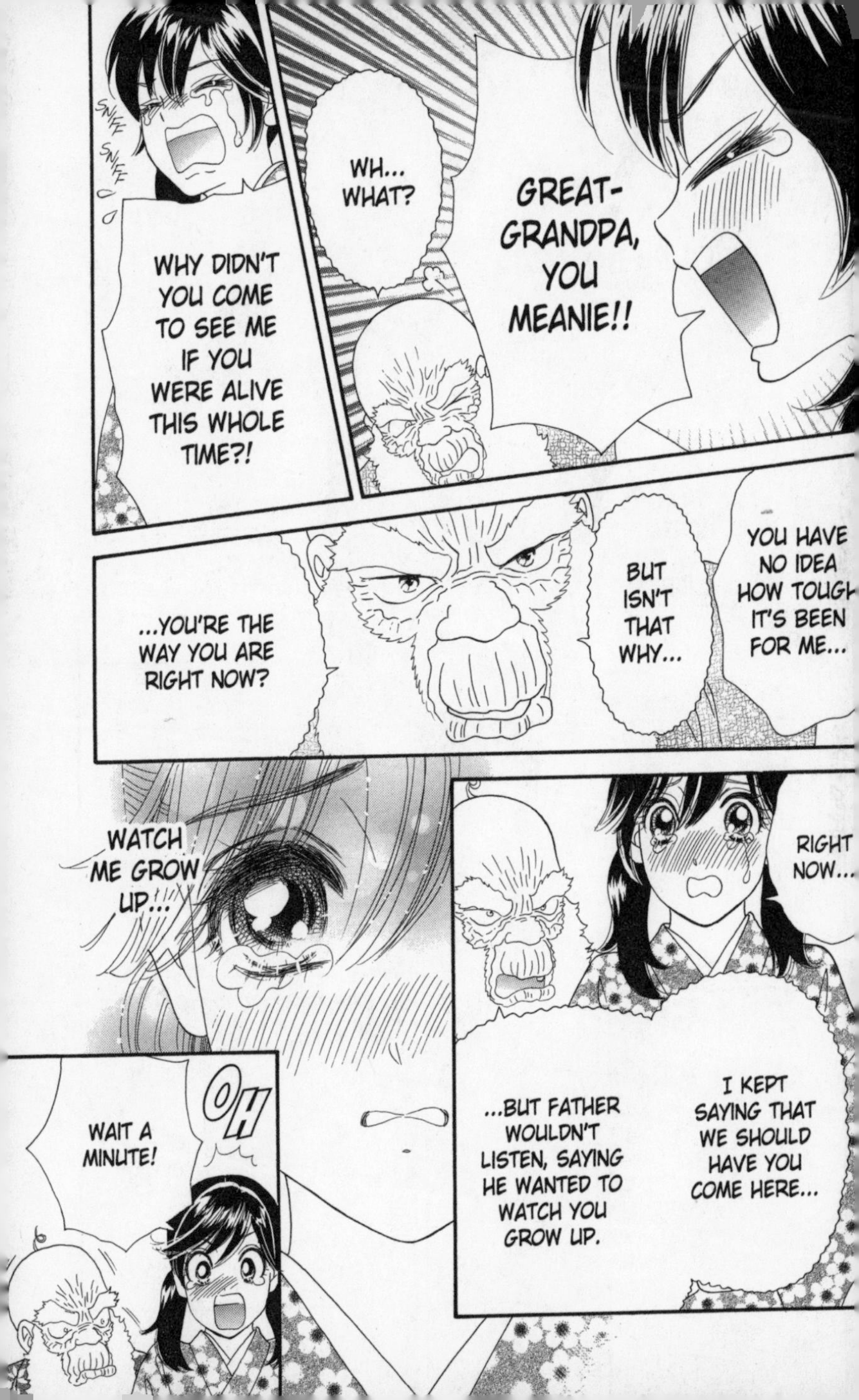
GREAT-GRANDPA, YOU MEANIE!!
WH... WHAT?
SNIFF SNIFF
WHY DIDN'T YOU COME TO SEE ME IF YOU WERE ALIVE THIS WHOLE TIME?!
YOU HAVE NO IDEA HOW TOUGH IT'S BEEN FOR ME...
BUT ISN'T THAT WHY...
...YOU'RE THE WAY YOU ARE RIGHT NOW?
RIGHT NOW...
I KEPT SAYING THAT WE SHOULD HAVE YOU COME HERE...
...BUT FATHER WOULDN'T LISTEN, SAYING HE WANTED TO WATCH YOU GROW UP.
WATCH ME GROW UP...
OH
WAIT A MINUTE!

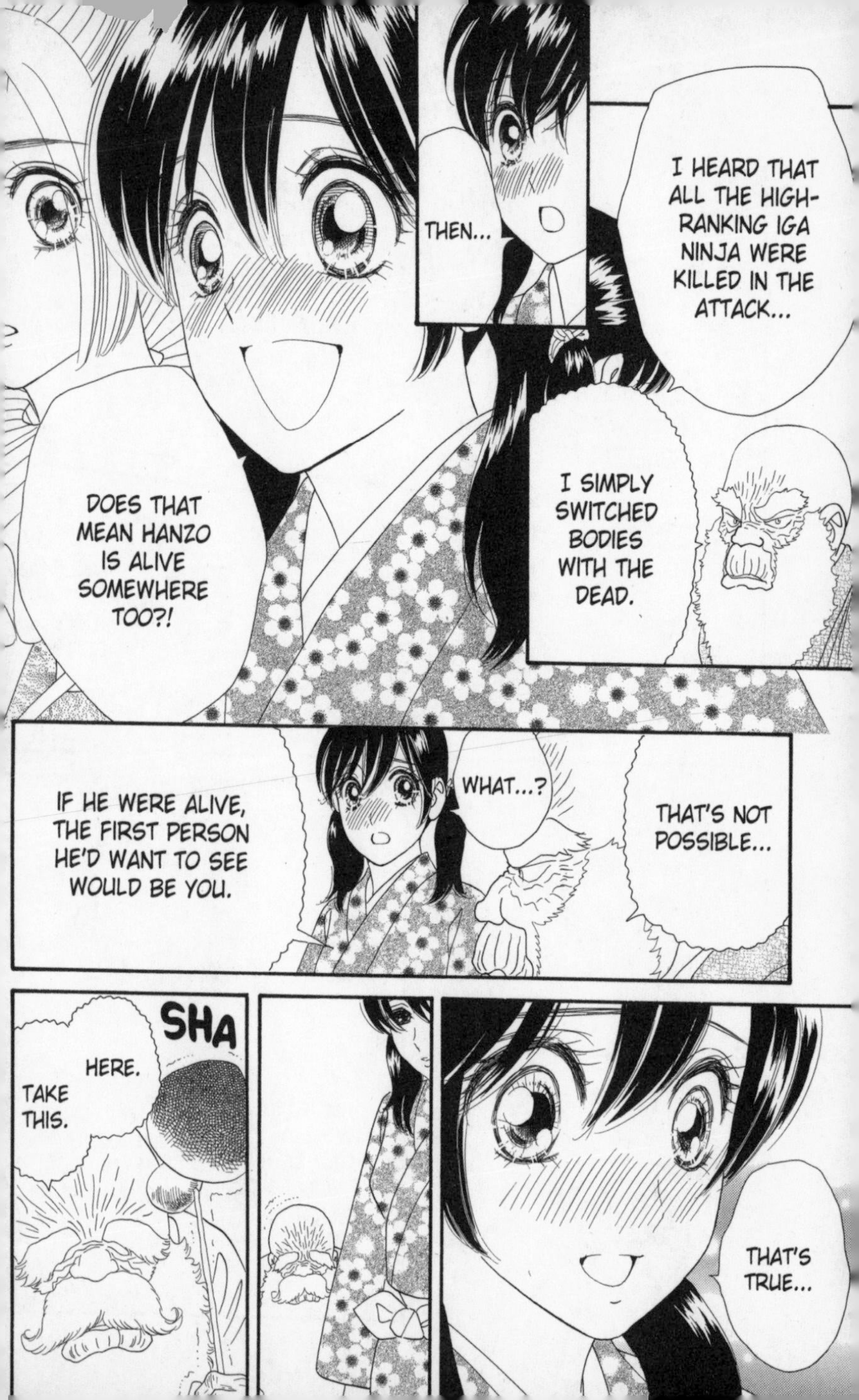
I HEARD THAT ALL THE HIGH-RANKING IGA NINJA WERE KILLED IN THE ATTACK...
I SIMPLY SWITCHED BODIES WITH THE DEAD.
THEN...
DOES THAT MEAN HANZO IS ALIVE SOMEWHERE TOO?!
THAT'S NOT POSSIBLE...
WHAT...?
IF HE WERE ALIVE, THE FIRST PERSON HE'D WANT TO SEE WOULD BE YOU.
THAT'S TRUE...
SHA
HERE.
TAKE THIS.

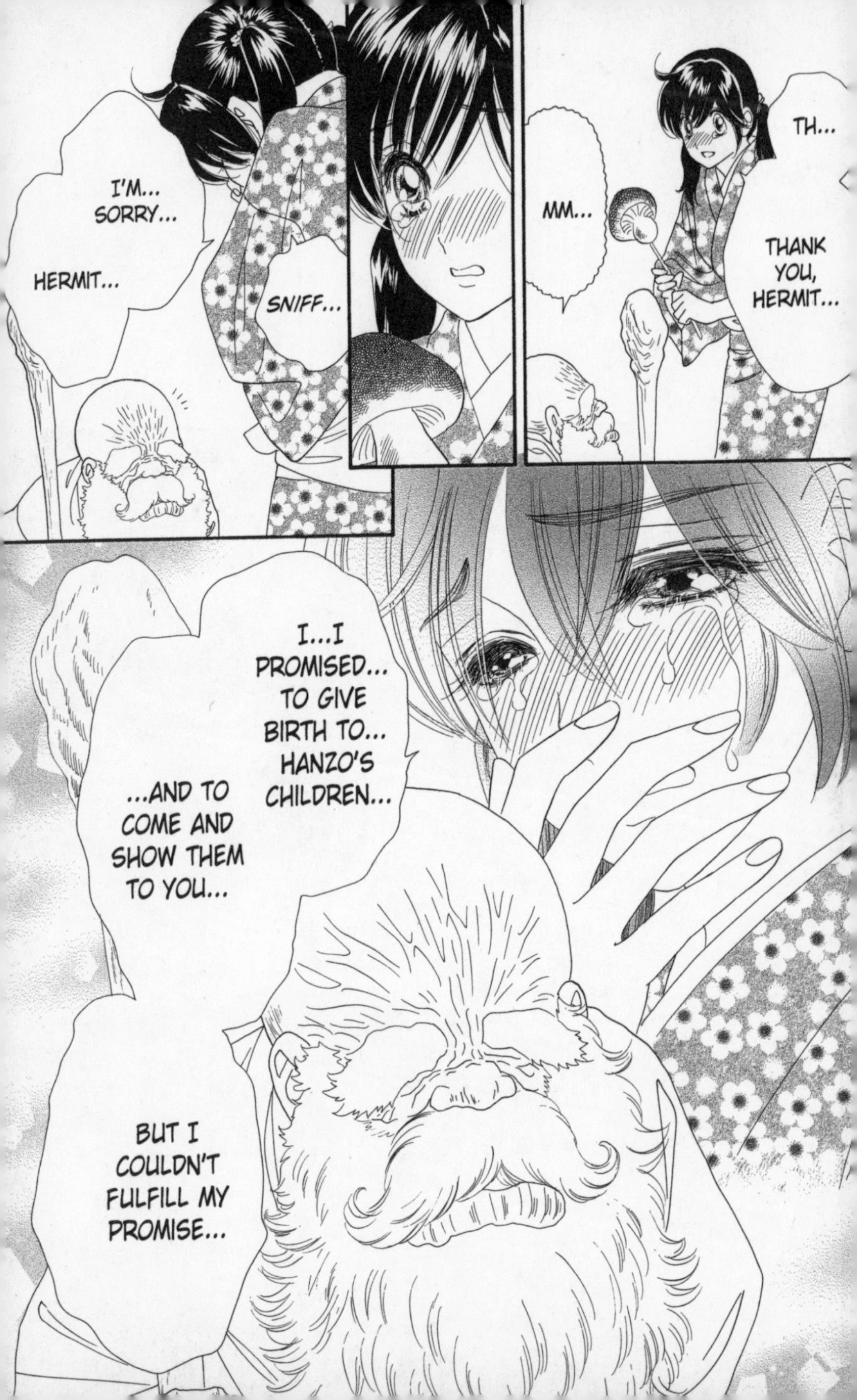
TH...
THANK YOU, HERMIT...
MM...
SNIFF...
I'M... SORRY... HERMIT...
I...I PROMISED... TO GIVE BIRTH TO... HANZO'S CHILDREN...
...AND TO COME AND SHOW THEM TO YOU...
BUT I COULDN'T FULFILL MY PROMISE...

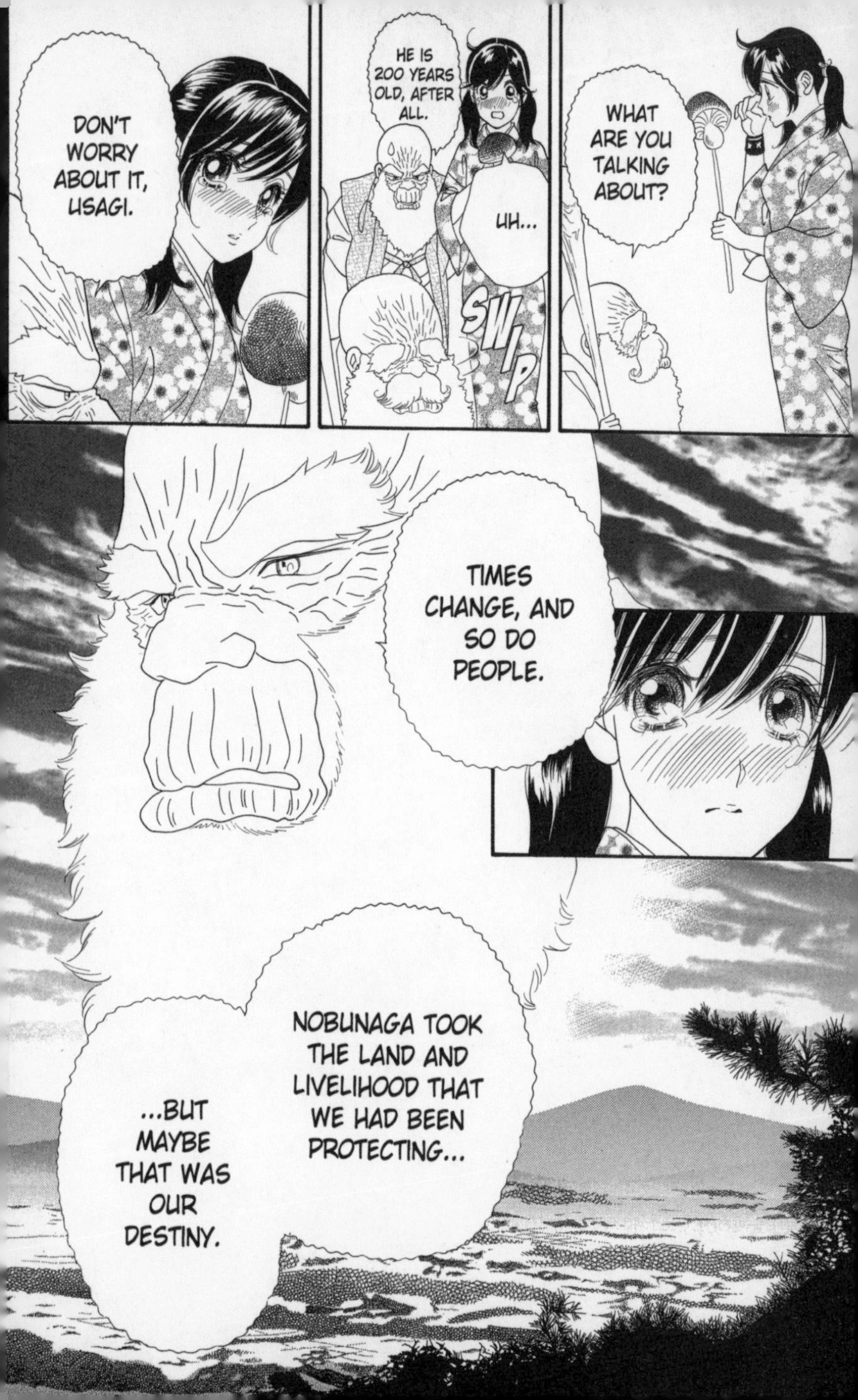
WHAT ARE YOU TALKING ABOUT?
HE IS 200 YEARS OLD, AFTER ALL.
UH...
SWIP
DON'T WORRY ABOUT IT, USAGI.
TIMES CHANGE, AND SO DO PEOPLE.
NOBUNAGA TOOK THE LAND AND LIVELIHOOD THAT WE HAD BEEN PROTECTING...
...BUT MAYBE THAT WAS OUR DESTINY.

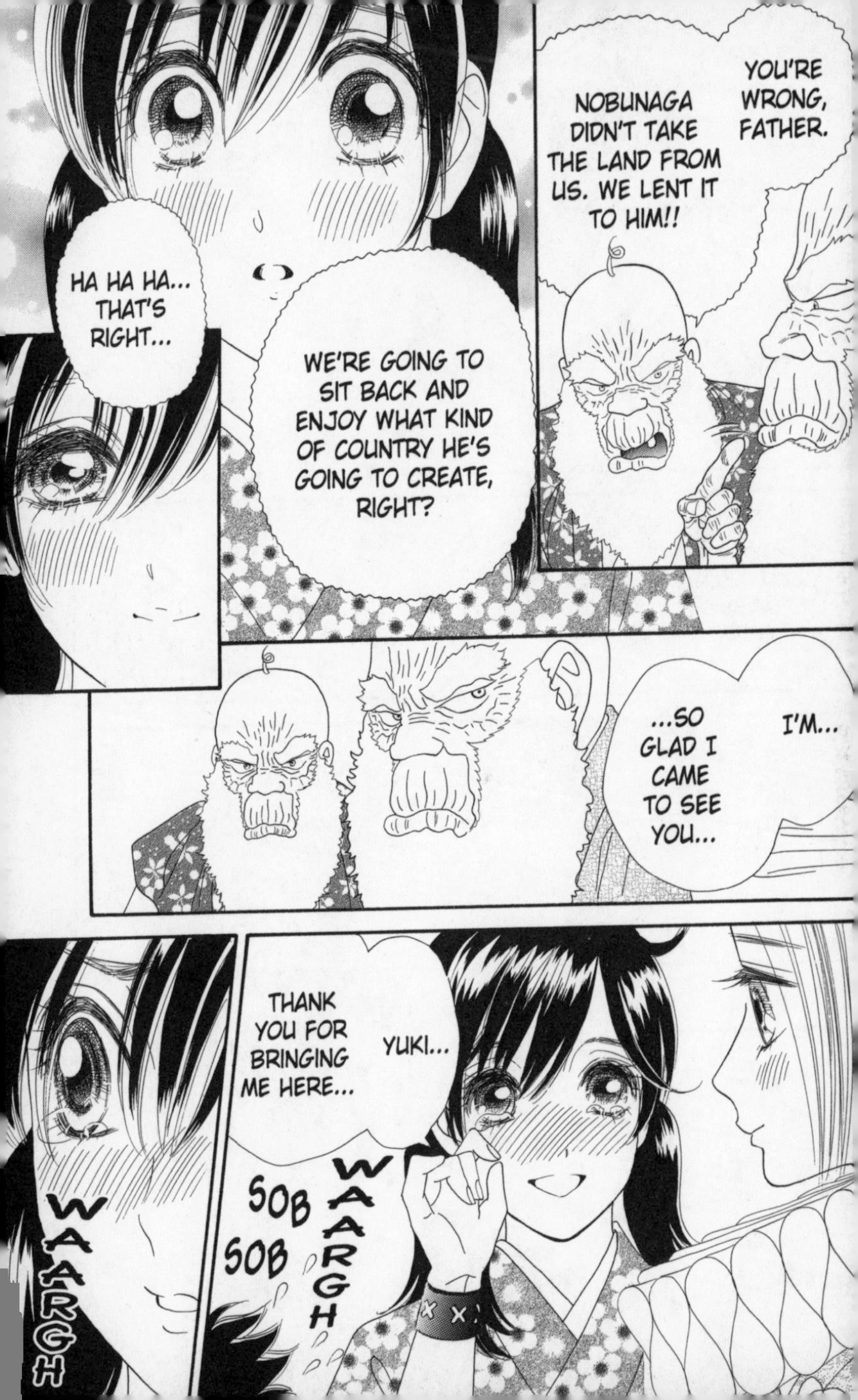
YOU'RE WRONG, FATHER.
NOBUNAGA DIDN'T TAKE THE LAND FROM US. WE LENT IT TO HIM!!
HA HA HA... THAT'S RIGHT...
WE'RE GOING TO SIT BACK AND ENJOY WHAT KIND OF COUNTRY HE'S GOING TO CREATE, RIGHT?
I'M...
...SO GLAD I CAME TO SEE YOU...
YUKI...
THANK YOU FOR BRINGING ME HERE...
WAARGH
SOB SOB
WAARGH

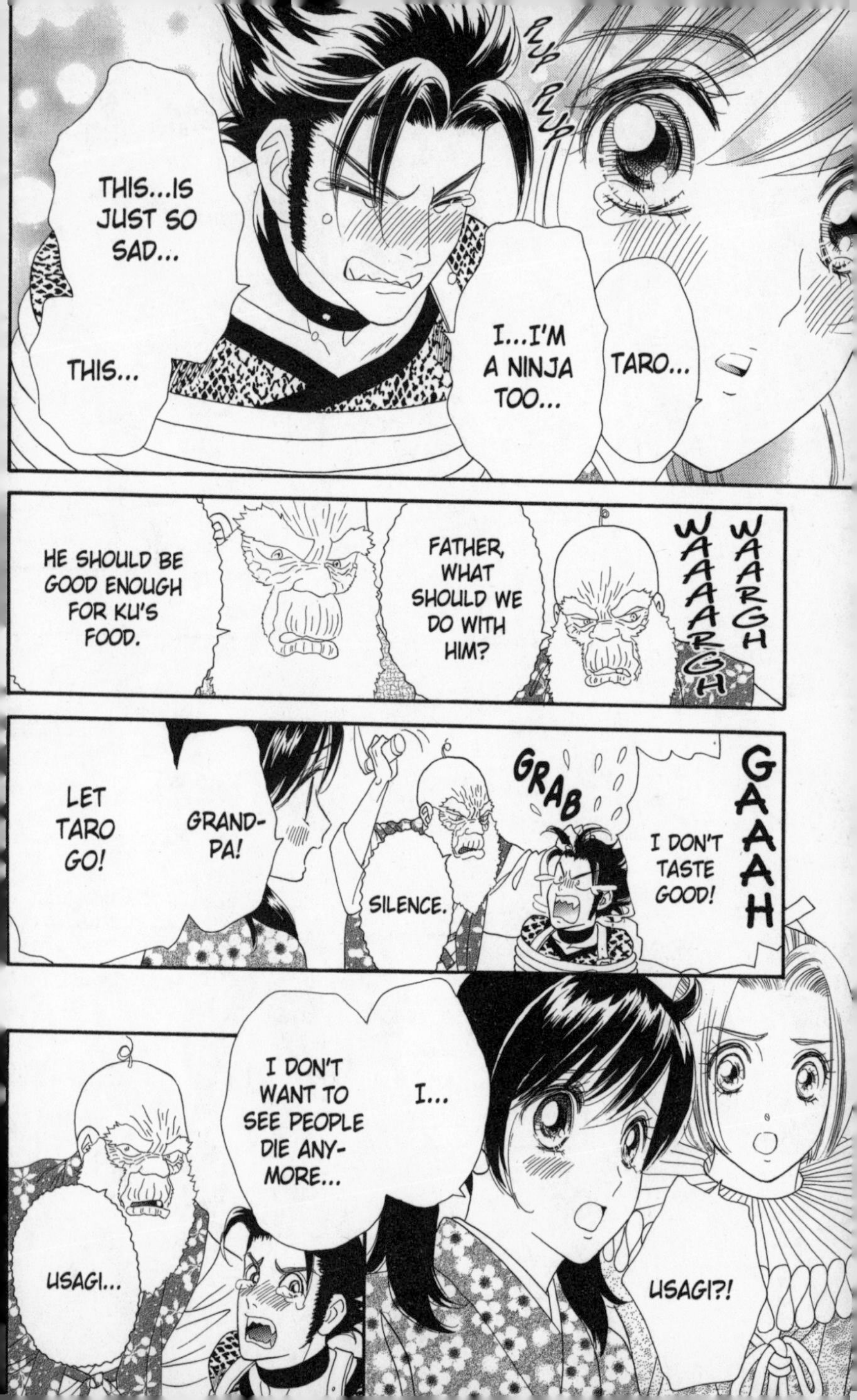
PLIP PLIP
TARO...
I...I'M A NINJA TOO...
THIS...IS JUST SO SAD...
THIS...
WAAARGH
WAAAAARGH
FATHER, WHAT SHOULD WE DO WITH HIM?
HE SHOULD BE GOOD ENOUGH FOR KU'S FOOD.
GAAAH
I DON'T TASTE GOOD!
GRAB
SILENCE.
GRAND-PA!
LET TARO GO!
USAGI?!
I...
I DON'T WANT TO SEE PEOPLE DIE ANY-MORE...
USAGI...

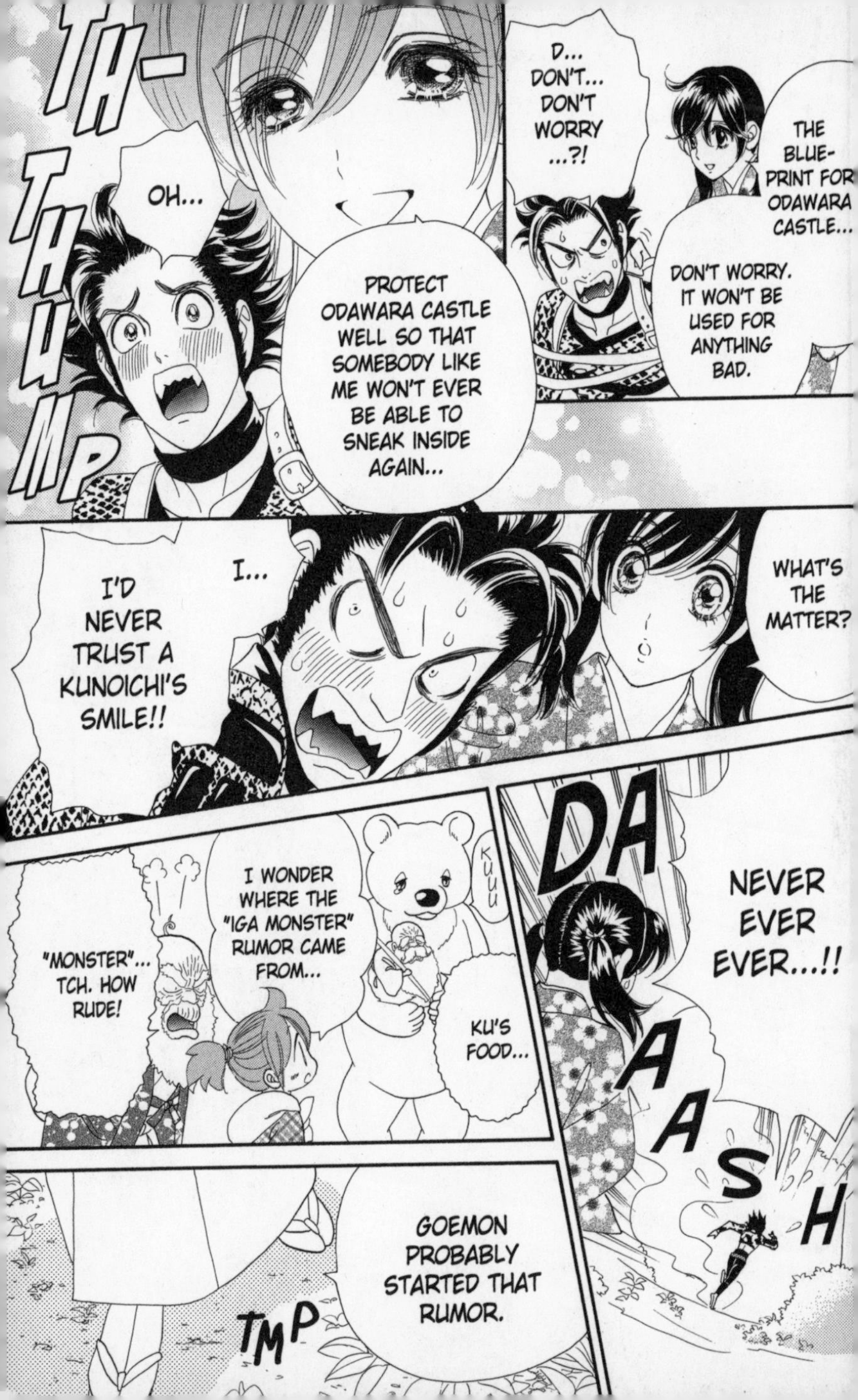
THE BLUE-PRINT FOR ODAWARA CASTLE...
DON'T WORRY. IT WON'T BE USED FOR ANYTHING BAD.
D... DON'T... DON'T WORRY ...?!
PROTECT ODAWARA CASTLE WELL SO THAT SOMEBODY LIKE ME WON'T EVER BE ABLE TO SNEAK INSIDE AGAIN...
OH...
TH-THUMP
WHAT'S THE MATTER?
I...
I'D NEVER TRUST A KUNOICHI'S SMILE!!
NEVER EVER EVER...!!
DAAASH
KUUU
I WONDER WHERE THE "IGA MONSTER" RUMOR CAME FROM...
KU'S FOOD...
"MONSTER"... TCH. HOW RUDE!
GOEMON PROBABLY STARTED THAT RUMOR.
TMP

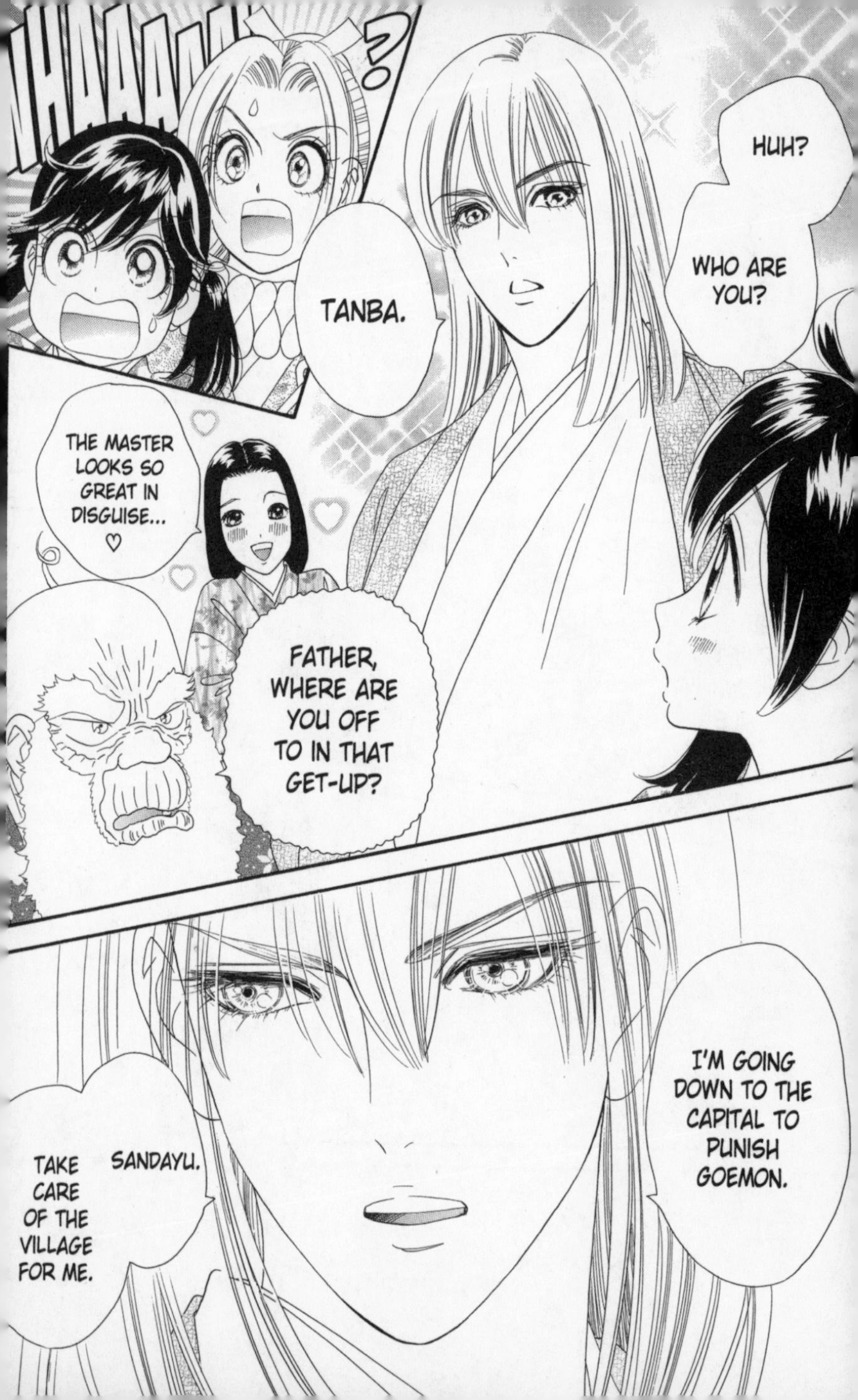
HUH?
WHO ARE YOU?
TANBA.
WHAAAA
?!
FATHER, WHERE ARE YOU OFF TO IN THAT GET-UP?
THE MASTER LOOKS SO GREAT IN DISGUISE... ♡
I'M GOING DOWN TO THE CAPITAL TO PUNISH GOEMON.
SANDAYU.
TAKE CARE OF THE VILLAGE FOR ME.

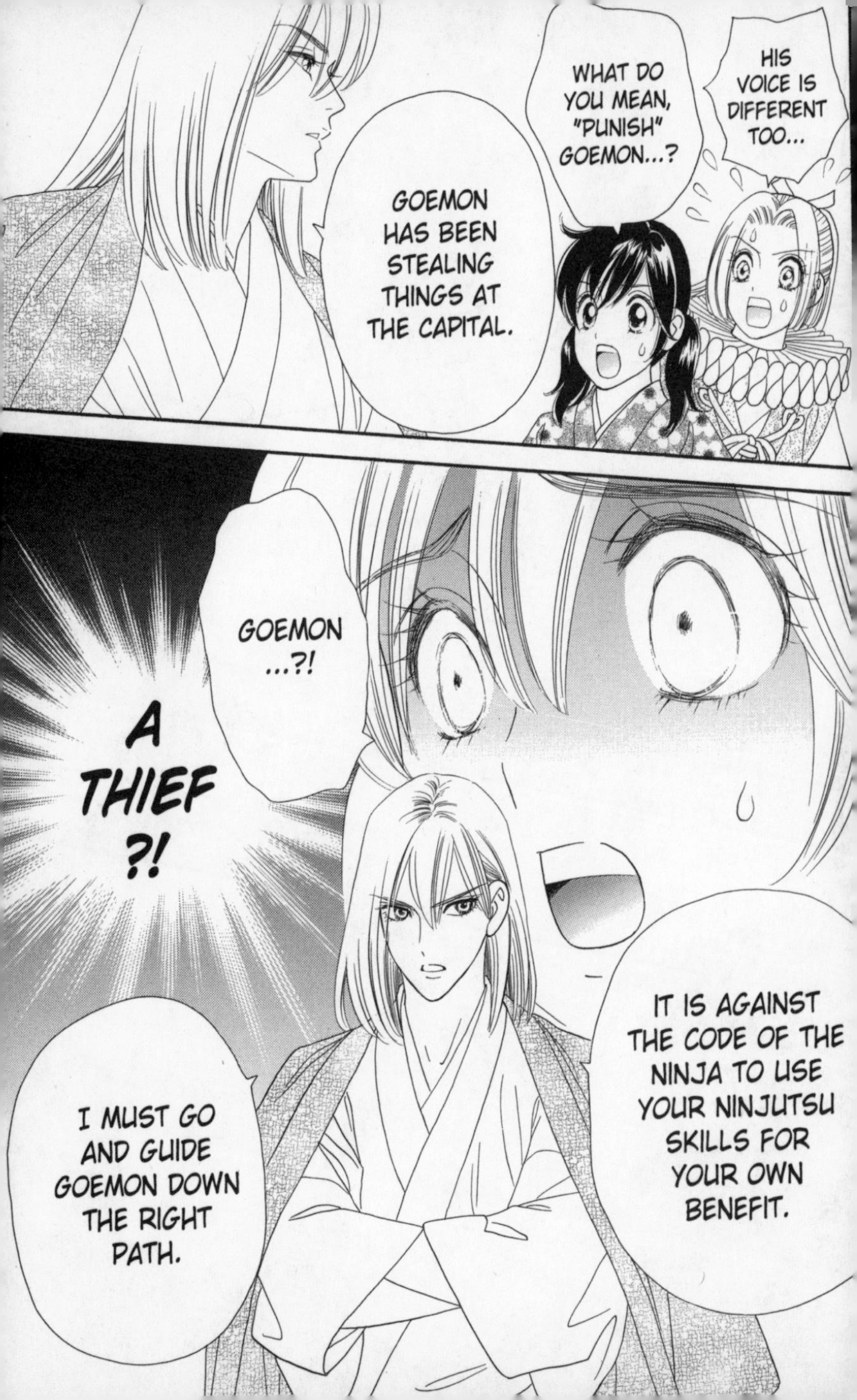

HIS VOICE IS DIFFERENT TOO...
WHAT DO YOU MEAN, "PUNISH" GOEMON...?
GOEMON HAS BEEN STEALING THINGS AT THE CAPITAL.
GOEMON ...?!
A THIEF ?!
IT IS AGAINST THE CODE OF THE NINJA TO USE YOUR NINJUTSU SKILLS FOR YOUR OWN BENEFIT.
I MUST GO AND GUIDE GOEMON DOWN THE RIGHT PATH.

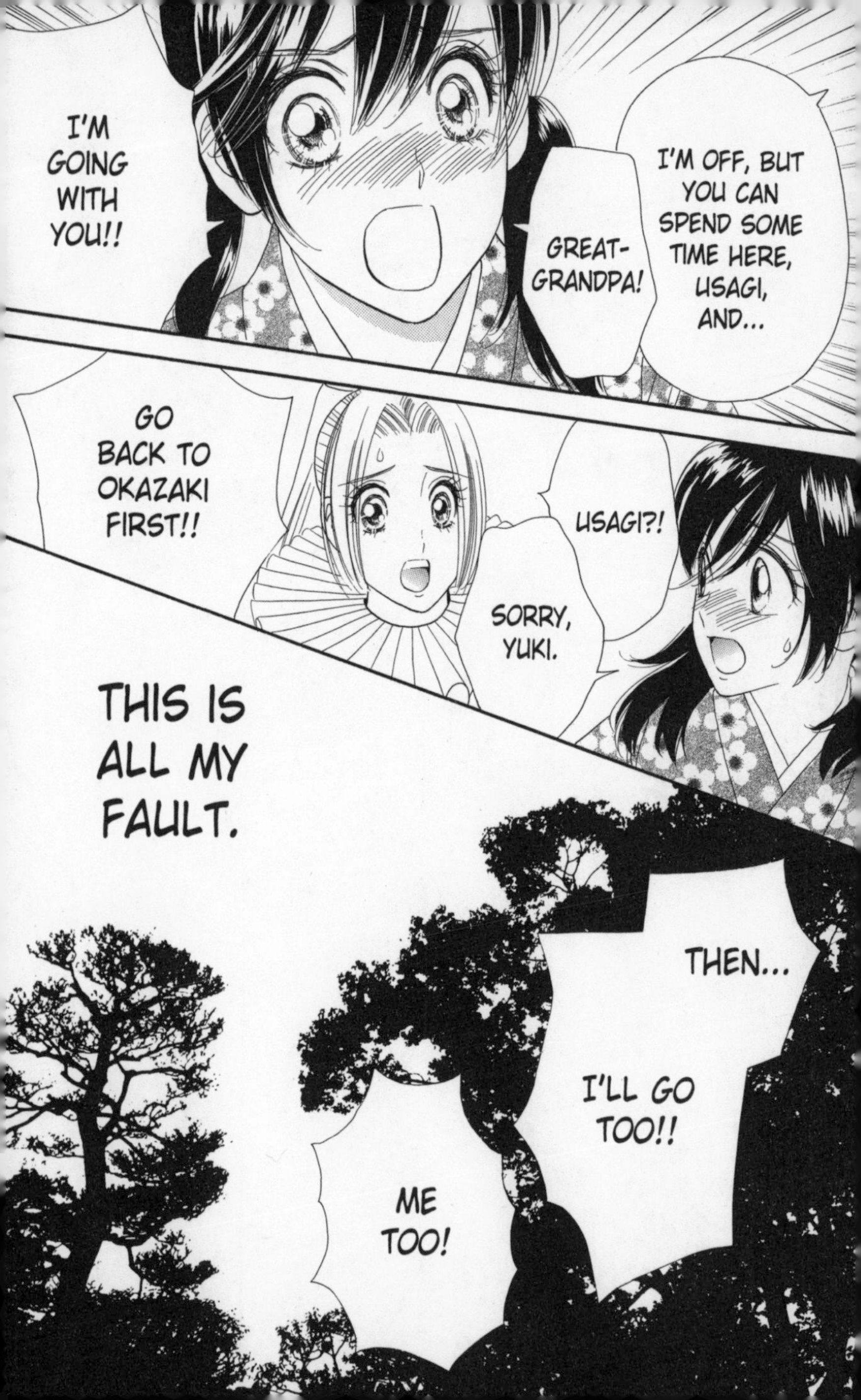
I'M OFF, BUT YOU CAN SPEND SOME TIME HERE, USAGI, AND...
GREAT-GRANDPA!
I'M GOING WITH YOU!!
USAGI?!
SORRY, YUKI.
GO BACK TO OKAZAKI FIRST!!
THIS IS ALL MY FAULT.
THEN...
I'LL GO TOO!!
ME TOO!

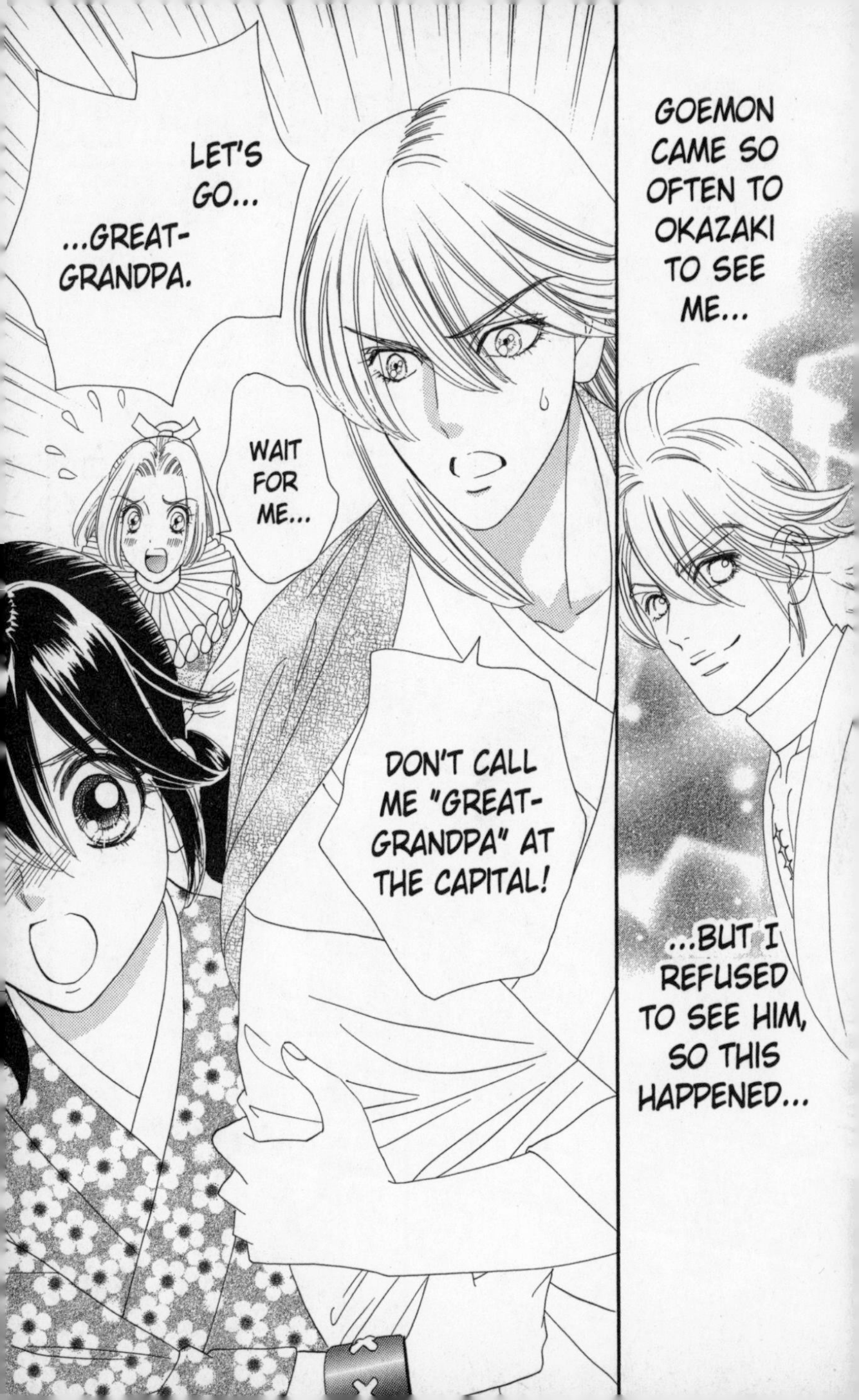
GOEMON CAME SO OFTEN TO OKAZAKI TO SEE ME...
...BUT I REFUSED TO SEE HIM, SO THIS HAPPENED...
LET'S GO... ...GREAT-GRANDPA.
WAIT FOR ME...
DON'T CALL ME "GREAT-GRANDPA" AT THE CAPITAL!

LET'S GO!

LITTLE HANZO

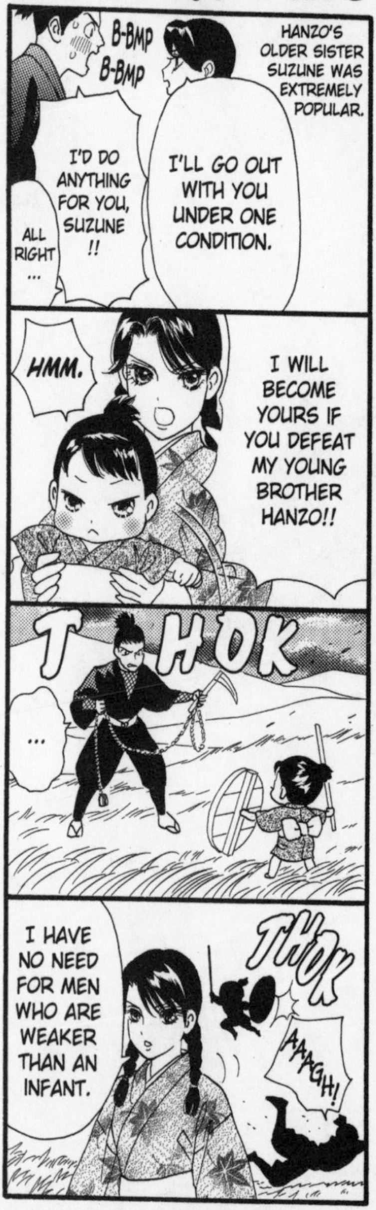
HANZO'S OLDER SISTER SUZUNE WAS EXTREMELY POPULAR.
B-BMP
B-BMP
I'LL GO OUT WITH YOU UNDER ONE CONDITION.
I'D DO ANYTHING FOR YOU, SUZUNE!!
ALL RIGHT...
I WILL BECOME YOURS IF YOU DEFEAT MY YOUNG BROTHER HANZO!!
HMM.
THOK
...
THOK
AAAGH!
I HAVE NO NEED FOR MEN WHO ARE WEAKER THAN AN INFANT.

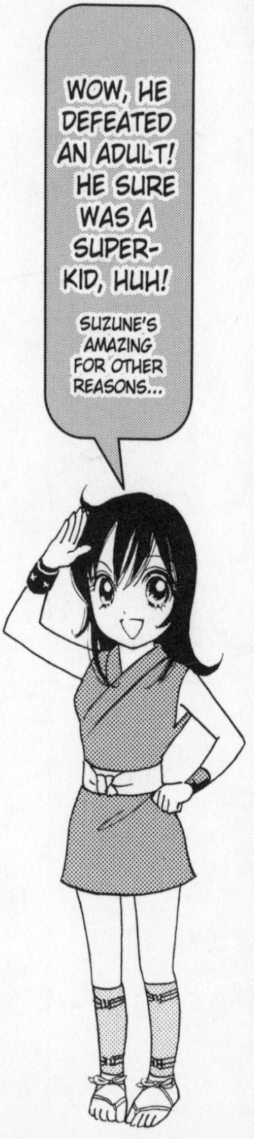
WOW, HE DEFEATED AN ADULT! HE SURE WAS A SUPER-KID, HUH!
SUZUNE'S AMAZING FOR OTHER REASONS...

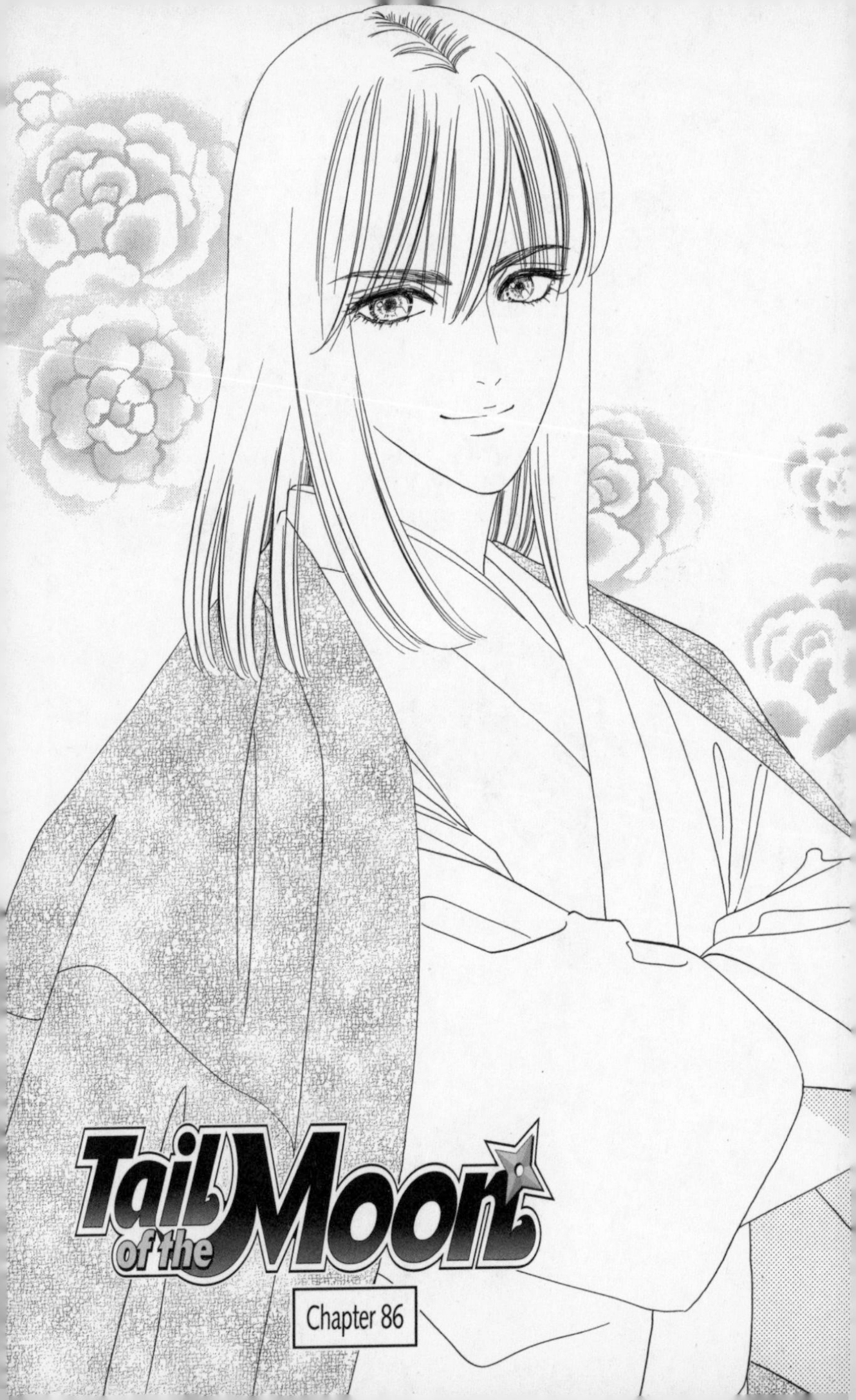
Tail of the Moon
Chapter 86

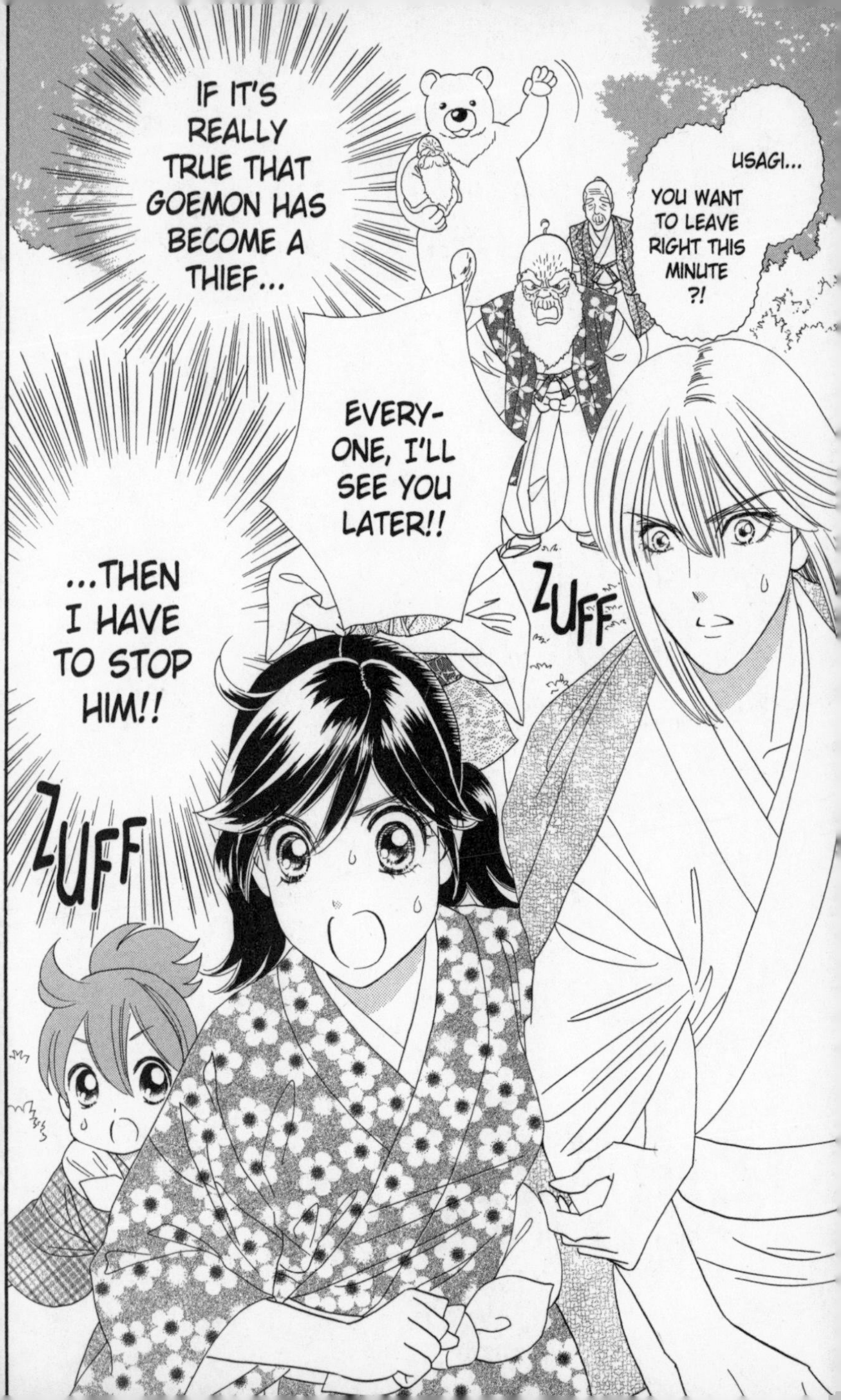
USAGI... YOU WANT TO LEAVE RIGHT THIS MINUTE ?!
IF IT'S REALLY TRUE THAT GOEMON HAS BECOME A THIEF...
EVERY-ONE, I'LL SEE YOU LATER!!
ZUFF
...THEN I HAVE TO STOP HIM!!
ZUFF

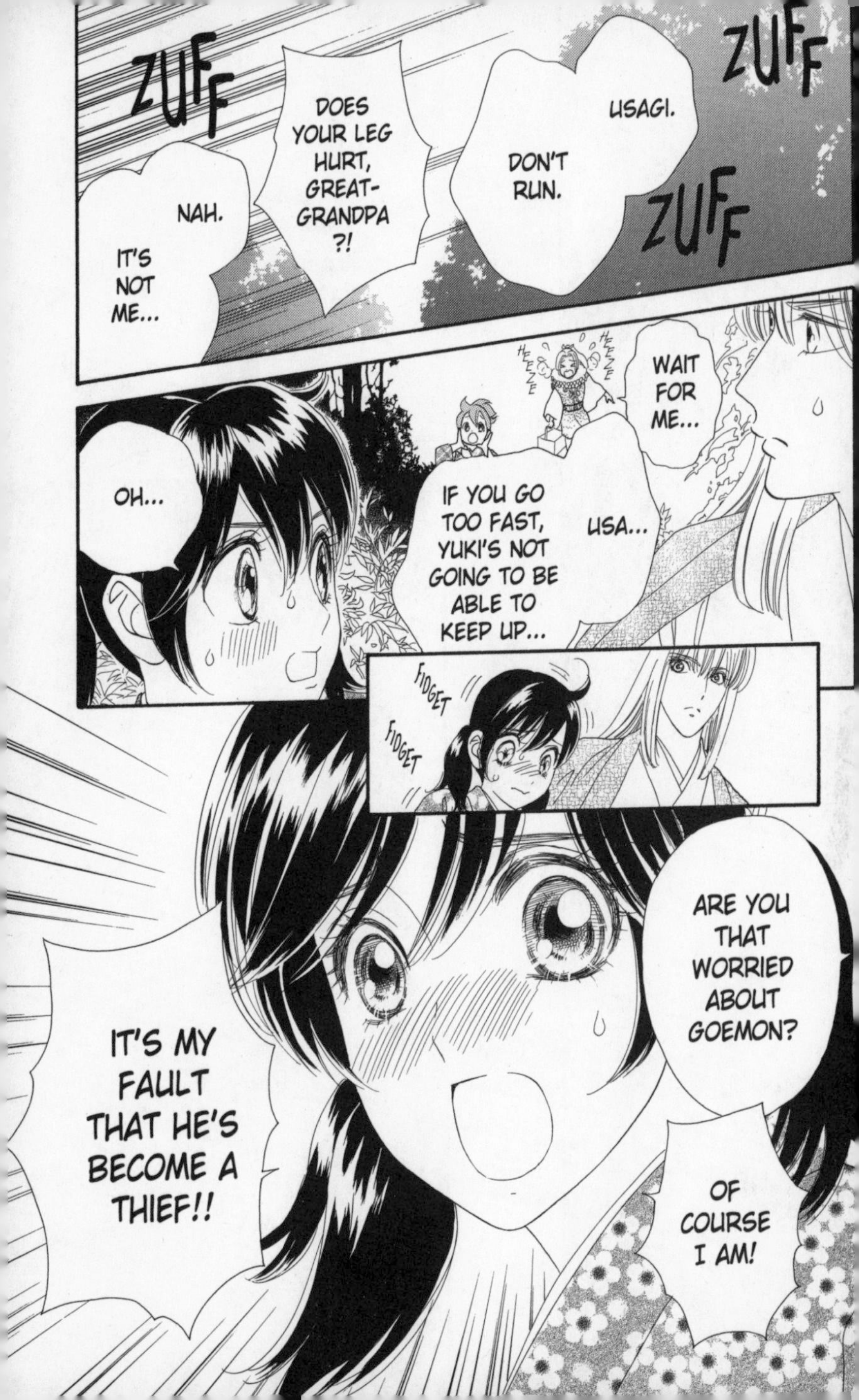
ZUFF
USAGI.
DON'T RUN.
ZUFF
DOES YOUR LEG HURT, GREAT-GRANDPA?!
NAH.
IT'S NOT ME...
WAIT FOR ME...
HEEZE
HEEZE
USA...
IF YOU GO TOO FAST, YUKI'S NOT GOING TO BE ABLE TO KEEP UP...
OH...
FIDGET
FIDGET
ARE YOU THAT WORRIED ABOUT GOEMON?
OF COURSE I AM!
IT'S MY FAULT THAT HE'S BECOME A THIEF!!

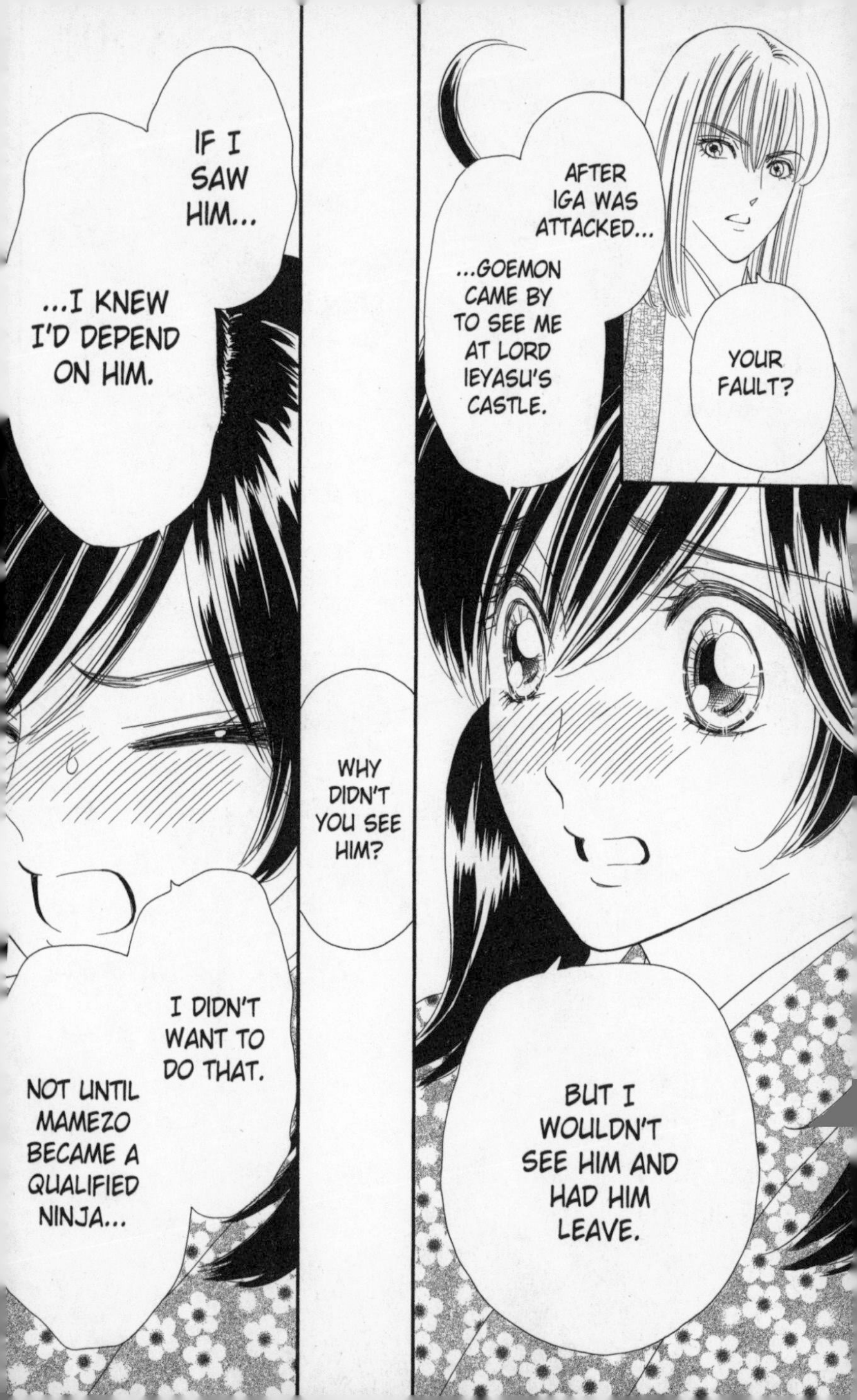
YOUR FAULT?
AFTER IGA WAS ATTACKED...
...GOEMON CAME BY TO SEE ME AT LORD IEYASU'S CASTLE.
BUT I WOULDN'T SEE HIM AND HAD HIM LEAVE.
WHY DIDN'T YOU SEE HIM?
IF I SAW HIM...
...I KNEW I'D DEPEND ON HIM.
I DIDN'T WANT TO DO THAT.
NOT UNTIL MAMEZO BECAME A QUALIFIED NINJA...

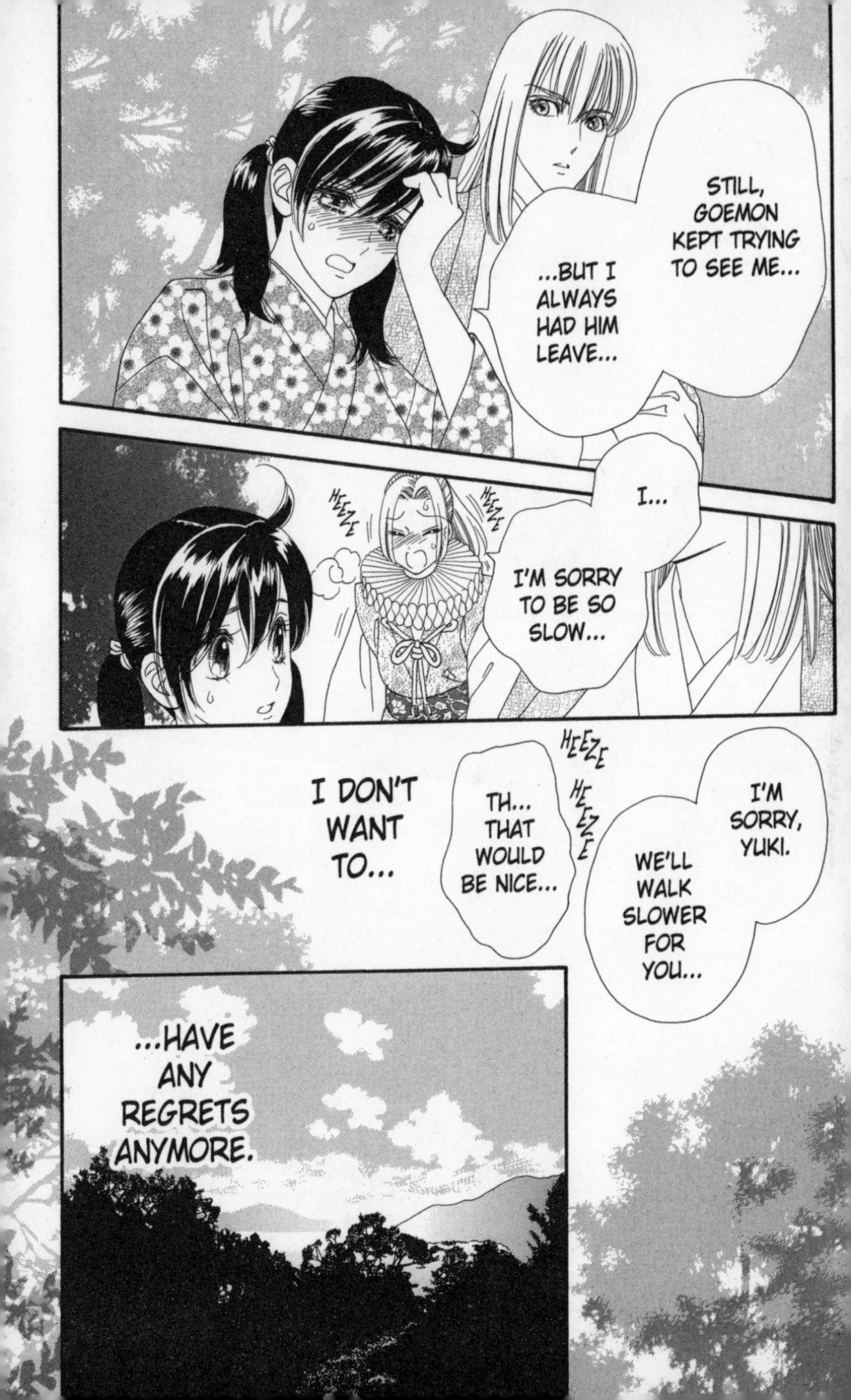
STILL, GOEMON KEPT TRYING TO SEE ME...
...BUT I ALWAYS HAD HIM LEAVE...
I...
I'M SORRY TO BE SO SLOW...
HEEZE
HEEZE
I'M SORRY, YUKI.
WE'LL WALK SLOWER FOR YOU...
HEEZE
HEEZE
TH... THAT WOULD BE NICE...
I DON'T WANT TO...
...HAVE ANY REGRETS ANYMORE.

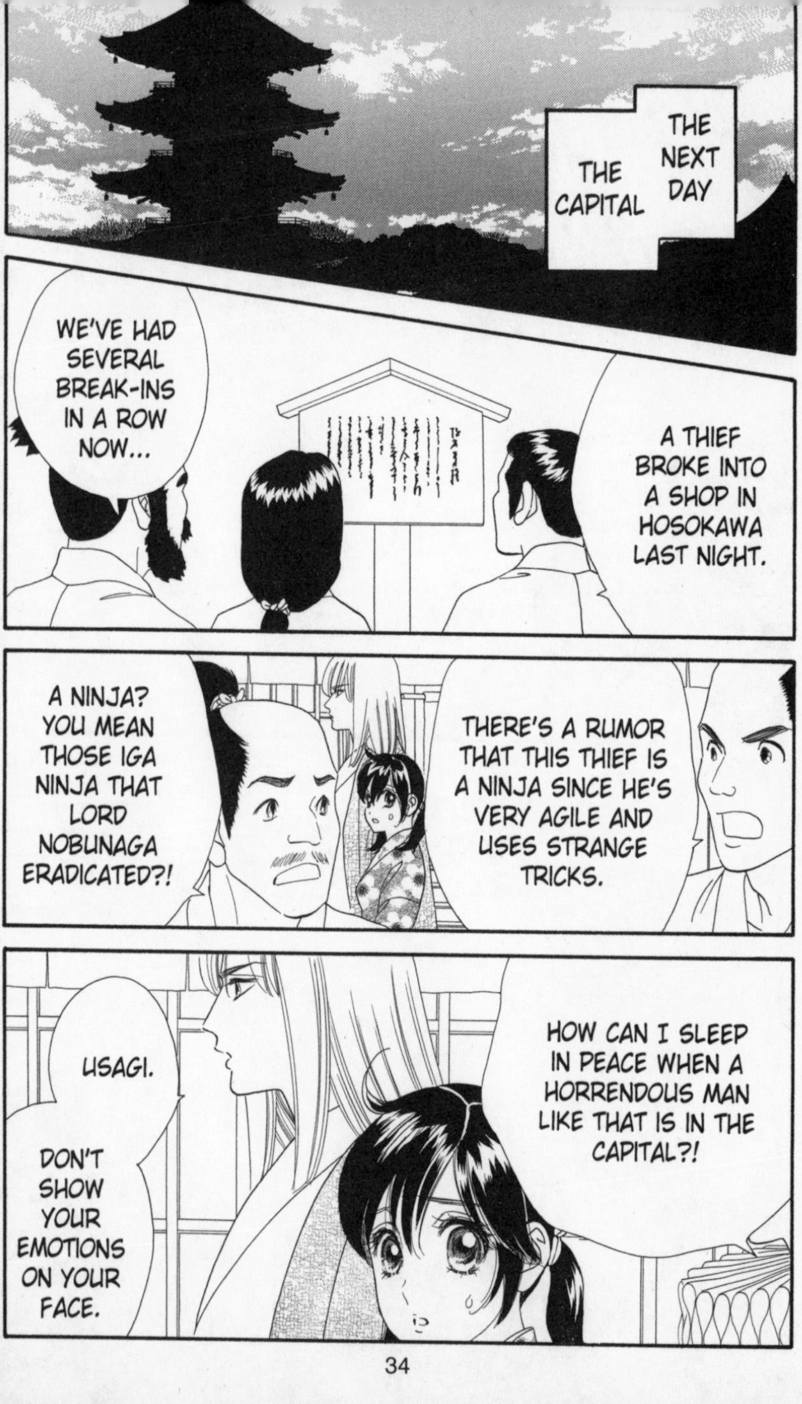
THE NEXT DAY
THE CAPITAL
A THIEF BROKE INTO A SHOP IN HOSOKAWA LAST NIGHT.
WE'VE HAD SEVERAL BREAK-INS IN A ROW NOW...
THERE'S A RUMOR THAT THIS THIEF IS A NINJA SINCE HE'S VERY AGILE AND USES STRANGE TRICKS.
A NINJA? YOU MEAN THOSE IGA NINJA THAT LORD NOBUNAGA ERADICATED?!
HOW CAN I SLEEP IN PEACE WHEN A HORRENDOUS MAN LIKE THAT IS IN THE CAPITAL?!
USAGI.
DON'T SHOW YOUR EMOTIONS ON YOUR FACE.

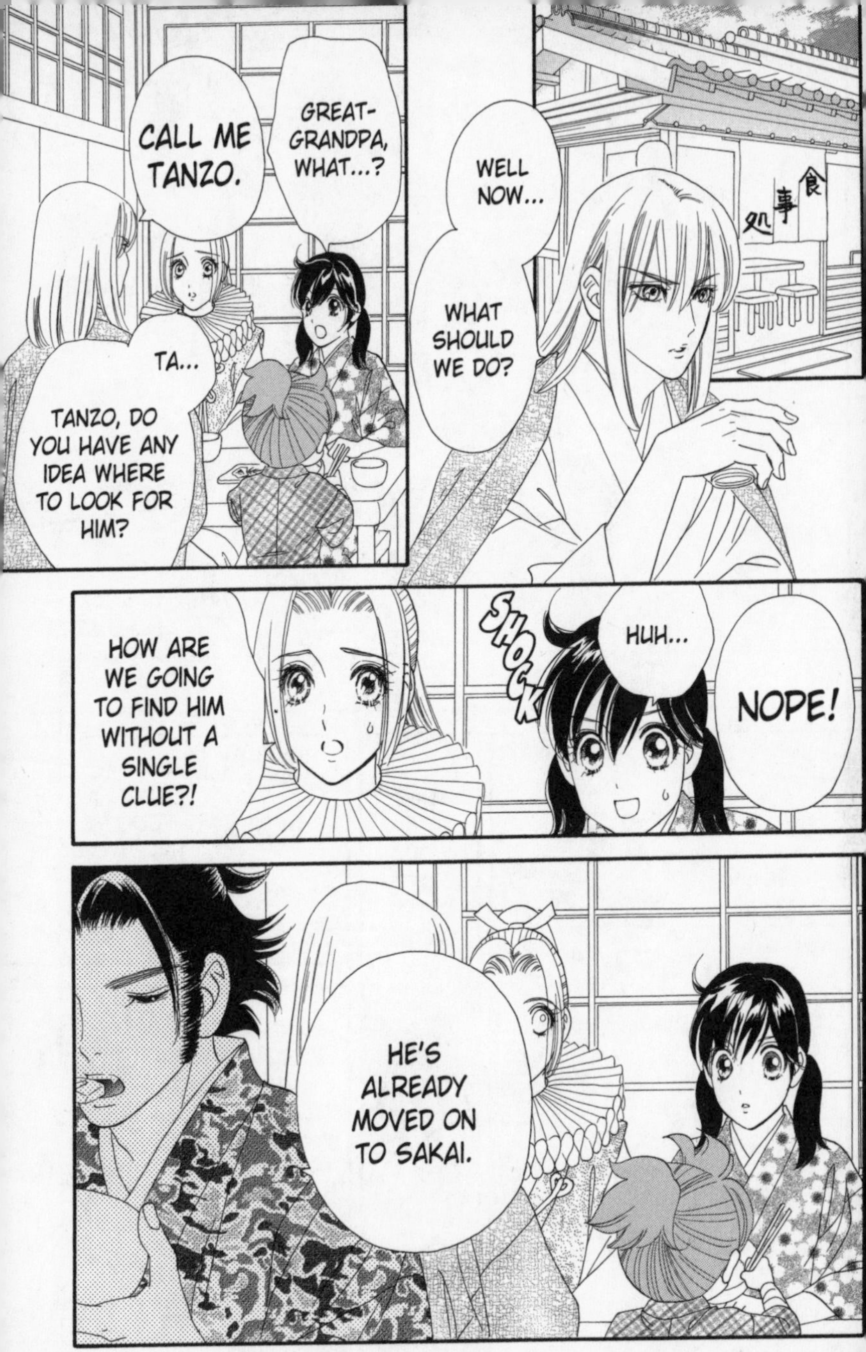
食事処
WELL NOW...
WHAT SHOULD WE DO?
GREAT-GRANDPA, WHAT...?
CALL ME TANZO.
TA...
TANZO, DO YOU HAVE ANY IDEA WHERE TO LOOK FOR HIM?
NOPE!
HUH...
SHOCK
HOW ARE WE GOING TO FIND HIM WITHOUT A SINGLE CLUE?!
HE'S ALREADY MOVED ON TO SAKAI.

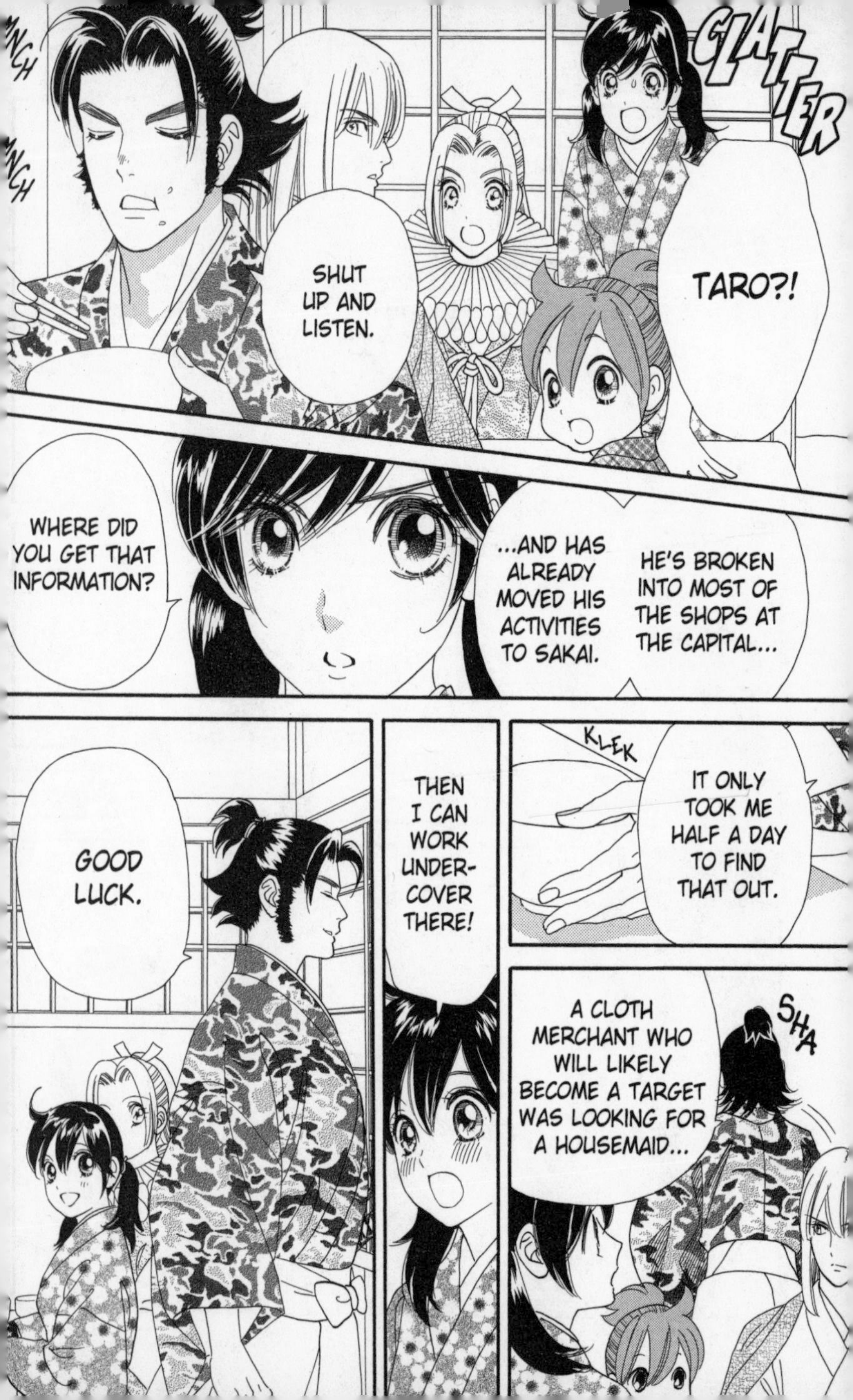
CLATTER
TARO?!
SHUT UP AND LISTEN.
MNCH
MNCH
HE'S BROKEN INTO MOST OF THE SHOPS AT THE CAPITAL...
...AND HAS ALREADY MOVED HIS ACTIVITIES TO SAKAI.
WHERE DID YOU GET THAT INFORMATION?
KLEK
IT ONLY TOOK ME HALF A DAY TO FIND THAT OUT.
SHA
A CLOTH MERCHANT WHO WILL LIKELY BECOME A TARGET WAS LOOKING FOR A HOUSEMAID...
THEN I CAN WORK UNDER-COVER THERE!
GOOD LUCK.

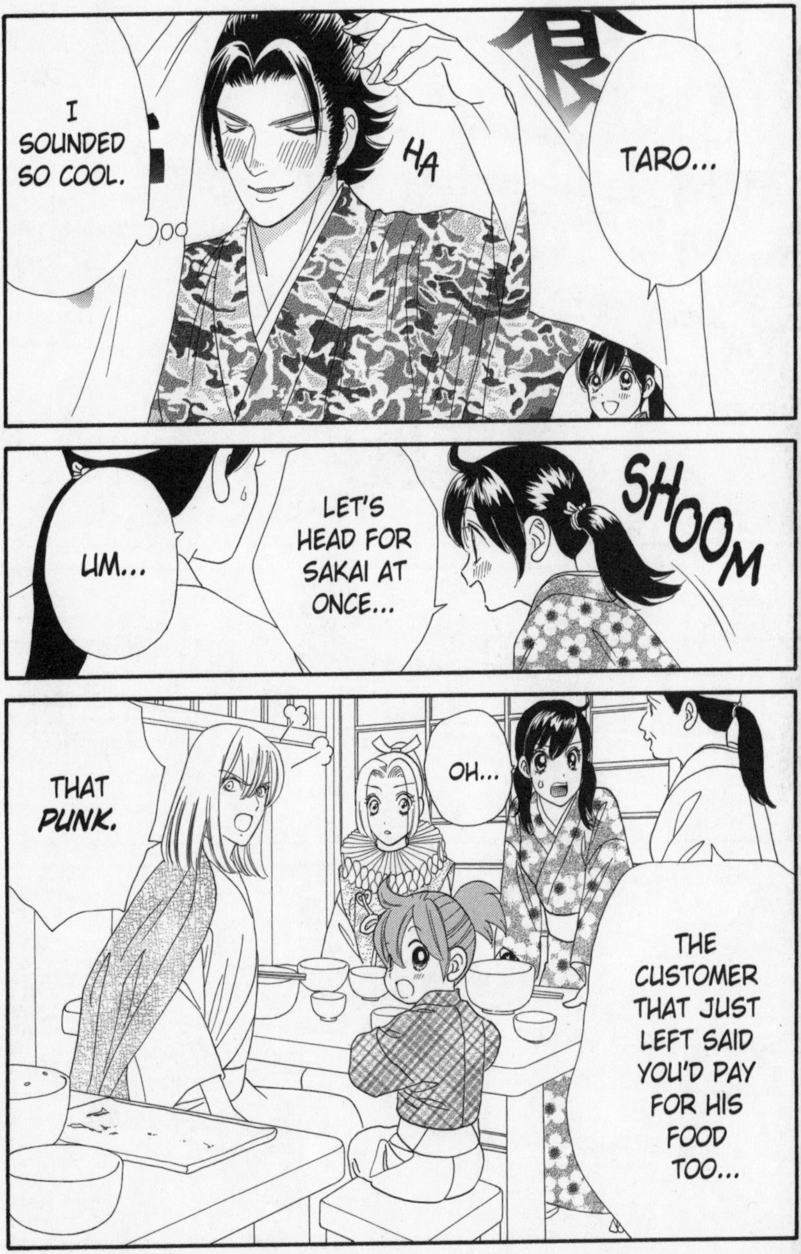
TARO...
HA
I SOUNDED SO COOL.
SHOOM
LET'S HEAD FOR SAKAI AT ONCE...
UM...
THE CUSTOMER THAT JUST LEFT SAID YOU'D PAY FOR HIS FOOD TOO...
OH...
THAT *PUNK.*

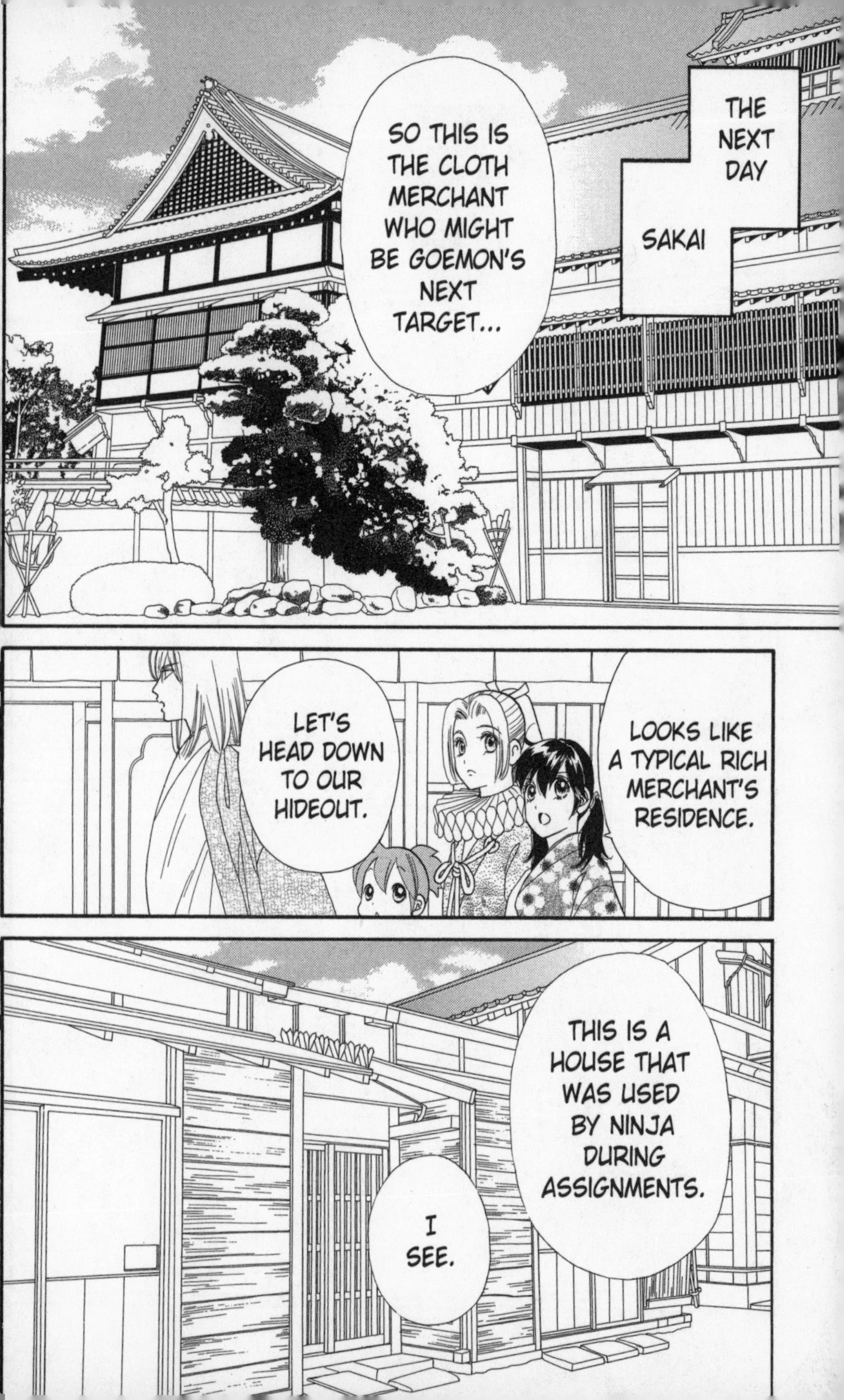
THE NEXT DAY
SAKAI
SO THIS IS THE CLOTH MERCHANT WHO MIGHT BE GOEMON'S NEXT TARGET...
LOOKS LIKE A TYPICAL RICH MERCHANT'S RESIDENCE.
LET'S HEAD DOWN TO OUR HIDEOUT.
THIS IS A HOUSE THAT WAS USED BY NINJA DURING ASSIGNMENTS.
I SEE.

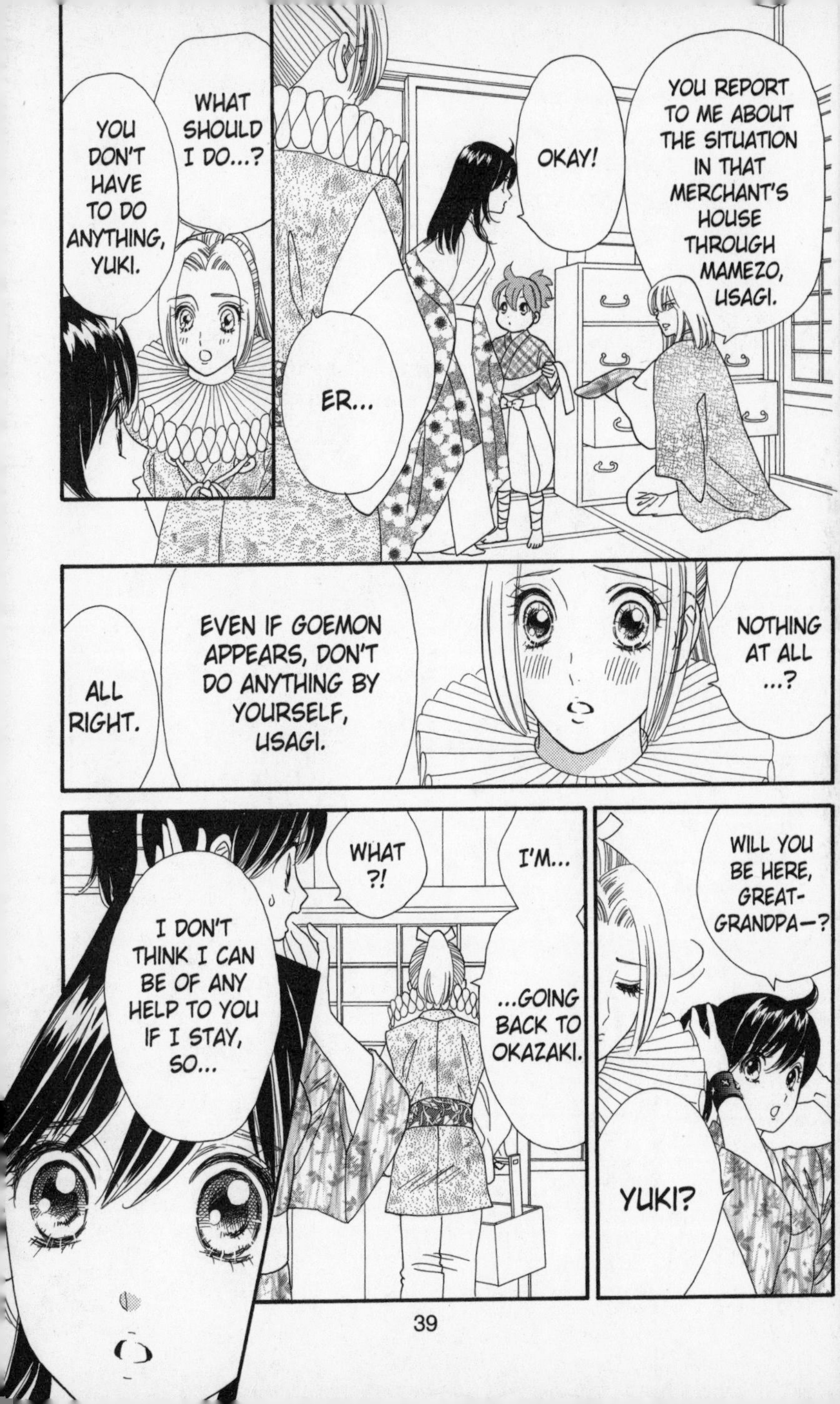
YOU REPORT TO ME ABOUT THE SITUATION IN THAT MERCHANT'S HOUSE THROUGH MAMEZO, USAGI.
OKAY!
ER...
WHAT SHOULD I DO...?
YOU DON'T HAVE TO DO ANYTHING, YUKI.
NOTHING AT ALL ...?
EVEN IF GOEMON APPEARS, DON'T DO ANYTHING BY YOURSELF, USAGI.
ALL RIGHT.
WILL YOU BE HERE, GREAT-GRANDPA—?
YUKI?
I'M...
WHAT ?!
...GOING BACK TO OKAZAKI.
I DON'T THINK I CAN BE OF ANY HELP TO YOU IF I STAY, SO...

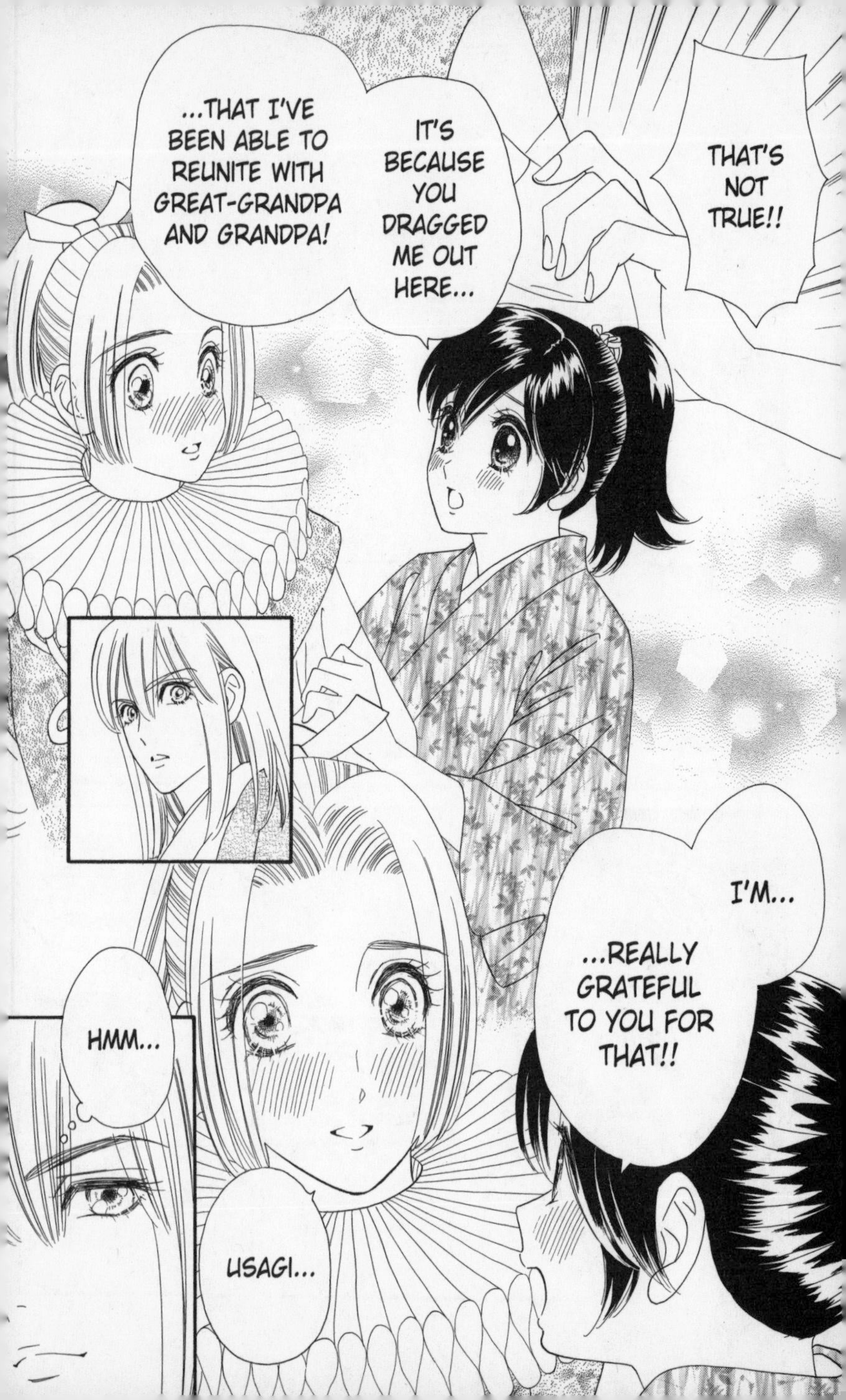
THAT'S NOT TRUE!!
IT'S BECAUSE YOU DRAGGED ME OUT HERE...
...THAT I'VE BEEN ABLE TO REUNITE WITH GREAT-GRANDPA AND GRANDPA!
I'M...
...REALLY GRATEFUL TO YOU FOR THAT!!
USAGI...
HMM...

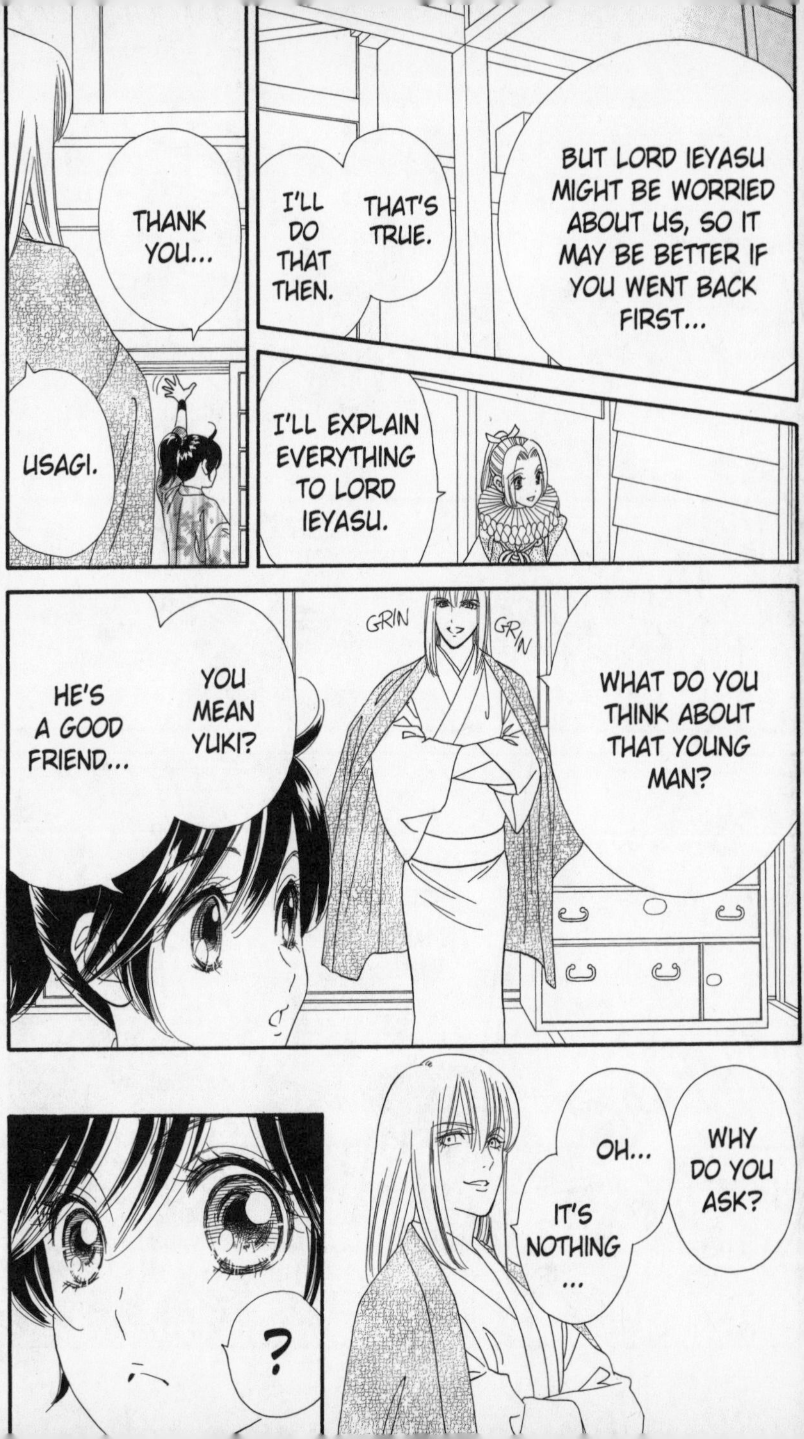
BUT LORD IEYASU MIGHT BE WORRIED ABOUT US, SO IT MAY BE BETTER IF YOU WENT BACK FIRST...
THAT'S TRUE.
I'LL DO THAT THEN.
I'LL EXPLAIN EVERYTHING TO LORD IEYASU.
THANK YOU...
USAGI.
WHAT DO YOU THINK ABOUT THAT YOUNG MAN?
GRIN
GRIN
YOU MEAN YUKI?
HE'S A GOOD FRIEND...
WHY DO YOU ASK?
OH...
IT'S NOTHING ...
?

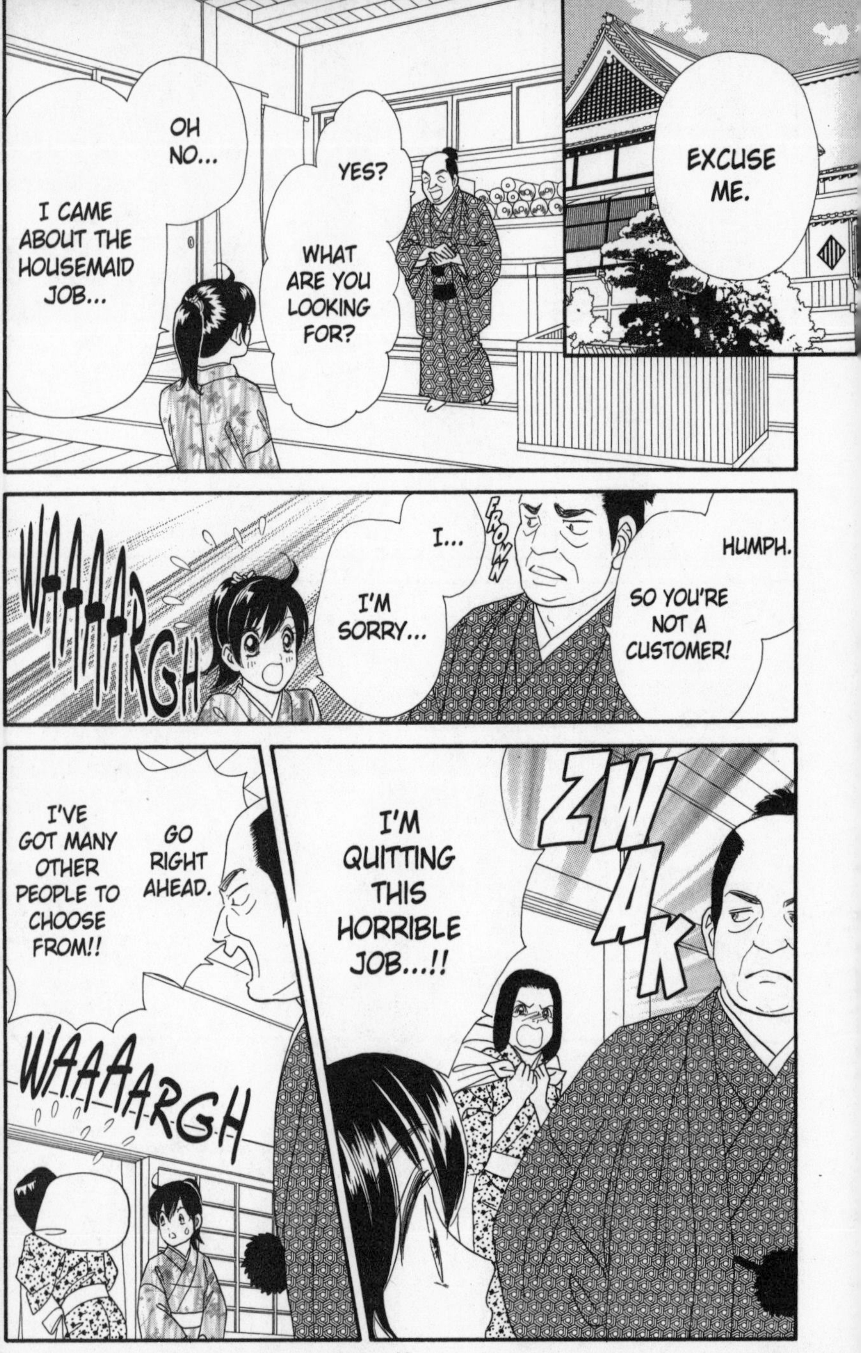
EXCUSE ME.
YES? WHAT ARE YOU LOOKING FOR?
OH NO... I CAME ABOUT THE HOUSEMAID JOB...
HUMPH. SO YOU'RE NOT A CUSTOMER!
FROWN
I... I'M SORRY...
WAAAARGH
ZWAK
I'M QUITTING THIS HORRIBLE JOB...!!
GO RIGHT AHEAD.
I'VE GOT MANY OTHER PEOPLE TO CHOOSE FROM!!
WAAAARGH

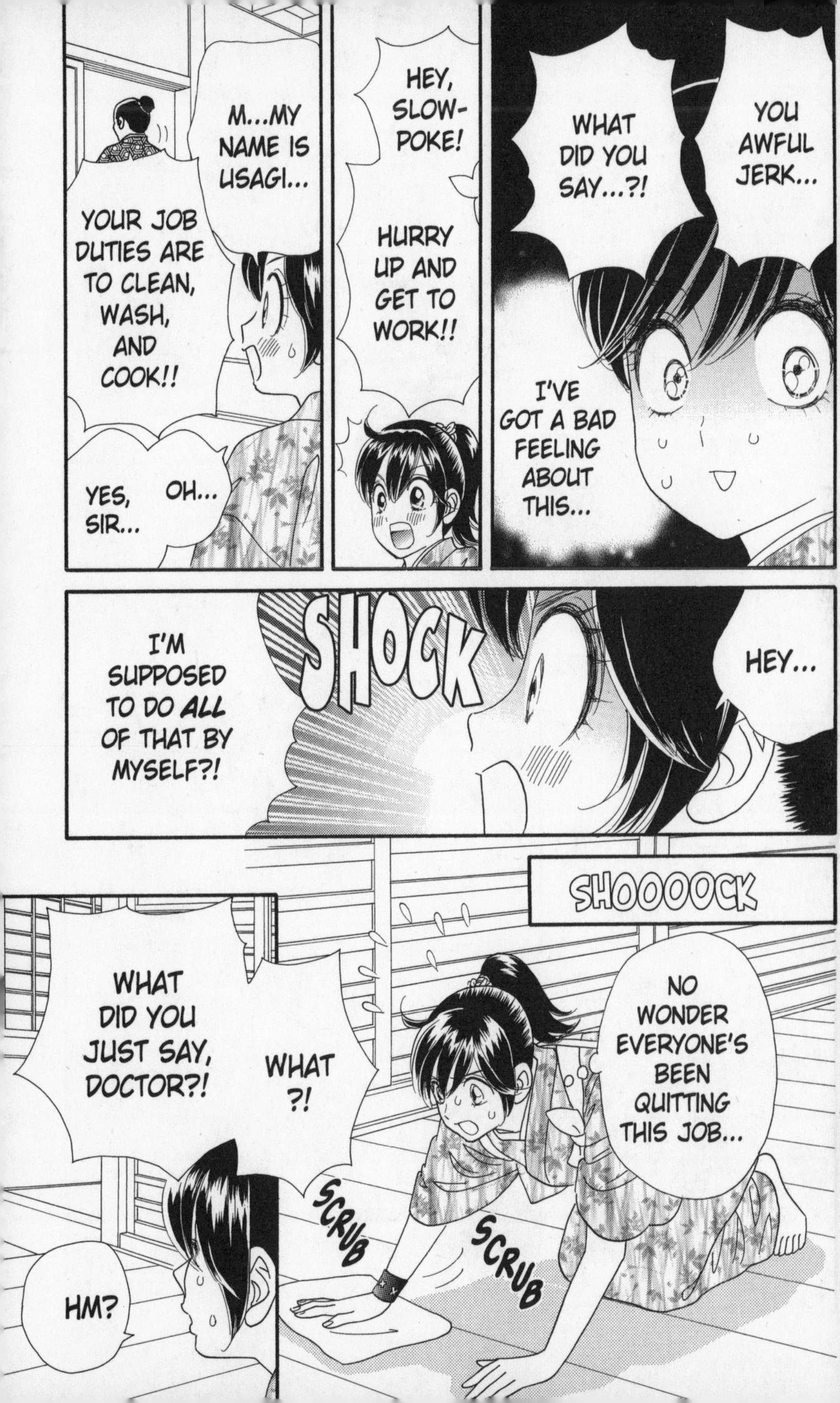
YOU AWFUL JERK...
WHAT DID YOU SAY...?!
I'VE GOT A BAD FEELING ABOUT THIS...
HEY, SLOW-POKE!
HURRY UP AND GET TO WORK!!
M...MY NAME IS USAGI...
YOUR JOB DUTIES ARE TO CLEAN, WASH, AND COOK!!
OH...
YES, SIR...
HEY...
SHOCK
I'M SUPPOSED TO DO **ALL** OF THAT BY MYSELF?!
SHOOOOCK
NO WONDER EVERYONE'S BEEN QUITTING THIS JOB...
WHAT ?!
WHAT DID YOU JUST SAY, DOCTOR?!
SCRUB
SCRUB
HM?

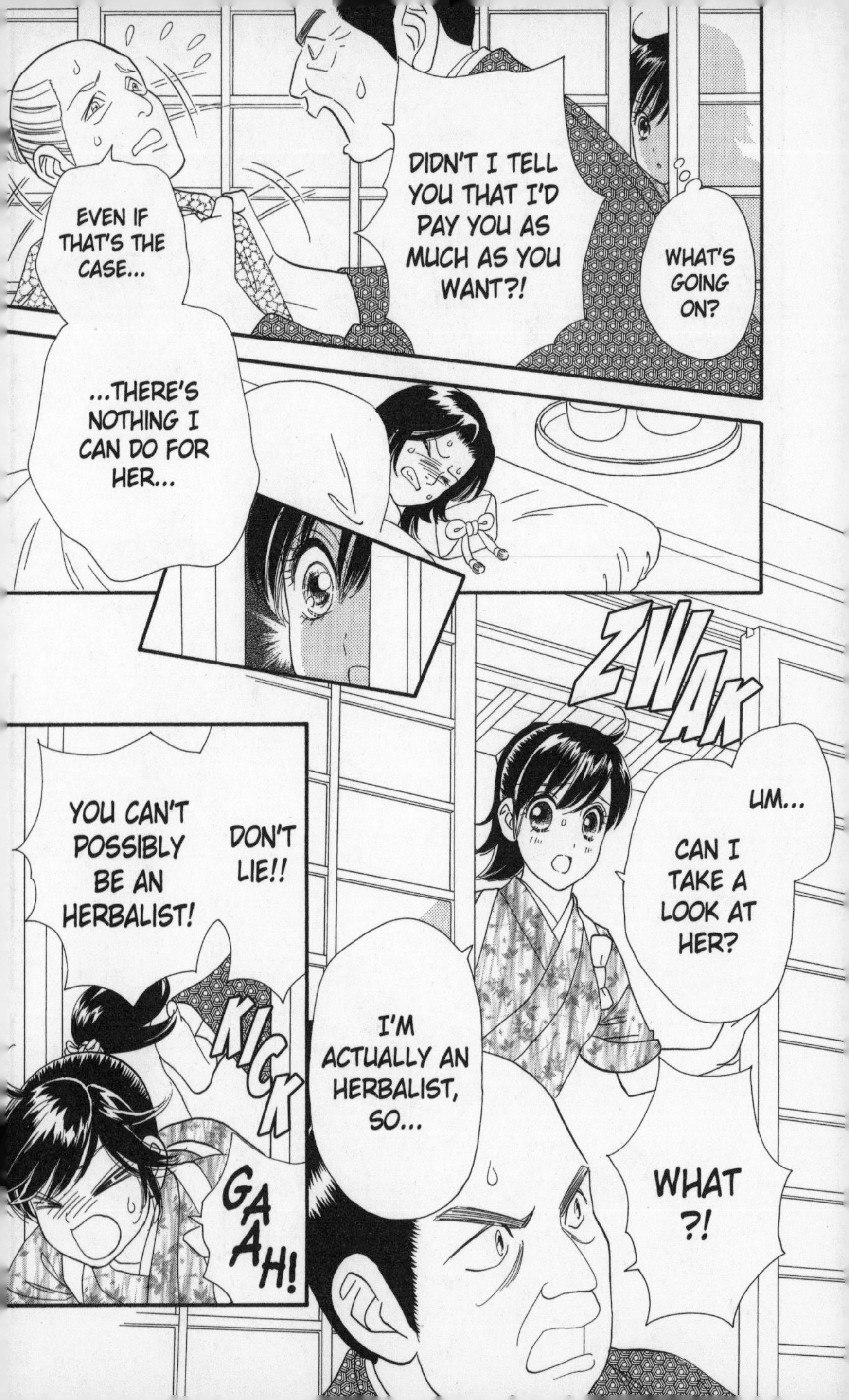
WHAT'S GOING ON?
DIDN'T I TELL YOU THAT I'D PAY YOU AS MUCH AS YOU WANT?!
EVEN IF THAT'S THE CASE...
...THERE'S NOTHING I CAN DO FOR HER...
ZWAK
UM...
CAN I TAKE A LOOK AT HER?
I'M ACTUALLY AN HERBALIST, SO...
WHAT ?!
DON'T LIE!!
YOU CAN'T POSSIBLY BE AN HERBALIST!
KICK
GAAH!

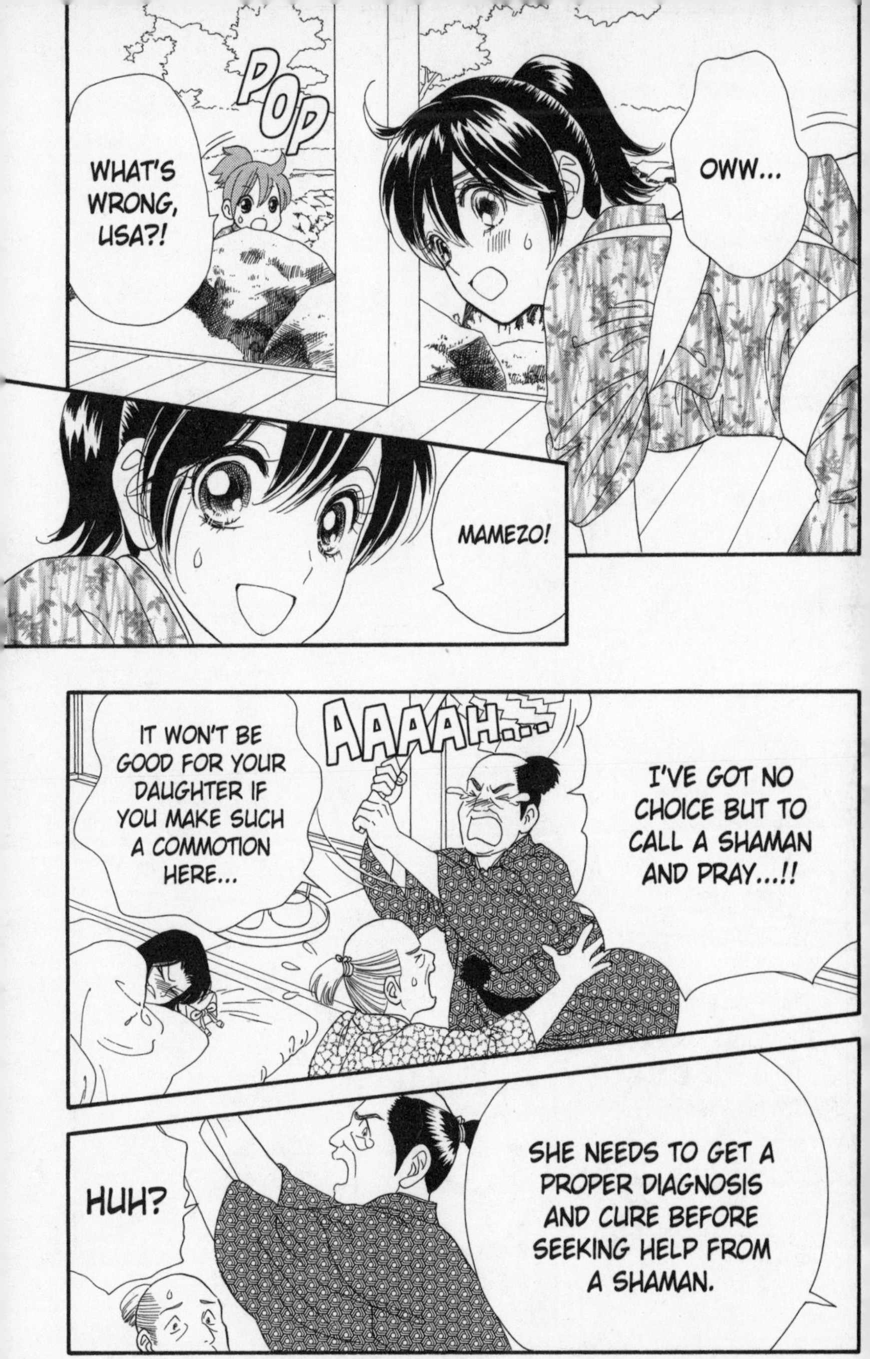
OWW...
POP
WHAT'S WRONG, USA?!
MAMEZO!
I'VE GOT NO CHOICE BUT TO CALL A SHAMAN AND PRAY...!!
AAAAH...
IT WON'T BE GOOD FOR YOUR DAUGHTER IF YOU MAKE SUCH A COMMOTION HERE...
SHE NEEDS TO GET A PROPER DIAGNOSIS AND CURE BEFORE SEEKING HELP FROM A SHAMAN.
HUH?

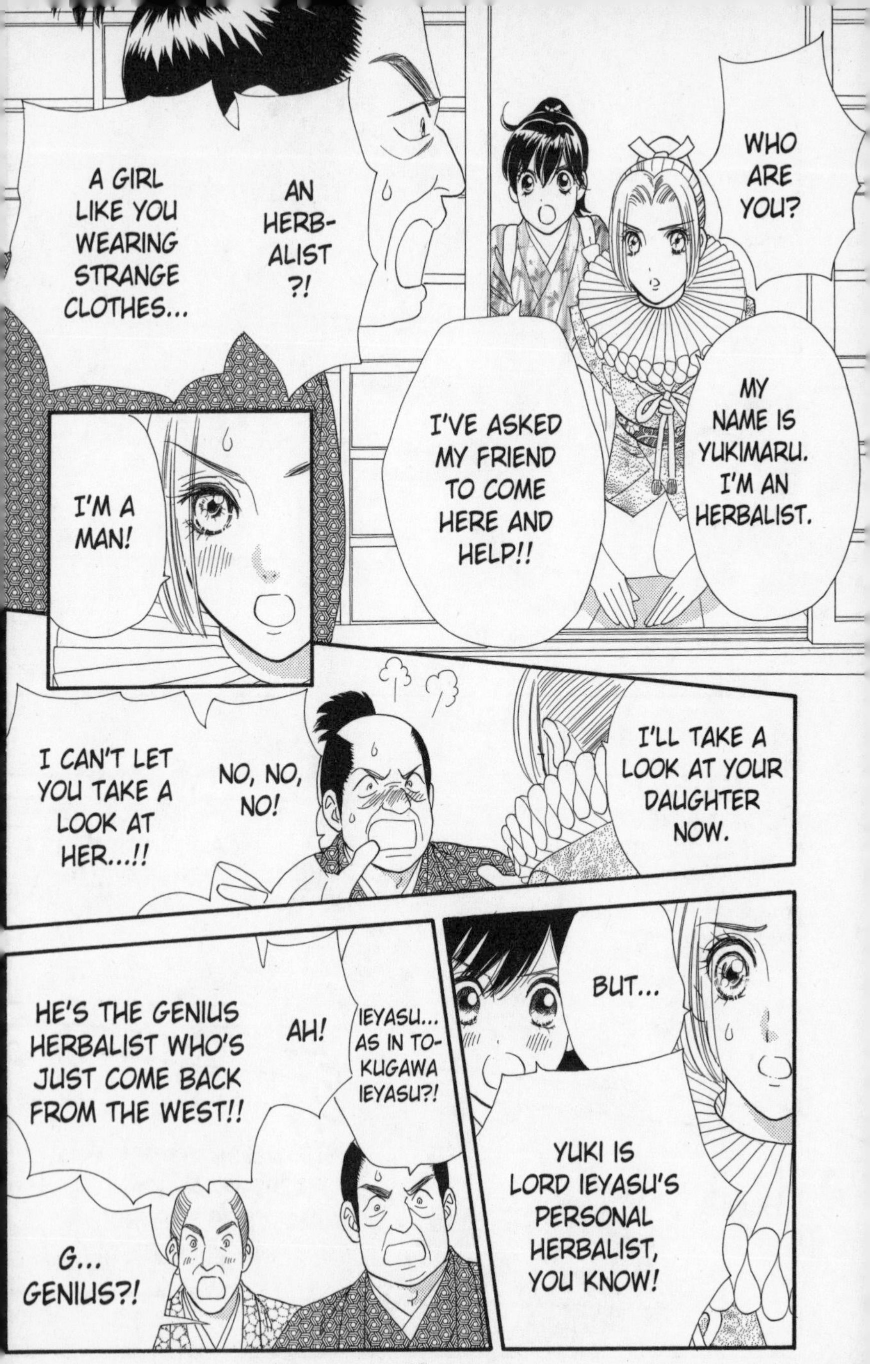
WHO ARE YOU?
MY NAME IS YUKIMARU. I'M AN HERBALIST.
I'VE ASKED MY FRIEND TO COME HERE AND HELP!!
AN HERB-ALIST?!
A GIRL LIKE YOU WEARING STRANGE CLOTHES...
I'M A MAN!
I'LL TAKE A LOOK AT YOUR DAUGHTER NOW.
NO, NO, NO!
I CAN'T LET YOU TAKE A LOOK AT HER...!!
BUT...
YUKI IS LORD IEYASU'S PERSONAL HERBALIST, YOU KNOW!
IEYASU... AS IN TO-KUGAWA IEYASU?!
AH!
HE'S THE GENIUS HERBALIST WHO'S JUST COME BACK FROM THE WEST!!
G... GENIUS?!

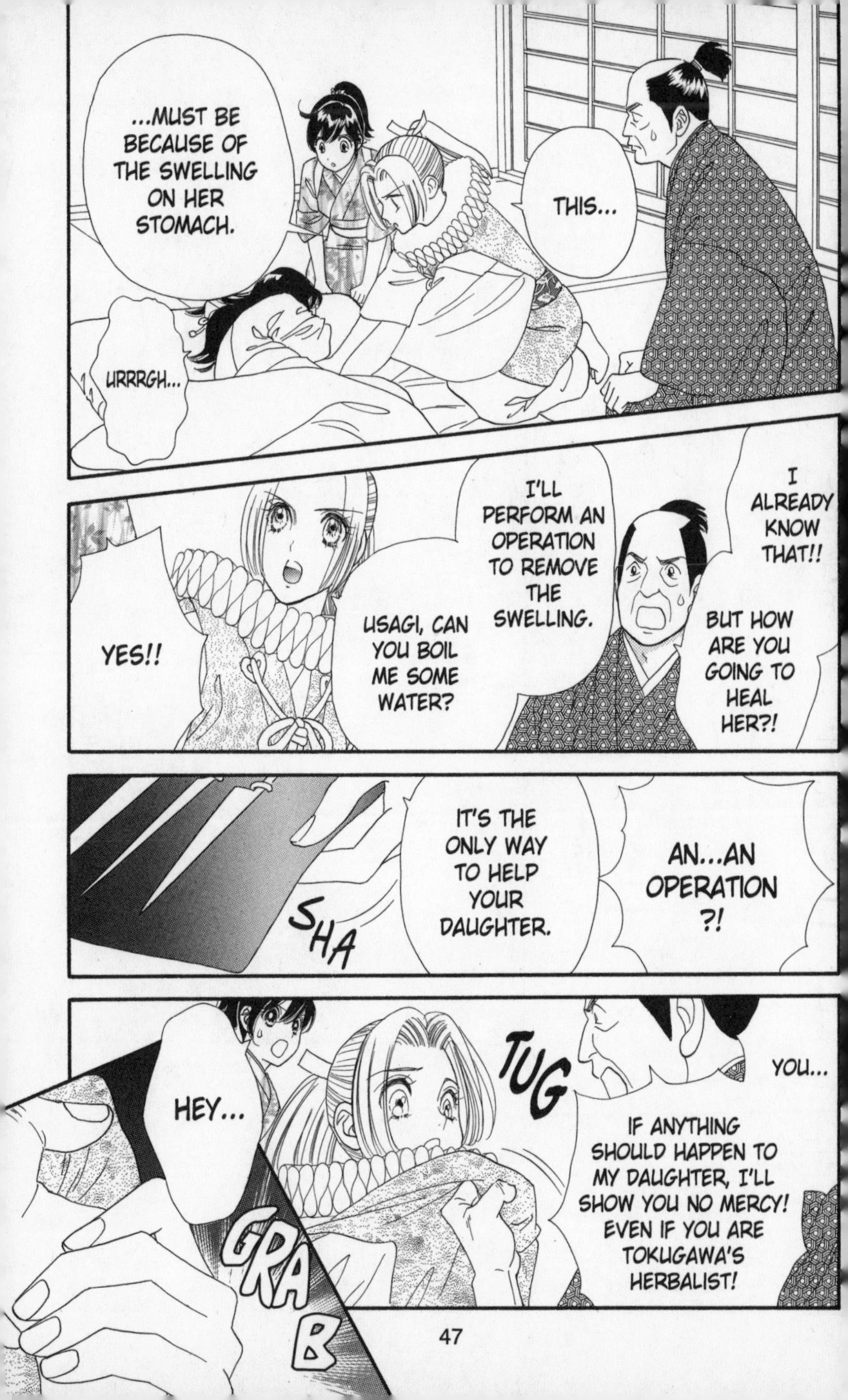
THIS...
...MUST BE BECAUSE OF THE SWELLING ON HER STOMACH.
URRRGH...
I ALREADY KNOW THAT!!
BUT HOW ARE YOU GOING TO HEAL HER?!
I'LL PERFORM AN OPERATION TO REMOVE THE SWELLING.
USAGI, CAN YOU BOIL ME SOME WATER?
YES!!
AN...AN OPERATION ?!
IT'S THE ONLY WAY TO HELP YOUR DAUGHTER.
SHA
YOU...
IF ANYTHING SHOULD HAPPEN TO MY DAUGHTER, I'LL SHOW YOU NO MERCY! EVEN IF YOU ARE TOKUGAWA'S HERBALIST!
TUG
HEY...
GRAB

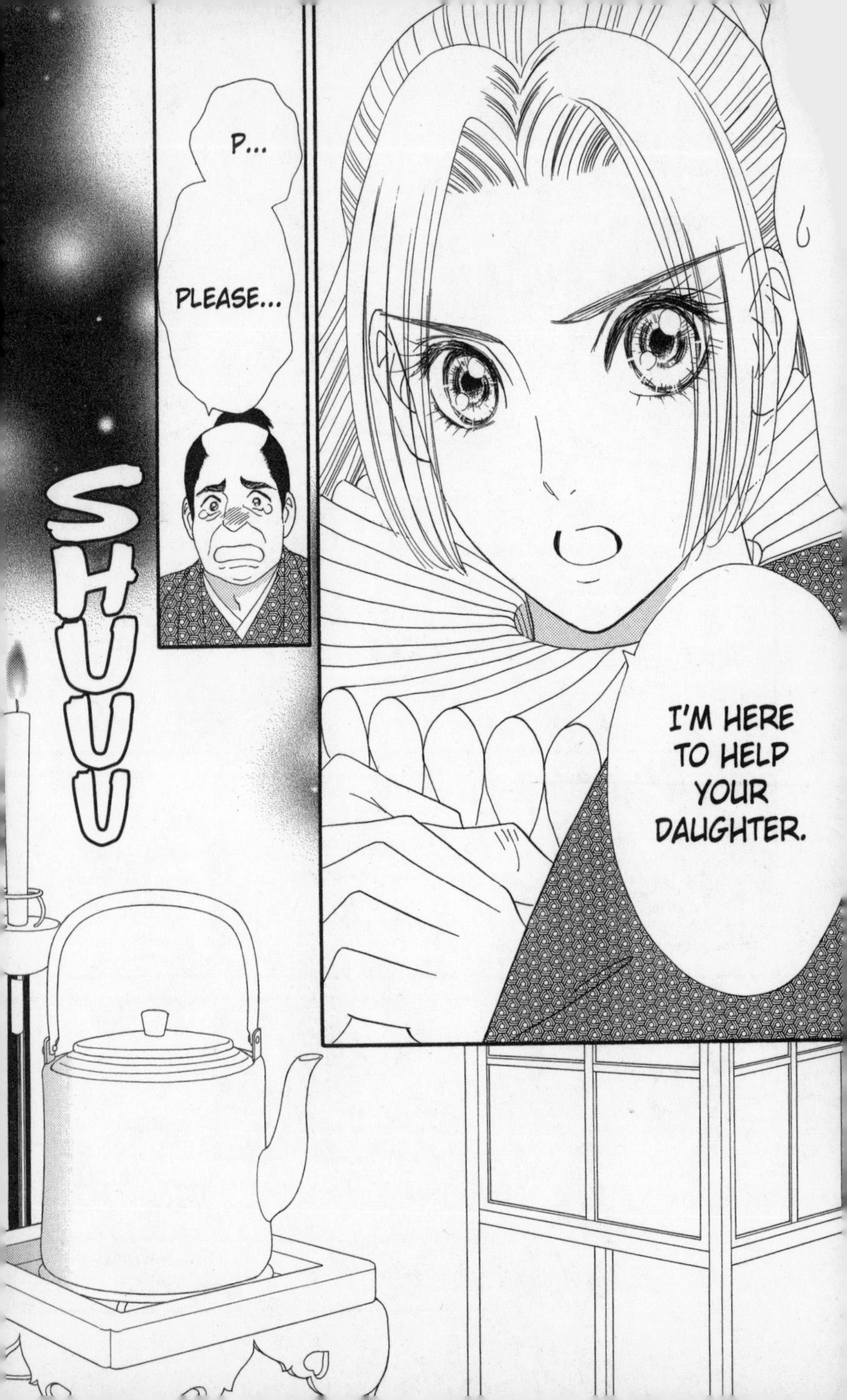
I'M HERE TO HELP YOUR DAUGHTER.
P...
PLEASE...
SHUUU

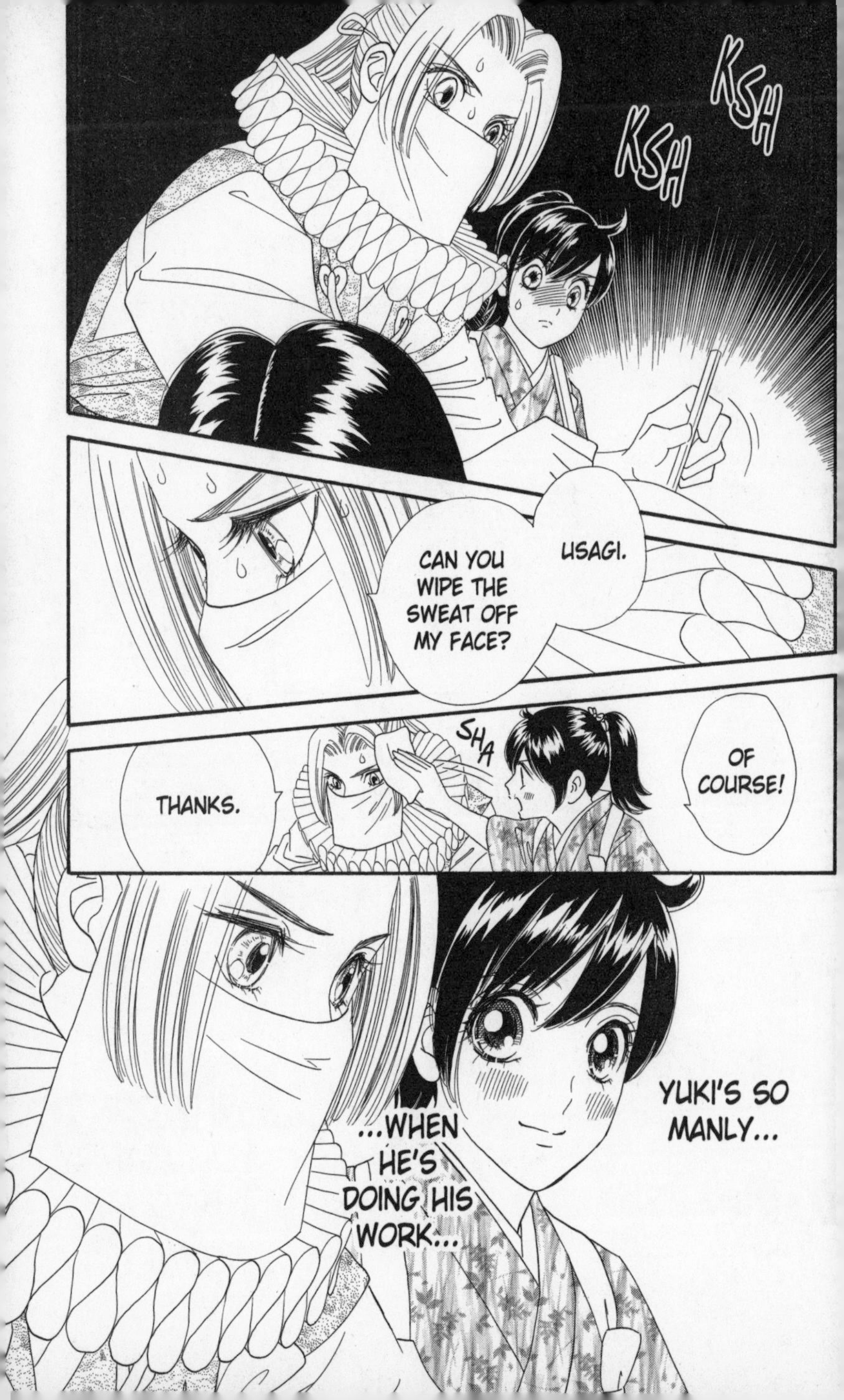
KSH
KSH
USAGI.
CAN YOU WIPE THE SWEAT OFF MY FACE?
OF COURSE!
SHA
THANKS.
YUKI'S SO MANLY...
...WHEN HE'S DOING HIS WORK...

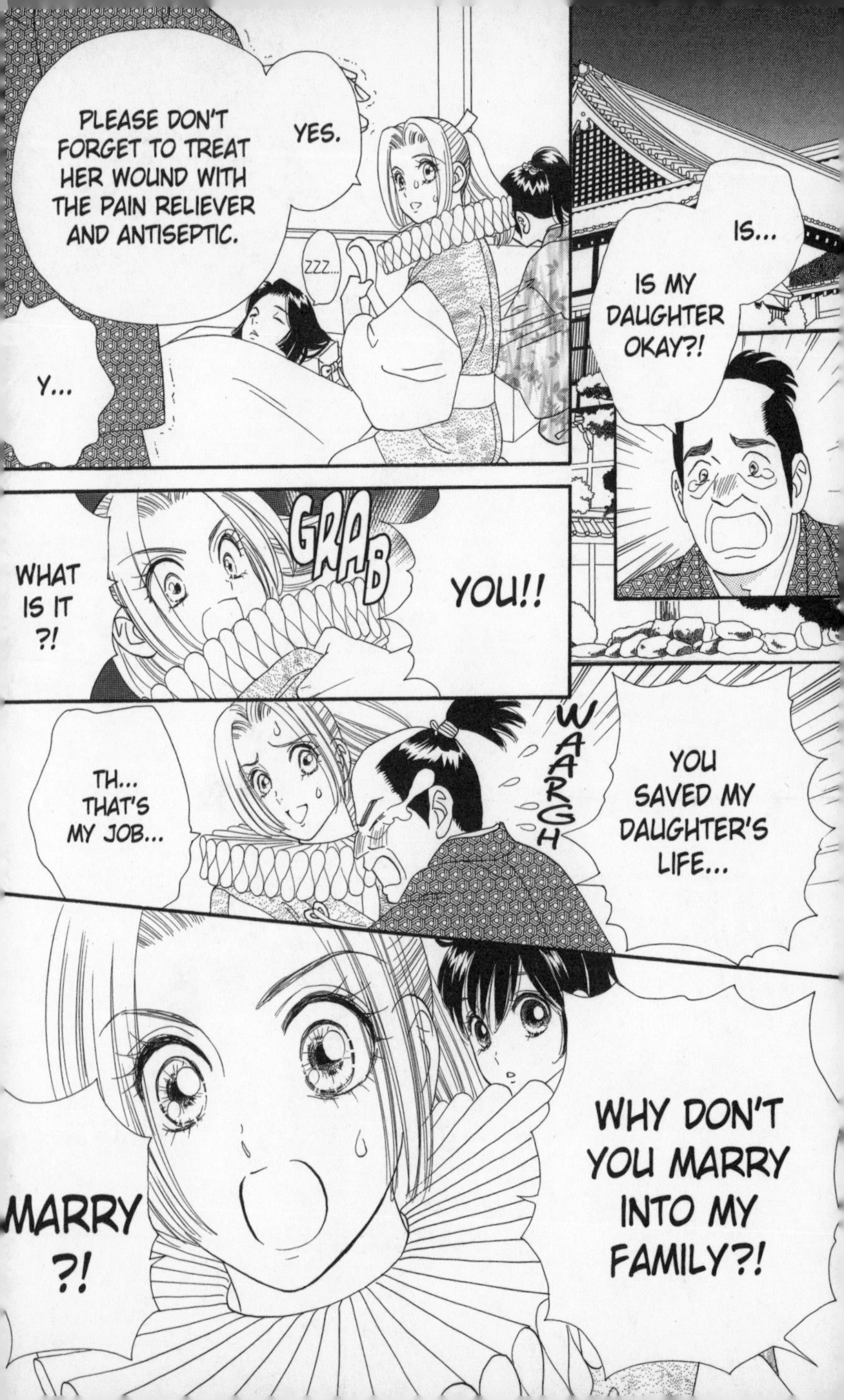
IS...
IS MY DAUGHTER OKAY?!
YES.
PLEASE DON'T FORGET TO TREAT HER WOUND WITH THE PAIN RELIEVER AND ANTISEPTIC.
ZZZ...
Y...
YOU!!
GRAB
WHAT IS IT ?!
YOU SAVED MY DAUGHTER'S LIFE...
WAARGH
TH... THAT'S MY JOB...
WHY DON'T YOU MARRY INTO MY FAMILY?!
MARRY ?!

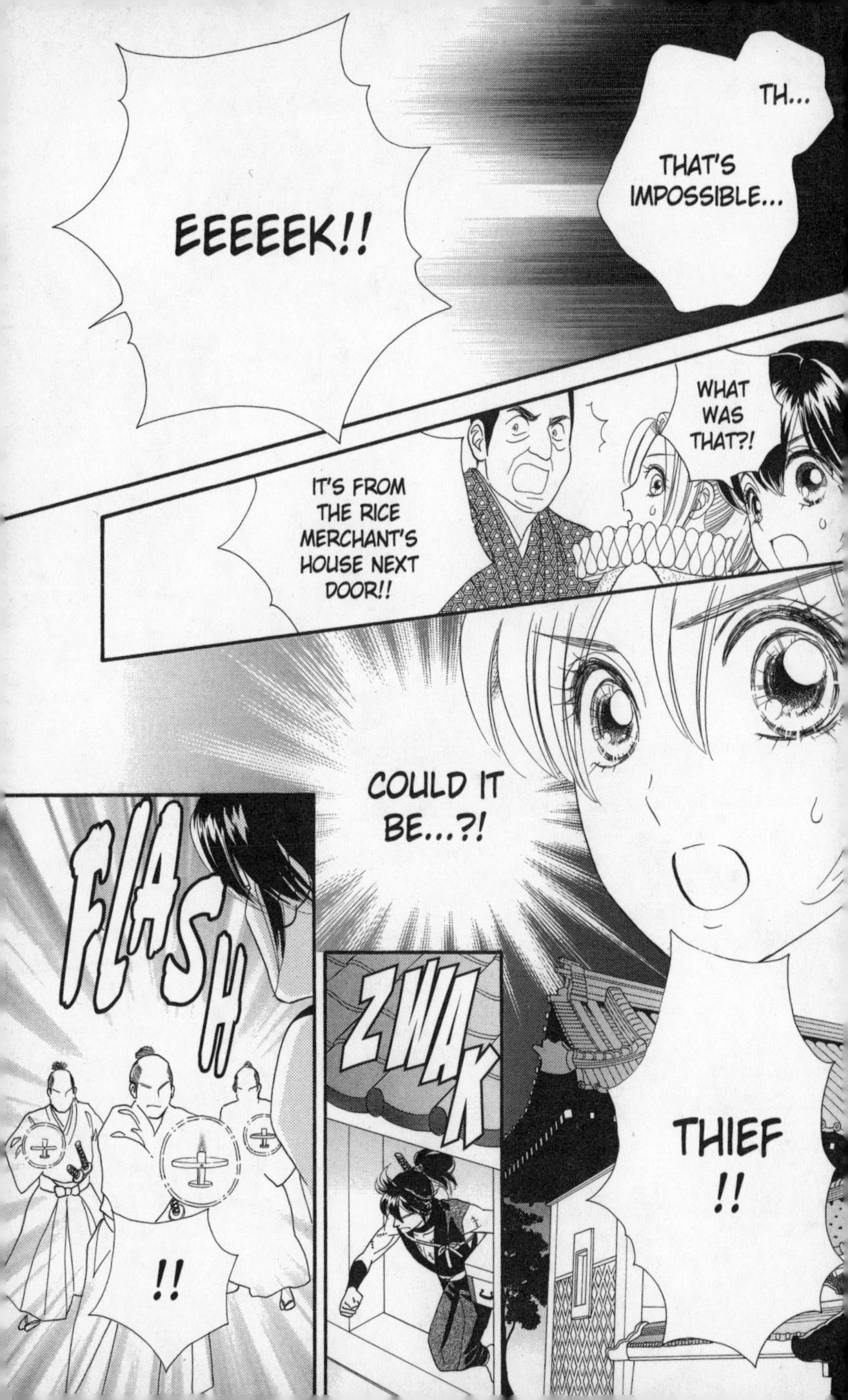
TH...
THAT'S IMPOSSIBLE...
EEEEEK!!
WHAT WAS THAT?!
IT'S FROM THE RICE MERCHANT'S HOUSE NEXT DOOR!!
COULD IT BE...?!
THIEF !!
ZWAK
FLASH
!!

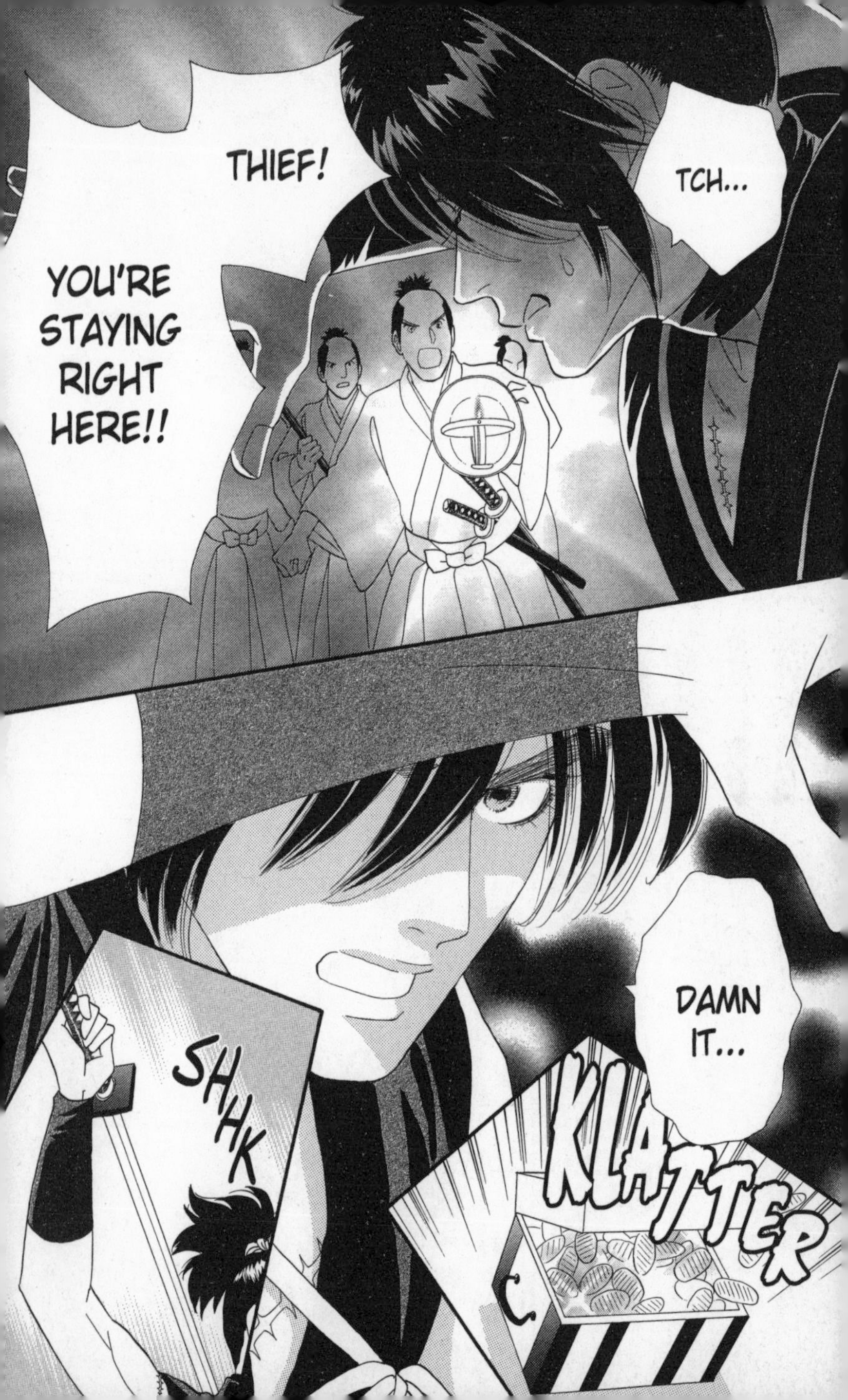
TCH...
THIEF!
YOU'RE STAYING RIGHT HERE!!
DAMN IT...
KLATTER
SHHK

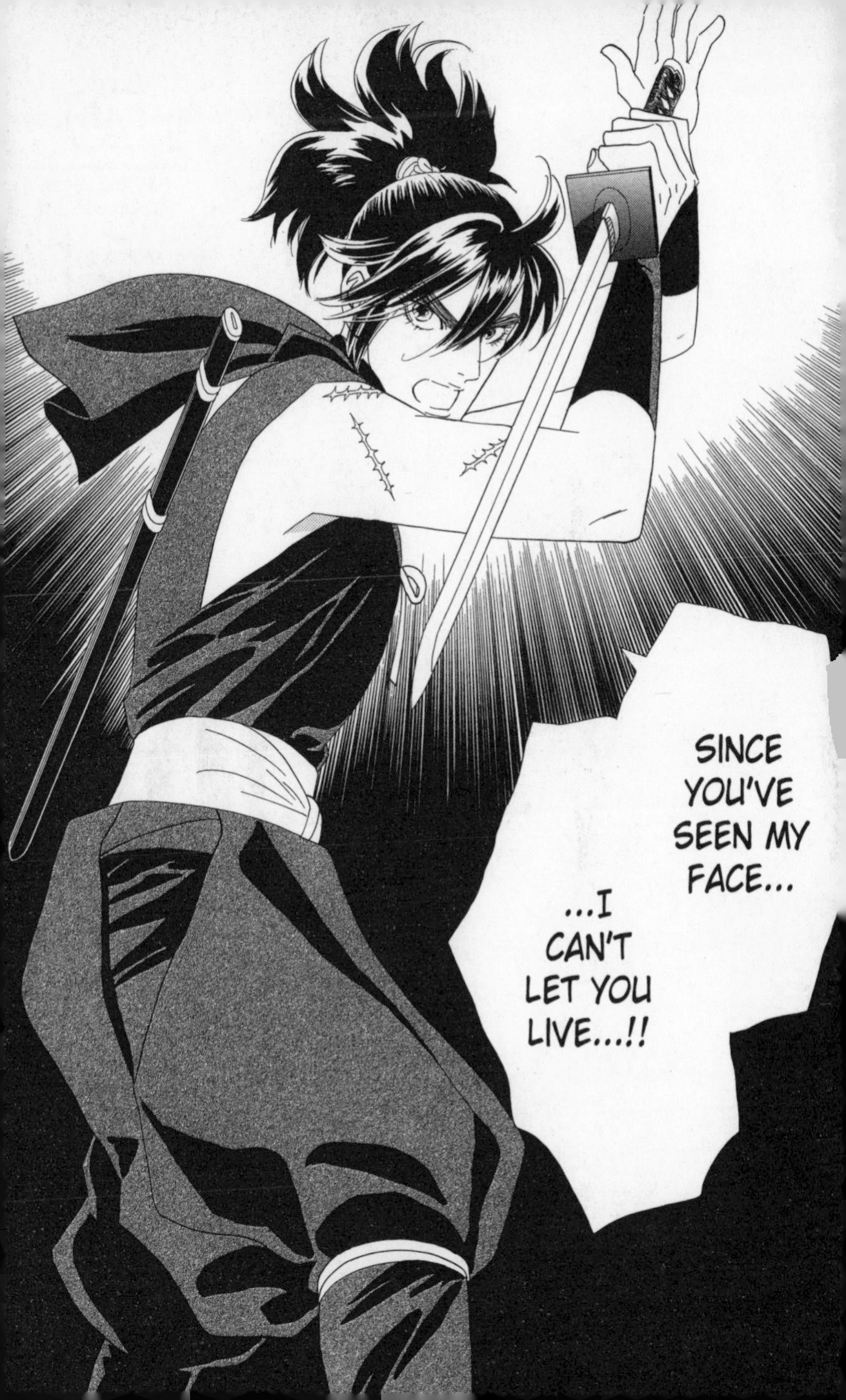
SINCE YOU'VE SEEN MY FACE...
...I CAN'T LET YOU LIVE...!!

LET'S GO!

LITTLE HANZO

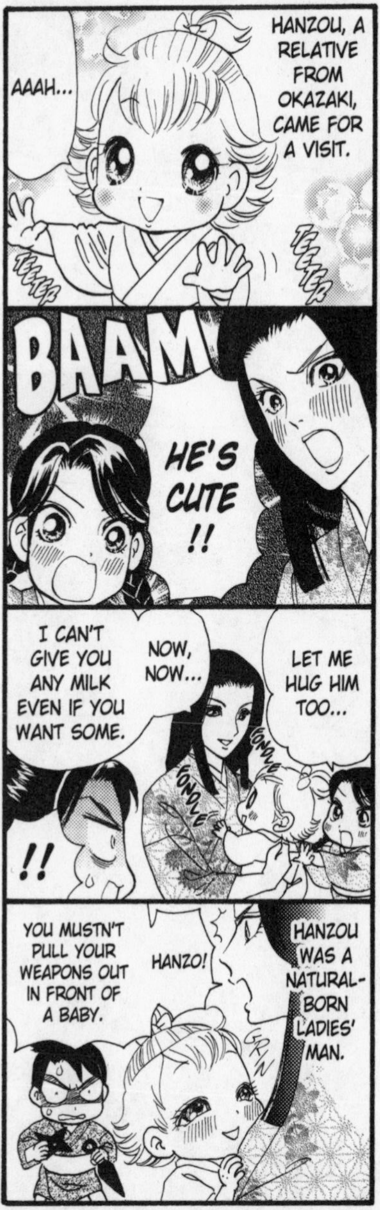
HANZOU, A RELATIVE FROM OKAZAKI, CAME FOR A VISIT.
AAAH...
TEETER
TEETER
BAAM
HE'S CUTE !!
LET ME HUG HIM TOO...
NOW, NOW...
I CAN'T GIVE YOU ANY MILK EVEN IF YOU WANT SOME.
FONDLE
FONDLE
!!
HANZOU WAS A NATURAL-BORN LADIES' MAN.
GRIN
HANZO!
YOU MUSTN'T PULL YOUR WEAPONS OUT IN FRONT OF A BABY.

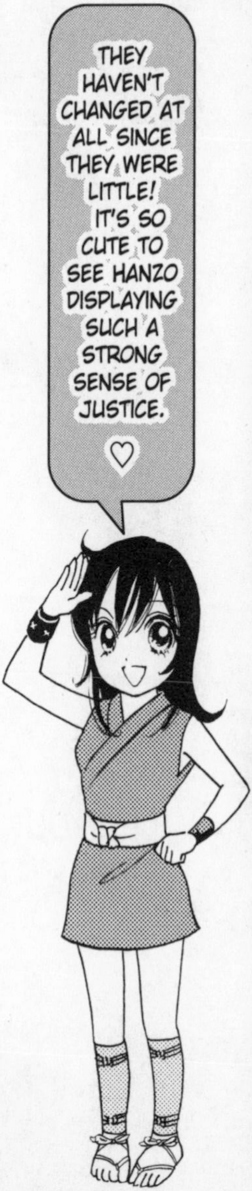
THEY HAVEN'T CHANGED AT ALL SINCE THEY WERE LITTLE! IT'S SO CUTE TO SEE HANZO DISPLAYING SUCH A STRONG SENSE OF JUSTICE. ♡

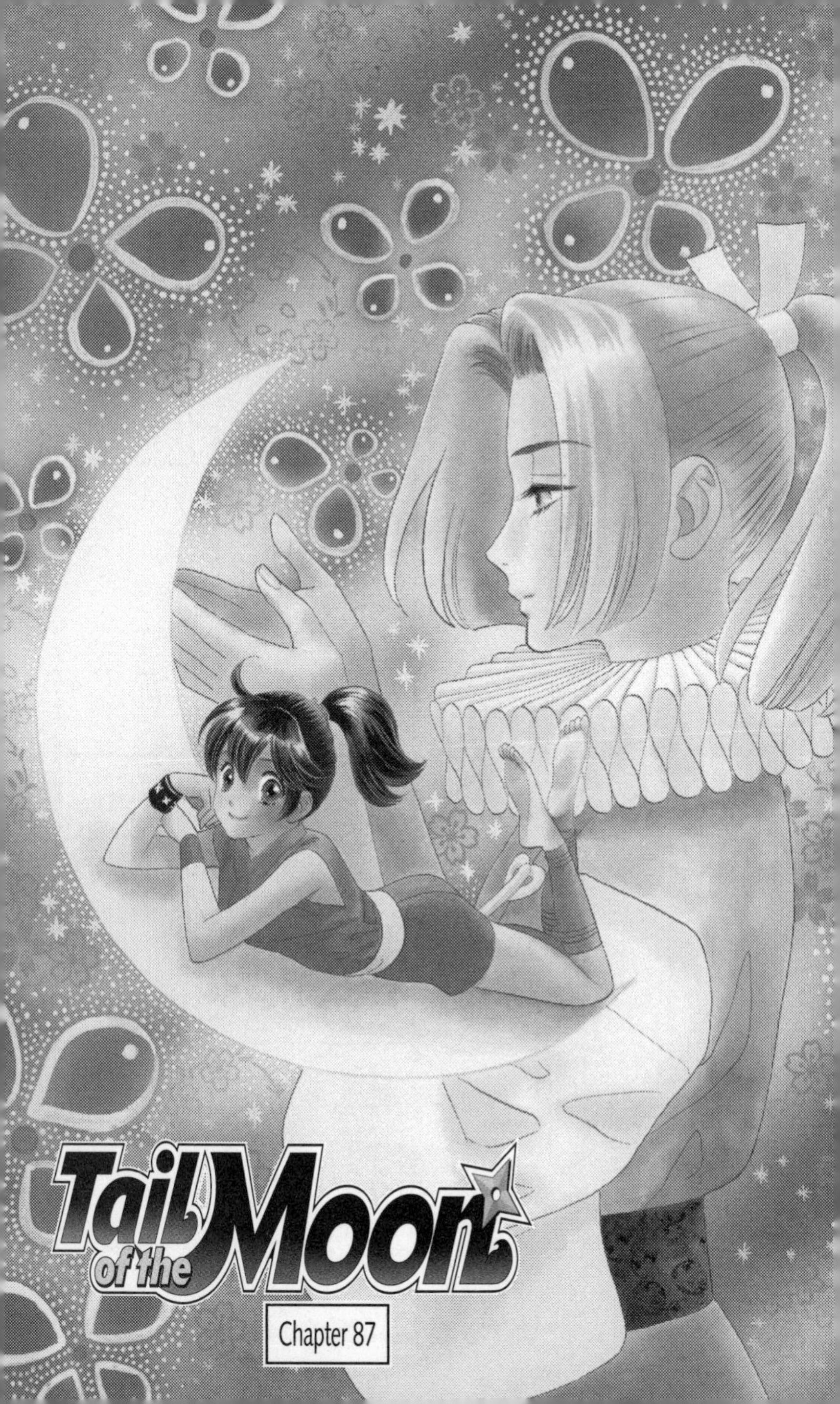

Tail of the Moon
Chapter 87

LET'S GO!

LITTLE HANZO

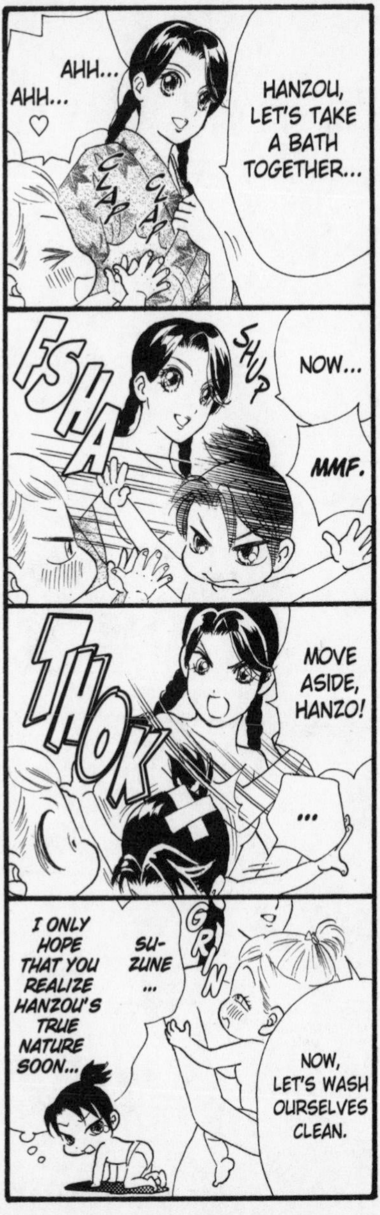
HANZOU, LET'S TAKE A BATH TOGETHER...
AHH... AHH... ♡
CLAP CLAP
NOW...
SHUP
FSHA
MMF.
MOVE ASIDE, HANZO!
THOK
...
GRIN
NOW, LET'S WASH OURSELVES CLEAN.
SU-ZUNE...
I ONLY HOPE THAT YOU REALIZE HANZOU'S TRUE NATURE SOON...

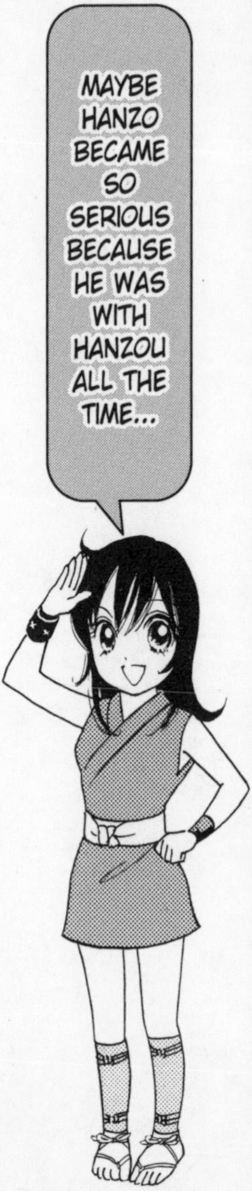
MAYBE HANZO BECAME SO SERIOUS BECAUSE HE WAS WITH HANZOU ALL THE TIME...

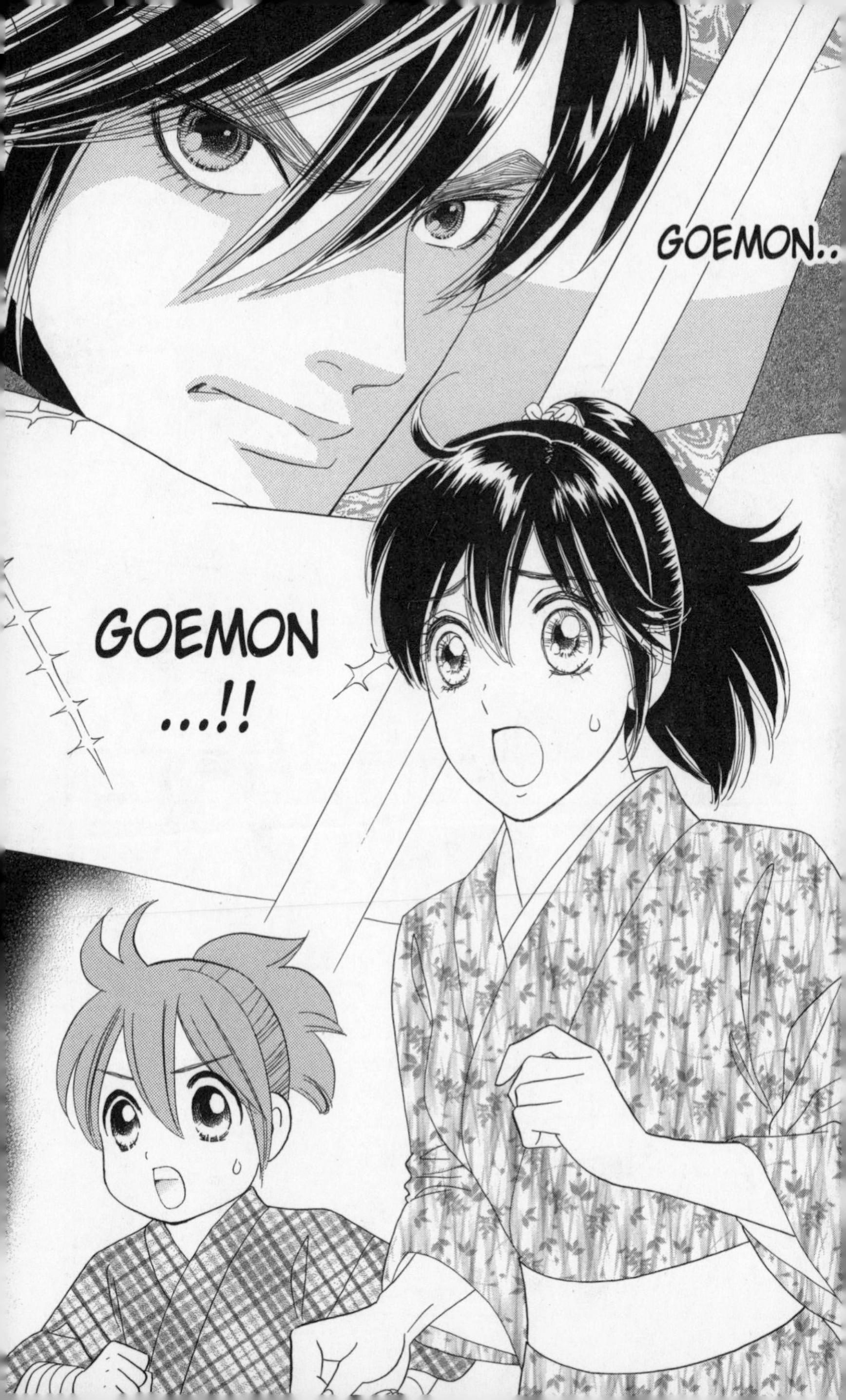
GOEMON..
GOEMON ...!!

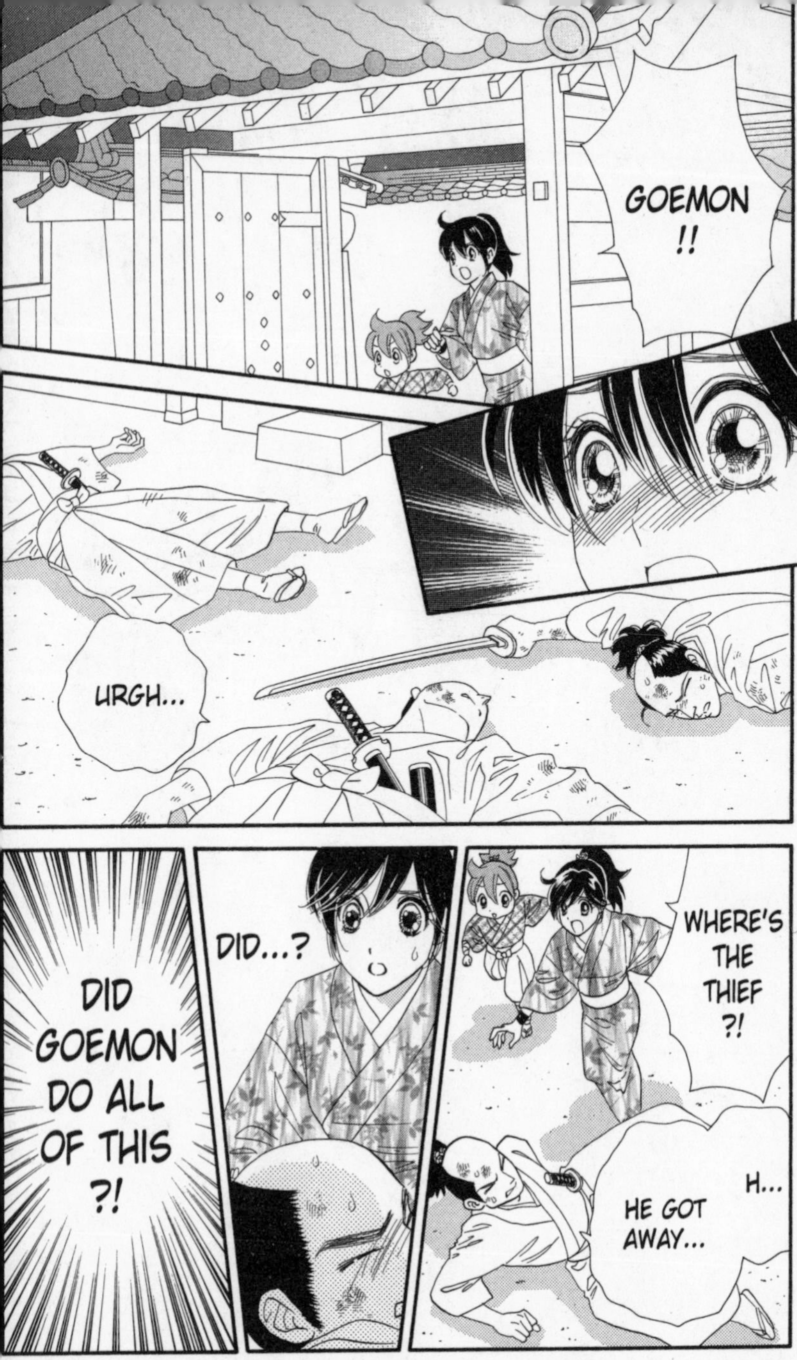
GOEMON !!
URGH...
WHERE'S THE THIEF ?!
H...
HE GOT AWAY...
DID...?
DID GOEMON DO ALL OF THIS ?!

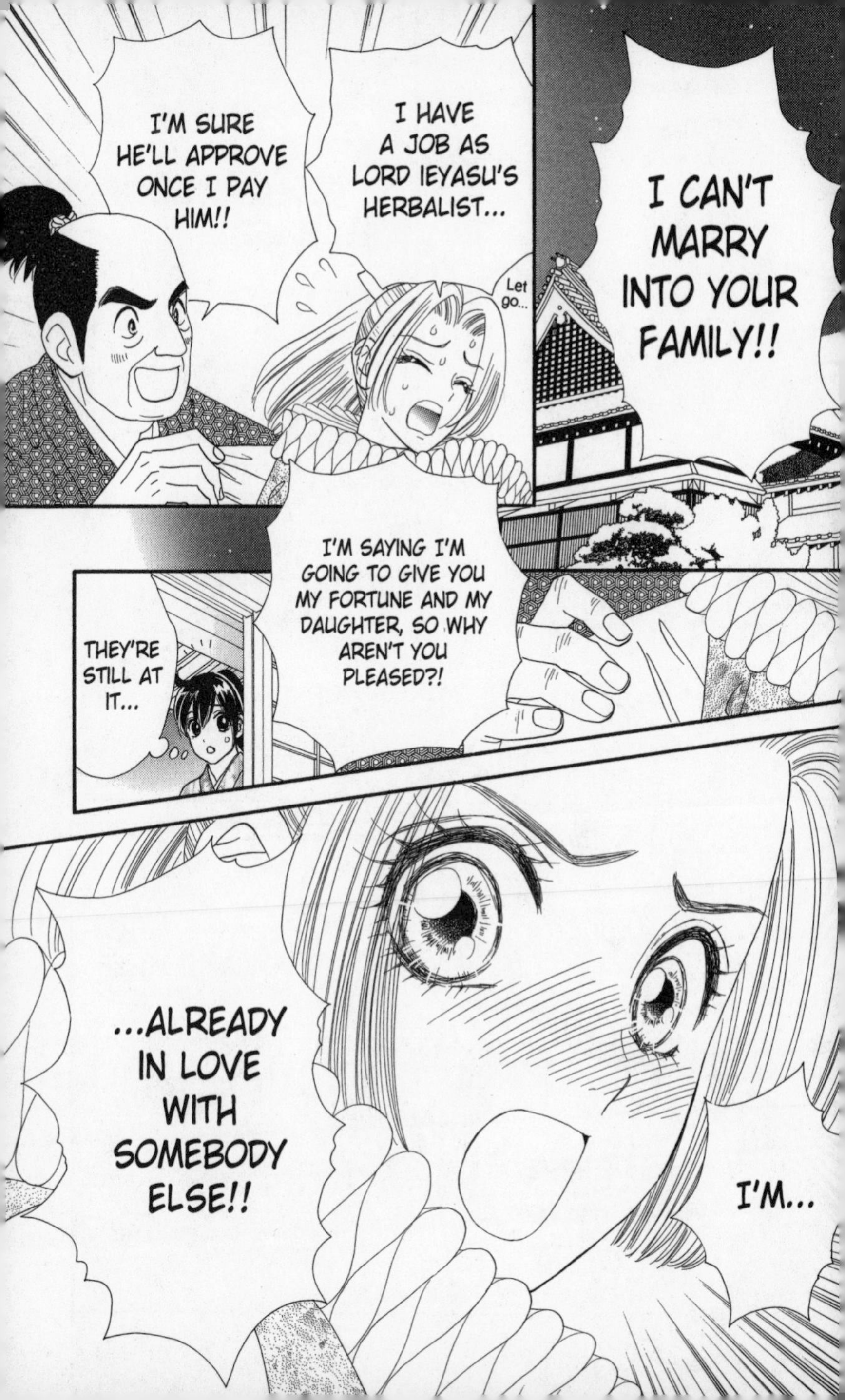
I CAN'T MARRY INTO YOUR FAMILY!!
I HAVE A JOB AS LORD IEYASU'S HERBALIST...
I'M SURE HE'LL APPROVE ONCE I PAY HIM!!
Let go...
I'M SAYING I'M GOING TO GIVE YOU MY FORTUNE AND MY DAUGHTER, SO WHY AREN'T YOU PLEASED?!
THEY'RE STILL AT IT...
I'M...
...ALREADY IN LOVE WITH SOMEBODY ELSE!!

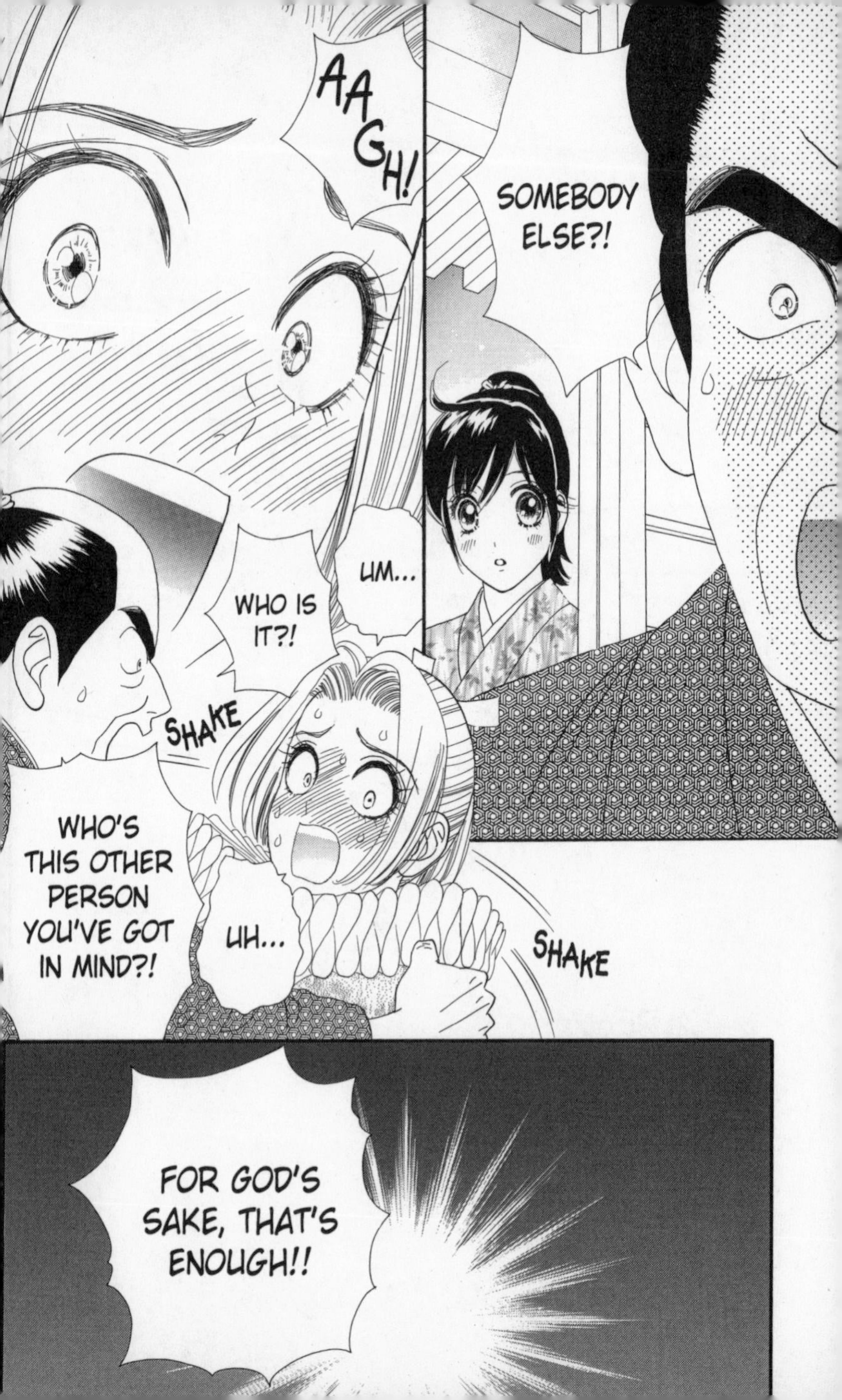
SOMEBODY ELSE?!
AAGH!
UM...
WHO IS IT?!
SHAKE
WHO'S THIS OTHER PERSON YOU'VE GOT IN MIND?!
UH...
SHAKE
FOR GOD'S SAKE, THAT'S ENOUGH!!

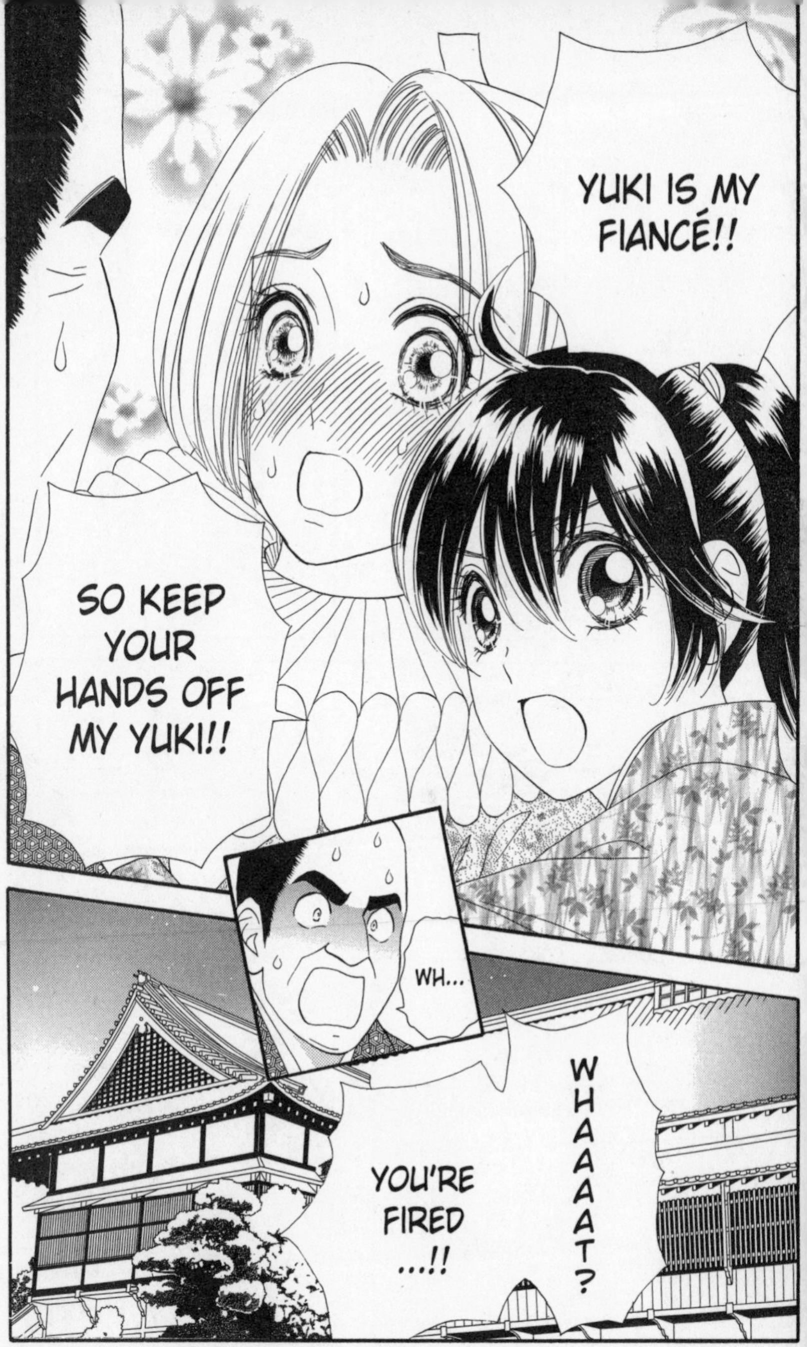
YUKI IS MY FIANCÉ!!
SO KEEP YOUR HANDS OFF MY YUKI!!
WH...
WHAAAAT?
YOU'RE FIRED ...!!

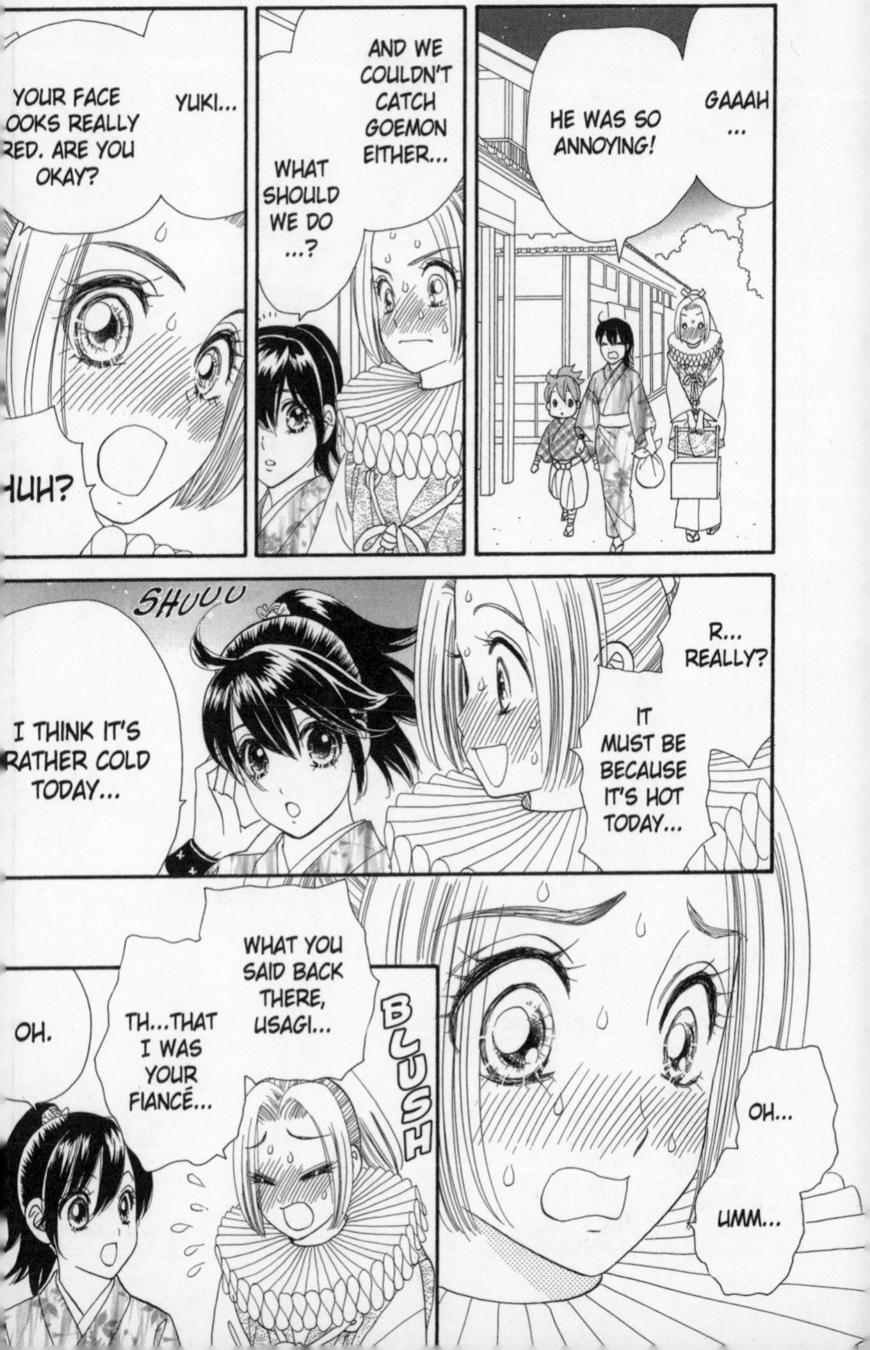
GAAAH ...
HE WAS SO ANNOYING!
AND WE COULDN'T CATCH GOEMON EITHER...
WHAT SHOULD WE DO ...?
YUKI...
YOUR FACE OOKS REALLY RED. ARE YOU OKAY?
HUH?
SHUUU
R... REALLY?
IT MUST BE BECAUSE IT'S HOT TODAY...
I THINK IT'S RATHER COLD TODAY...
OH...
UMM...
BLUSH
WHAT YOU SAID BACK THERE, USAGI...
TH...THAT I WAS YOUR FIANCÉ...
OH.

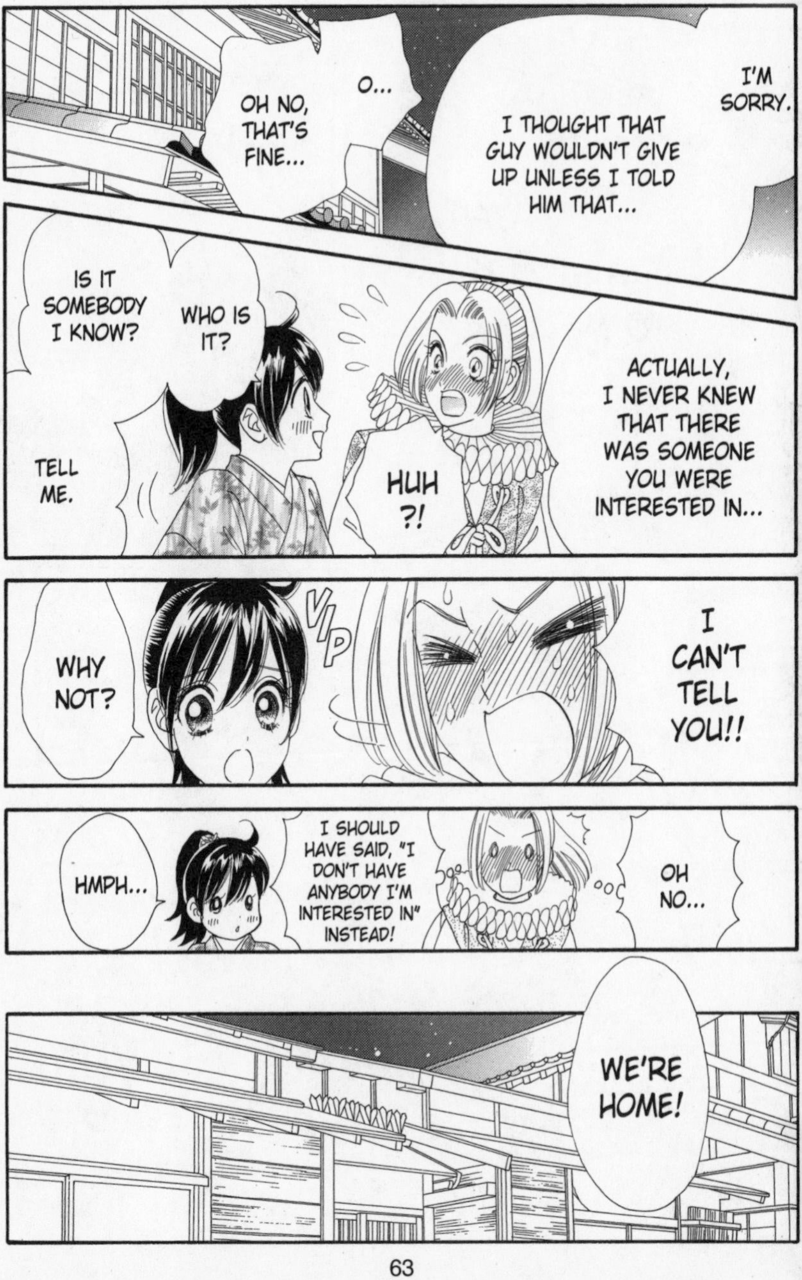
I'M SORRY.
I THOUGHT THAT GUY WOULDN'T GIVE UP UNLESS I TOLD HIM THAT...
O...
OH NO, THAT'S FINE...
ACTUALLY, I NEVER KNEW THAT THERE WAS SOMEONE YOU WERE INTERESTED IN...
HUH ?!
WHO IS IT?
IS IT SOMEBODY I KNOW?
TELL ME.
I CAN'T TELL YOU!!
VIP
WHY NOT?
OH NO...
I SHOULD HAVE SAID, "I DON'T HAVE ANYBODY I'M INTERESTED IN" INSTEAD!
HMPH...
WE'RE HOME!

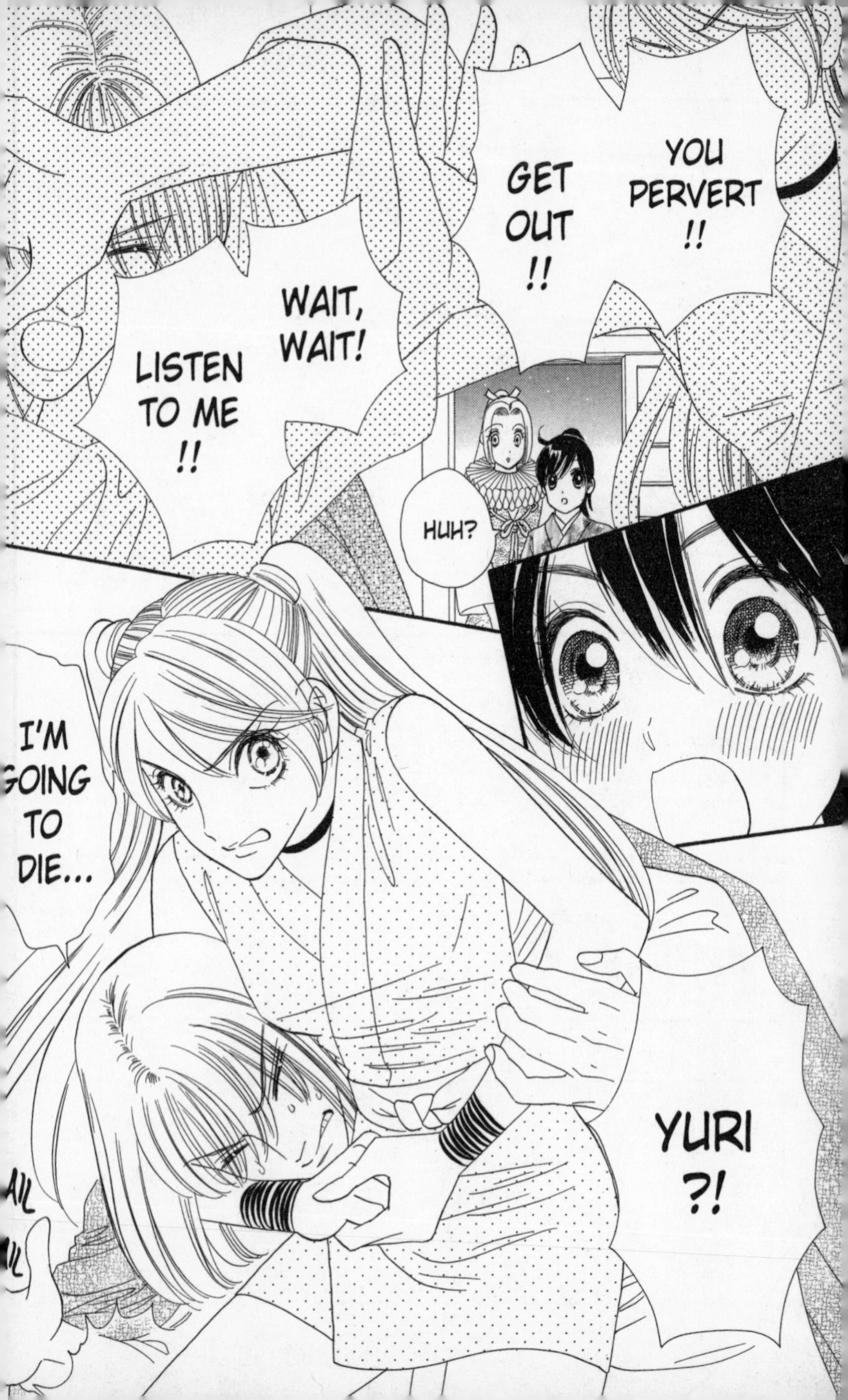
YOU PERVERT!!
GET OUT!!
WAIT, WAIT!
LISTEN TO ME!!
HUH?
YURI?!
I'M GOING TO DIE...

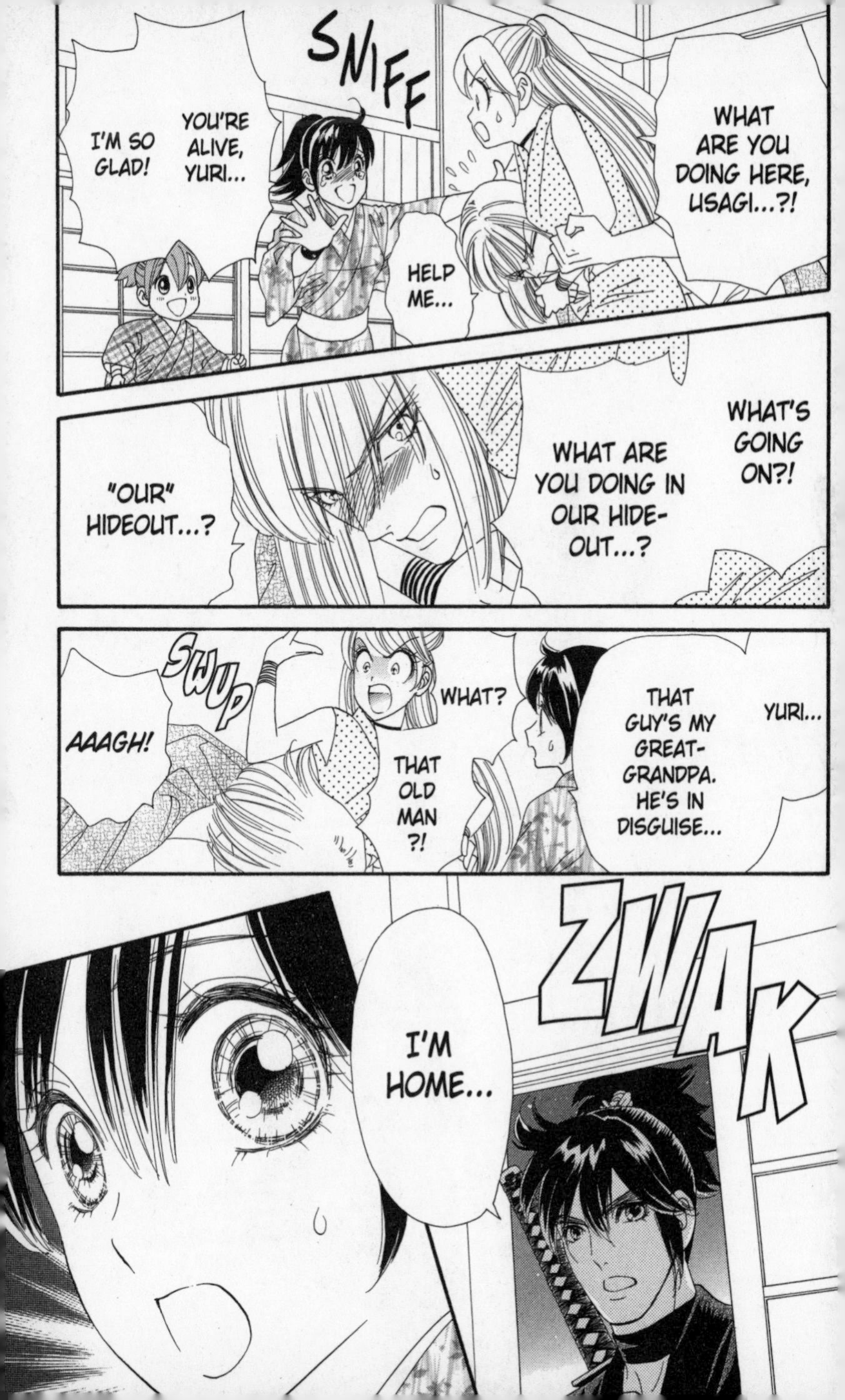

WHAT ARE YOU DOING HERE, USAGI...?!
SNIFF
YOU'RE ALIVE, YURI...
I'M SO GLAD!
HELP ME...
WHAT'S GOING ON?!
WHAT ARE YOU DOING IN OUR HIDE-OUT...?
"OUR" HIDEOUT...?
YURI...
THAT GUY'S MY GREAT-GRANDPA. HE'S IN DISGUISE...
WHAT?
THAT OLD MAN ?!
SWUP
AAAGH!
ZWAK
I'M HOME...

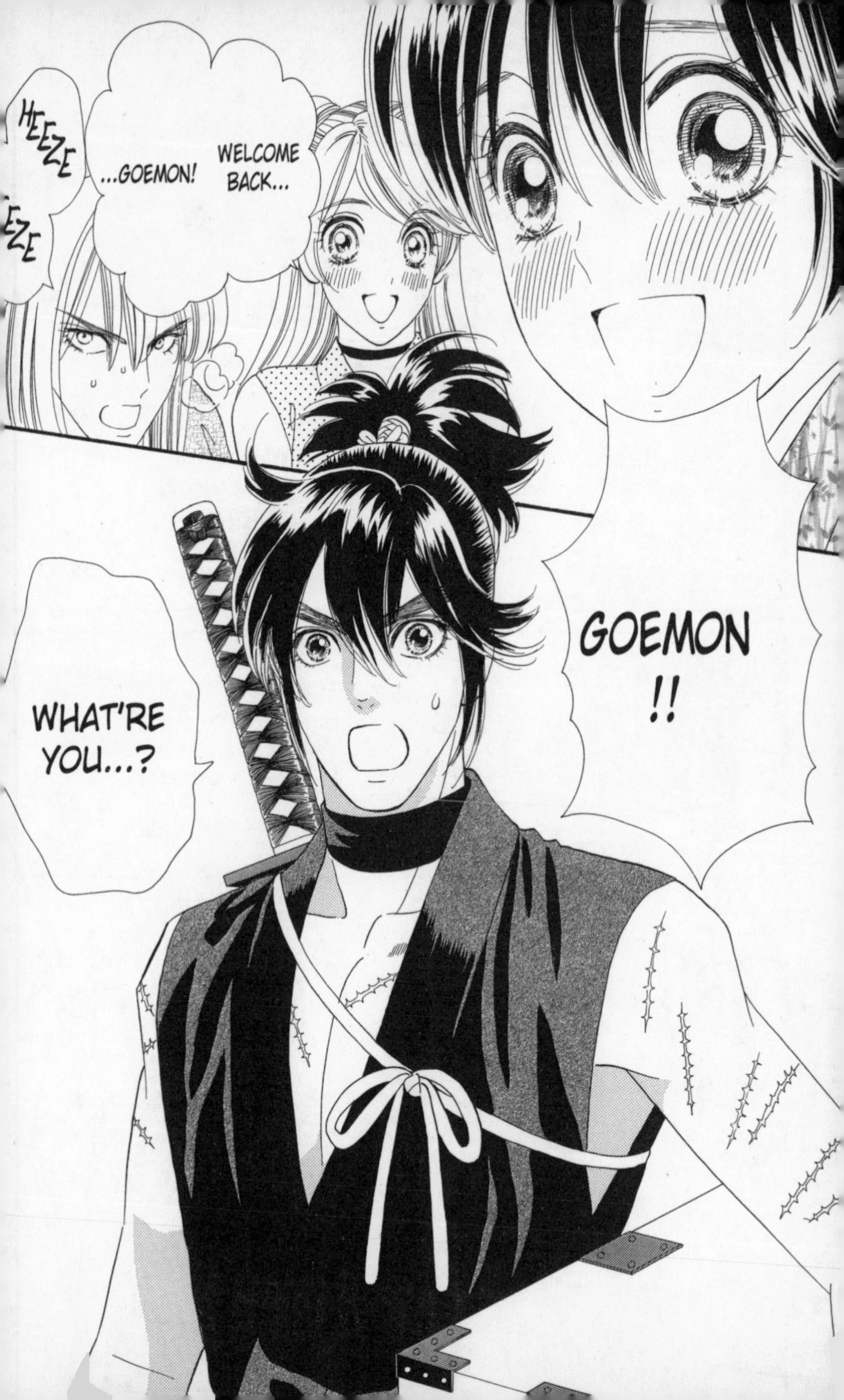
GOEMON !!
WELCOME BACK...
...GOEMON!
HEEZE
EEZE
WHAT'RE YOU...?

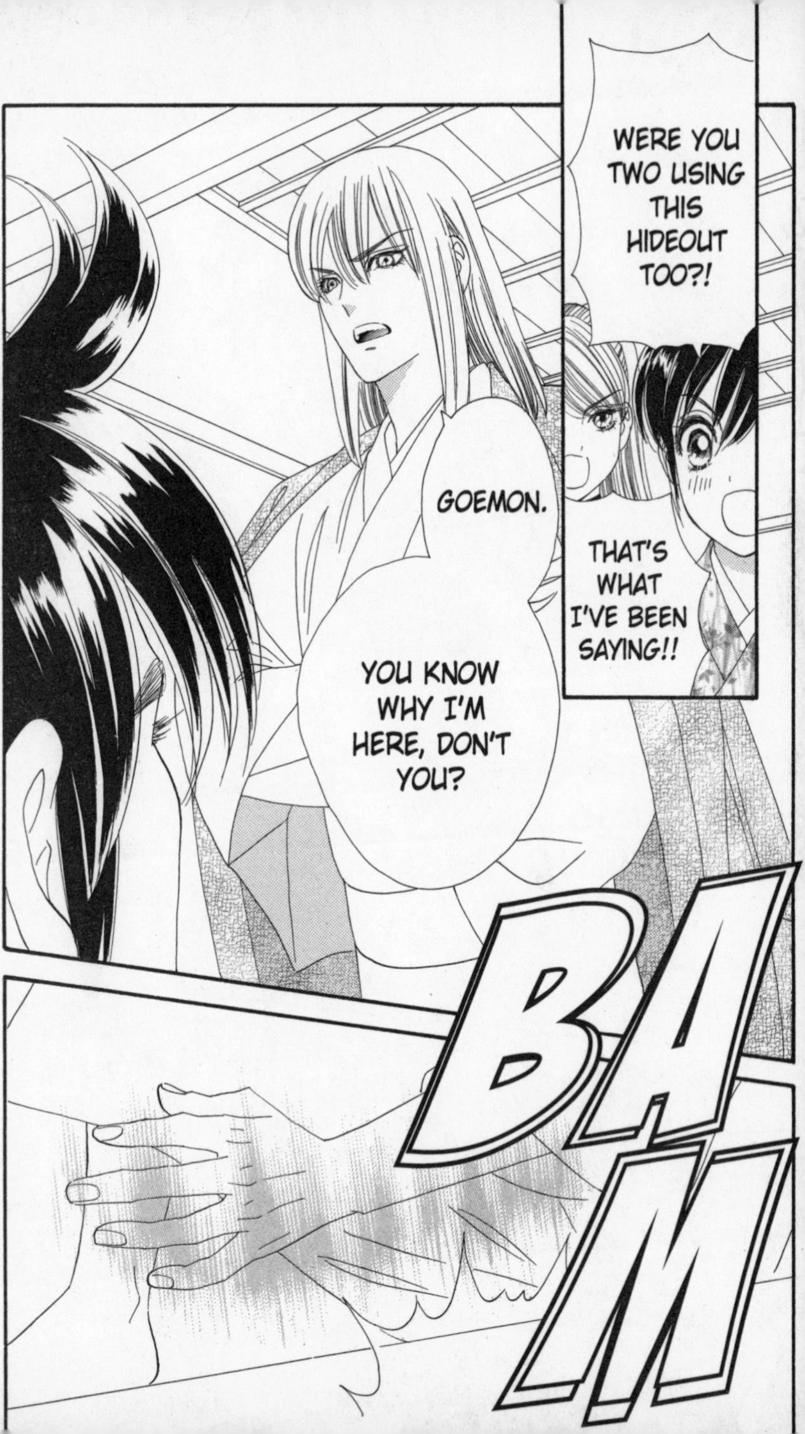
WERE YOU TWO USING THIS HIDEOUT TOO?!
THAT'S WHAT I'VE BEEN SAYING!!
GOEMON.
YOU KNOW WHY I'M HERE, DON'T YOU?
BAM

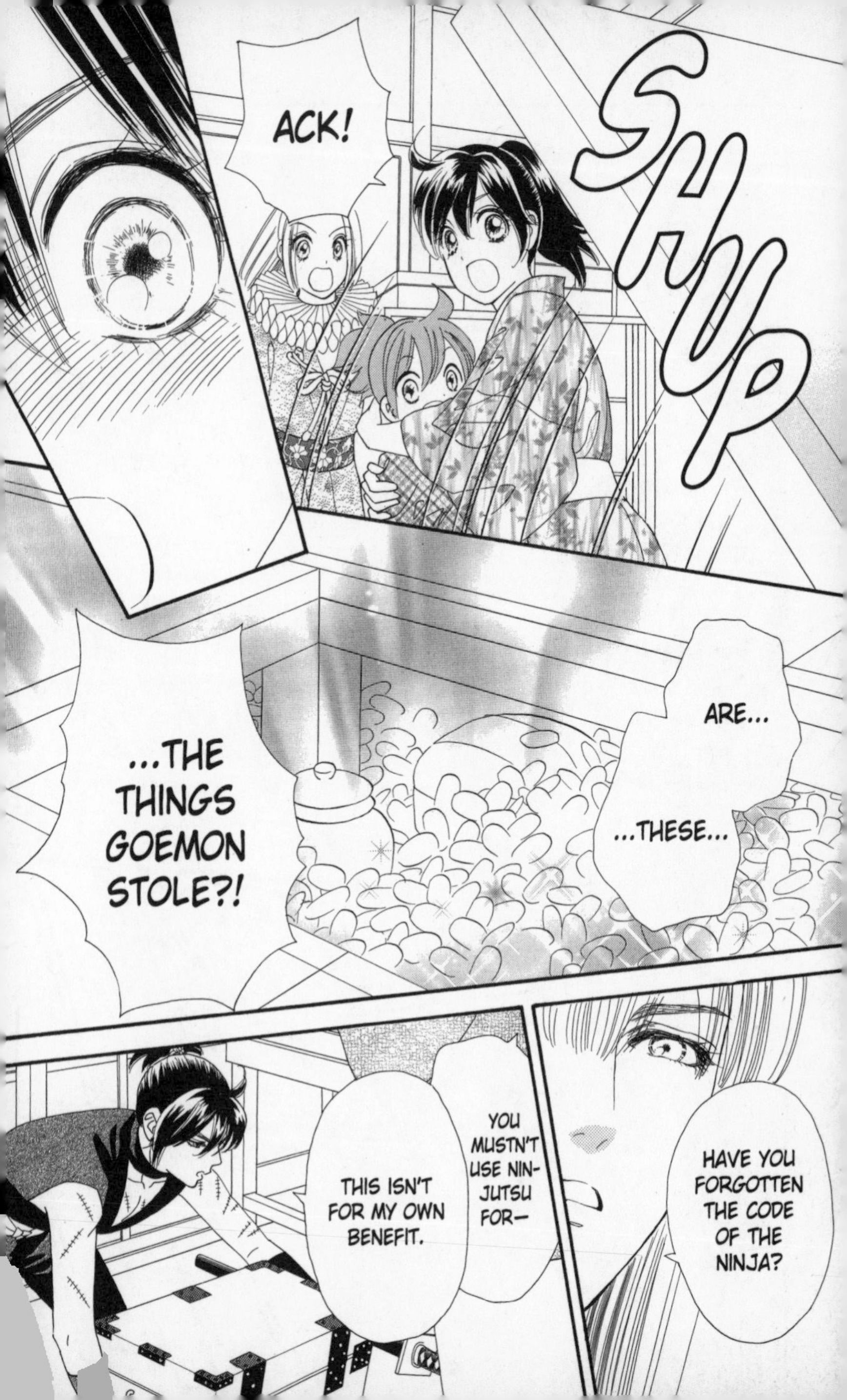
SHUP
ACK!
ARE...
...THESE...
...THE THINGS GOEMON STOLE?!
HAVE YOU FORGOTTEN THE CODE OF THE NINJA?
YOU MUSTN'T USE NIN-JUTSU FOR—
THIS ISN'T FOR MY OWN BENEFIT.

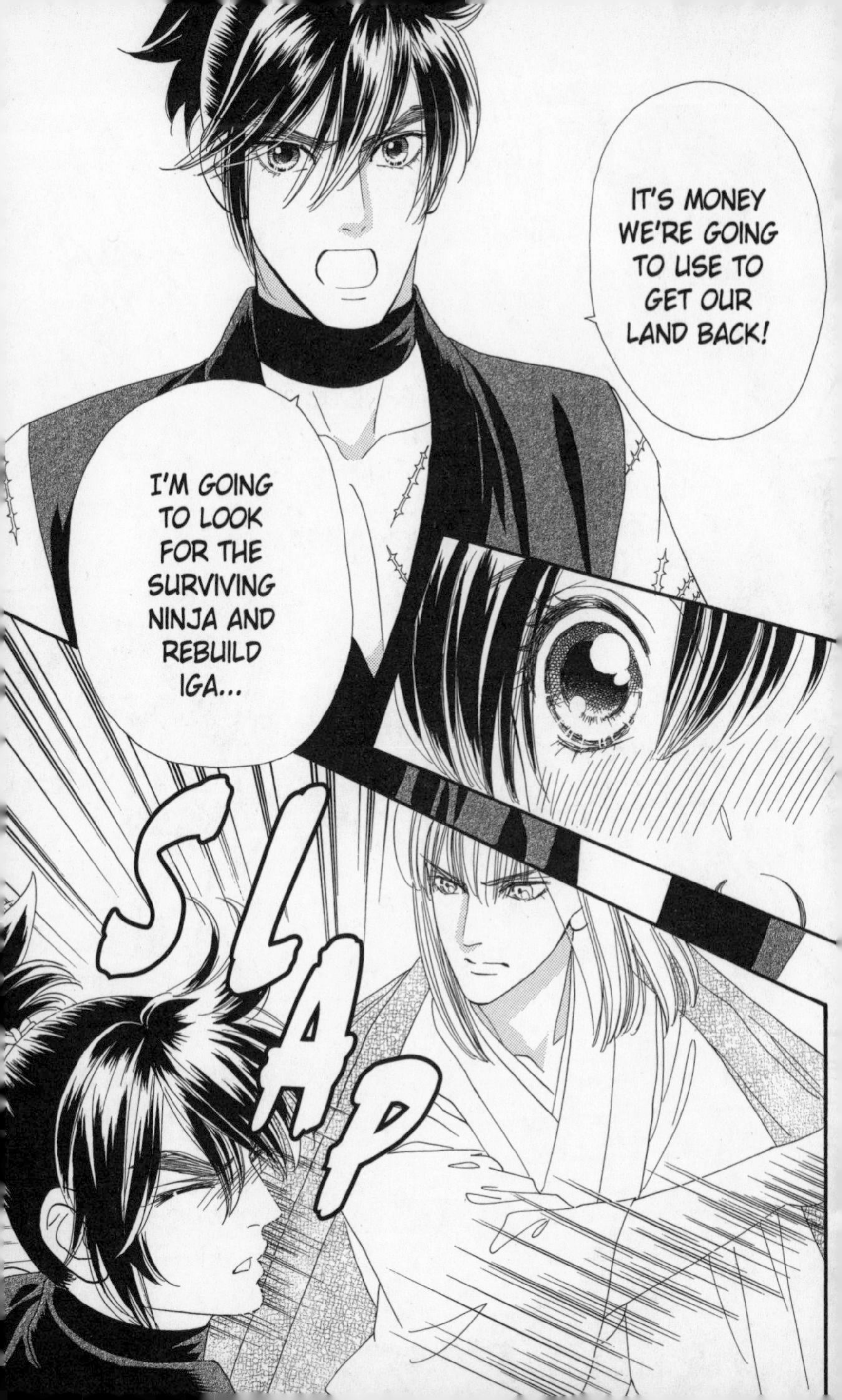
IT'S MONEY WE'RE GOING TO USE TO GET OUR LAND BACK!
I'M GOING TO LOOK FOR THE SURVIVING NINJA AND REBUILD IGA...
SLAP

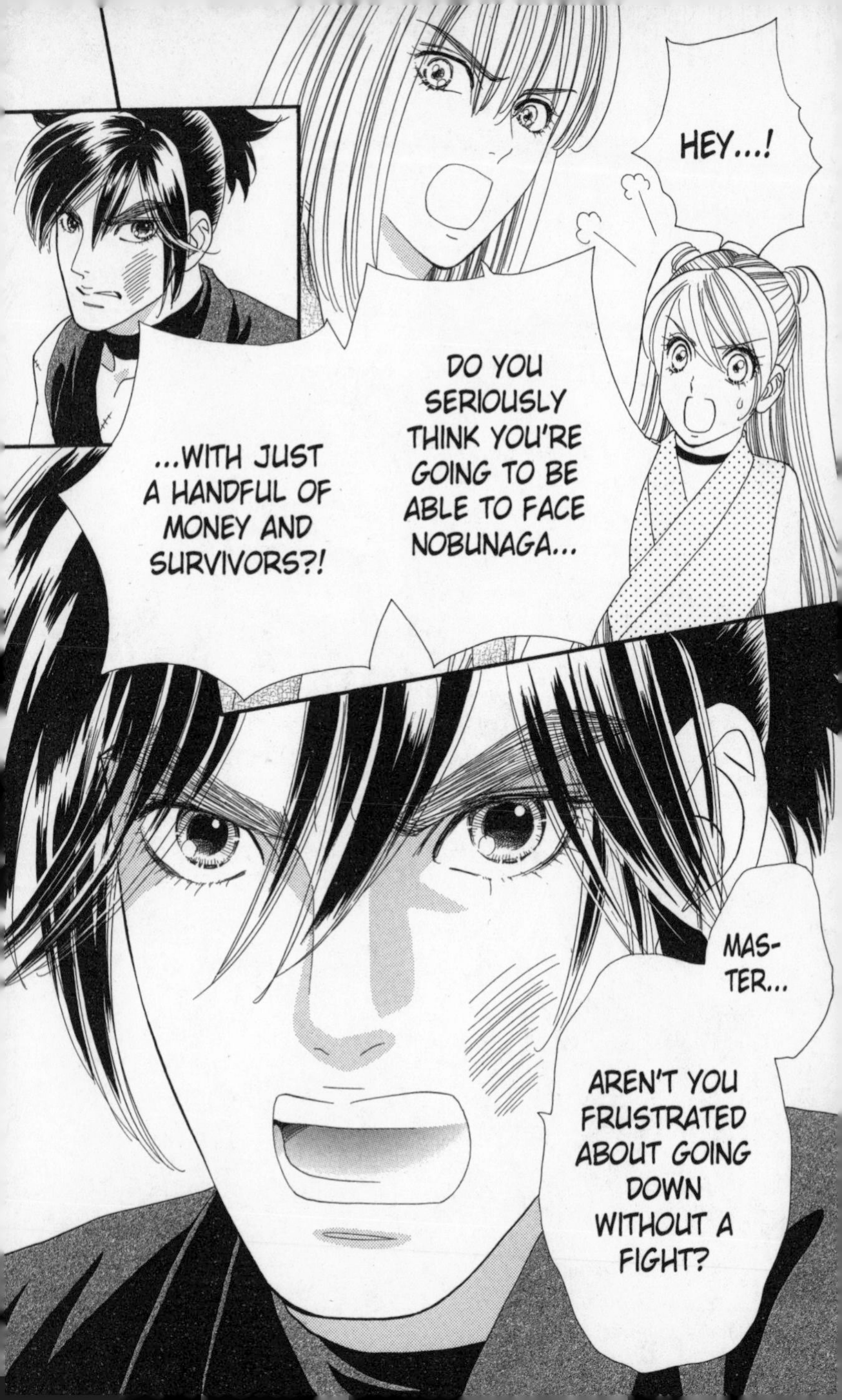
HEY...!
DO YOU SERIOUSLY THINK YOU'RE GOING TO BE ABLE TO FACE NOBUNAGA...
...WITH JUST A HANDFUL OF MONEY AND SURVIVORS?!
MAS-TER...
AREN'T YOU FRUSTRATED ABOUT GOING DOWN WITHOUT A FIGHT?

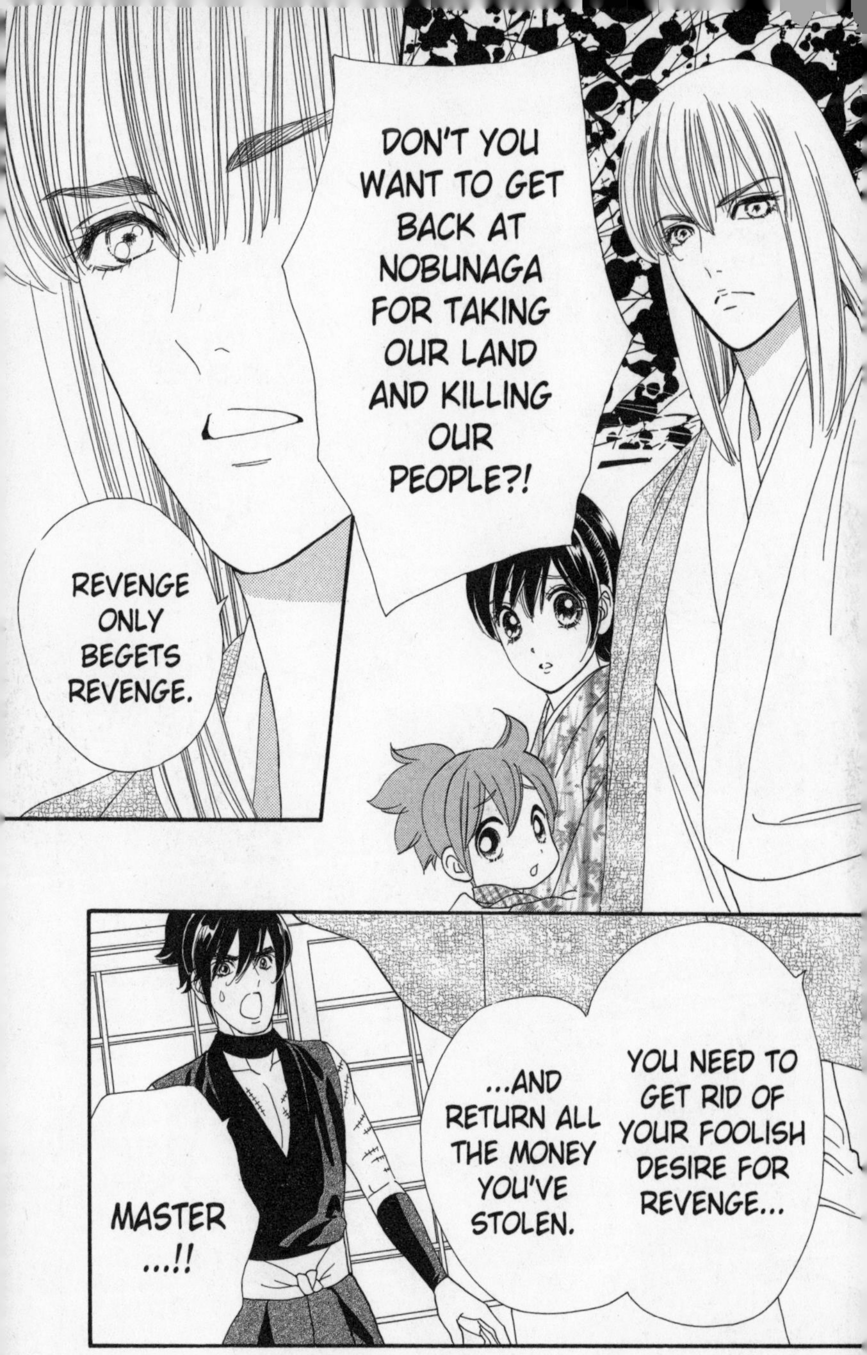
DON'T YOU WANT TO GET BACK AT NOBUNAGA FOR TAKING OUR LAND AND KILLING OUR PEOPLE?!
REVENGE ONLY BEGETS REVENGE.
YOU NEED TO GET RID OF YOUR FOOLISH DESIRE FOR REVENGE...
...AND RETURN ALL THE MONEY YOU'VE STOLEN.
MASTER ...!!

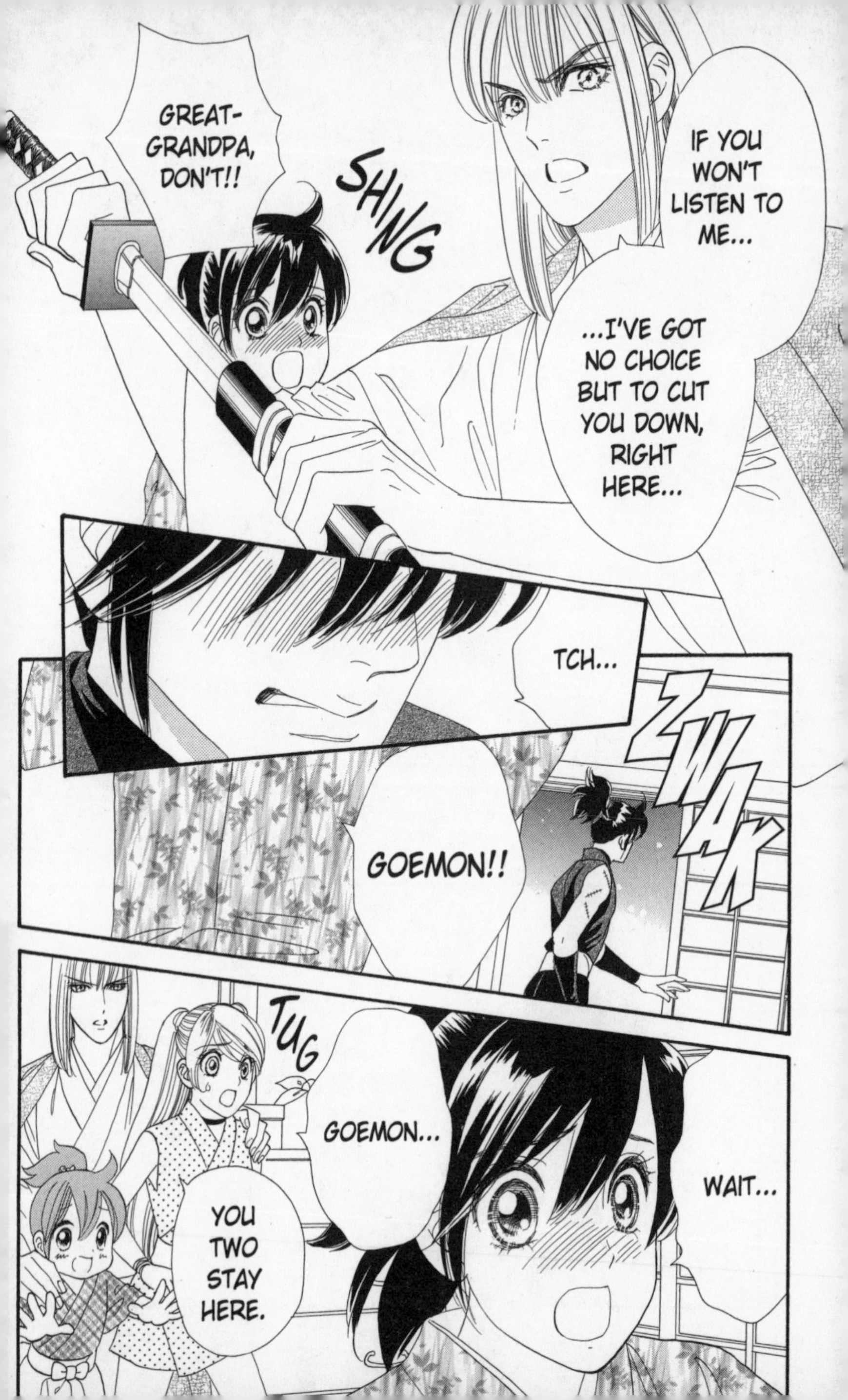
IF YOU WON'T LISTEN TO ME...
...I'VE GOT NO CHOICE BUT TO CUT YOU DOWN, RIGHT HERE...
SHING
GREAT-GRANDPA, DON'T!!
TCH...
ZWAK
GOEMON!!
WAIT...
GOEMON...
TUG
YOU TWO STAY HERE.

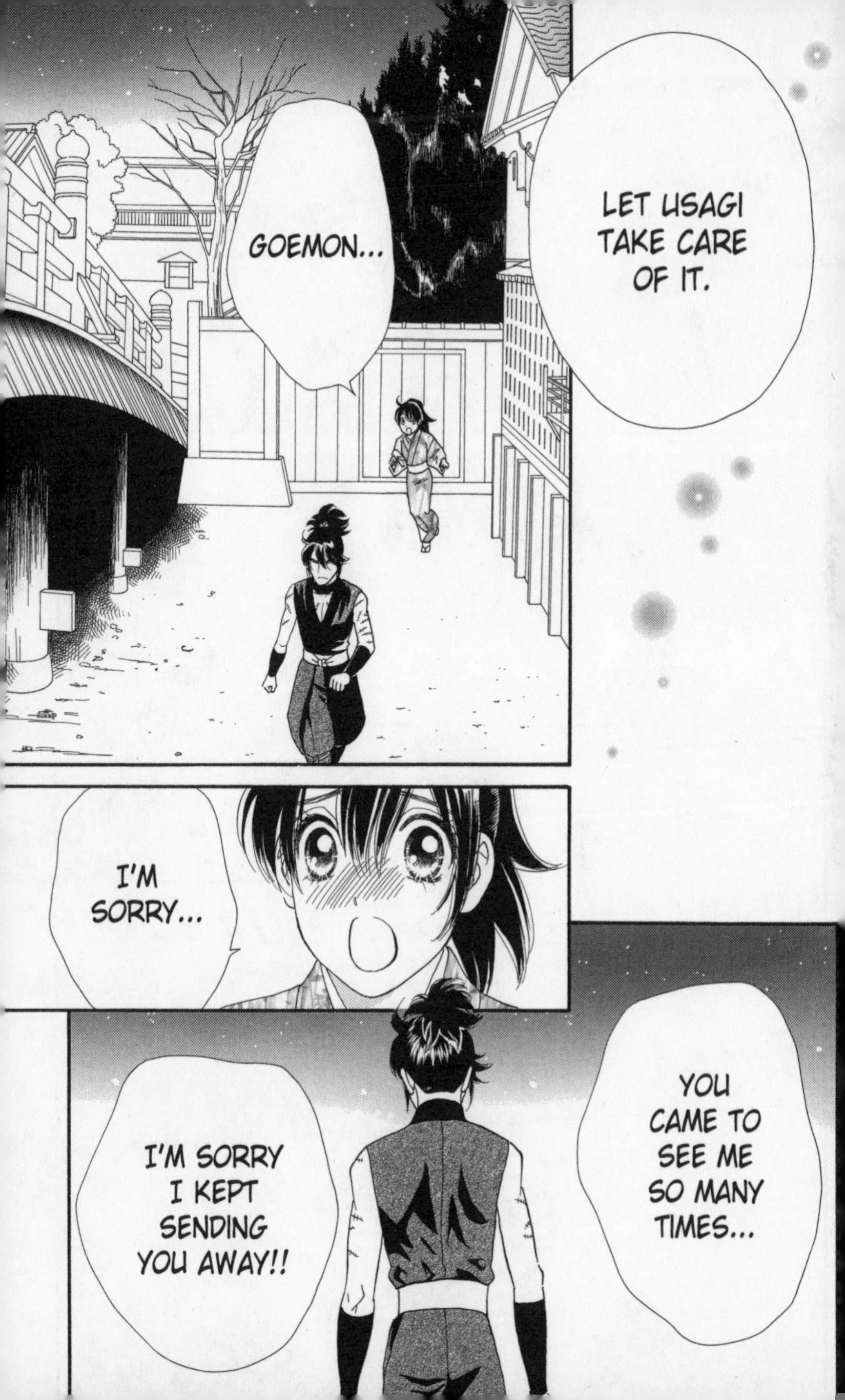
LET USAGI TAKE CARE OF IT.
GOEMON...
I'M SORRY...
YOU CAME TO SEE ME SO MANY TIMES...
I'M SORRY I KEPT SENDING YOU AWAY!!

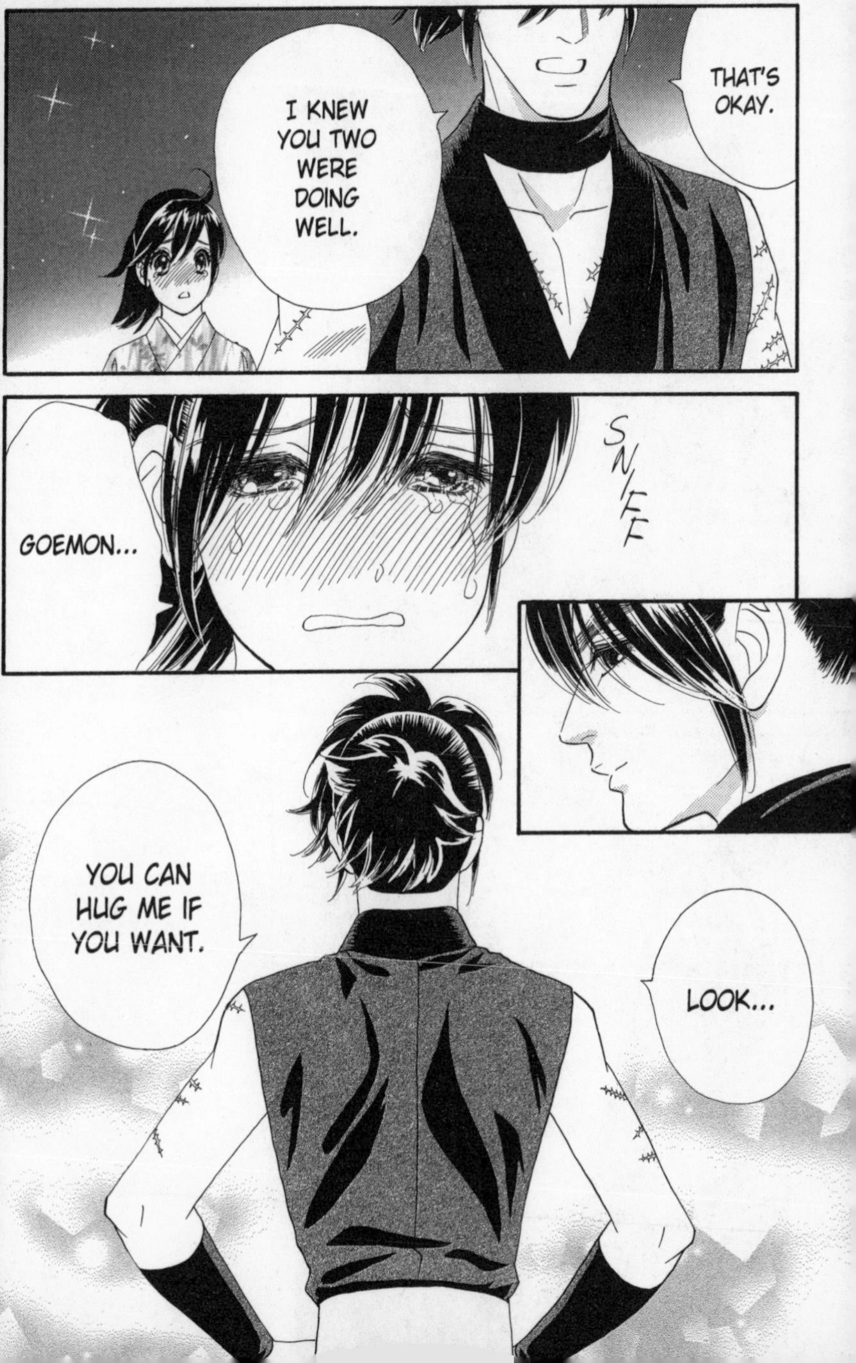
THAT'S OKAY.
I KNEW YOU TWO WERE DOING WELL.
SNIFF
GOEMON...
LOOK...
YOU CAN HUG ME IF YOU WANT.

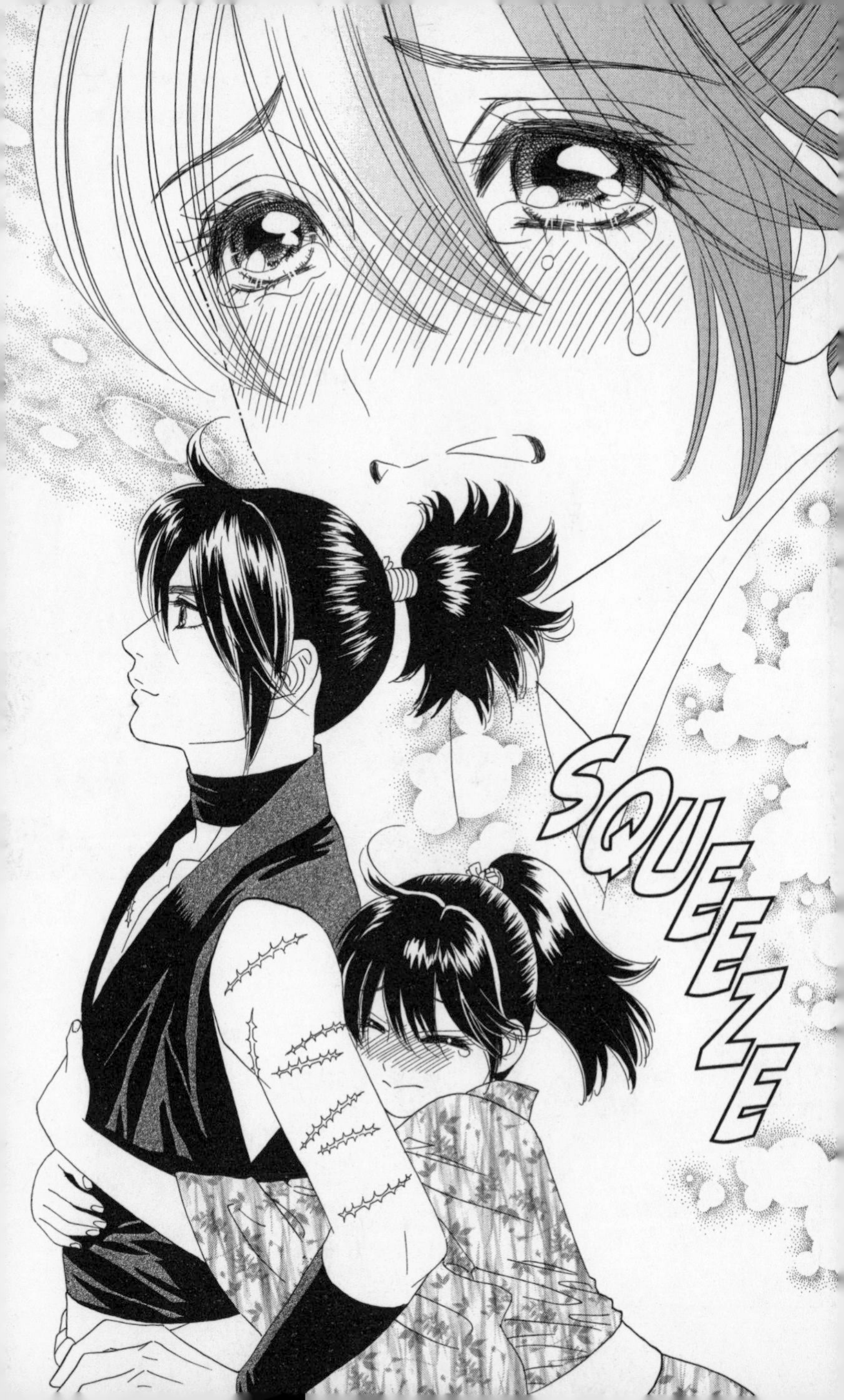
SQUEEZE

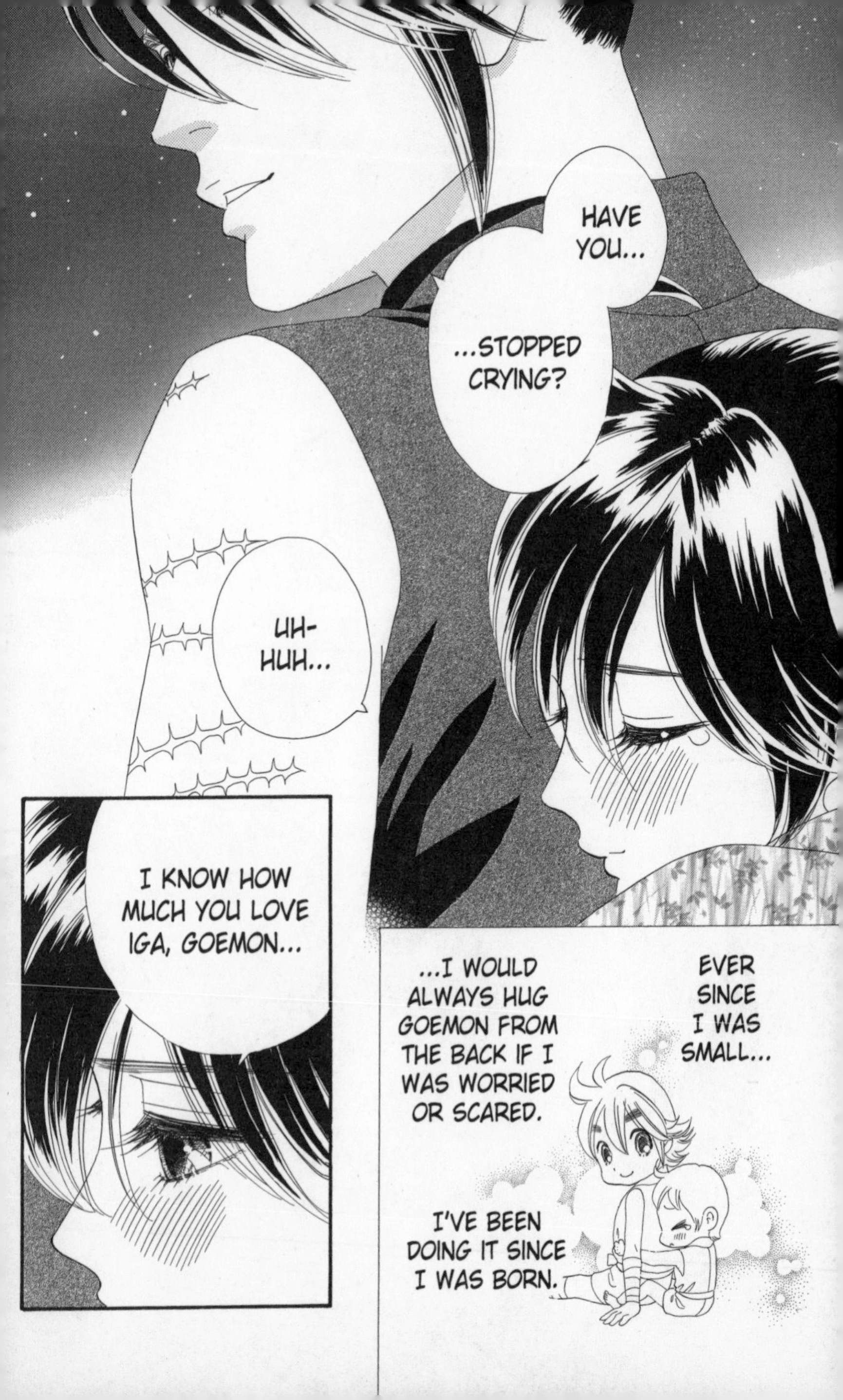
HAVE YOU...
...STOPPED CRYING?
UH-HUH...
I KNOW HOW MUCH YOU LOVE IGA, GOEMON...
EVER SINCE I WAS SMALL...
...I WOULD ALWAYS HUG GOEMON FROM THE BACK IF I WAS WORRIED OR SCARED.
I'VE BEEN DOING IT SINCE I WAS BORN.

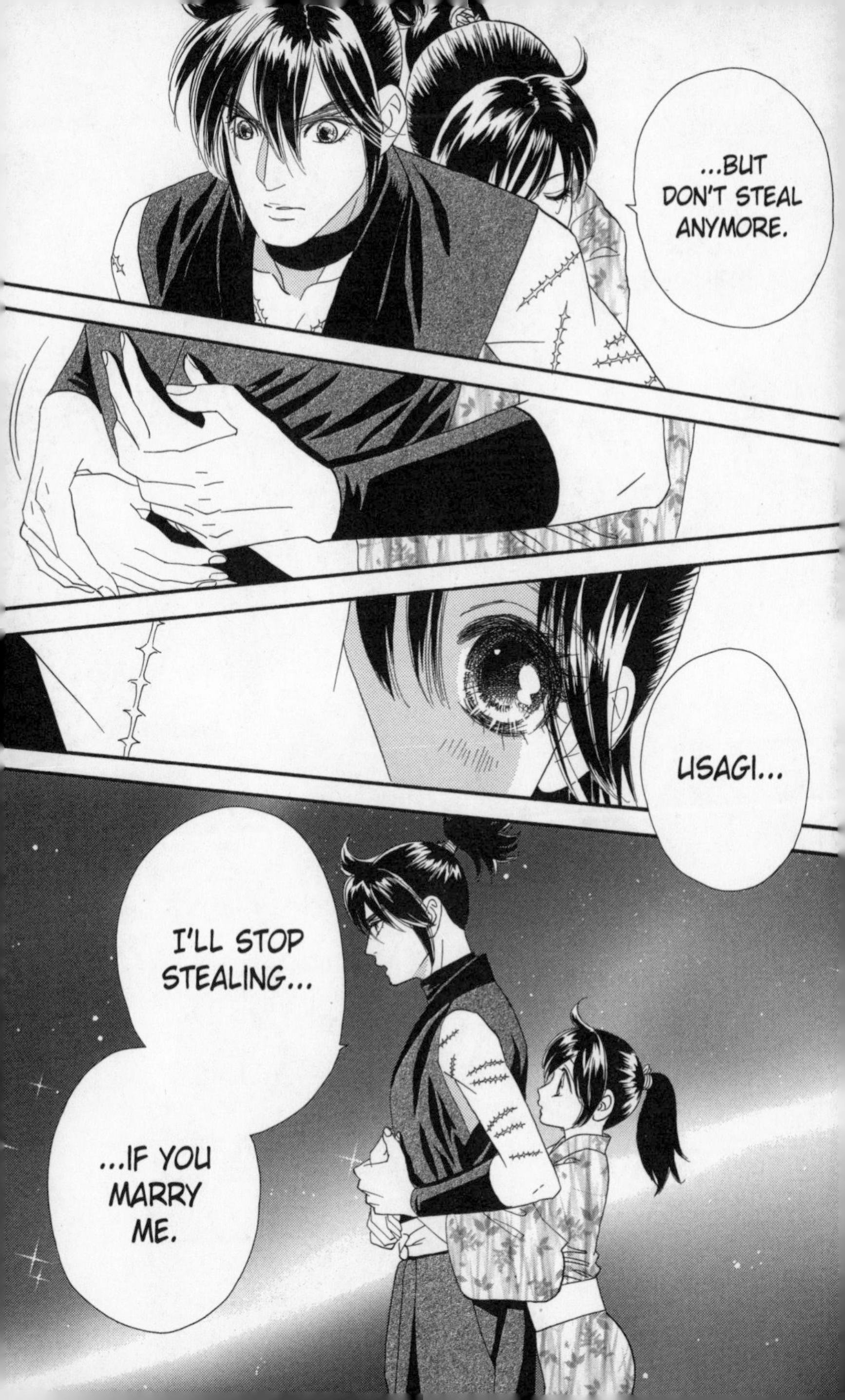
...BUT DON'T STEAL ANYMORE.
USAGI...
I'LL STOP STEALING...
...IF YOU MARRY ME.

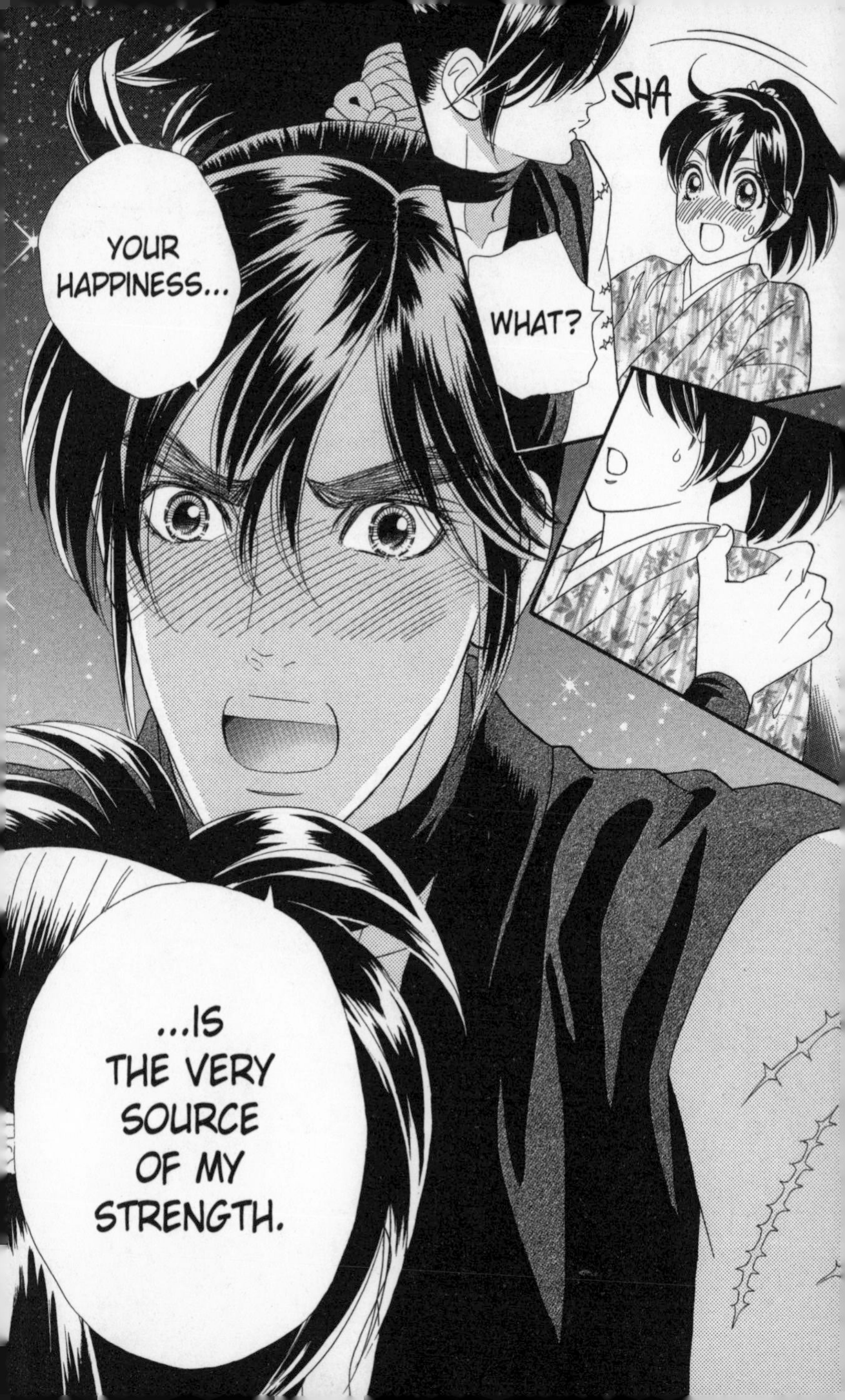
SHA
WHAT?
YOUR HAPPINESS...
...IS THE VERY SOURCE OF MY STRENGTH.

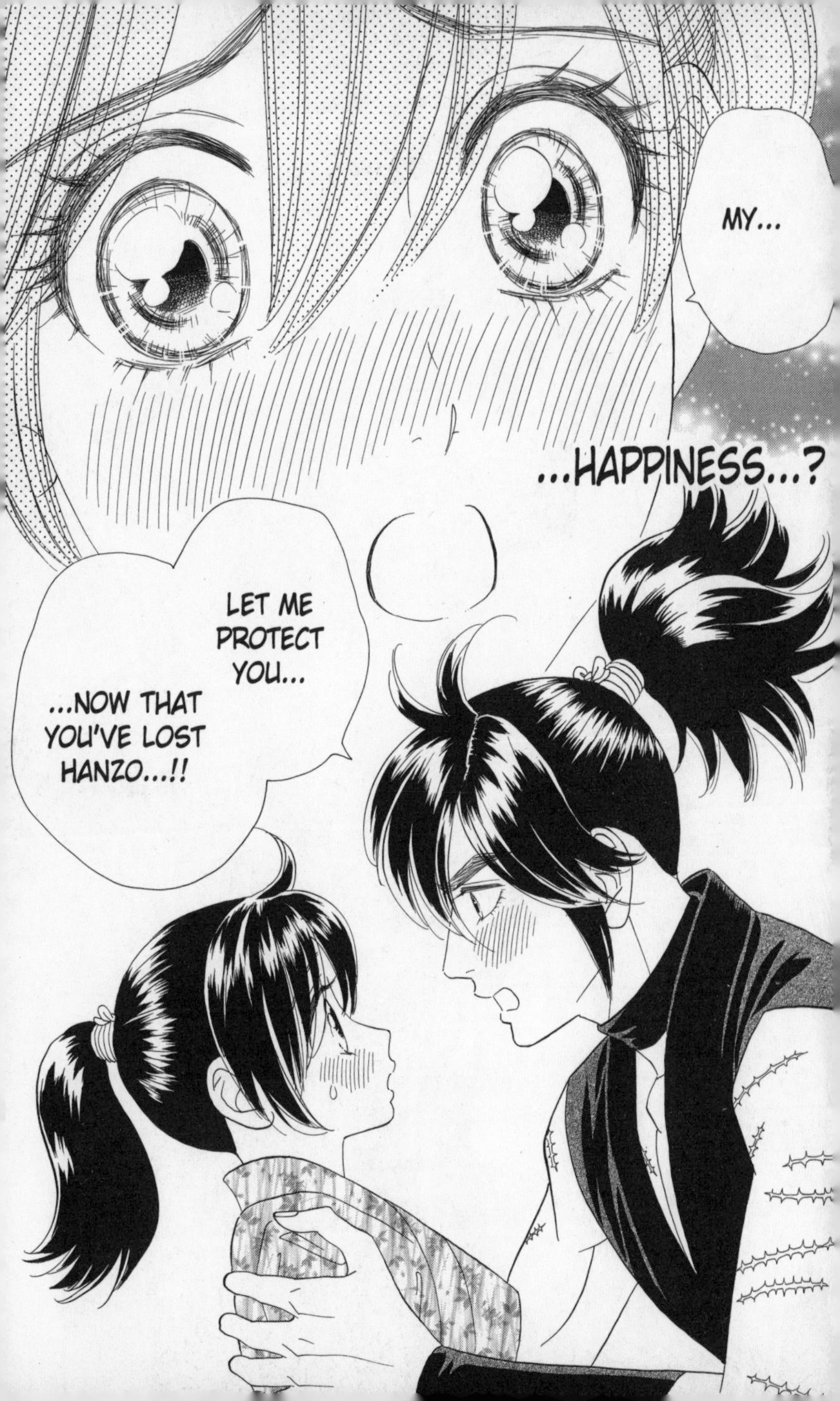
MY...
...HAPPINESS...?
LET ME PROTECT YOU...
...NOW THAT YOU'VE LOST HANZO...!!

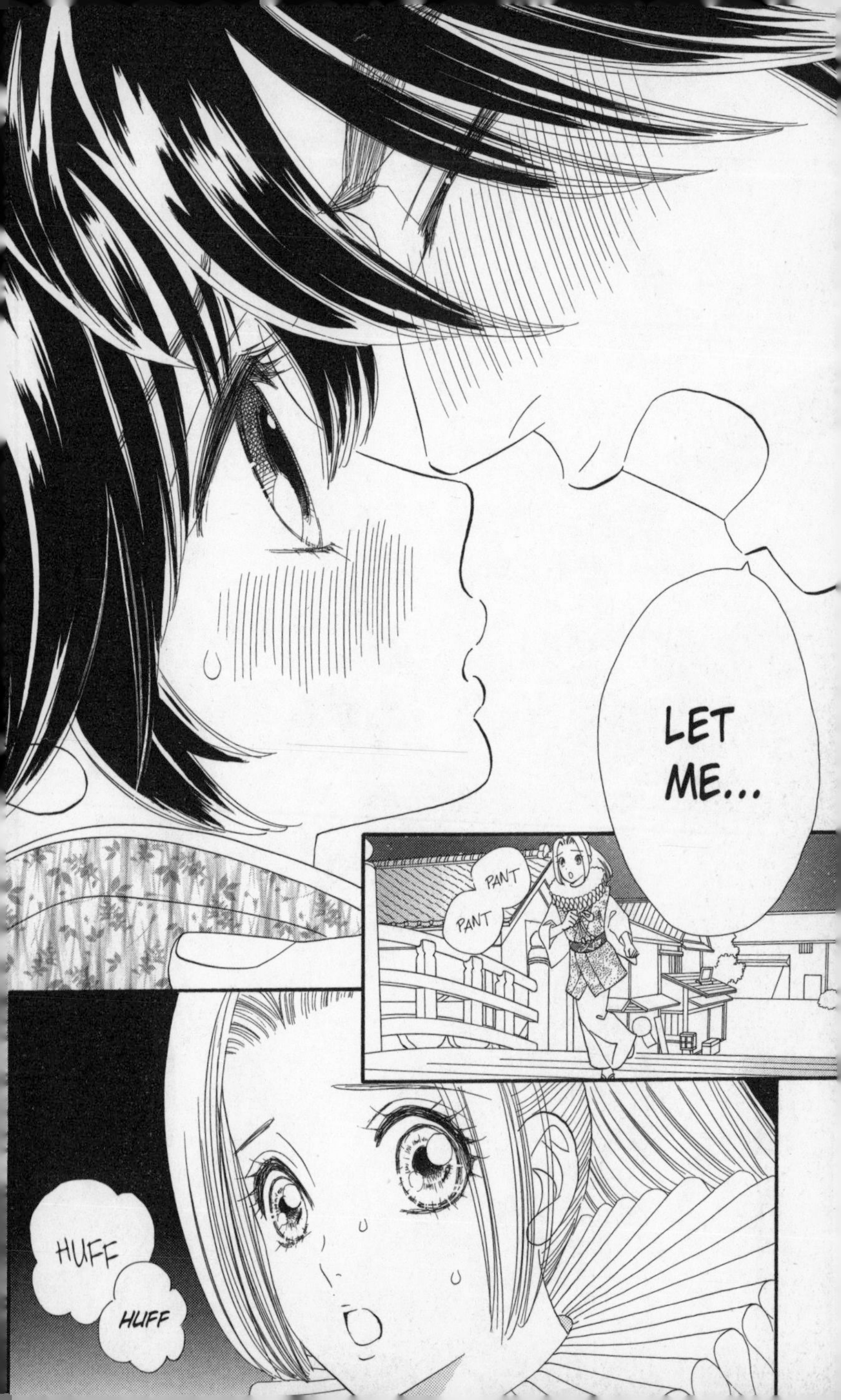
LET ME...
PANT
PANT
HUFF
HUFF

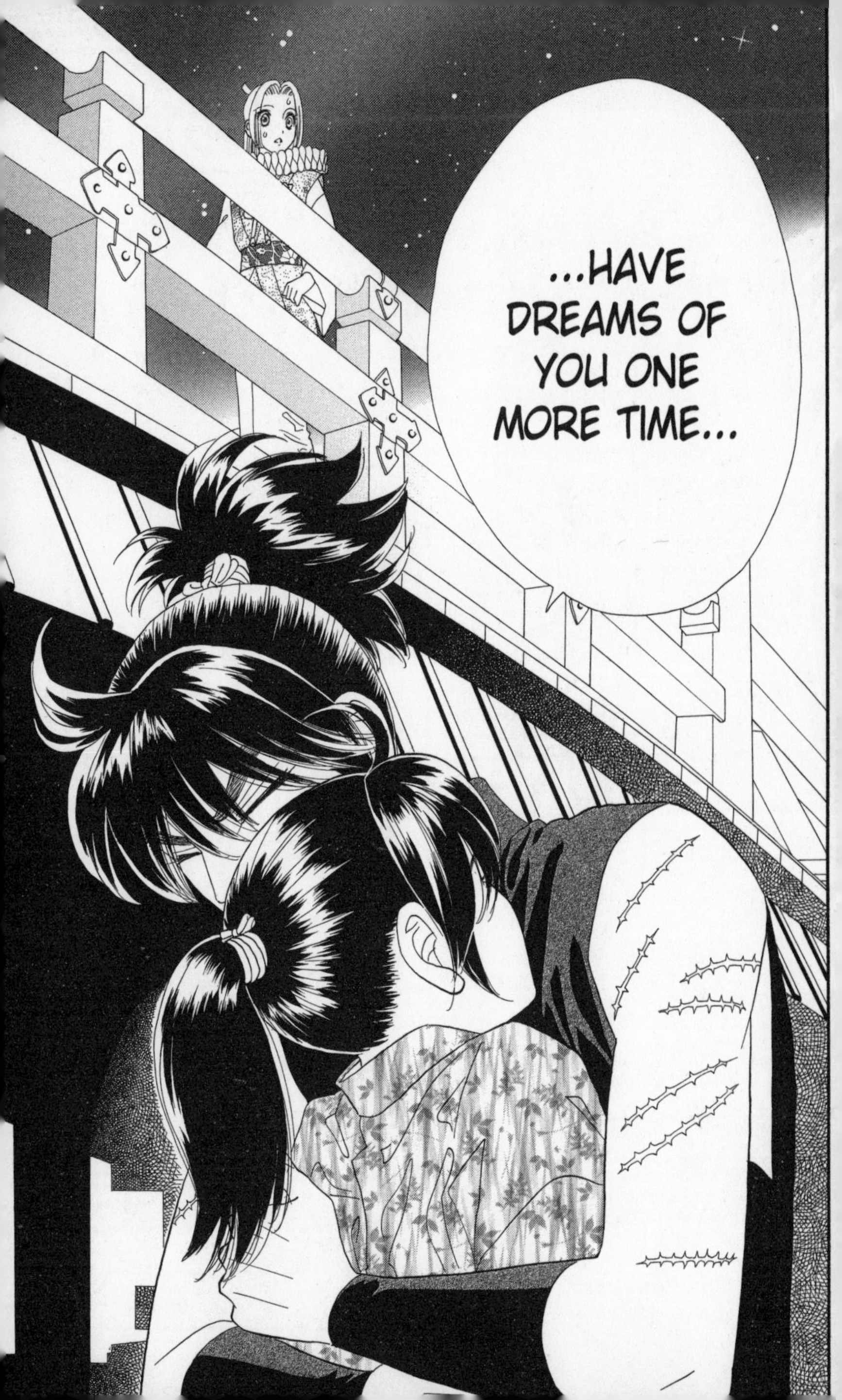
...HAVE DREAMS OF YOU ONE MORE TIME...

LET'S GO!

LITTLE HANZO

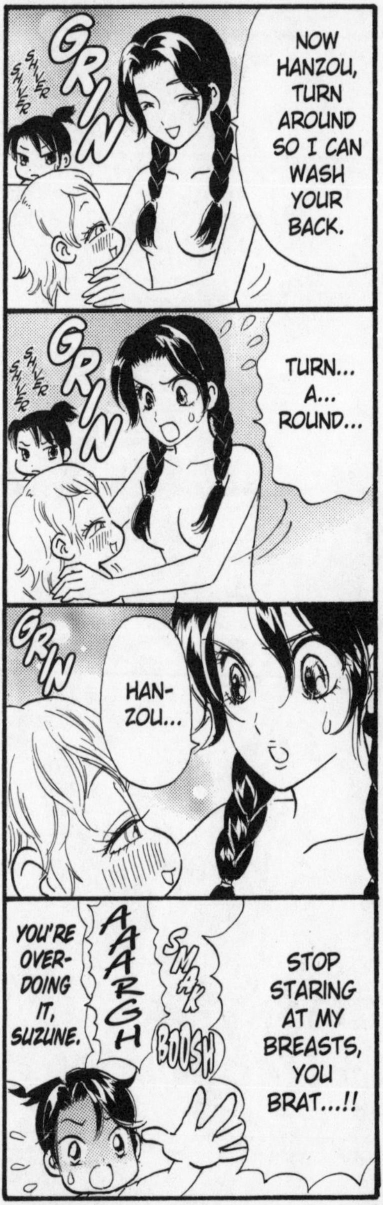
NOW HANZOU, TURN AROUND SO I CAN WASH YOUR BACK.
GRIN
SHIVER SHIVER
TURN... A... ROUND...
GRIN
SHIVER SHIVER
HAN-ZOU...
GRIN
STOP STARING AT MY BREASTS, YOU BRAT...!!
SMAK
BOOSH
AAARGH
YOU'RE OVER-DOING IT, SUZUNE.

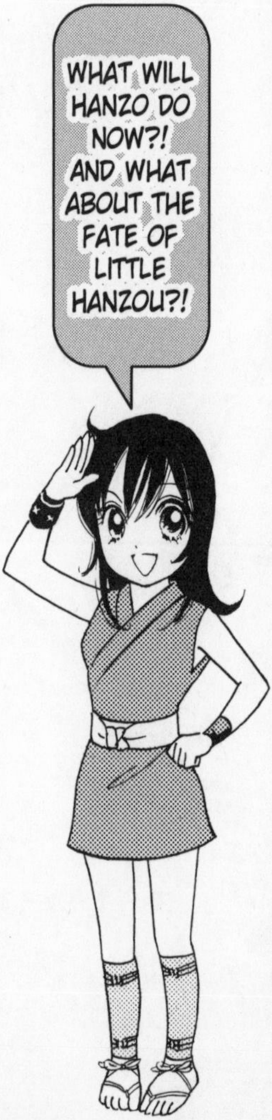
WHAT WILL HANZO DO NOW?! AND WHAT ABOUT THE FATE OF LITTLE HANZOU?!

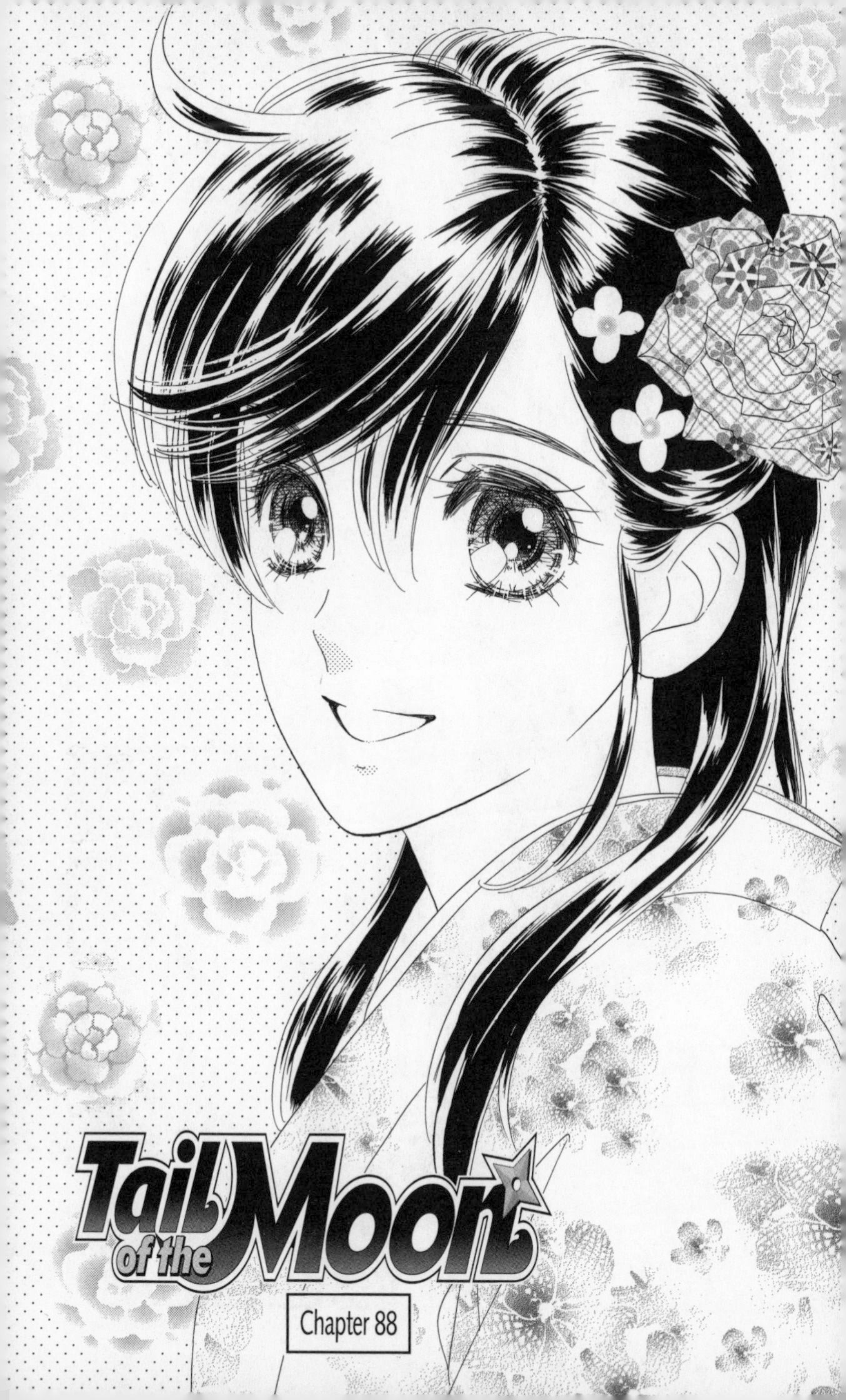
Tail of the Moon
Chapter 88

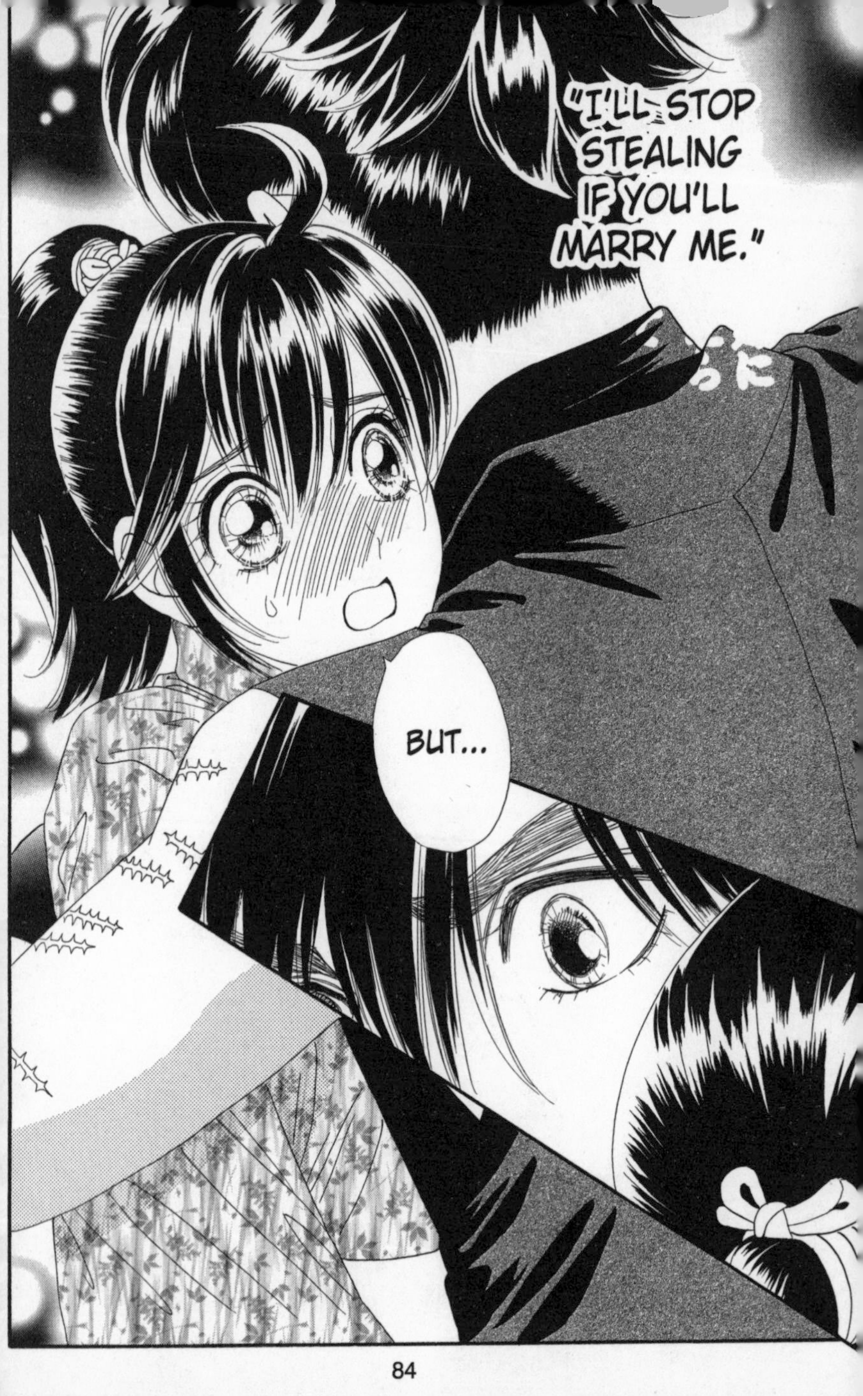
"I'LL STOP STEALING IF YOU'LL MARRY ME."
BUT...

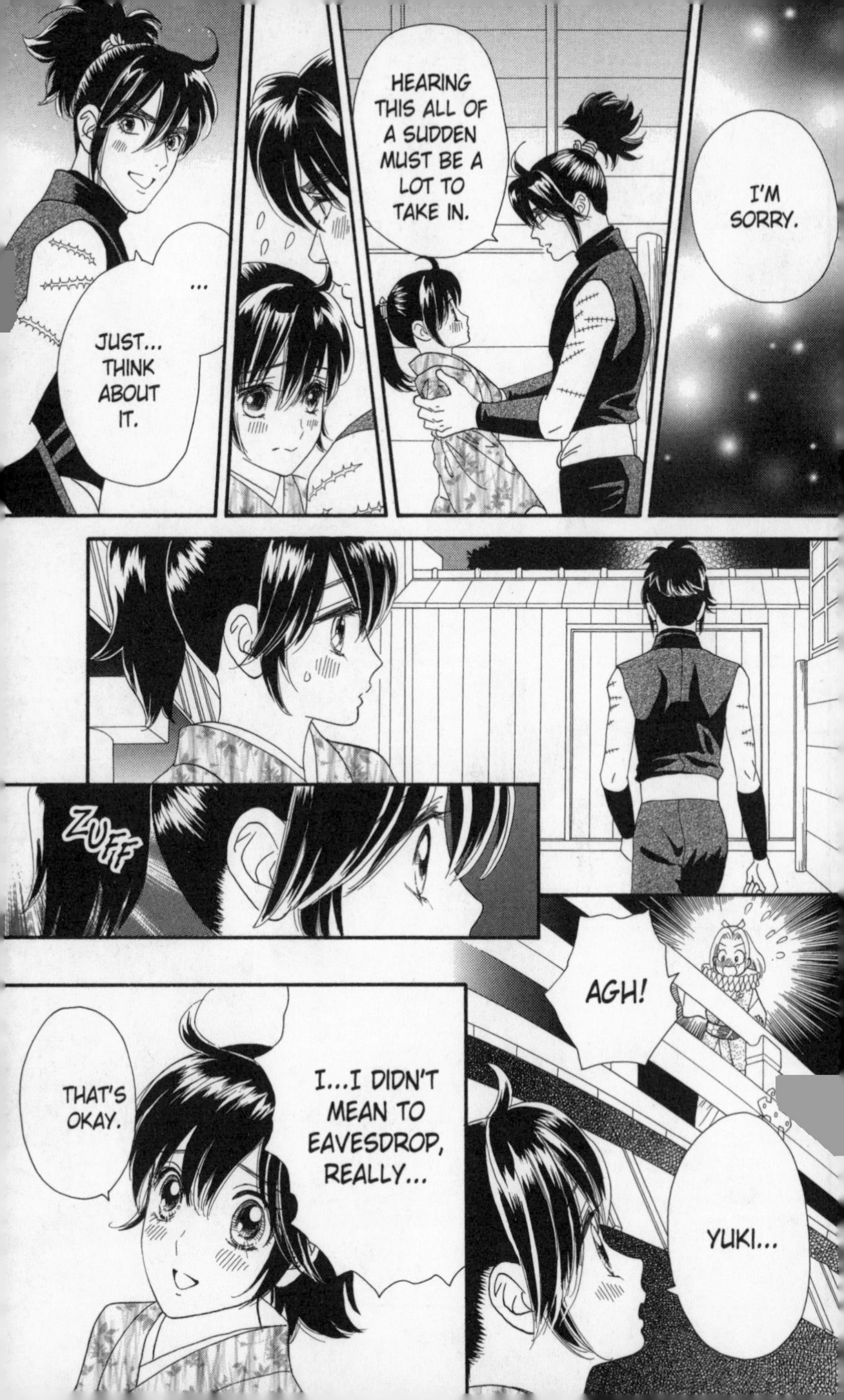
I'M SORRY.
HEARING THIS ALL OF A SUDDEN MUST BE A LOT TO TAKE IN.
...
JUST... THINK ABOUT IT.
ZUFF
AGH!
YUKI...
I...I DIDN'T MEAN TO EAVESDROP, REALLY...
THAT'S OKAY.

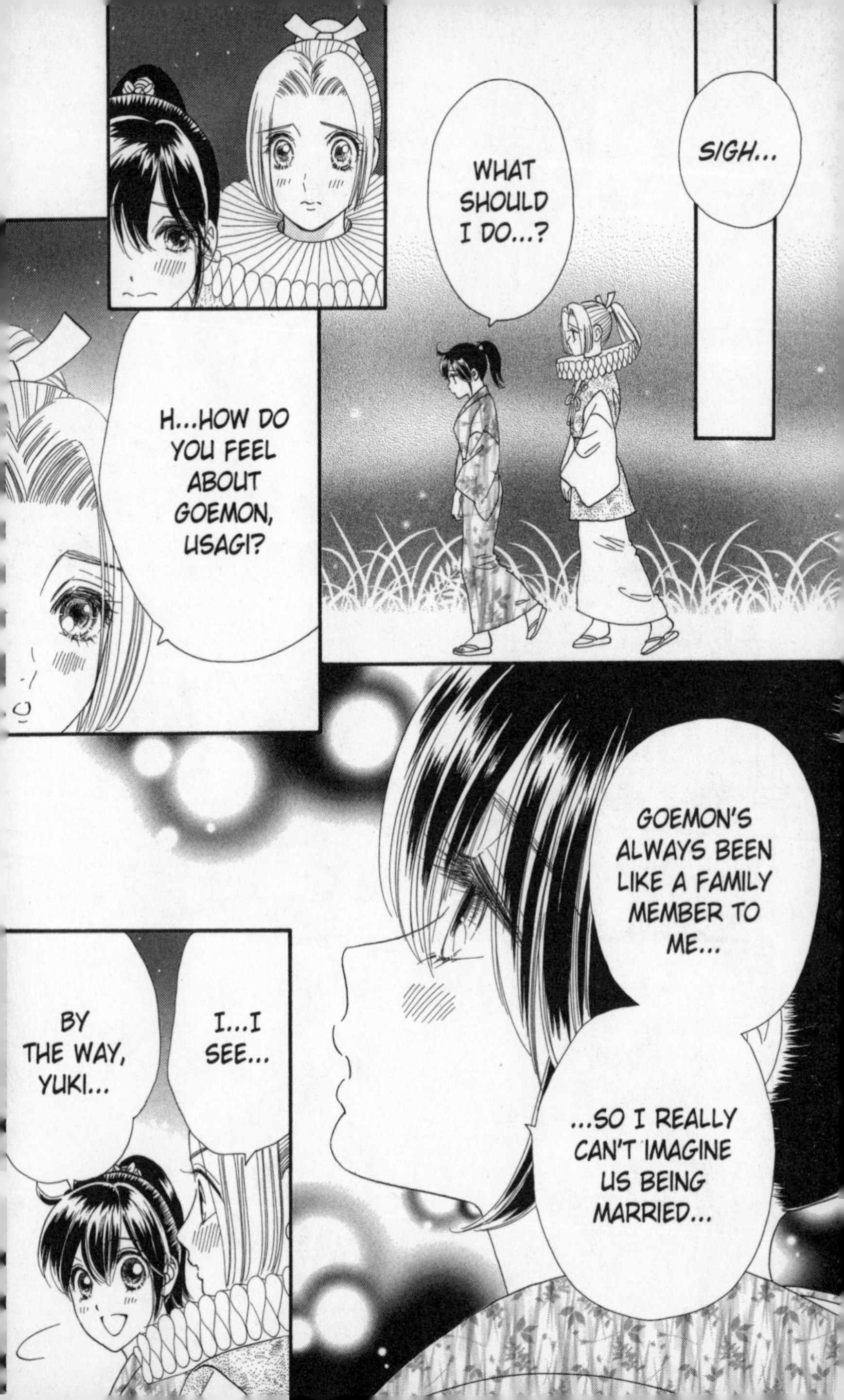
SIGH...
WHAT SHOULD I DO...?
H...HOW DO YOU FEEL ABOUT GOEMON, USAGI?
GOEMON'S ALWAYS BEEN LIKE A FAMILY MEMBER TO ME...
...SO I REALLY CAN'T IMAGINE US BEING MARRIED...
I...I SEE...
BY THE WAY, YUKI...

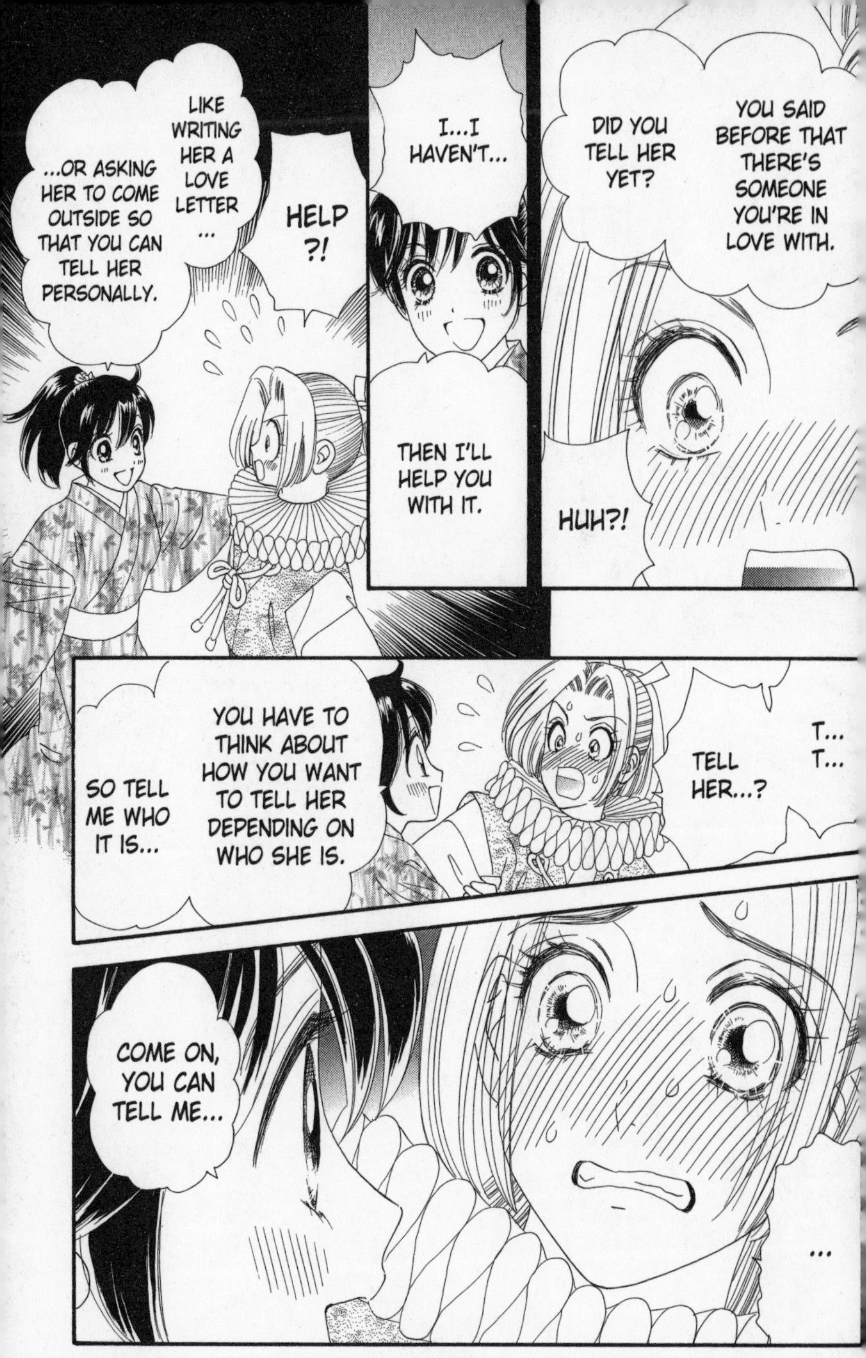
YOU SAID BEFORE THAT THERE'S SOMEONE YOU'RE IN LOVE WITH.
DID YOU TELL HER YET?
HUH?!
I...I HAVEN'T...
THEN I'LL HELP YOU WITH IT.
HELP ?!
LIKE WRITING HER A LOVE LETTER ...
...OR ASKING HER TO COME OUTSIDE SO THAT YOU CAN TELL HER PERSONALLY.
T... T...
TELL HER...?
YOU HAVE TO THINK ABOUT HOW YOU WANT TO TELL HER DEPENDING ON WHO SHE IS.
SO TELL ME WHO IT IS...
...
COME ON, YOU CAN TELL ME...

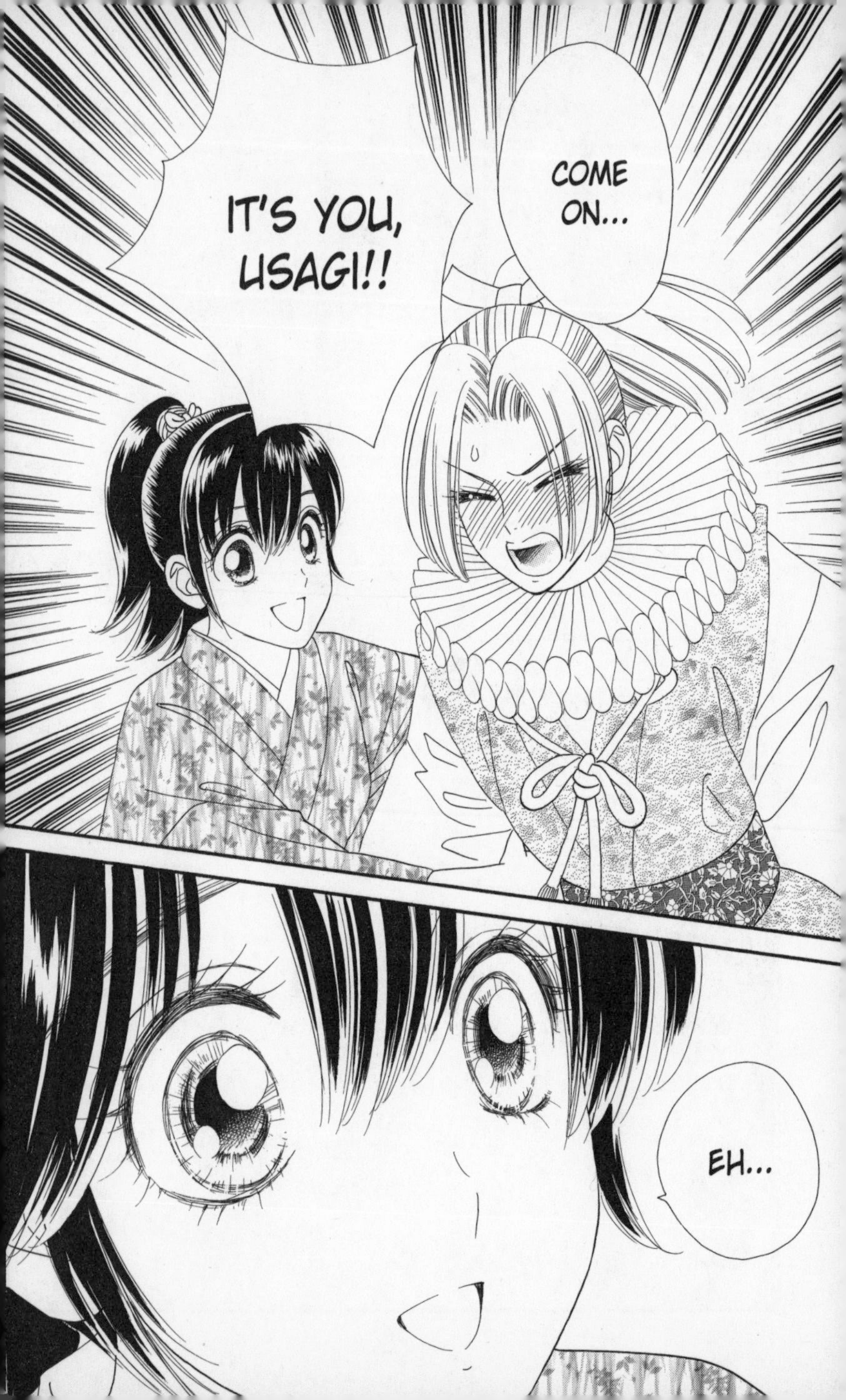
COME ON...
IT'S YOU, USAGI!!
EH...

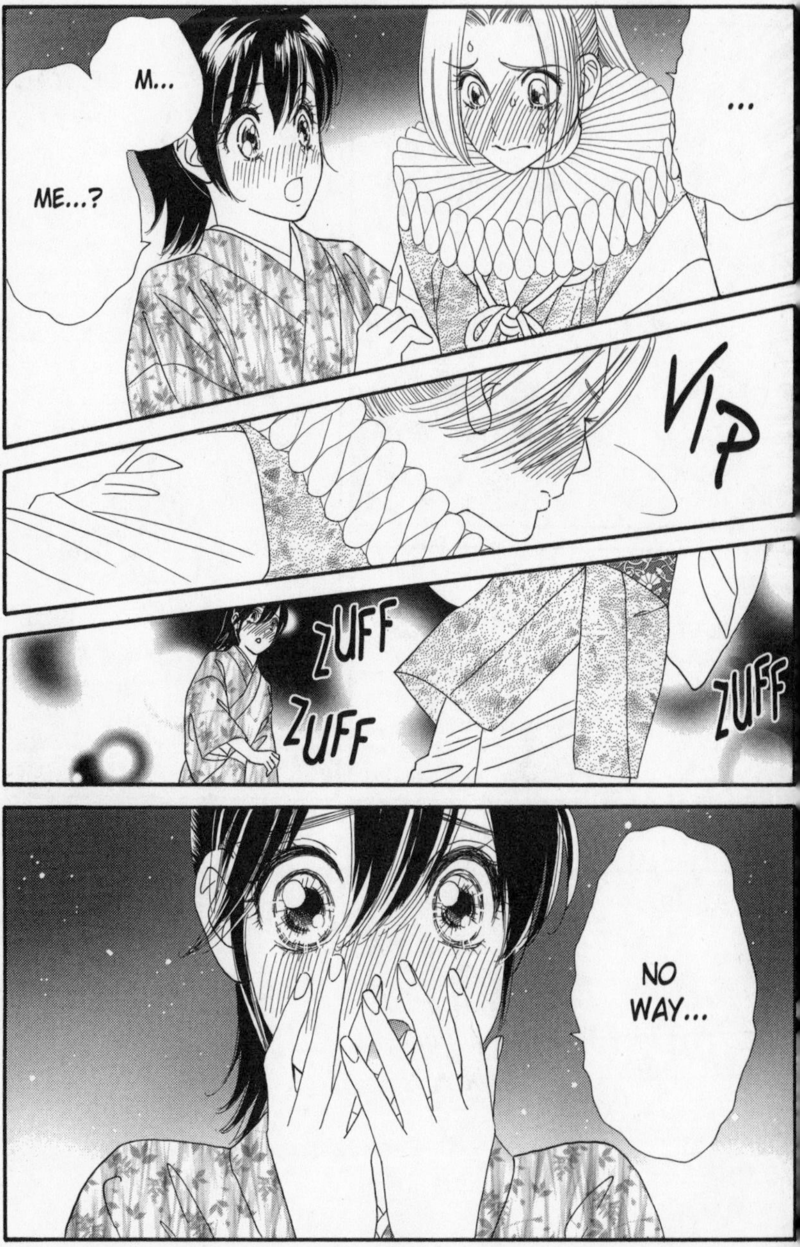
...
M...
ME...?
VIP
ZUFF
ZUFF
ZUFF
NO WAY...

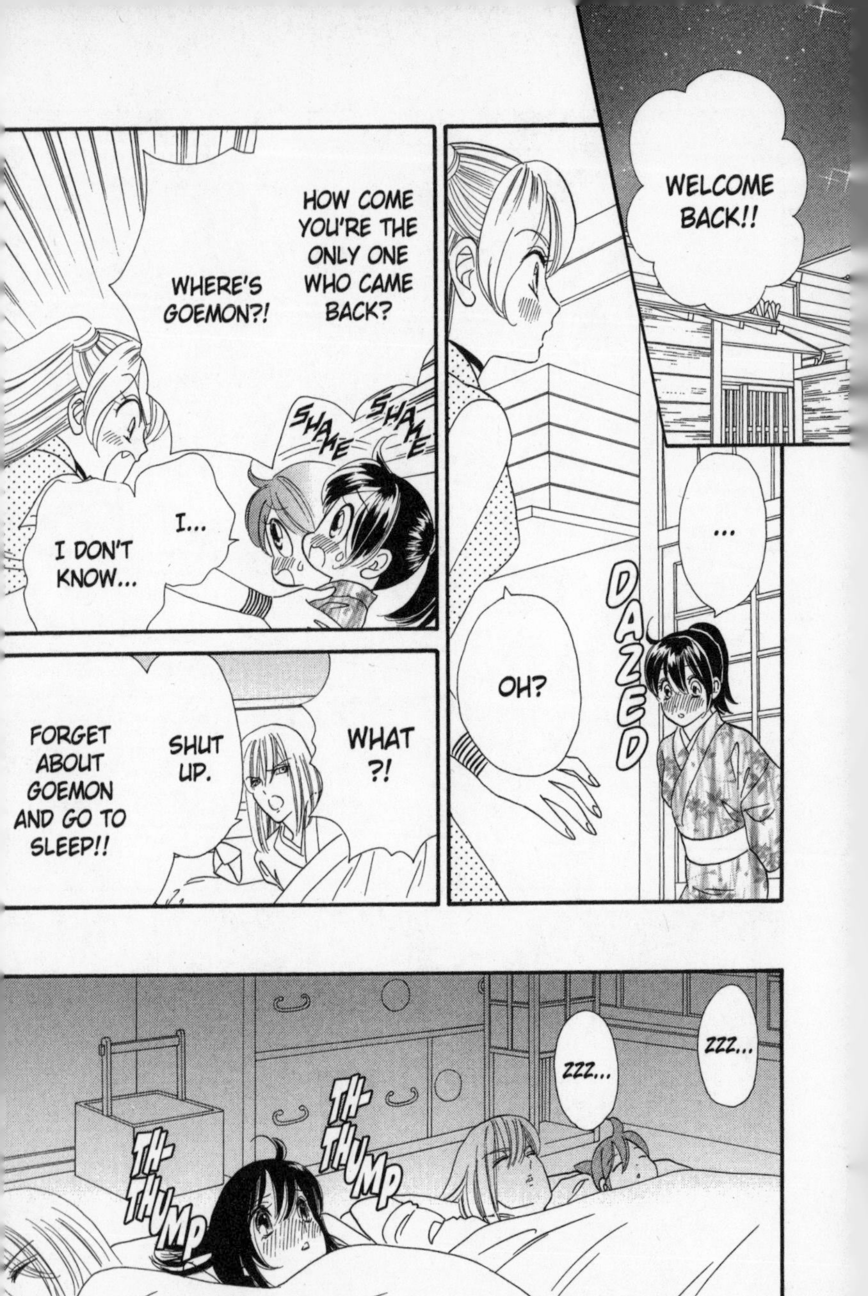
WELCOME BACK!!
...
DAZED
OH?
HOW COME YOU'RE THE ONLY ONE WHO CAME BACK?
WHERE'S GOEMON?!
SHAKE
SHAKE
I...
I DON'T KNOW...
WHAT?!
SHUT UP.
FORGET ABOUT GOEMON AND GO TO SLEEP!!
ZZZ...
ZZZ...
TH-THUMP
TH-THUMP

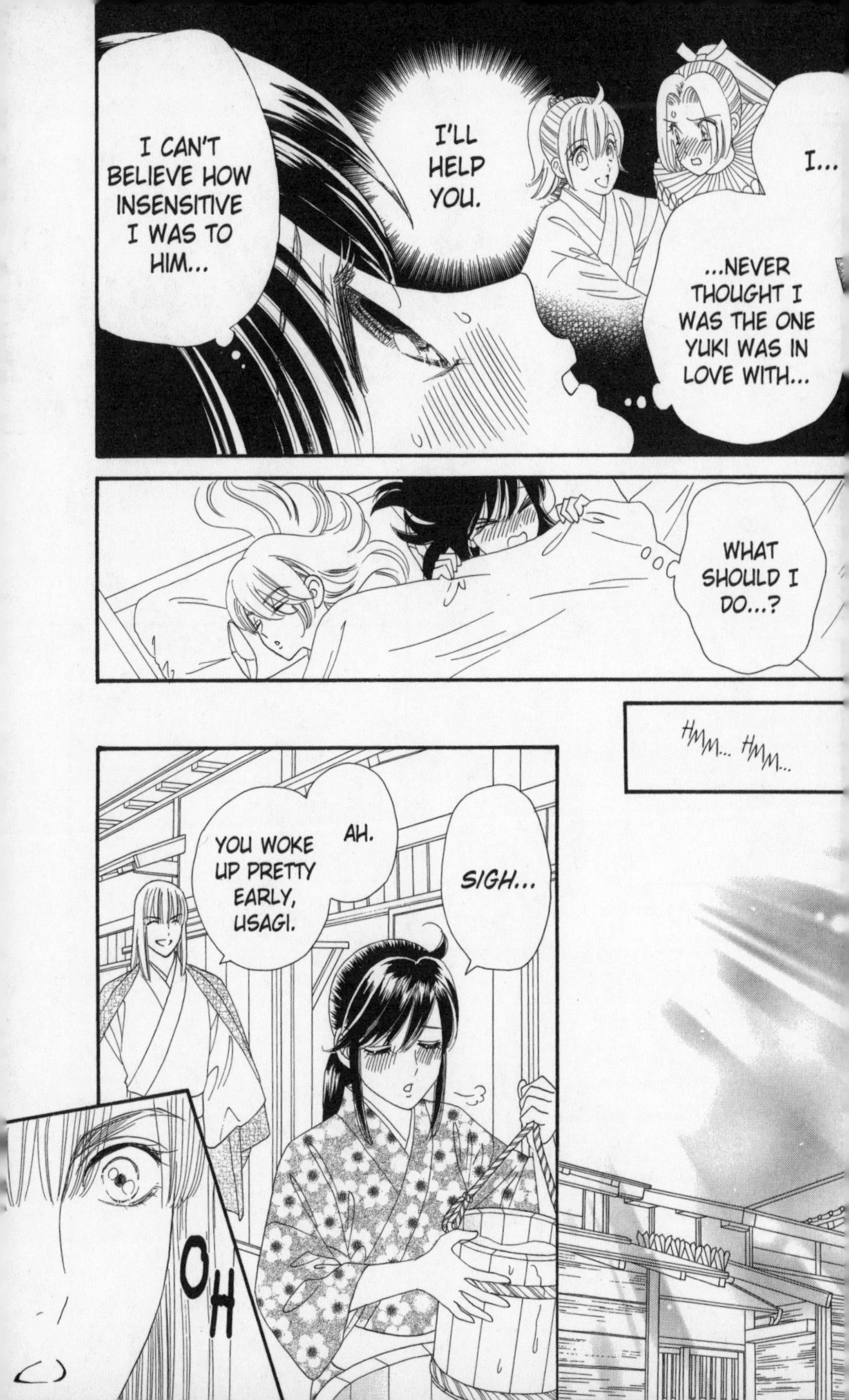
I...
...NEVER THOUGHT I WAS THE ONE YUKI WAS IN LOVE WITH...
I'LL HELP YOU.
I CAN'T BELIEVE HOW INSENSITIVE I WAS TO HIM...
WHAT SHOULD I DO...?
HMM... HMM...
SIGH...
AH.
YOU WOKE UP PRETTY EARLY, USAGI.
OH

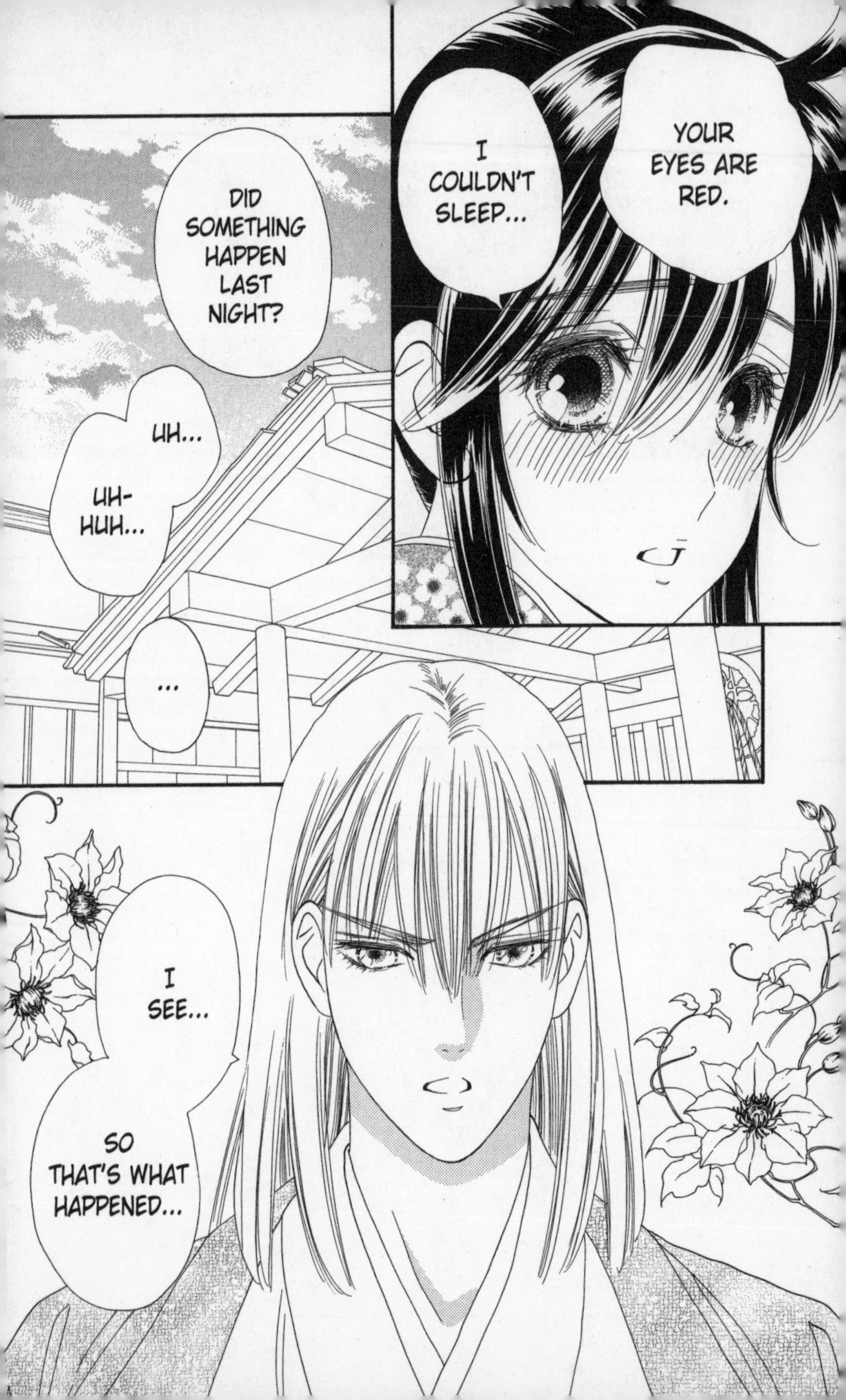
YOUR EYES ARE RED.
I COULDN'T SLEEP...
DID SOMETHING HAPPEN LAST NIGHT?
UH... UH-HUH...
...
I SEE...
SO THAT'S WHAT HAPPENED...

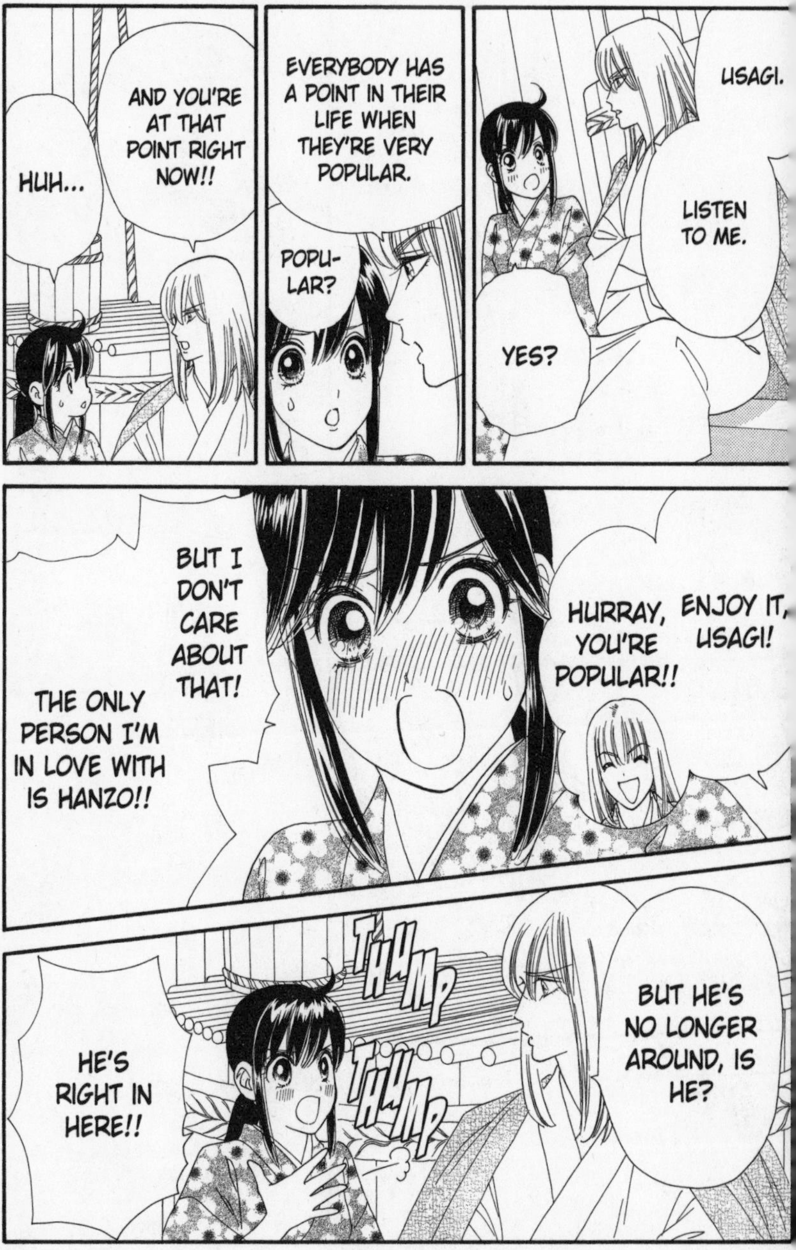
USAGI.
LISTEN TO ME.
YES?
EVERYBODY HAS A POINT IN THEIR LIFE WHEN THEY'RE VERY POPULAR.
POPU-LAR?
AND YOU'RE AT THAT POINT RIGHT NOW!!
HUH...
ENJOY IT, USAGI!
HURRAY, YOU'RE POPULAR!!
BUT I DON'T CARE ABOUT THAT!
THE ONLY PERSON I'M IN LOVE WITH IS HANZO!!
BUT HE'S NO LONGER AROUND, IS HE?
THUMP
THUMP
HE'S RIGHT IN HERE!!

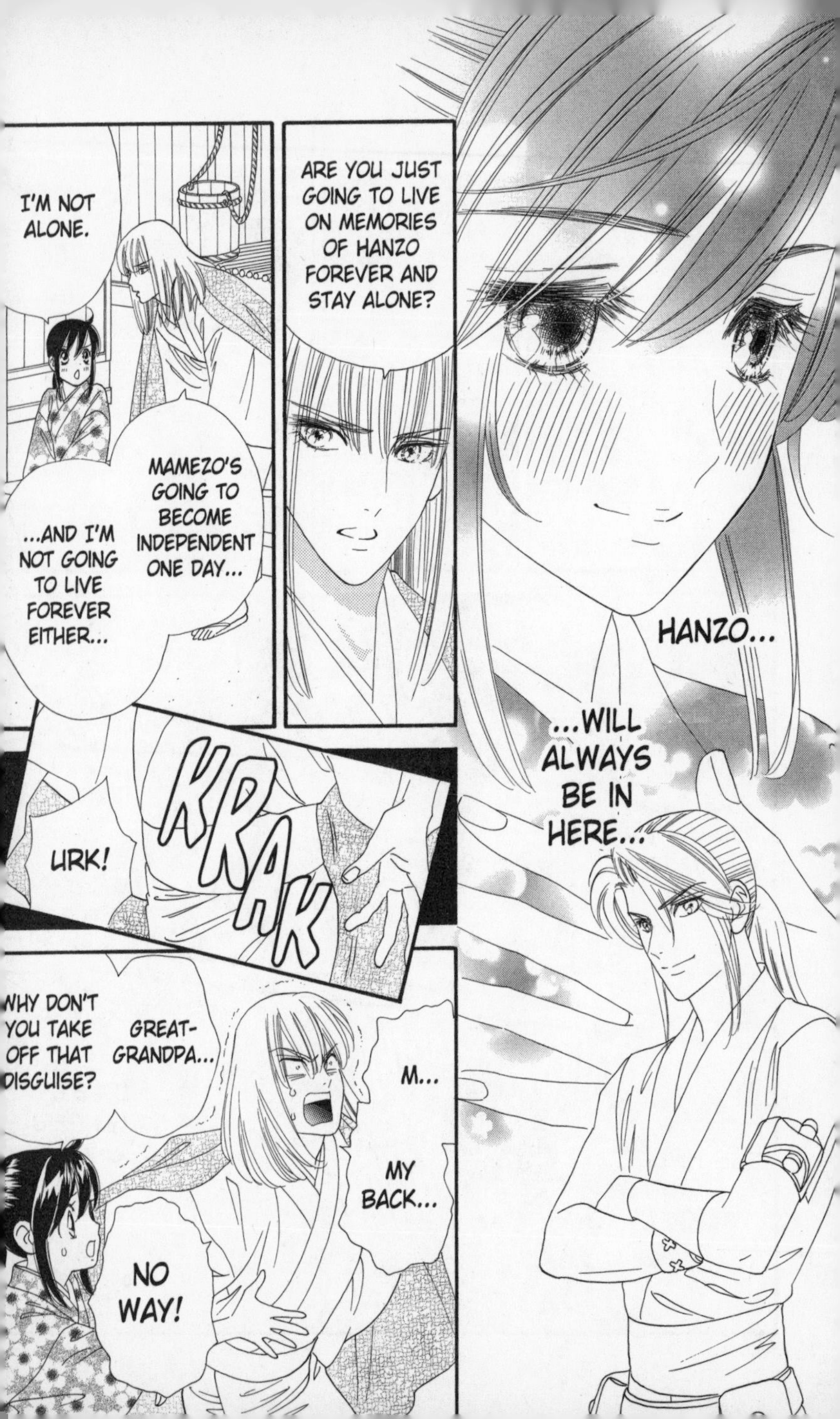
HANZO...
...WILL ALWAYS BE IN HERE...
ARE YOU JUST GOING TO LIVE ON MEMORIES OF HANZO FOREVER AND STAY ALONE?
I'M NOT ALONE.
MAMEZO'S GOING TO BECOME INDEPENDENT ONE DAY...
...AND I'M NOT GOING TO LIVE FOREVER EITHER...
KRAK
URK!
M...
MY BACK...
GREAT-GRANDPA...
WHY DON'T YOU TAKE OFF THAT DISGUISE?
NO WAY!

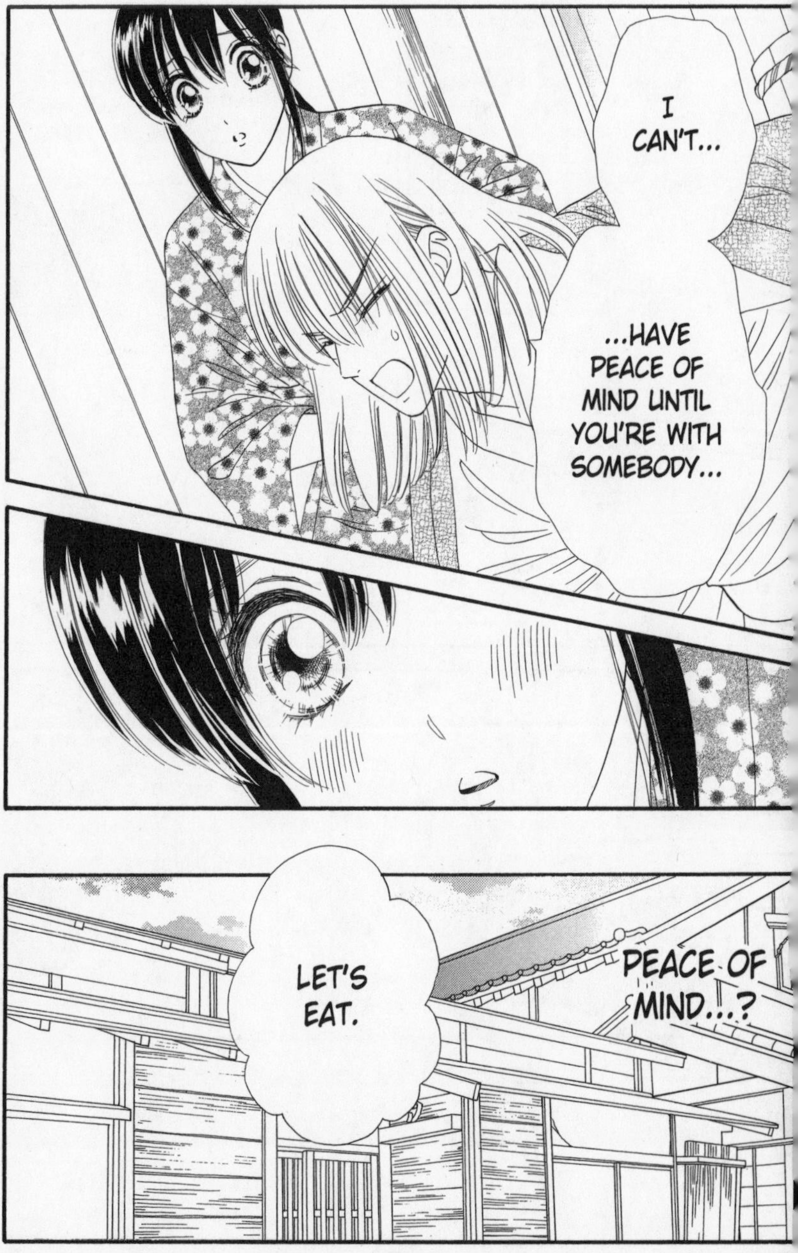
I CAN'T...
...HAVE PEACE OF MIND UNTIL YOU'RE WITH SOMEBODY...
PEACE OF MIND...?
LET'S EAT.

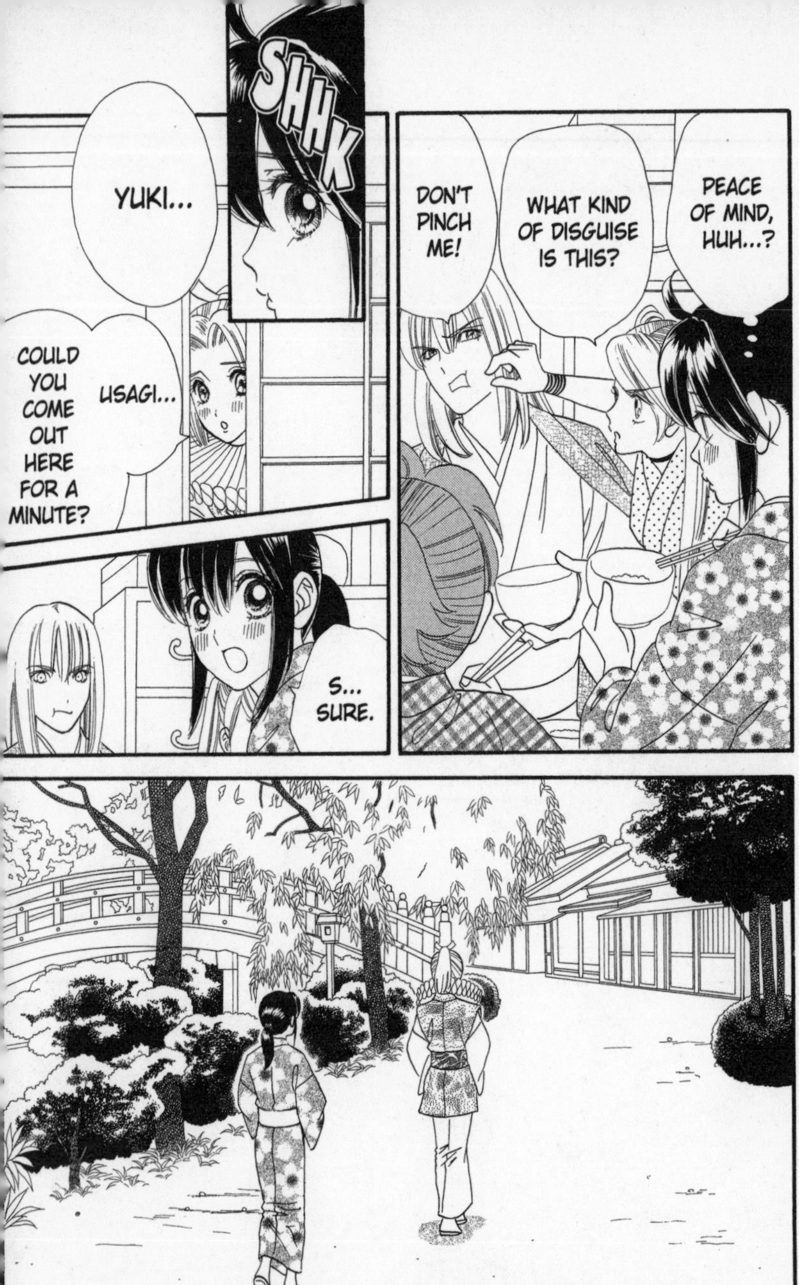
PEACE OF MIND, HUH...?
WHAT KIND OF DISGUISE IS THIS?
DON'T PINCH ME!
SHHK
YUKI...
USAGI...
COULD YOU COME OUT HERE FOR A MINUTE?
S... SURE.

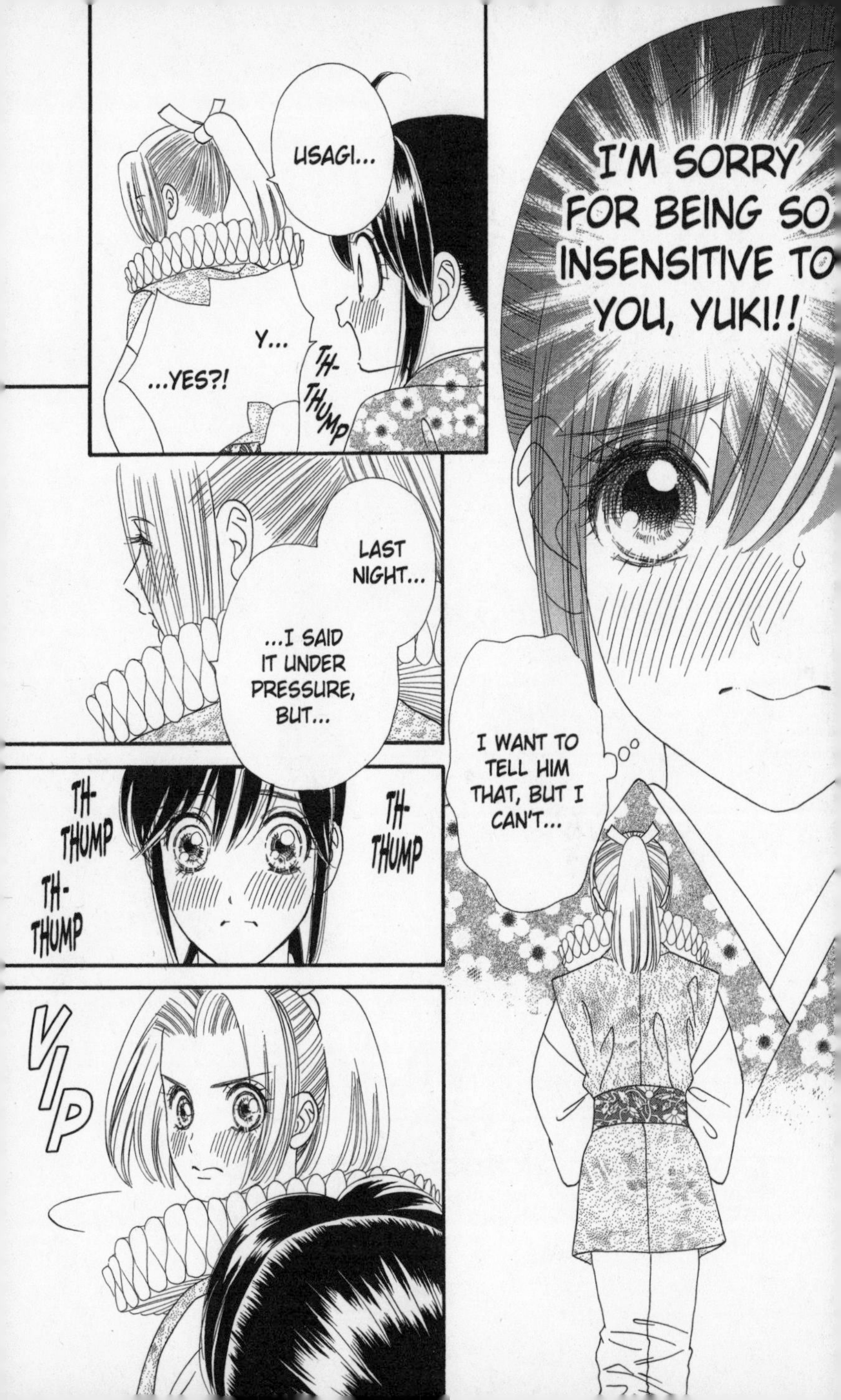
I'M SORRY FOR BEING SO INSENSITIVE TO YOU, YUKI!!
I WANT TO TELL HIM THAT, BUT I CAN'T...
USAGI...
Y...
...YES?!
TH-THUMP
LAST NIGHT...
...I SAID IT UNDER PRESSURE, BUT...
TH-THUMP
TH-THUMP
TH-THUMP
VIP

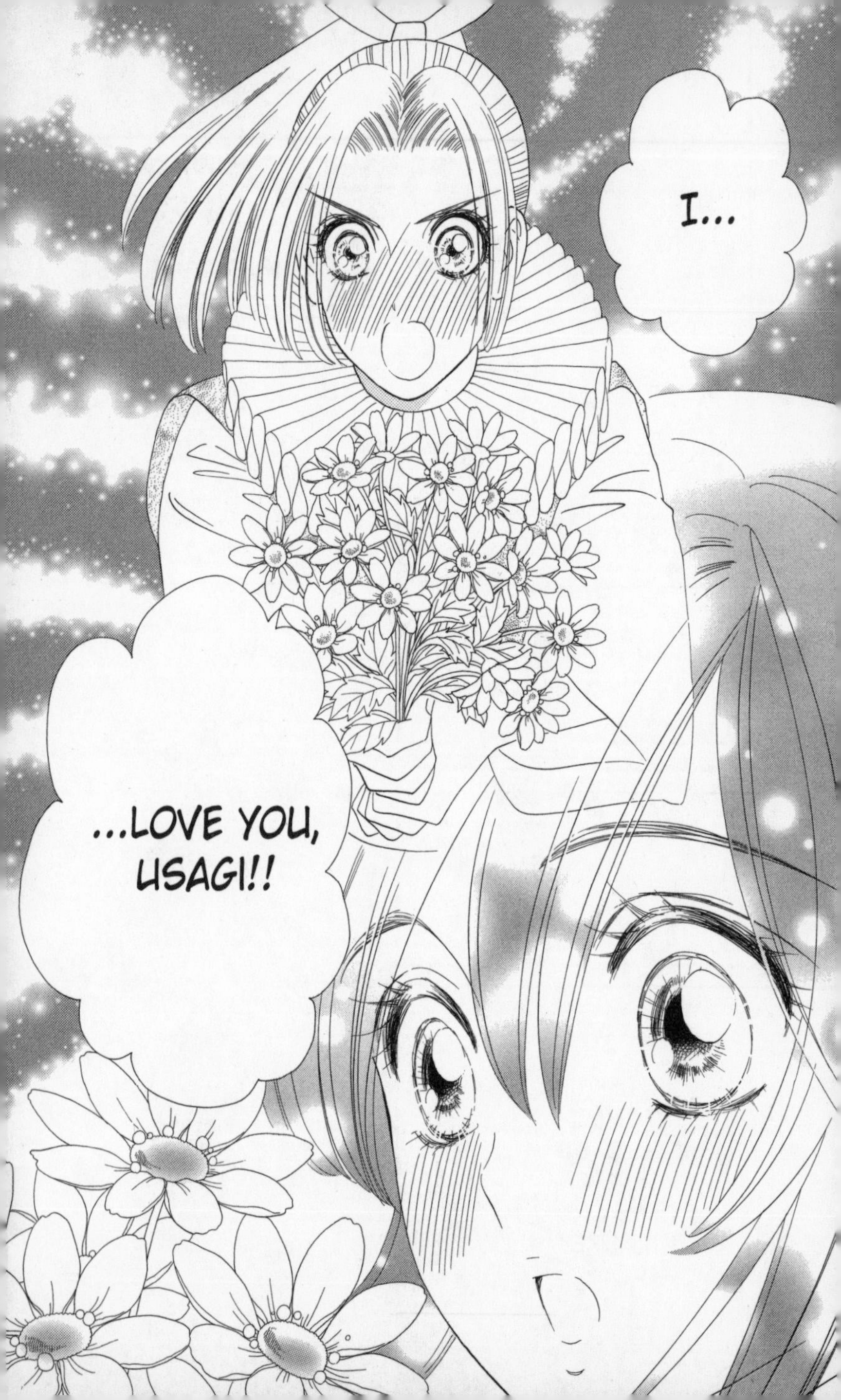
I...
...LOVE YOU, USAGI!!

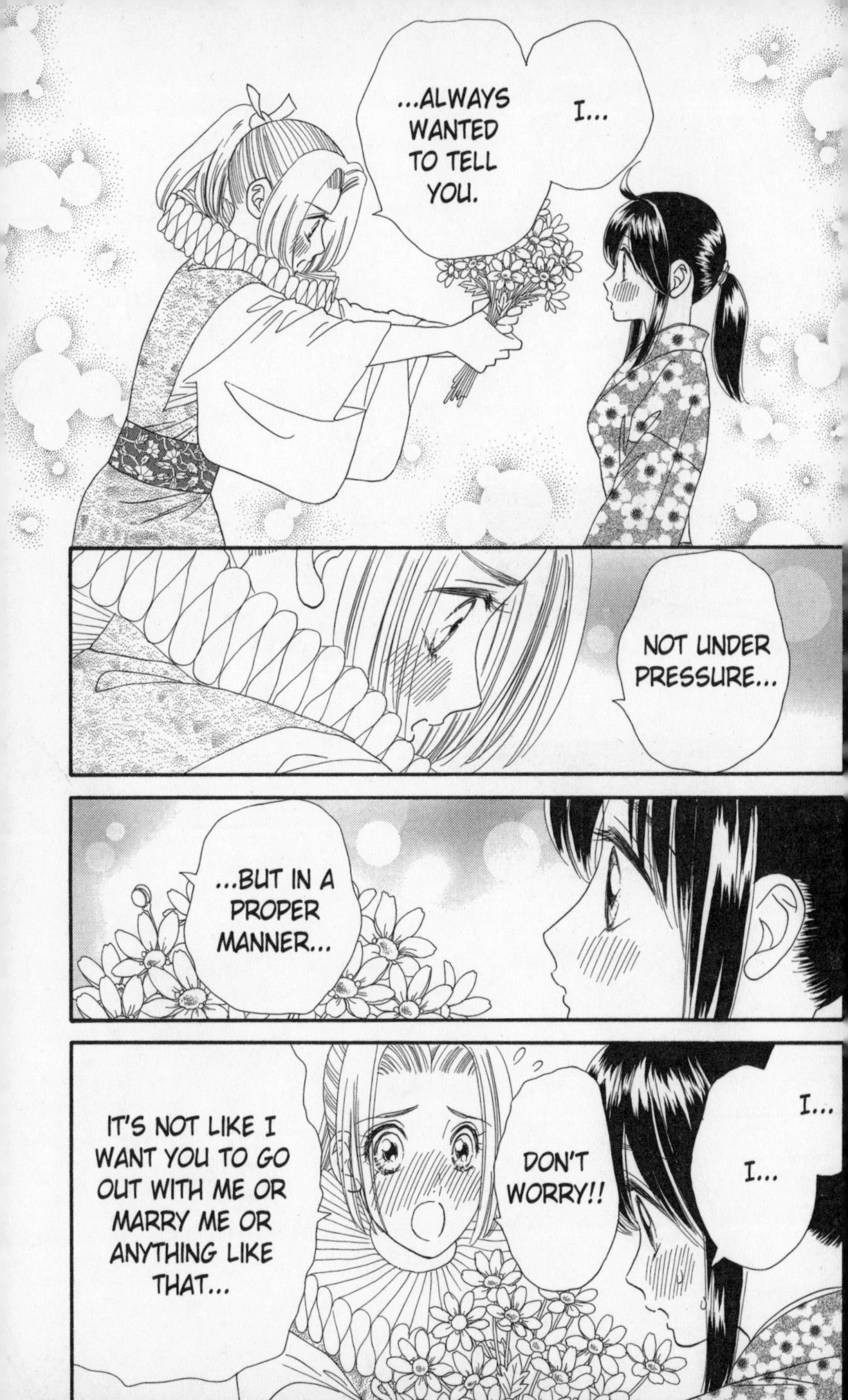
I...
...ALWAYS WANTED TO TELL YOU.
NOT UNDER PRESSURE...
...BUT IN A PROPER MANNER...
I...
I...
DON'T WORRY!!
IT'S NOT LIKE I WANT YOU TO GO OUT WITH ME OR MARRY ME OR ANYTHING LIKE THAT...

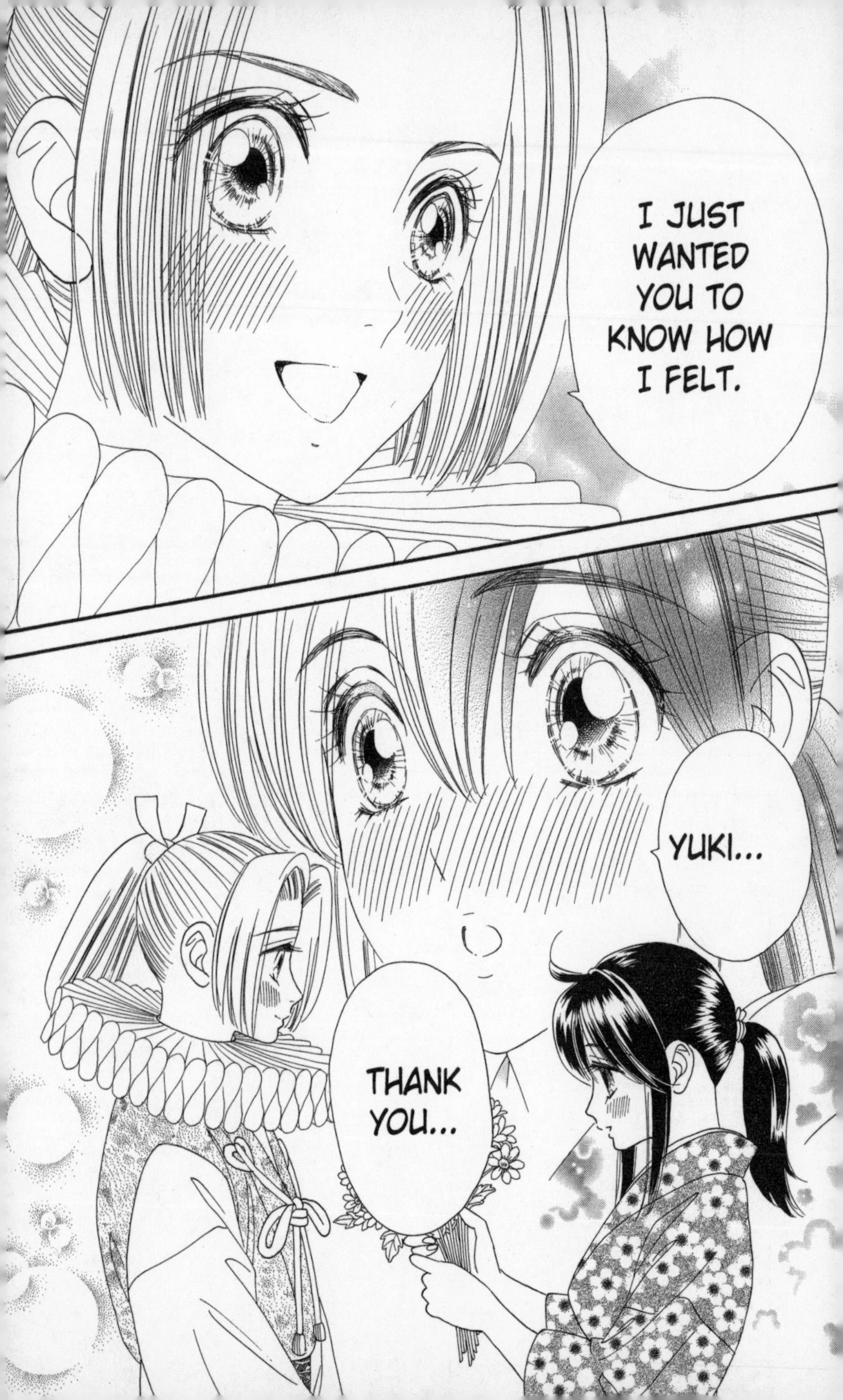
I JUST WANTED YOU TO KNOW HOW I FELT.
YUKI...
THANK YOU...

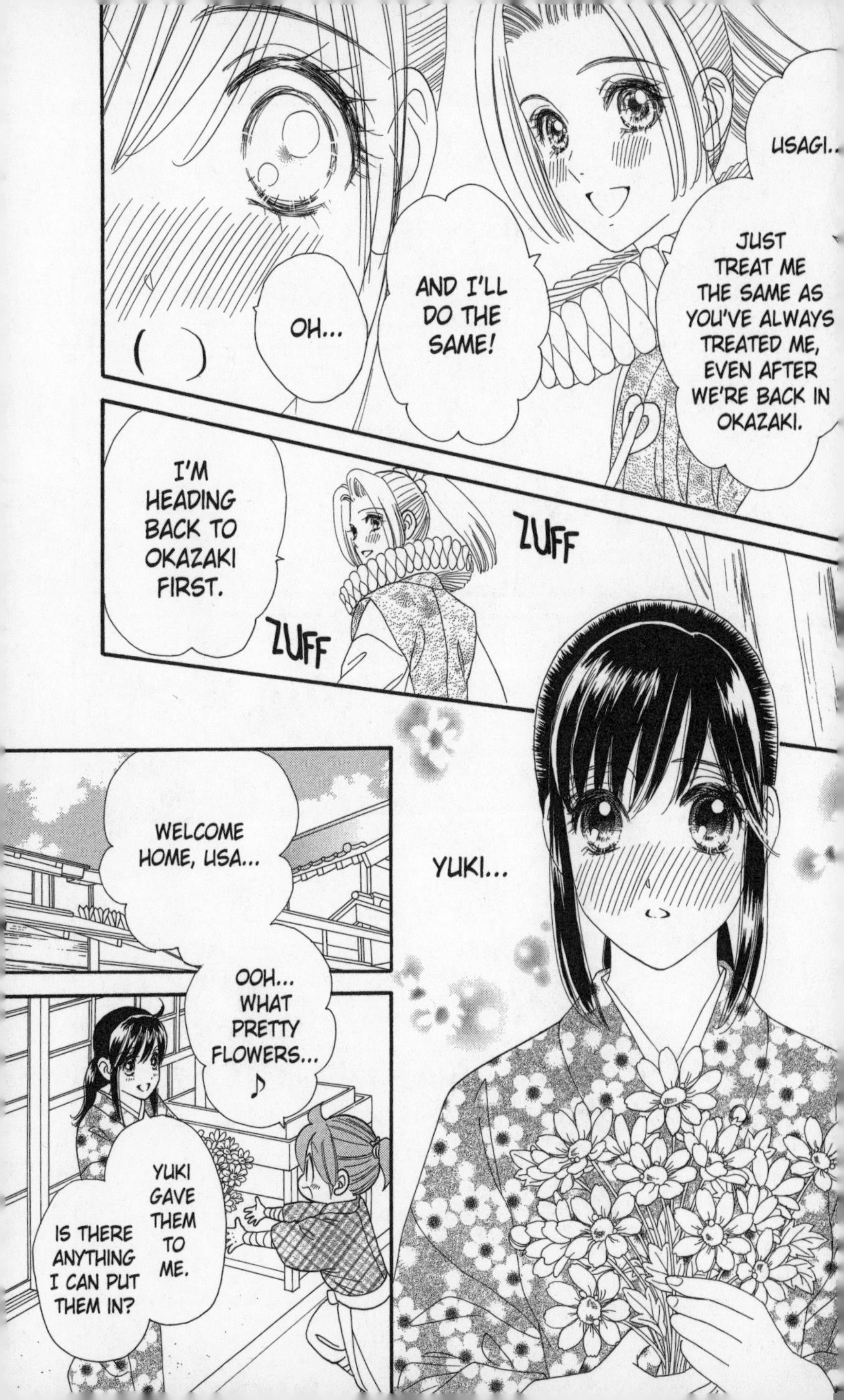
USAGI...
JUST TREAT ME THE SAME AS YOU'VE ALWAYS TREATED ME, EVEN AFTER WE'RE BACK IN OKAZAKI.
AND I'LL DO THE SAME!
OH...
ZUFF
I'M HEADING BACK TO OKAZAKI FIRST.
ZUFF
YUKI...
WELCOME HOME, USA...
OOH... WHAT PRETTY FLOWERS... ♪
YUKI GAVE THEM TO ME.
IS THERE ANYTHING I CAN PUT THEM IN?

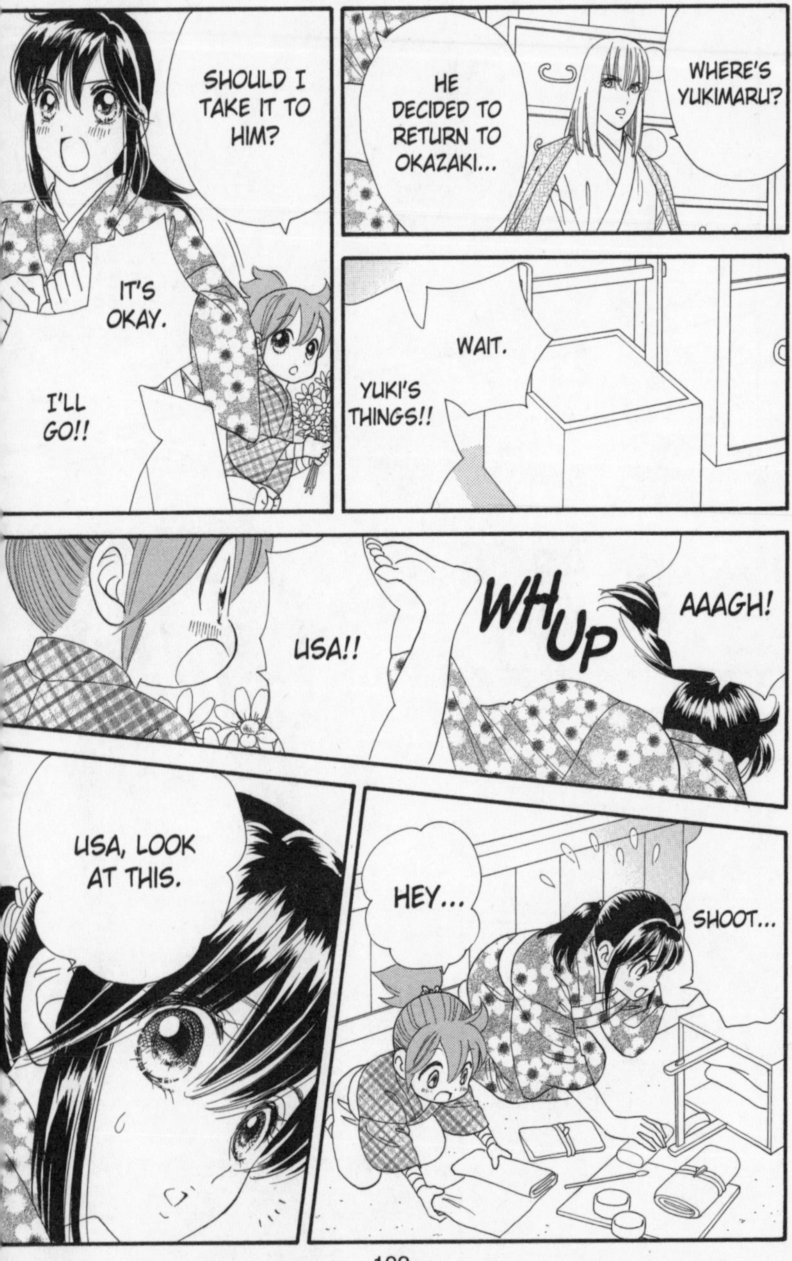
WHERE'S YUKIMARU?
HE DECIDED TO RETURN TO OKAZAKI...
WAIT.
YUKI'S THINGS!!
SHOULD I TAKE IT TO HIM?
IT'S OKAY.
I'LL GO!!
AAAGH!
WHUP
USA!!
SHOOT...
HEY...
USA, LOOK AT THIS.

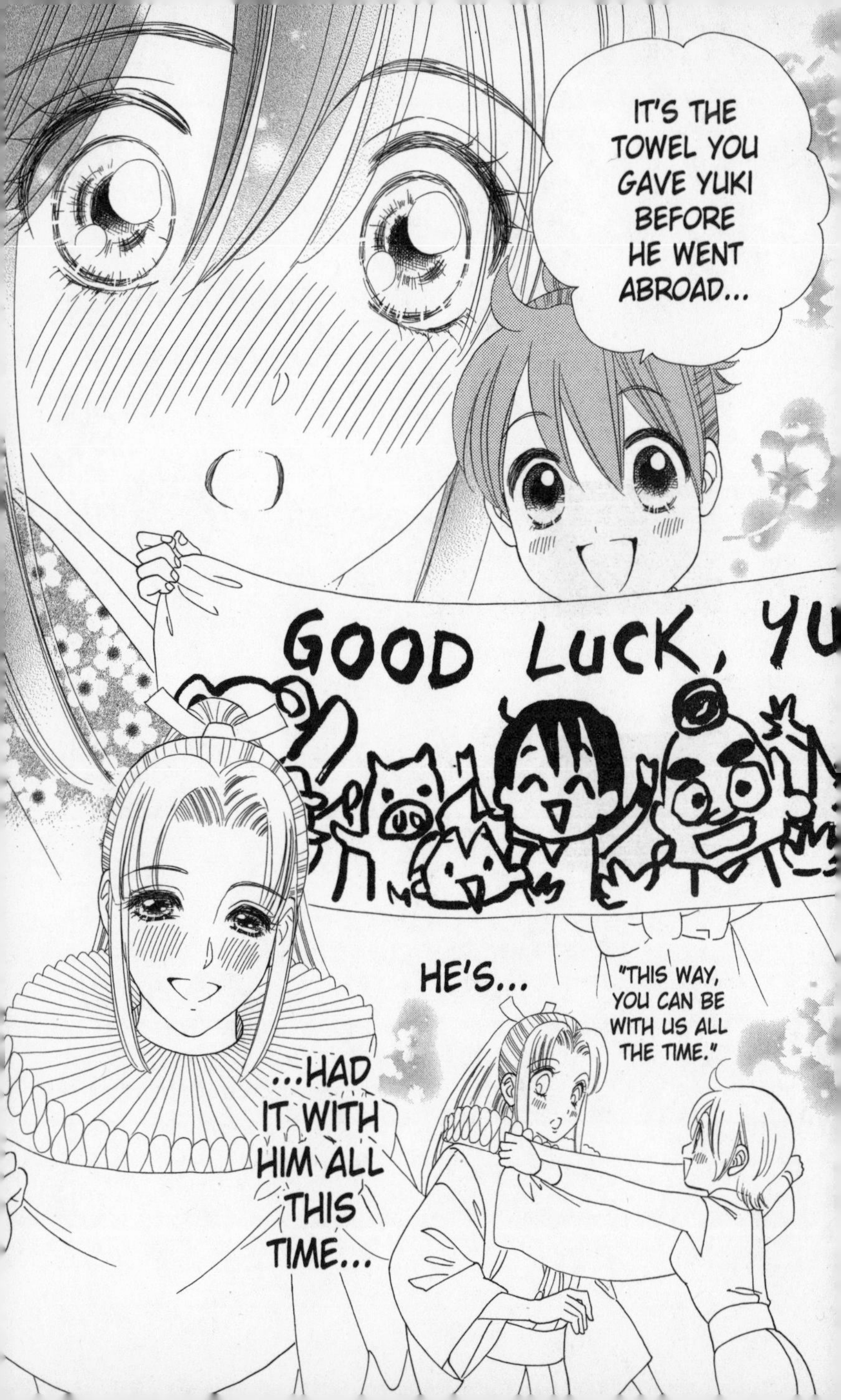
IT'S THE TOWEL YOU GAVE YUKI BEFORE HE WENT ABROAD...
GOOD LUCK, YU
"THIS WAY, YOU CAN BE WITH US ALL THE TIME."
HE'S...
...HAD IT WITH HIM ALL THIS TIME...

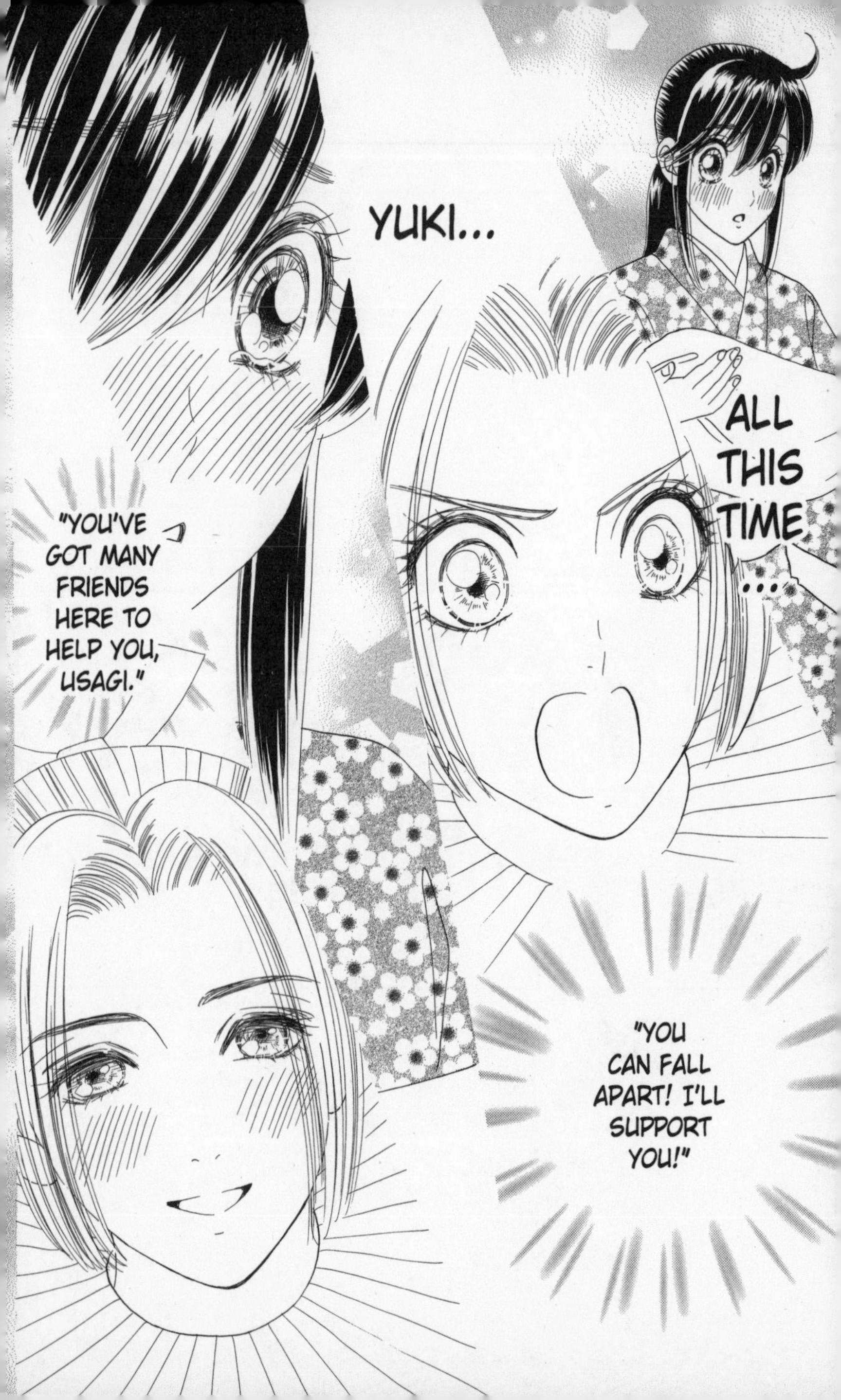
YUKI...
ALL THIS TIME...
"YOU'VE GOT MANY FRIENDS HERE TO HELP YOU, USAGI."
"YOU CAN FALL APART! I'LL SUPPORT YOU!"

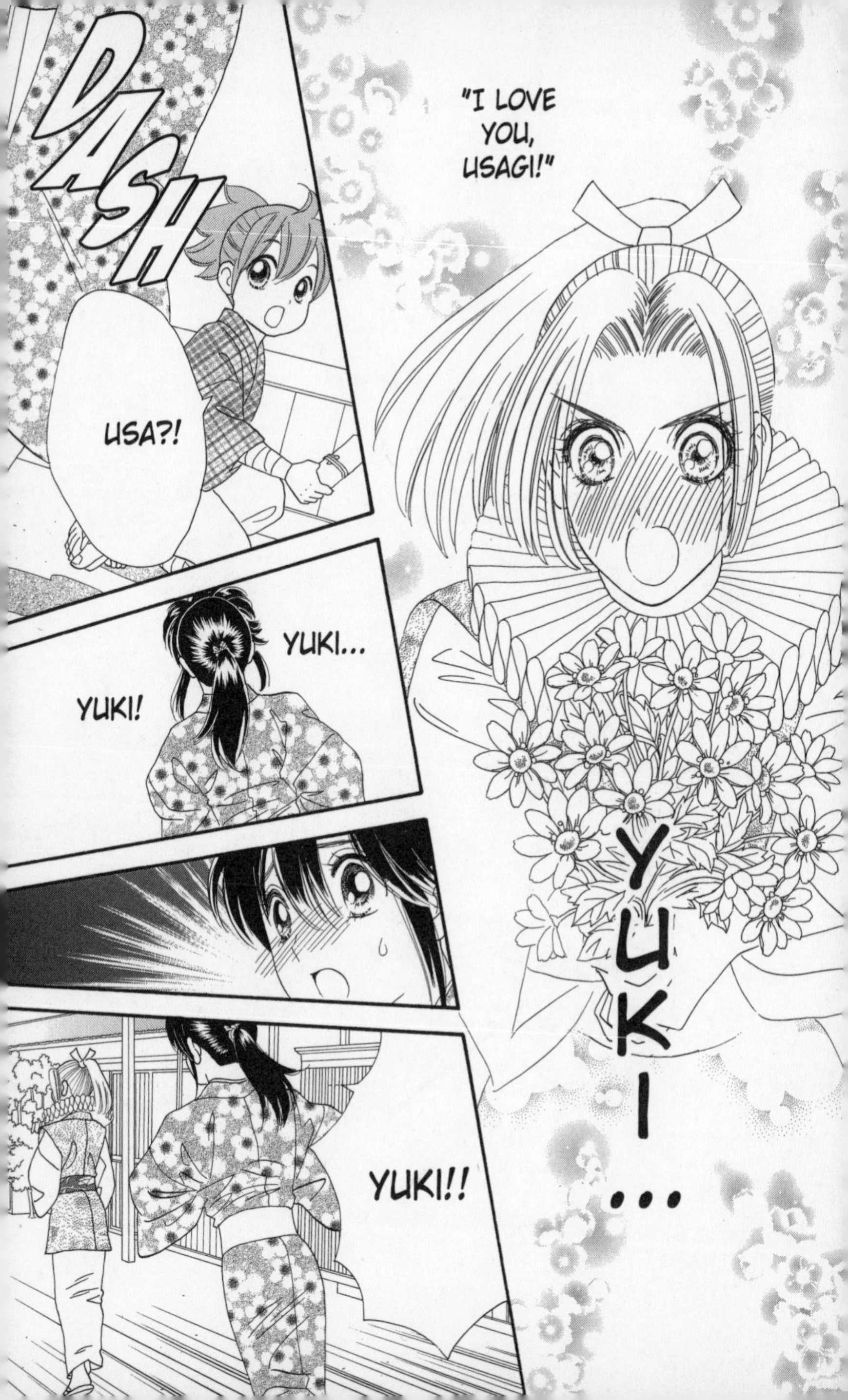
"I LOVE YOU, USAGI!"
YUKI...
DASH
USA?!
YUKI...
YUKI!
YUKI!!

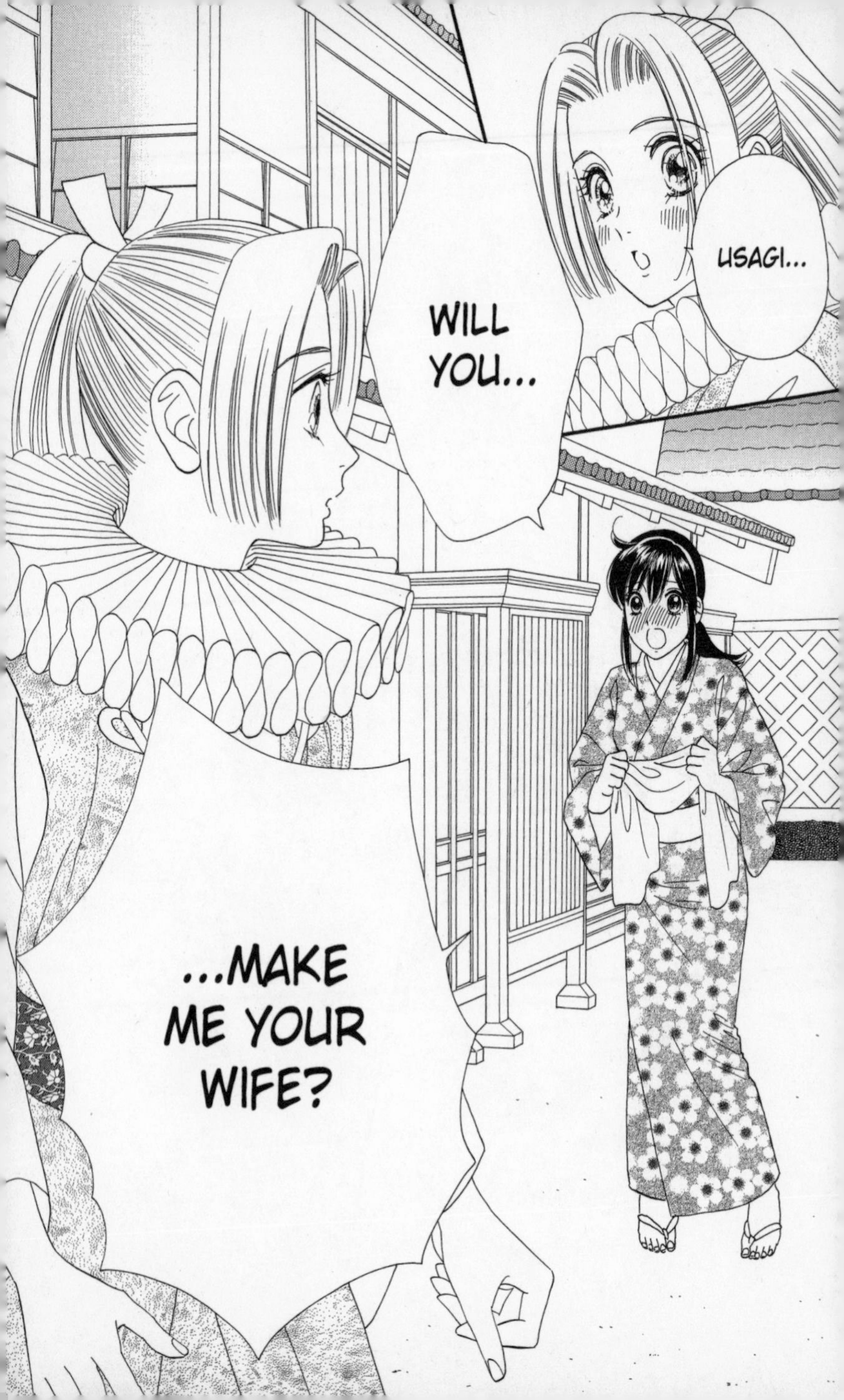
USAGI...
WILL YOU...
...MAKE ME YOUR WIFE?

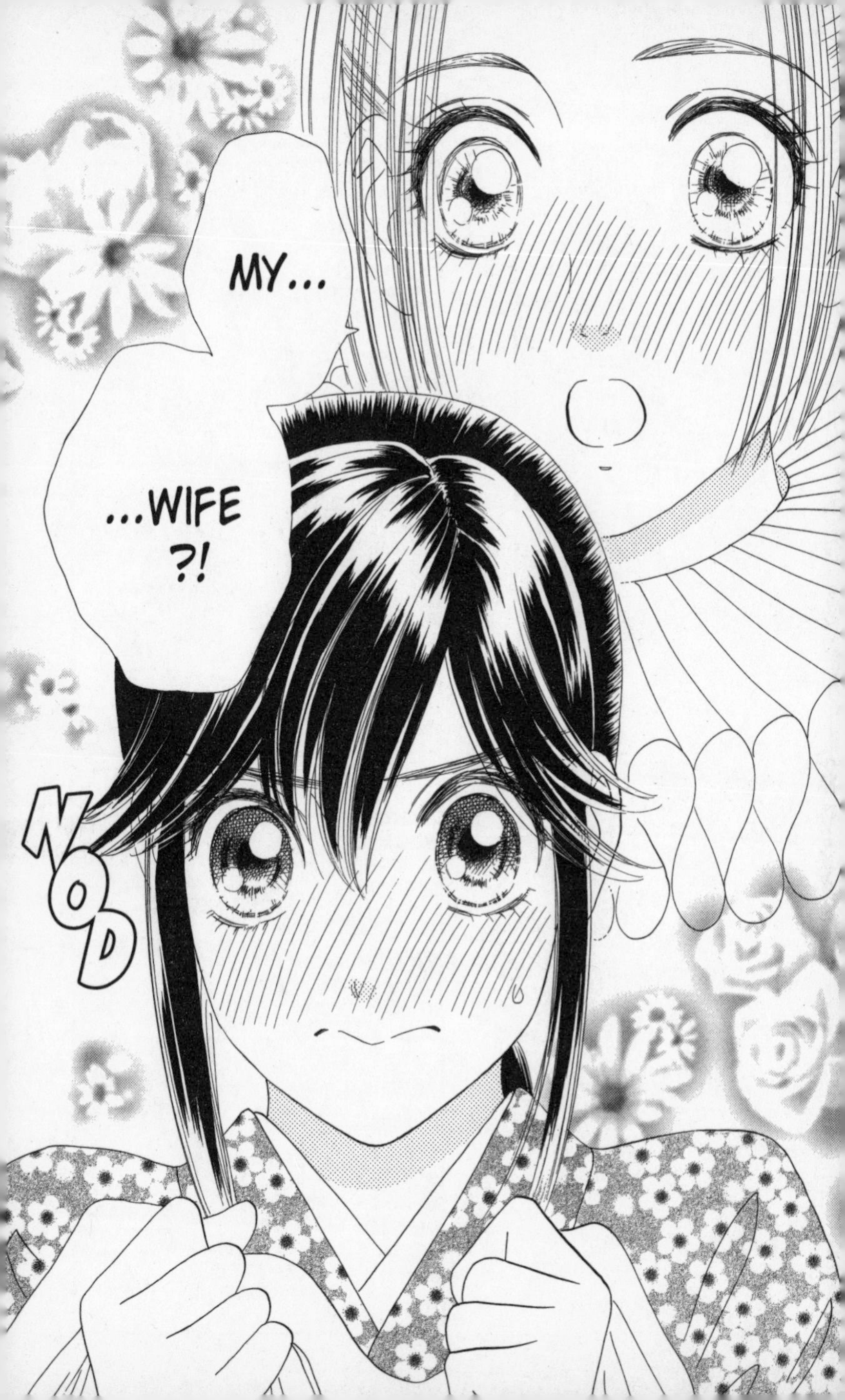
MY...
...WIFE ?!
NOD

LET'S GO! LITTLE HANZO

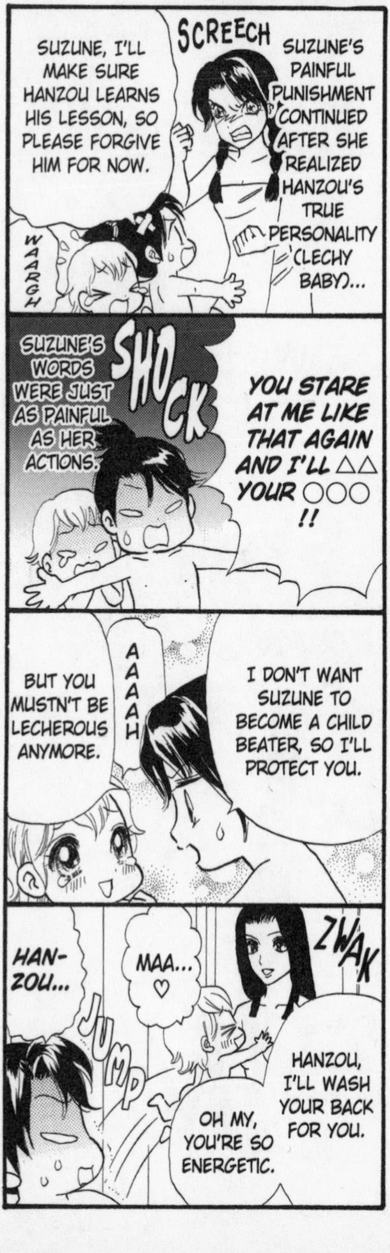
SUZUNE'S PAINFUL PUNISHMENT CONTINUED AFTER SHE REALIZED HANZOU'S TRUE PERSONALITY (LECHY BABY)...
SCREECH
SUZUNE, I'LL MAKE SURE HANZOU LEARNS HIS LESSON, SO PLEASE FORGIVE HIM FOR NOW.
WAARGH
YOU STARE AT ME LIKE THAT AGAIN AND I'LL △△ YOUR ○○○ !!
SHOCK
SUZUNE'S WORDS WERE JUST AS PAINFUL AS HER ACTIONS.
I DON'T WANT SUZUNE TO BECOME A CHILD BEATER, SO I'LL PROTECT YOU.
AAAAH
BUT YOU MUSTN'T BE LECHEROUS ANYMORE.
ZWAK
HANZOU, I'LL WASH YOUR BACK FOR YOU.
OH MY, YOU'RE SO ENERGETIC.
MAA... ♡
JUMP
HAN-ZOU...

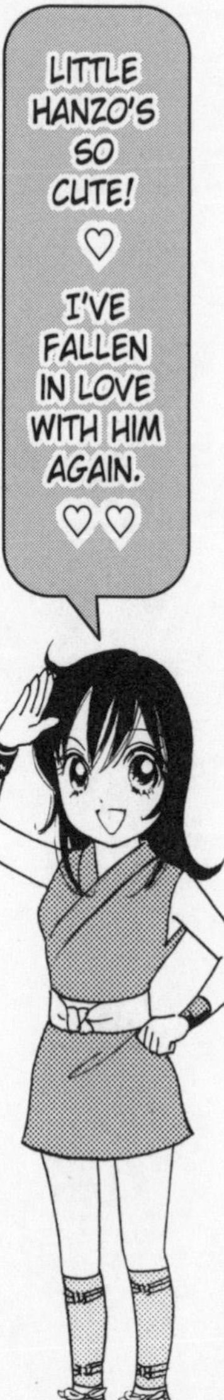
LITTLE HANZO'S SO CUTE! ♡ I'VE FALLEN IN LOVE WITH HIM AGAIN. ♡♡

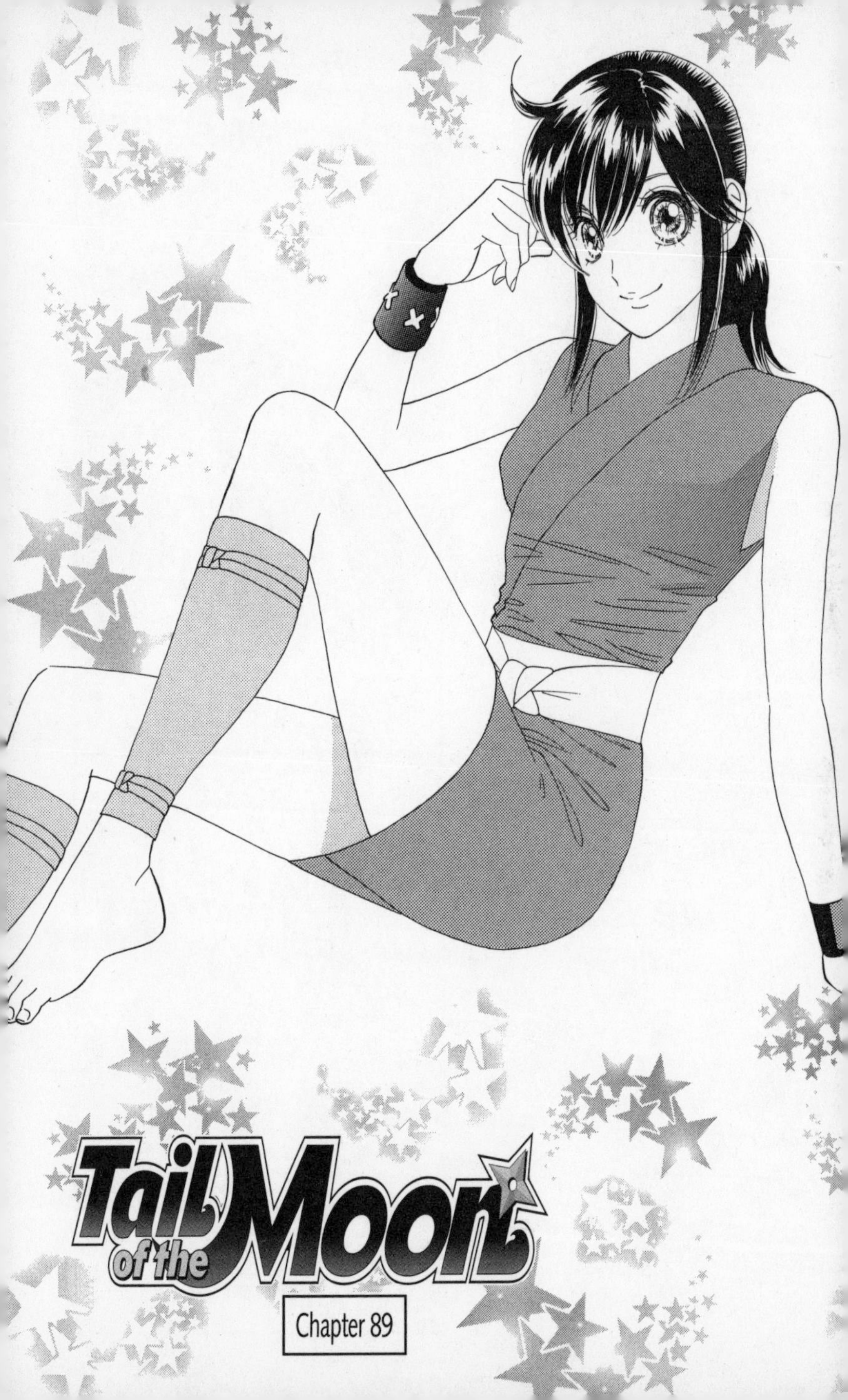

Tail of the Moon

Chapter 89

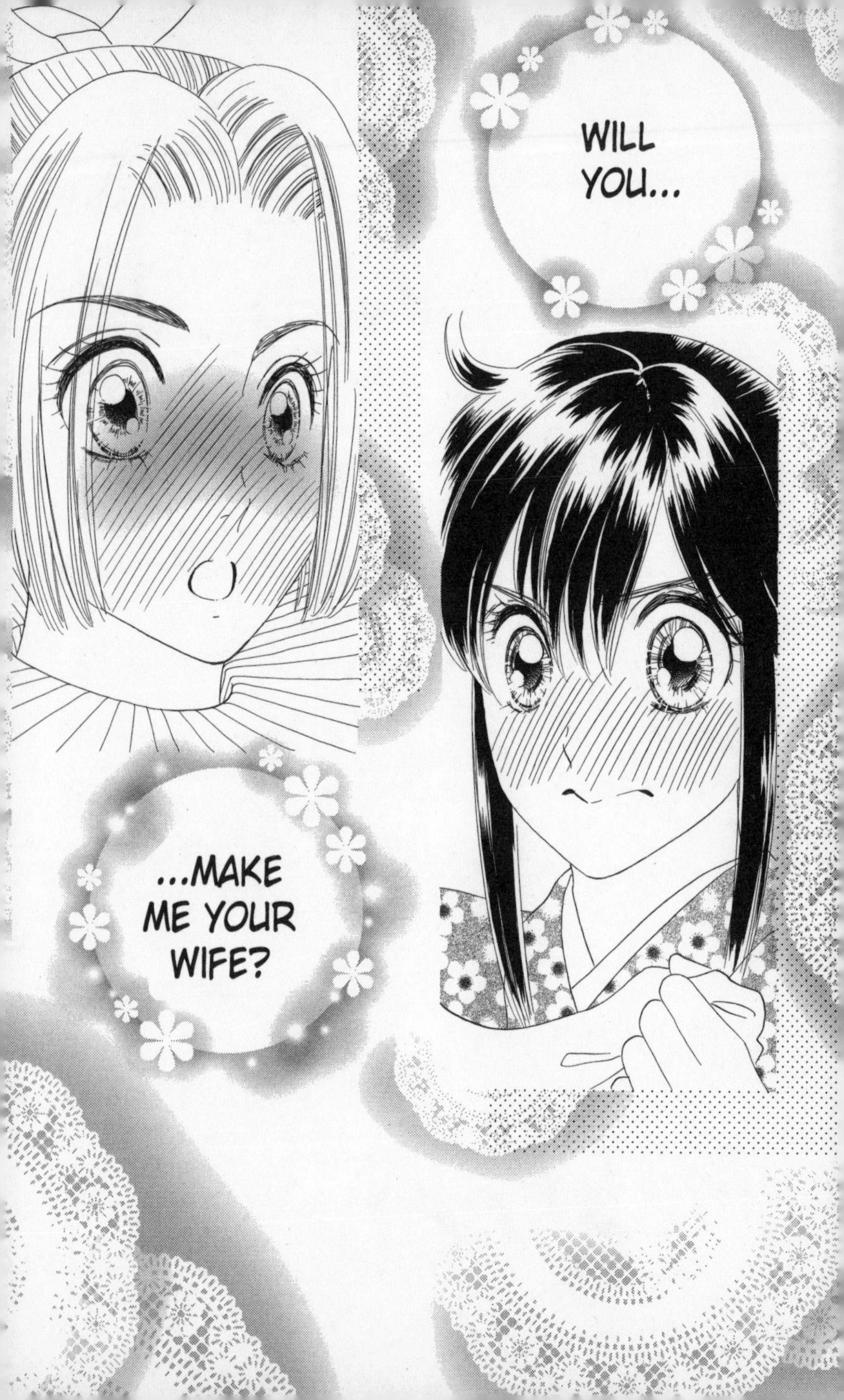
WILL YOU...
...MAKE ME YOUR WIFE?

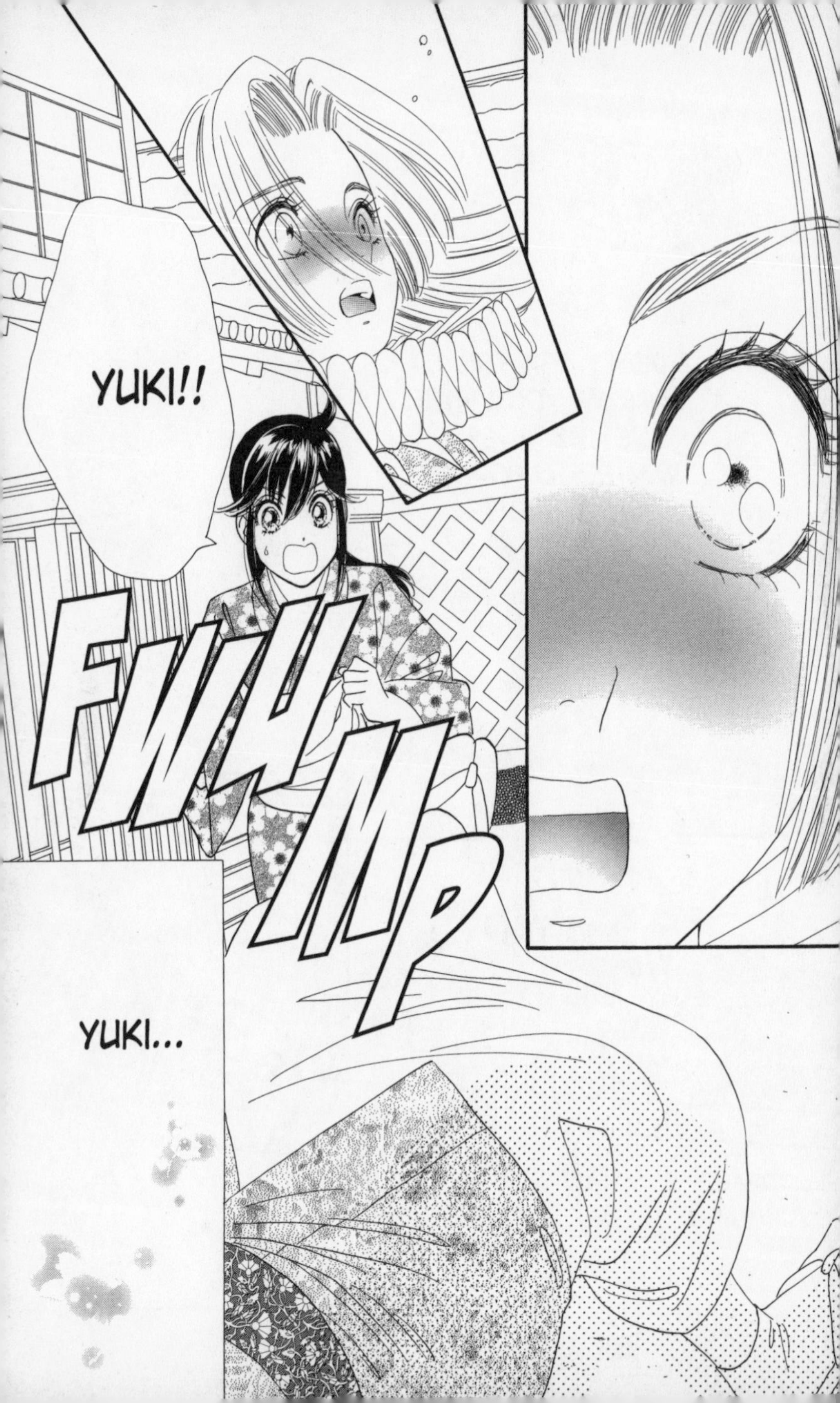
YUKI!!
FWUMP
YUKI...

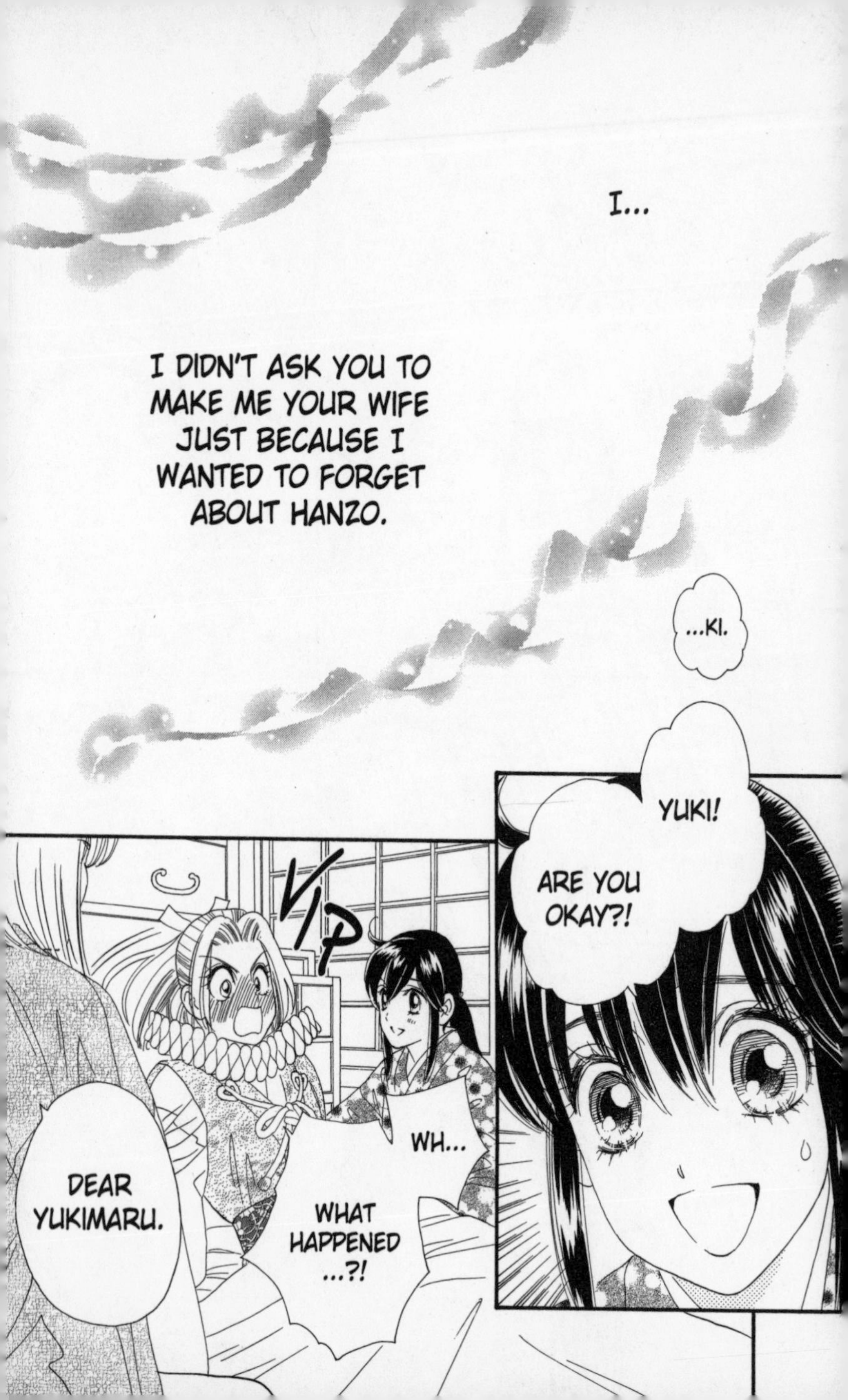
I...
I DIDN'T ASK YOU TO MAKE ME YOUR WIFE JUST BECAUSE I WANTED TO FORGET ABOUT HANZO.
...KI.
YUKI!
ARE YOU OKAY?!
VIP
WH...
WHAT HAPPENED ...?!
DEAR YUKIMARU.

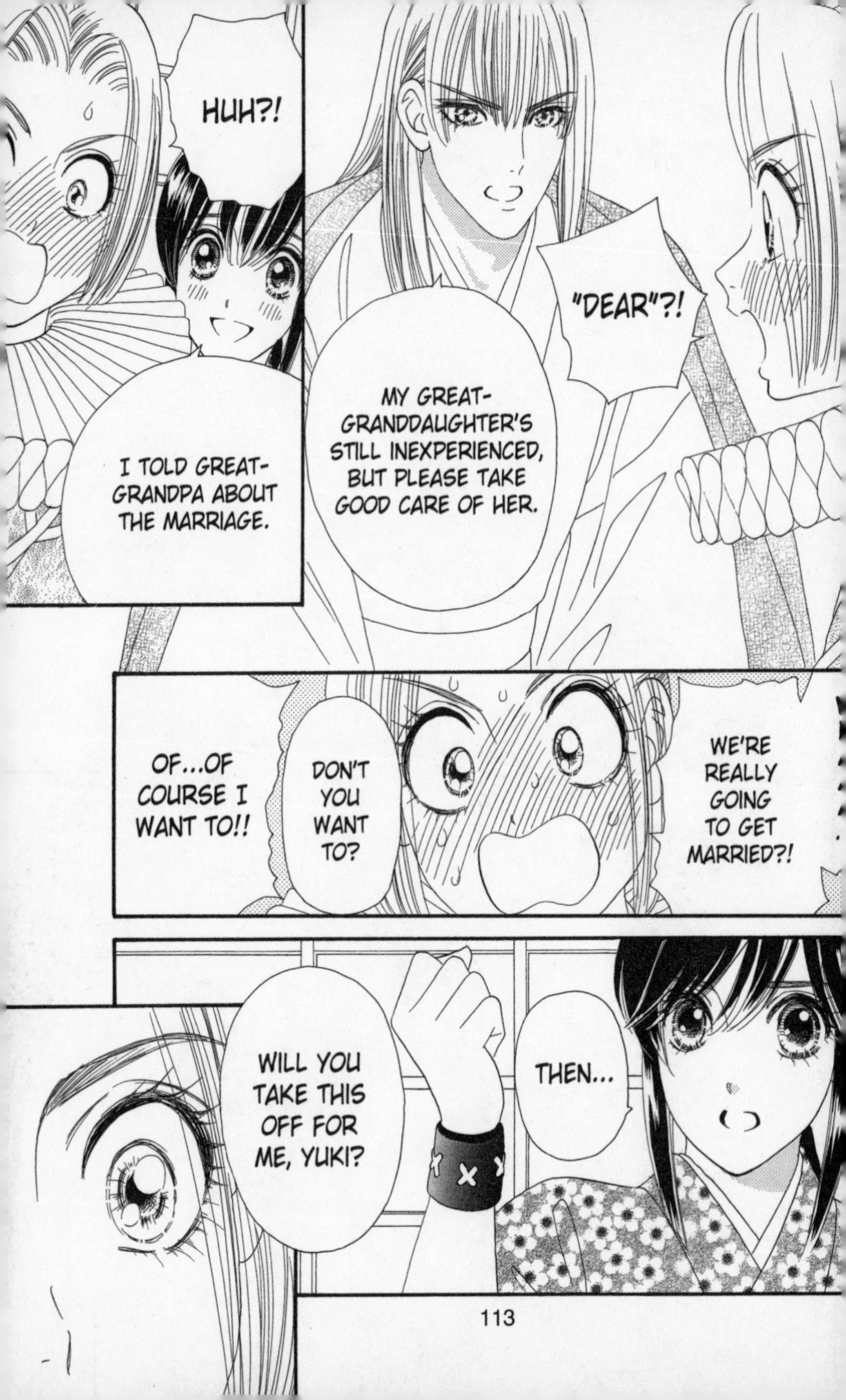
"DEAR"?!
MY GREAT-GRANDDAUGHTER'S STILL INEXPERIENCED, BUT PLEASE TAKE GOOD CARE OF HER.
HUH?!
I TOLD GREAT-GRANDPA ABOUT THE MARRIAGE.
WE'RE REALLY GOING TO GET MARRIED?!
DON'T YOU WANT TO?
OF...OF COURSE I WANT TO!!
THEN...
WILL YOU TAKE THIS OFF FOR ME, YUKI?

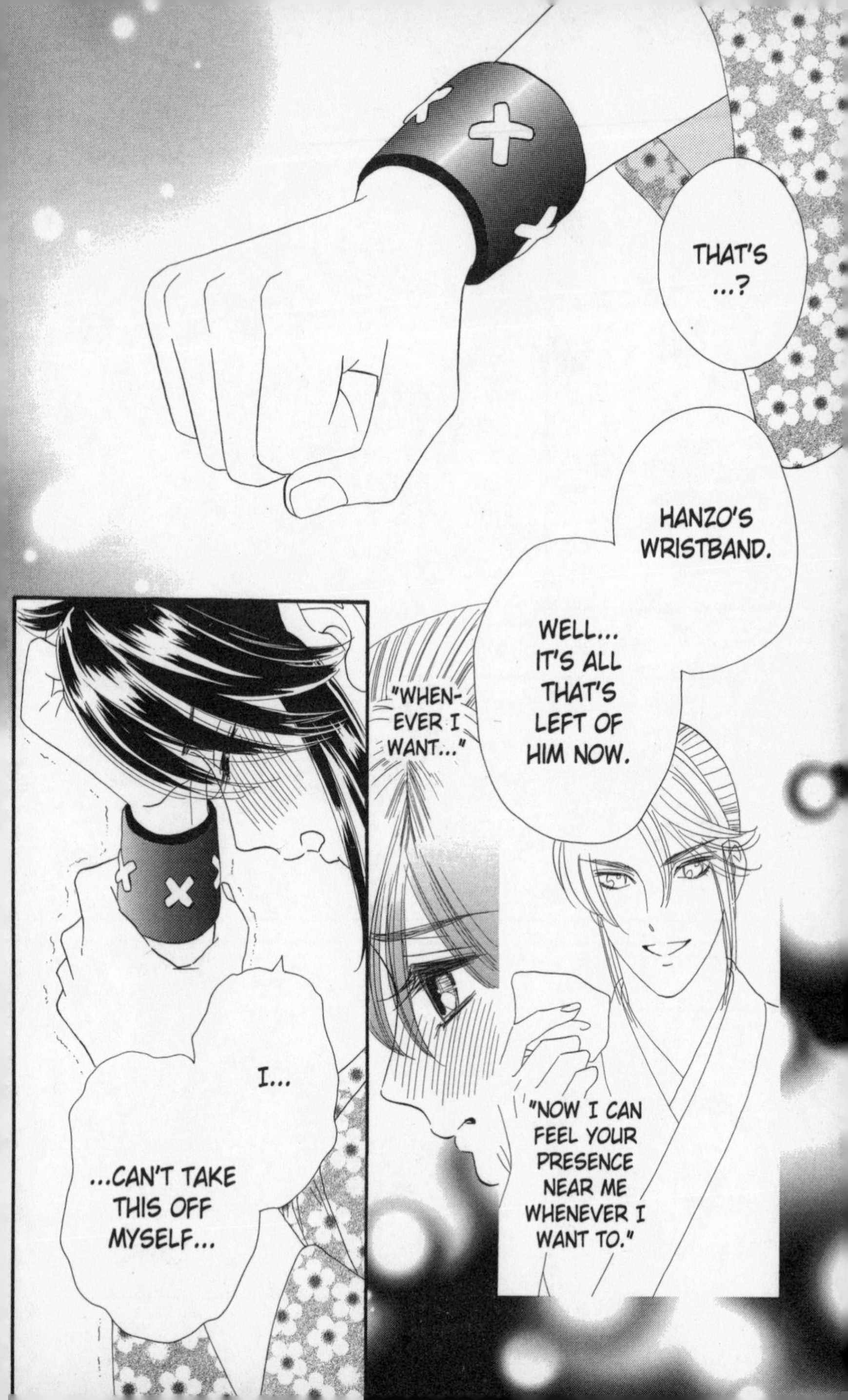
THAT'S ...?
HANZO'S WRISTBAND.
WELL... IT'S ALL THAT'S LEFT OF HIM NOW.
"NOW I CAN FEEL YOUR PRESENCE NEAR ME WHENEVER I WANT TO."
"WHEN-EVER I WANT..."
I...
...CAN'T TAKE THIS OFF MYSELF...

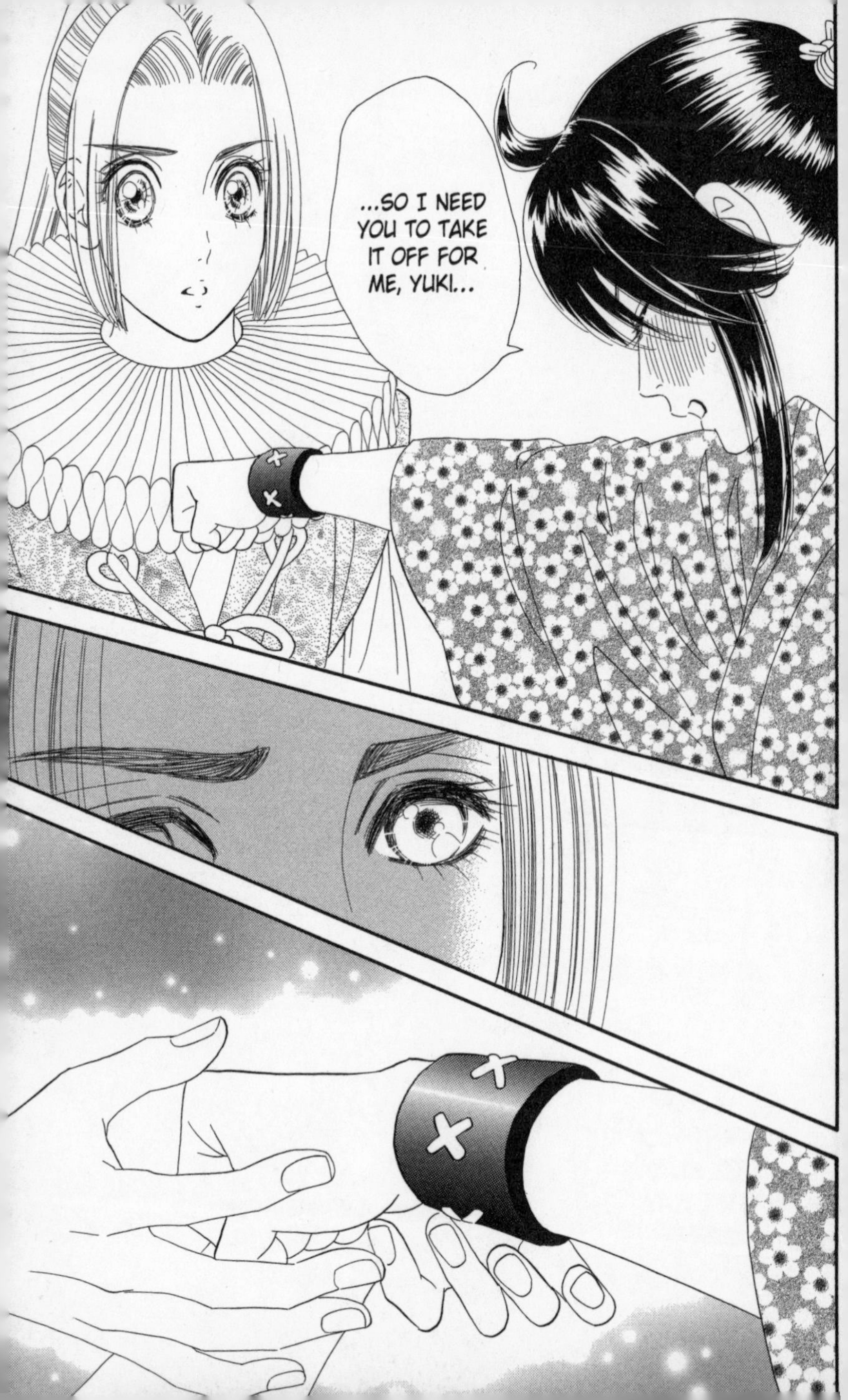
...SO I NEED YOU TO TAKE IT OFF FOR ME, YUKI...

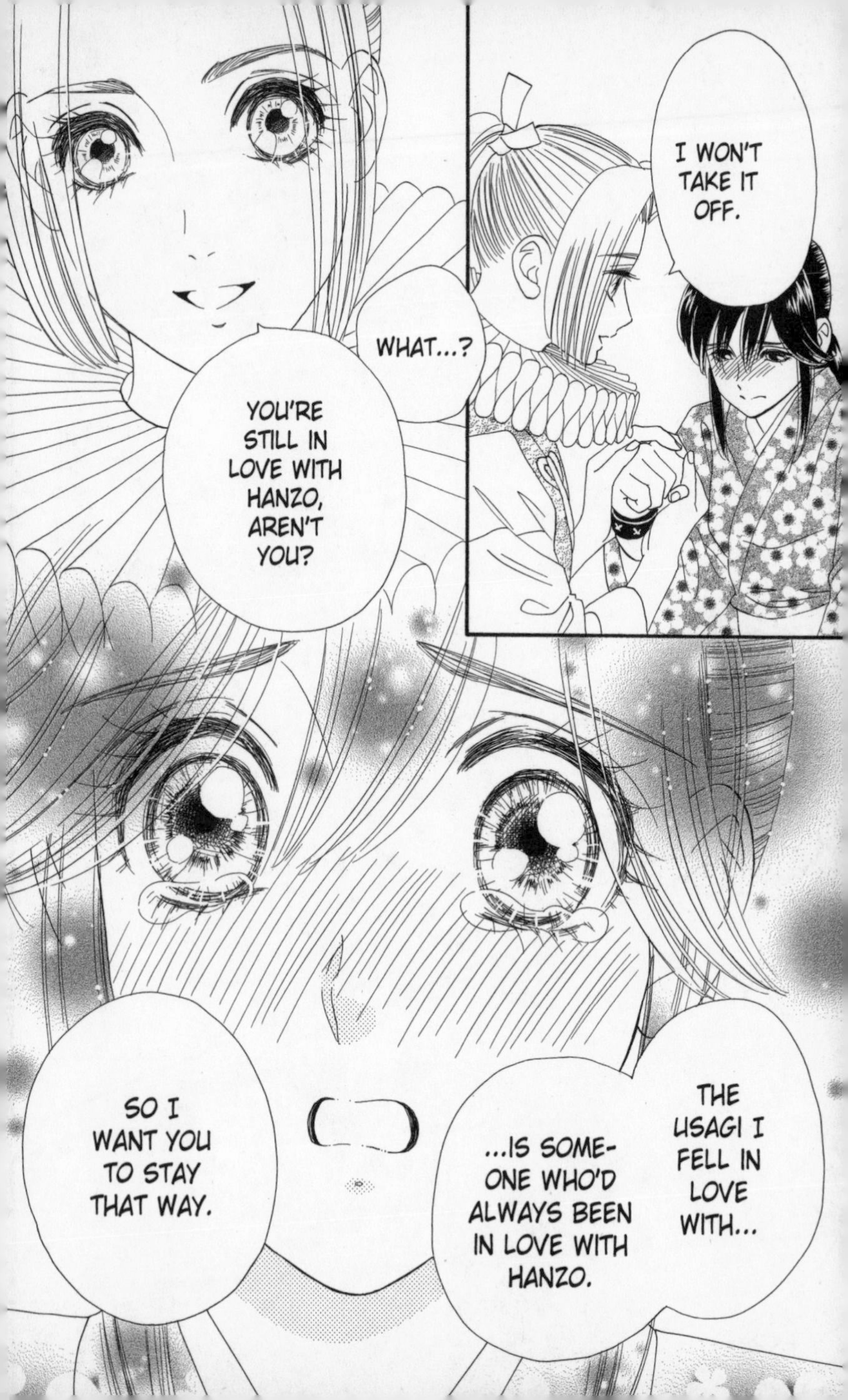
I WON'T TAKE IT OFF.
WHAT...?
YOU'RE STILL IN LOVE WITH HANZO, AREN'T YOU?
THE USAGI I FELL IN LOVE WITH...
...IS SOME-ONE WHO'D ALWAYS BEEN IN LOVE WITH HANZO.
SO I WANT YOU TO STAY THAT WAY.

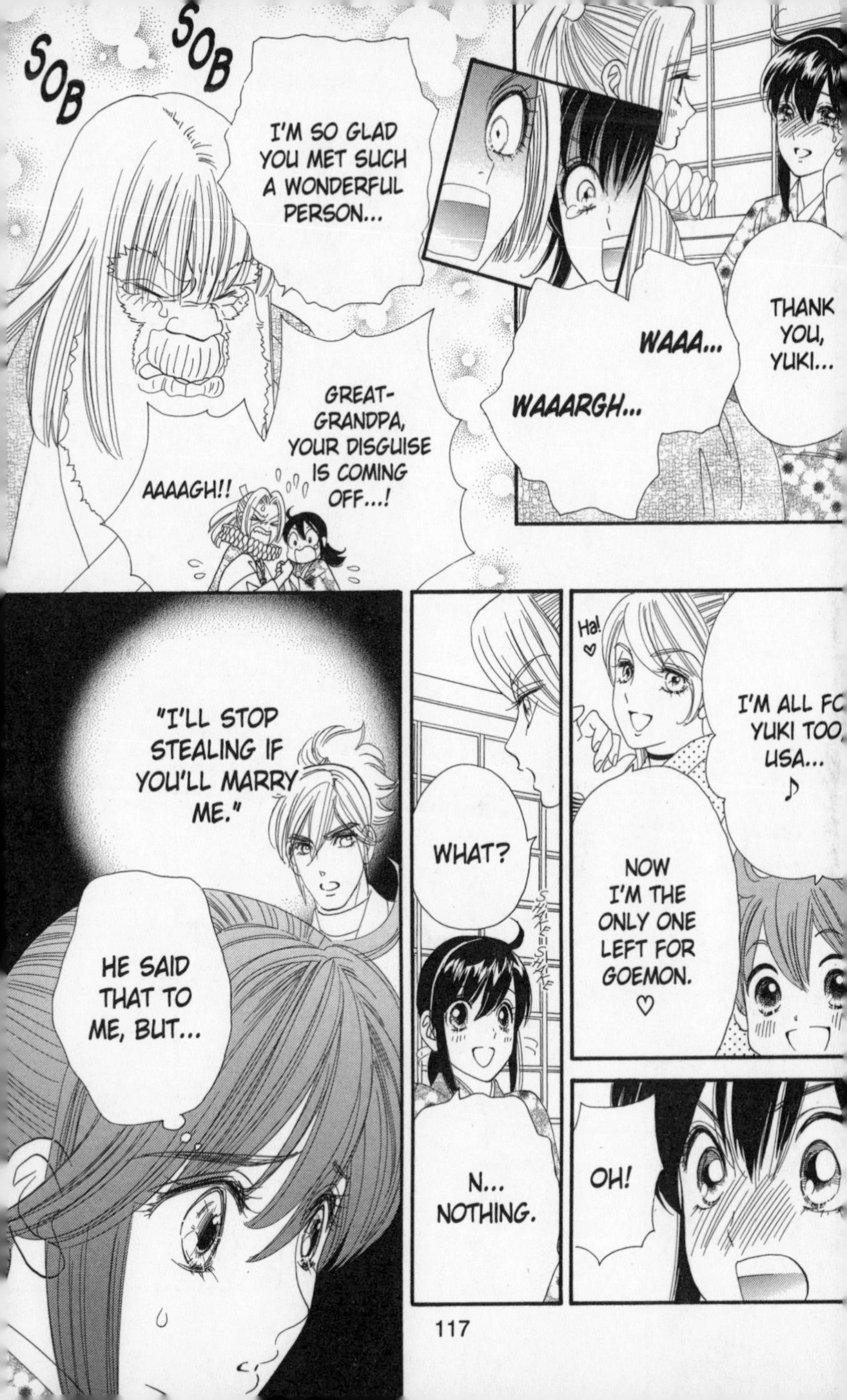
THANK YOU, YUKI...
WAAA...
WAAARGH...
SOB SOB
I'M SO GLAD YOU MET SUCH A WONDERFUL PERSON...
GREAT-GRANDPA, YOUR DISGUISE IS COMING OFF...!
AAAAGH!!
Ha! ♡
I'M ALL FO
YUKI TOO, USA... ♪
NOW I'M THE ONLY ONE LEFT FOR GOEMON. ♡
OH!
WHAT?
SHAKE SHAKE
N... NOTHING.
"I'LL STOP STEALING IF YOU'LL MARRY ME."
HE SAID THAT TO ME, BUT...

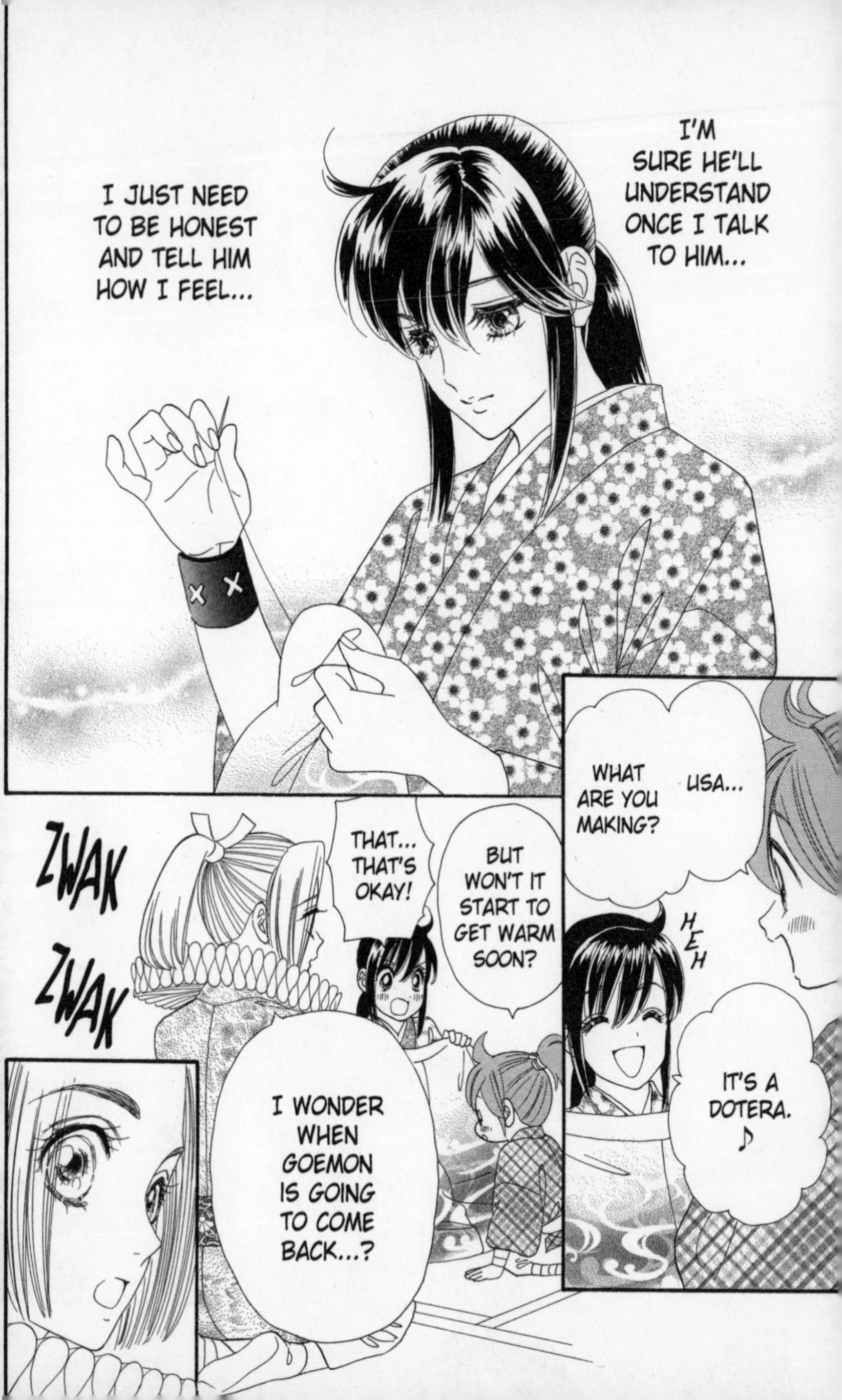
I'M SURE HE'LL UNDERSTAND ONCE I TALK TO HIM...
I JUST NEED TO BE HONEST AND TELL HIM HOW I FEEL...
USA...
WHAT ARE YOU MAKING?
HEH
IT'S A DOTERA. ♪
BUT WON'T IT START TO GET WARM SOON?
THAT... THAT'S OKAY!
ZWAK
ZWAK
I WONDER WHEN GOEMON IS GOING TO COME BACK...?

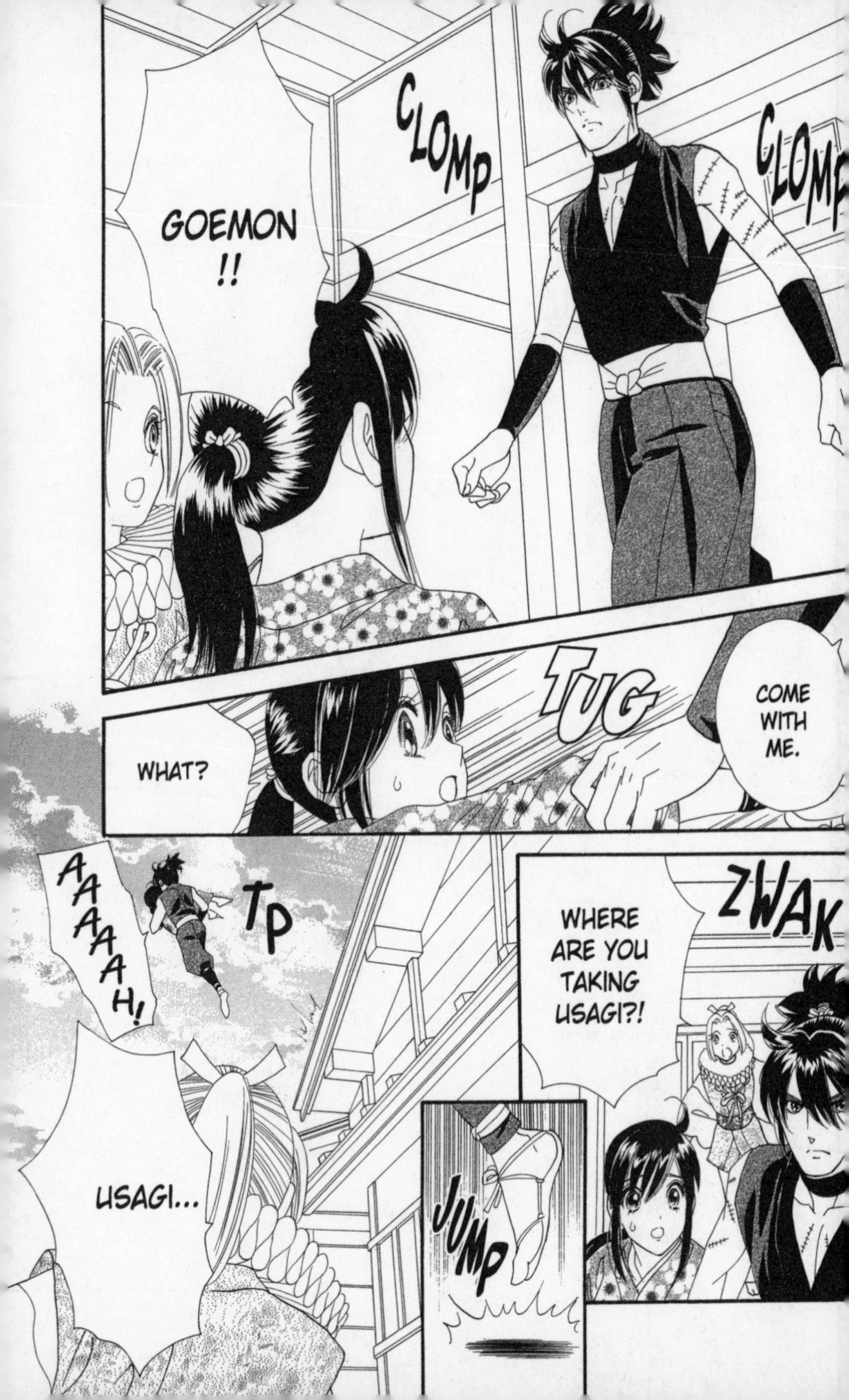
CLOMP
CLOMP
GOEMON !!
COME WITH ME.
TUG
WHAT?
ZWAK
WHERE ARE YOU TAKING USAGI?!
JUMP
TP
AAAAAH!
USAGI...

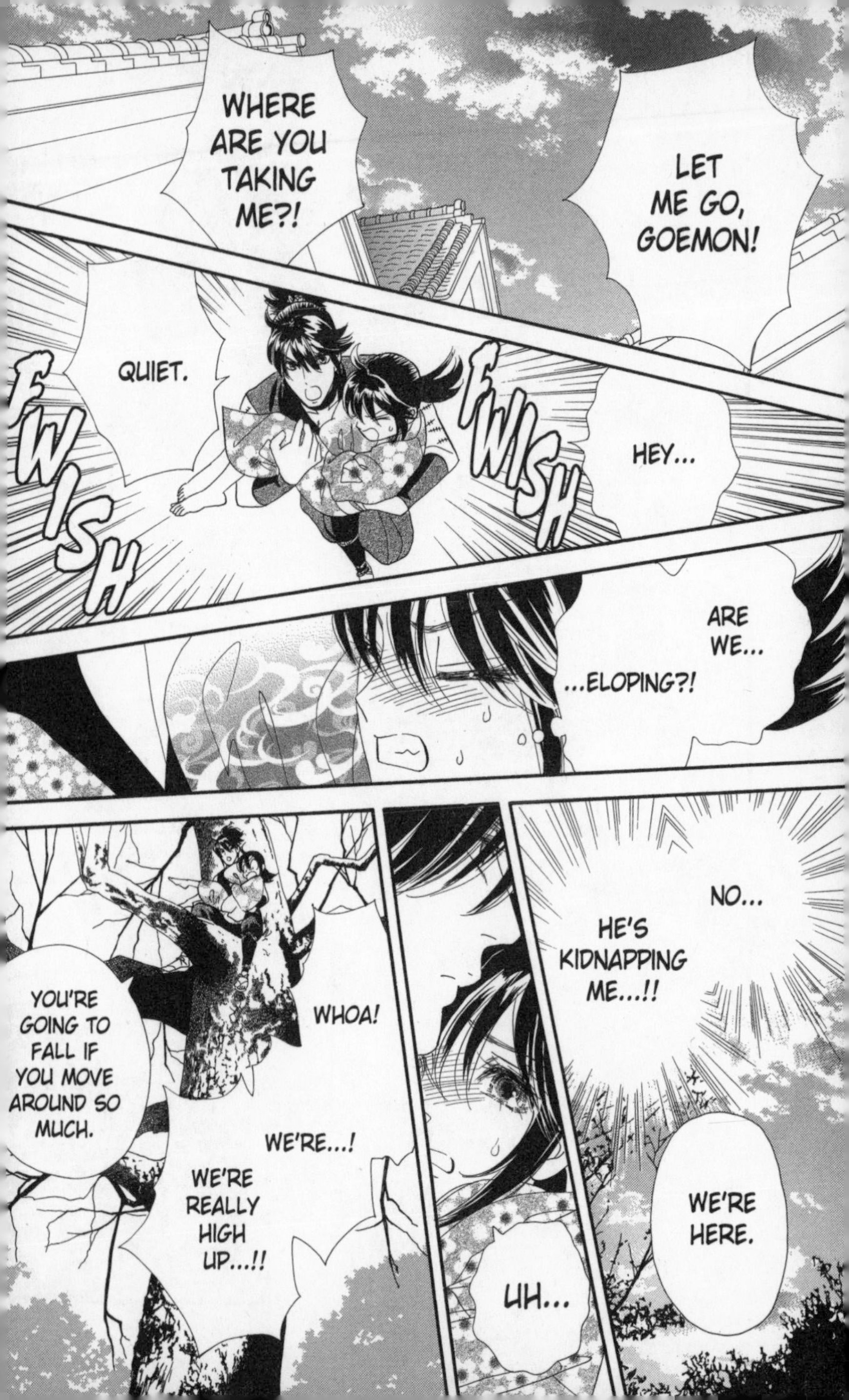
LET ME GO, GOEMON!
WHERE ARE YOU TAKING ME?!
FWISH
HEY...
QUIET.
FWISH
ARE WE...
...ELOPING?!
NO...
HE'S KIDNAPPING ME...!!
WE'RE HERE.
UH...
WHOA!
WE'RE...!
WE'RE REALLY HIGH UP...!!
YOU'RE GOING TO FALL IF YOU MOVE AROUND SO MUCH.

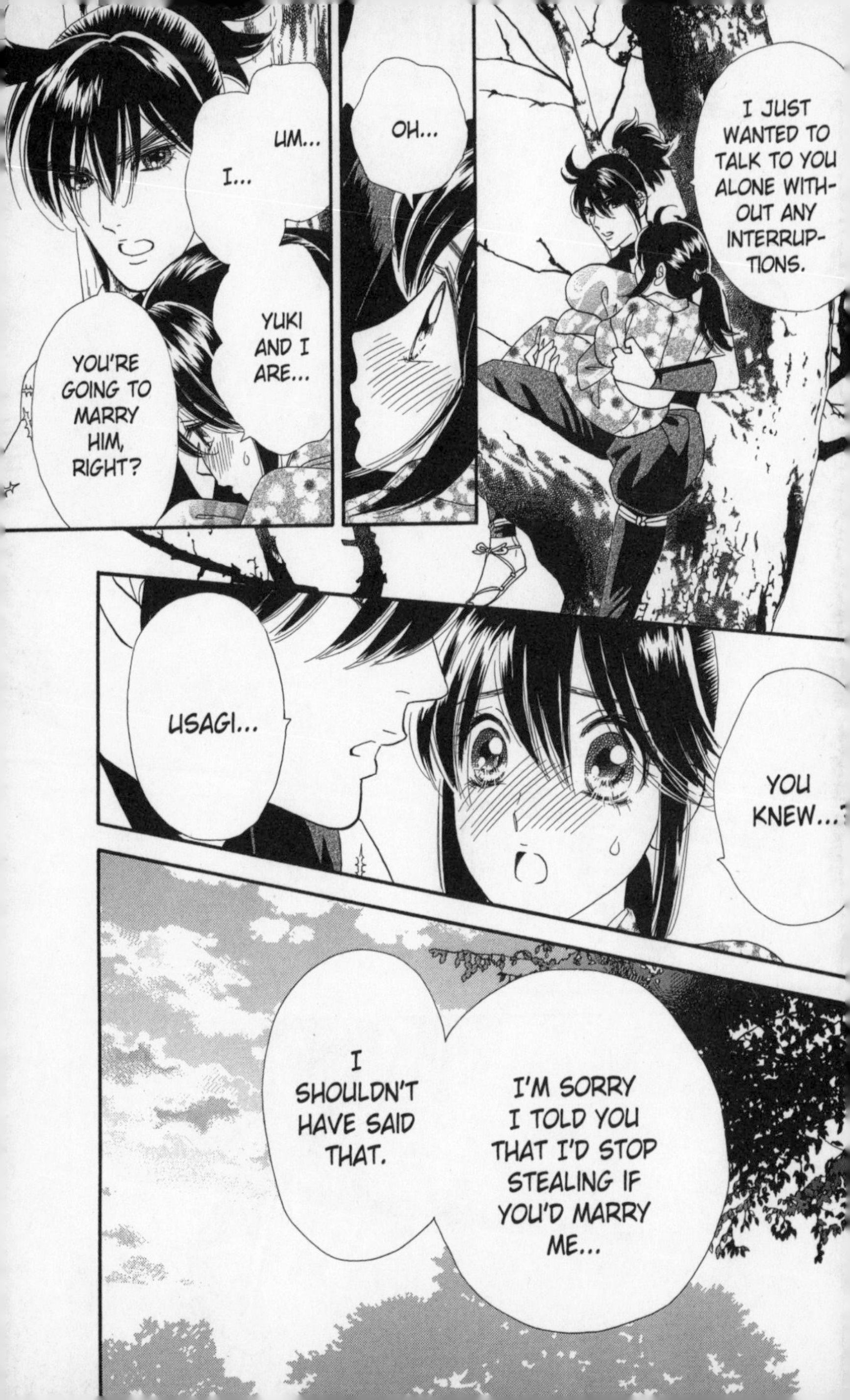
I JUST WANTED TO TALK TO YOU ALONE WITH-OUT ANY INTERRUP-TIONS.
OH...
UM... I...
YUKI AND I ARE...
YOU'RE GOING TO MARRY HIM, RIGHT?
YOU KNEW...?
USAGI...
I'M SORRY I TOLD YOU THAT I'D STOP STEALING IF YOU'D MARRY ME...
I SHOULDN'T HAVE SAID THAT.

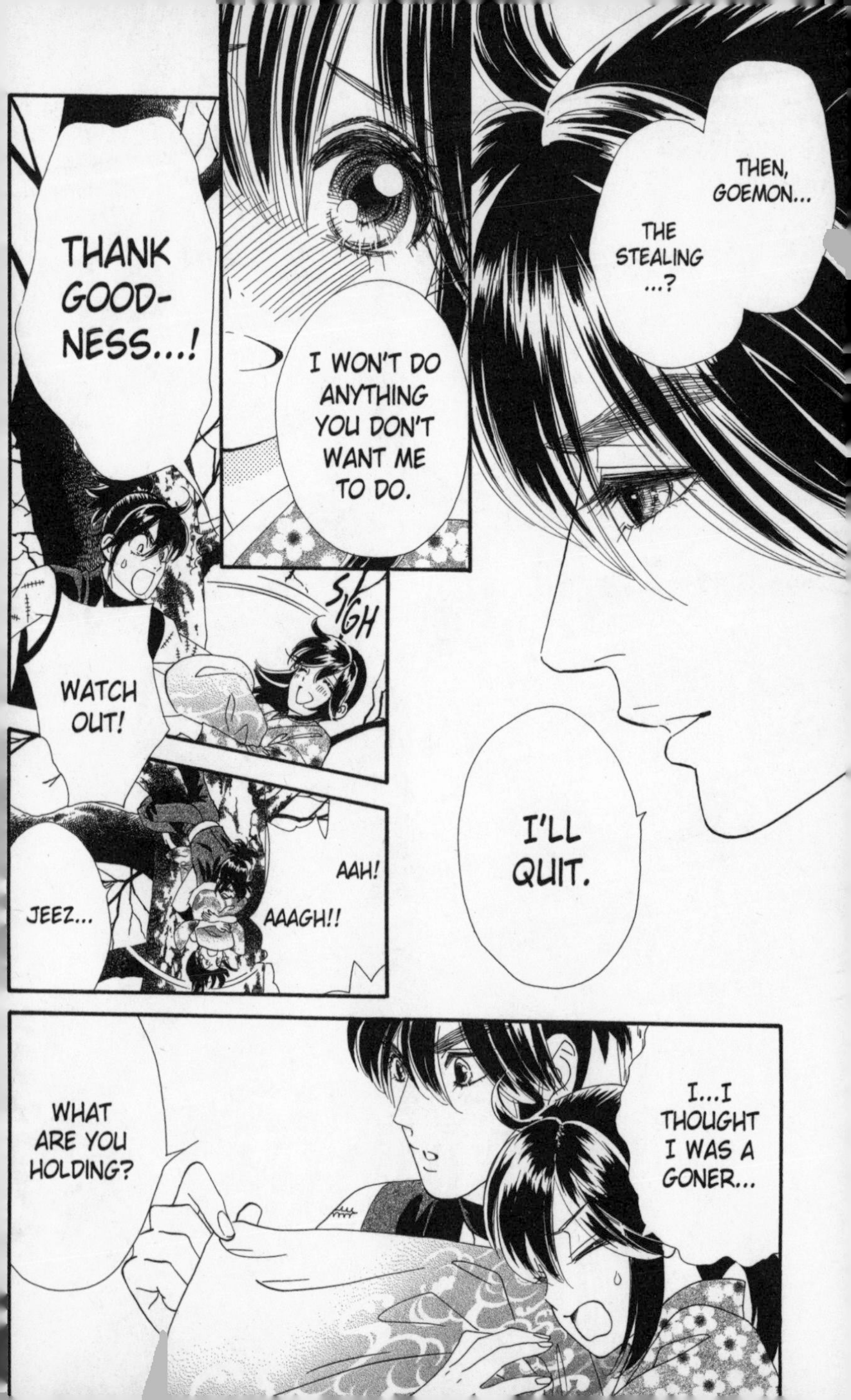
THEN, GOEMON...
THE STEALING ...?
I'LL QUIT.
I WON'T DO ANYTHING YOU DON'T WANT ME TO DO.
THANK GOOD-NESS...!
SIGH
WATCH OUT!
AAH!
AAAGH!!
JEEZ...
I...I THOUGHT I WAS A GONER...
WHAT ARE YOU HOLDING?

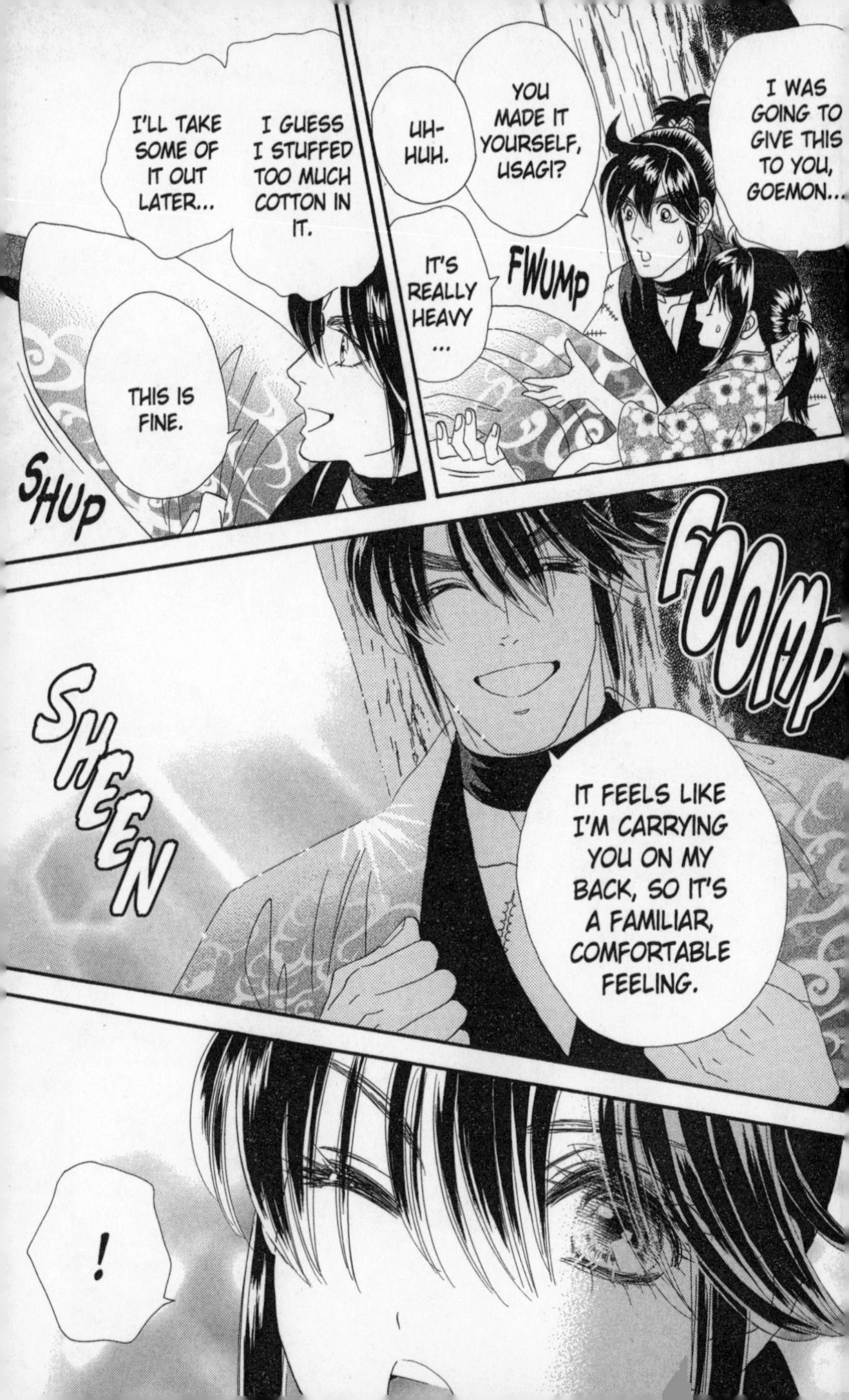
I WAS GOING TO GIVE THIS TO YOU, GOEMON...
YOU MADE IT YOURSELF, USAGI?
UH-HUH.
FWUMP
IT'S REALLY HEAVY...
I GUESS I STUFFED TOO MUCH COTTON IN IT.
I'LL TAKE SOME OF IT OUT LATER...
THIS IS FINE.
SHUP
FOOMP
SHEEN
IT FEELS LIKE I'M CARRYING YOU ON MY BACK, SO IT'S A FAMILIAR, COMFORTABLE FEELING.
!

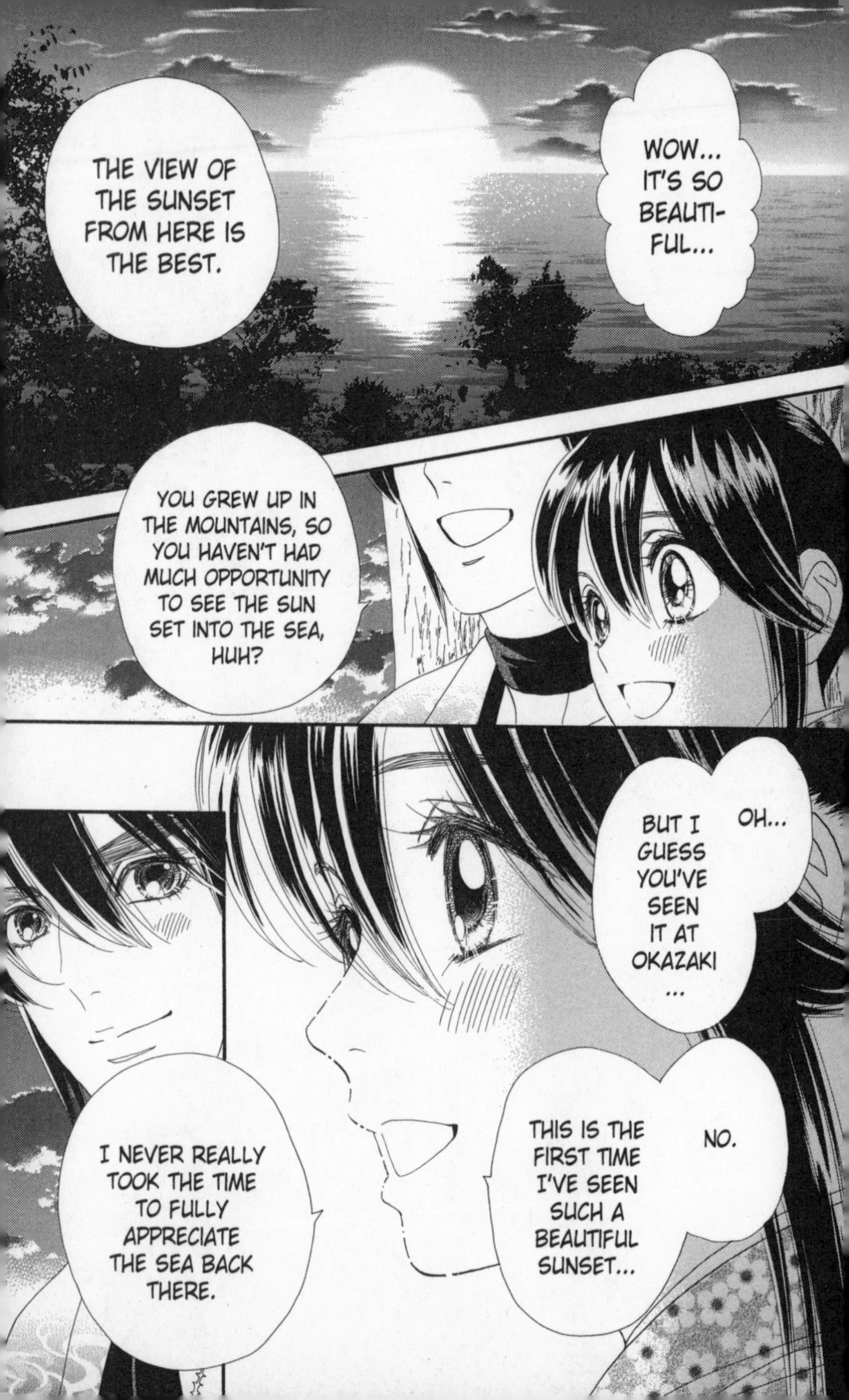
WOW... IT'S SO BEAUTIFUL...
THE VIEW OF THE SUNSET FROM HERE IS THE BEST.
YOU GREW UP IN THE MOUNTAINS, SO YOU HAVEN'T HAD MUCH OPPORTUNITY TO SEE THE SUN SET INTO THE SEA, HUH?
OH...
BUT I GUESS YOU'VE SEEN IT AT OKAZAKI...
NO.
THIS IS THE FIRST TIME I'VE SEEN SUCH A BEAUTIFUL SUNSET...
I NEVER REALLY TOOK THE TIME TO FULLY APPRECIATE THE SEA BACK THERE.

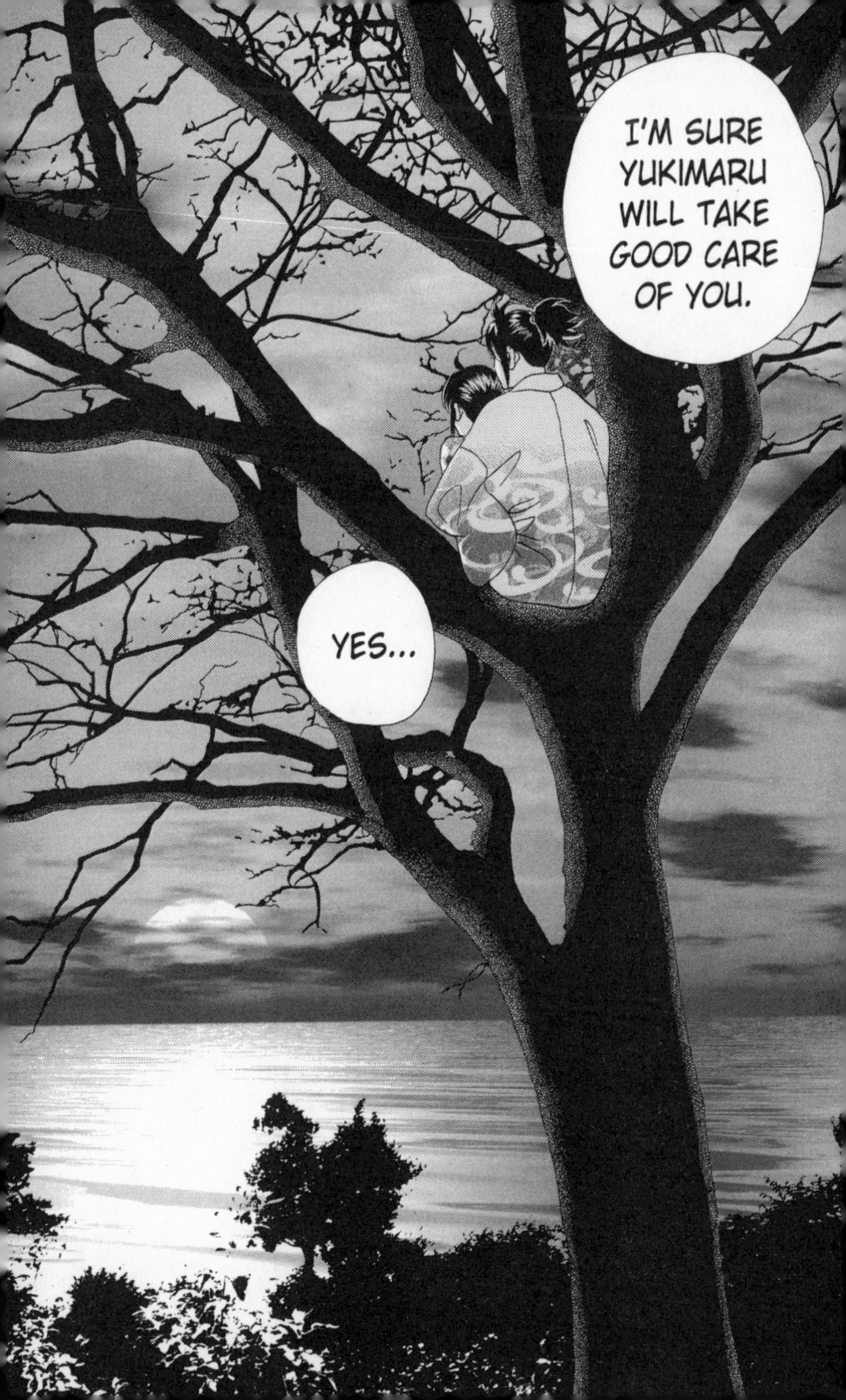
I'M SURE YUKIMARU WILL TAKE GOOD CARE OF YOU.
YES...

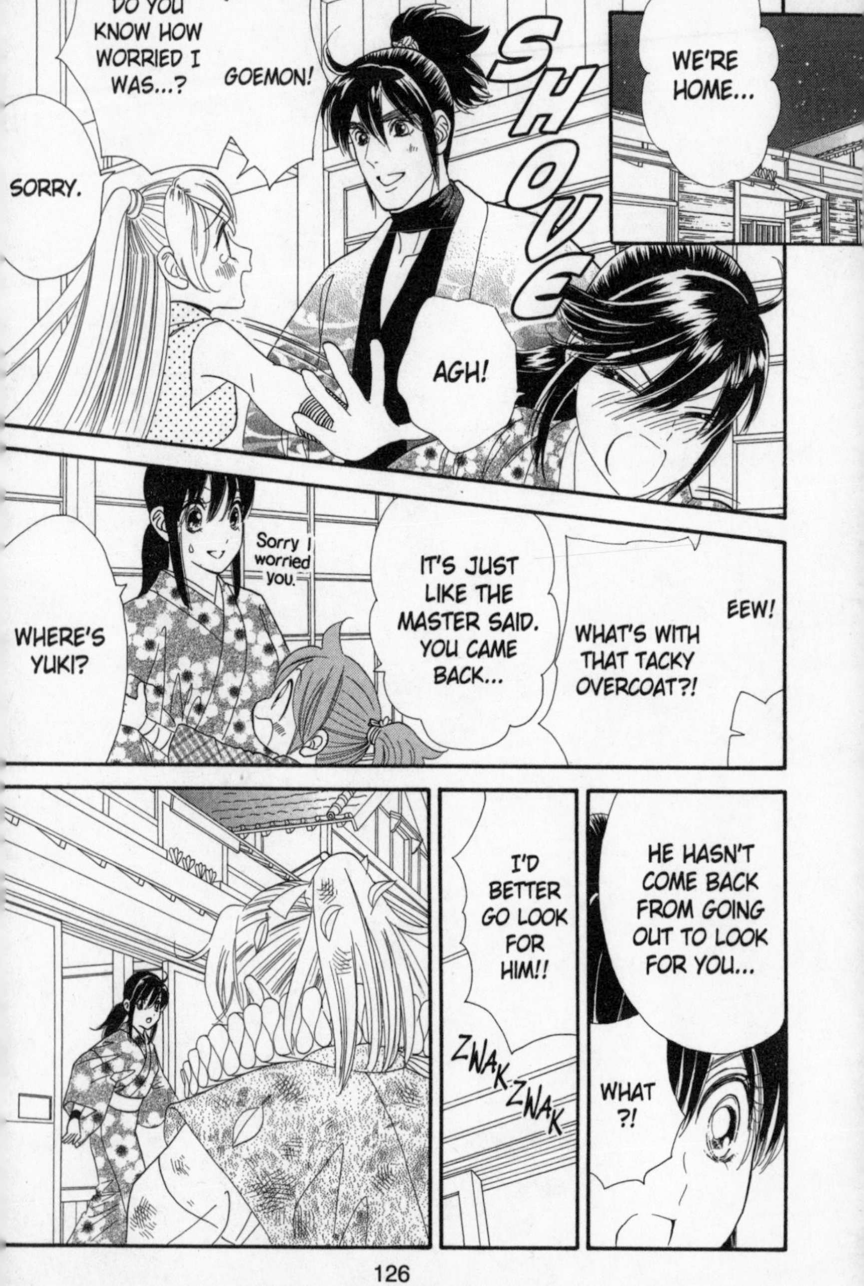
WE'RE HOME...
SHOUC
GOEMON!
DO YOU KNOW HOW WORRIED I WAS...?
SORRY.
AGH!
EEW!
WHAT'S WITH THAT TACKY OVERCOAT?!
IT'S JUST LIKE THE MASTER SAID. YOU CAME BACK...
Sorry I worried you.
WHERE'S YUKI?
HE HASN'T COME BACK FROM GOING OUT TO LOOK FOR YOU...
WHAT ?!
I'D BETTER GO LOOK FOR HIM!!
ZWAK ZWAK

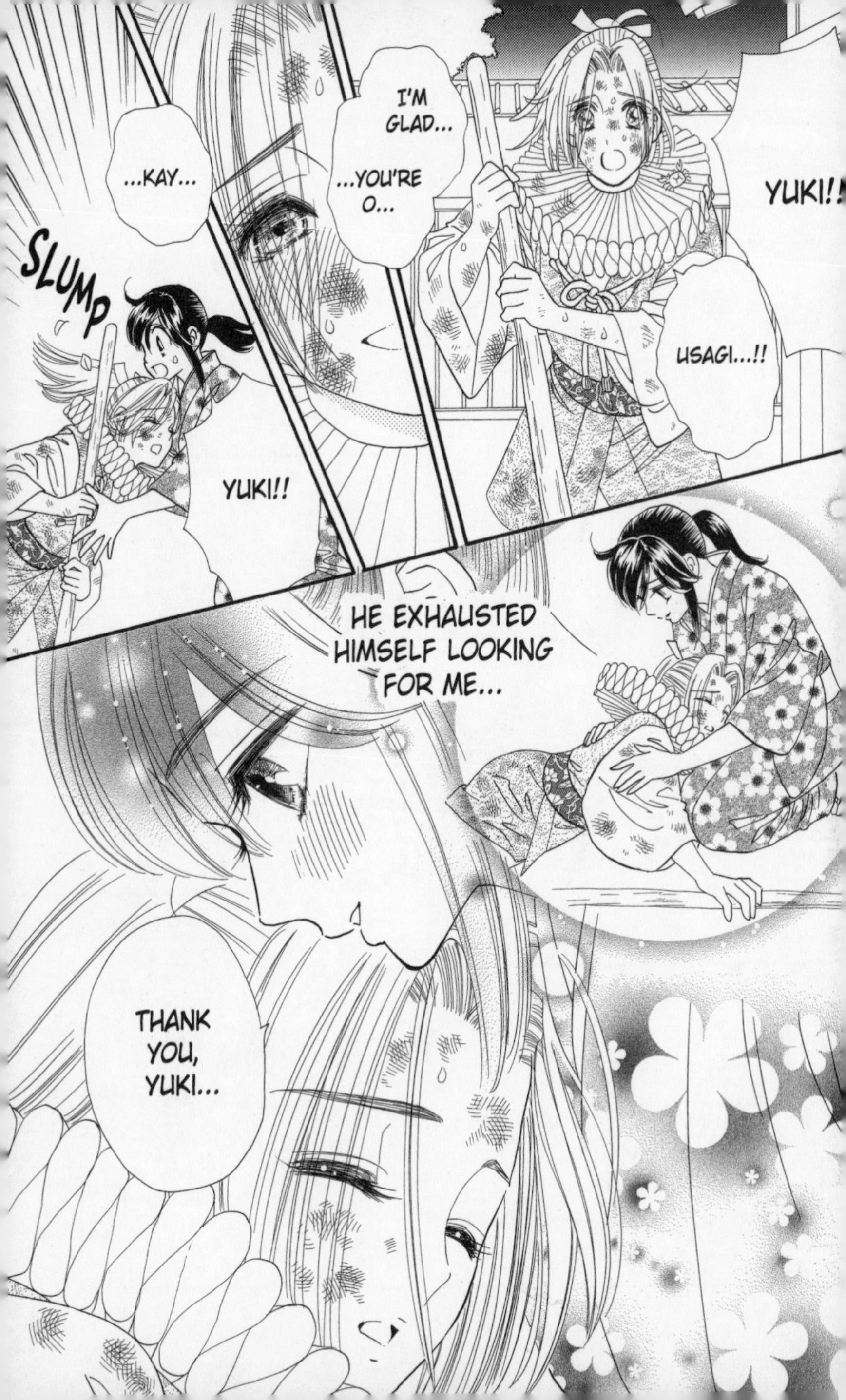
YUKI!!
USAGI...!!
I'M GLAD...
...YOU'RE O...
...KAY...
SLUMP
YUKI!!
HE EXHAUSTED HIMSELF LOOKING FOR ME...
THANK YOU, YUKI...

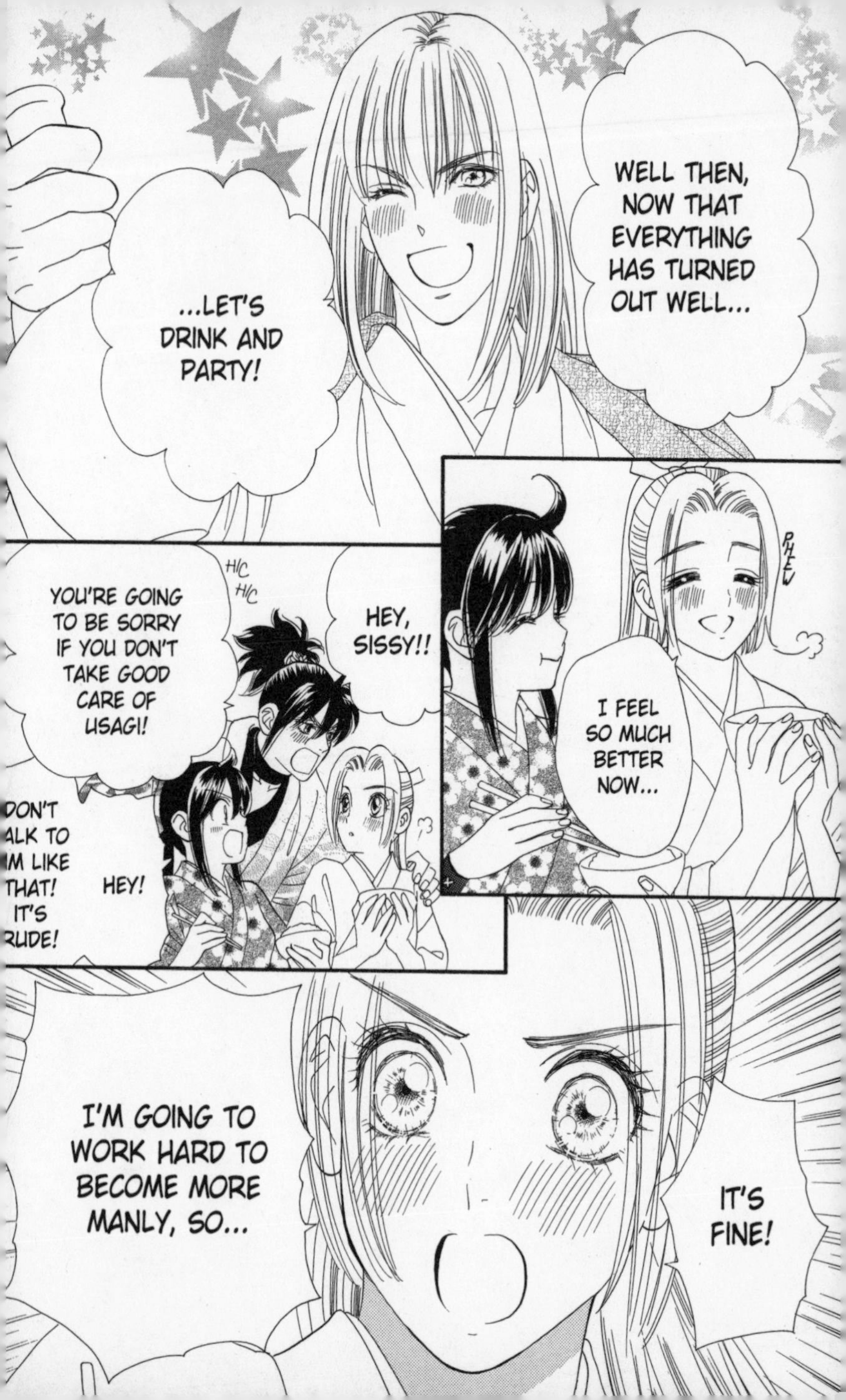
WELL THEN, NOW THAT EVERYTHING HAS TURNED OUT WELL...
...LET'S DRINK AND PARTY!
PHEW
I FEEL SO MUCH BETTER NOW...
HEY, SISSY!!
HIC HIC
YOU'RE GOING TO BE SORRY IF YOU DON'T TAKE GOOD CARE OF USAGI!
HEY!
DON'T ALK TO M LIKE THAT! IT'S RUDE!
IT'S FINE!
I'M GOING TO WORK HARD TO BECOME MORE MANLY, SO...

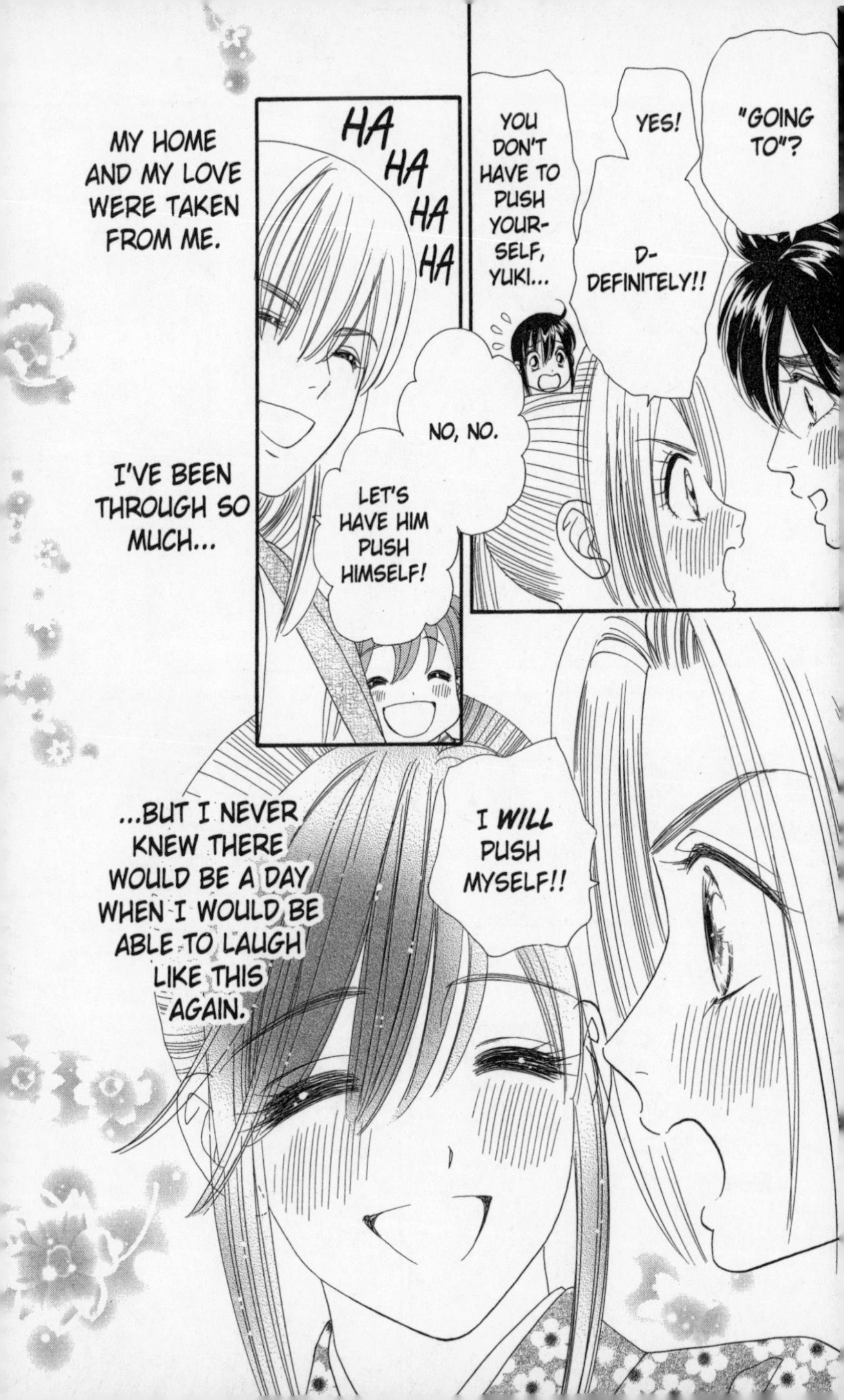
"GOING TO"?
YES!
D-DEFINITELY!!
YOU DON'T HAVE TO PUSH YOURSELF, YUKI...
NO, NO.
LET'S HAVE HIM PUSH HIMSELF!
HA HA HA HA
MY HOME AND MY LOVE WERE TAKEN FROM ME.
I'VE BEEN THROUGH SO MUCH...
I WILL PUSH MYSELF!!
...BUT I NEVER KNEW THERE WOULD BE A DAY WHEN I WOULD BE ABLE TO LAUGH LIKE THIS AGAIN.

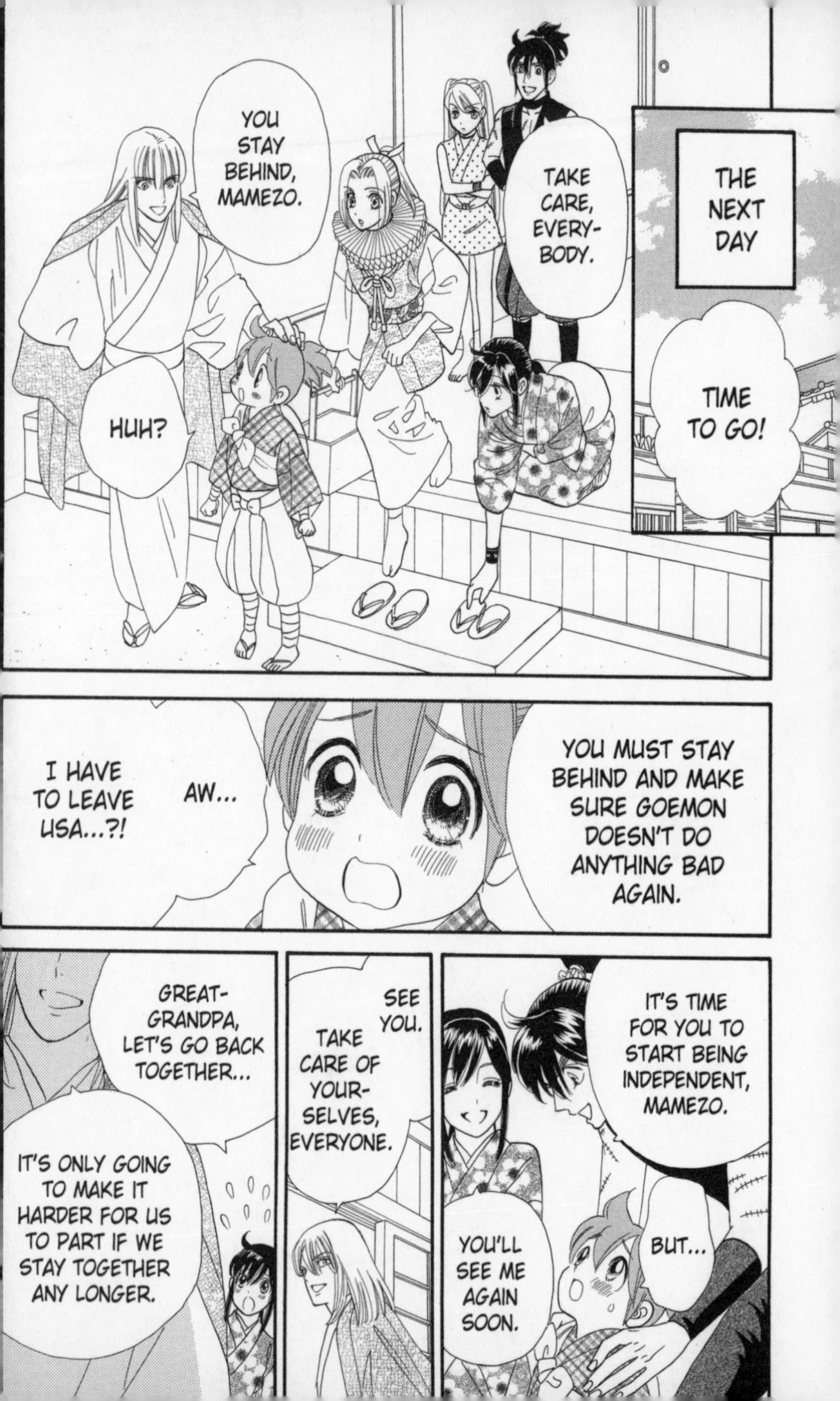
THE NEXT DAY
TIME TO GO!
TAKE CARE, EVERYBODY.
YOU STAY BEHIND, MAMEZO.
HUH?
YOU MUST STAY BEHIND AND MAKE SURE GOEMON DOESN'T DO ANYTHING BAD AGAIN.
AW...
I HAVE TO LEAVE USA...?!
IT'S TIME FOR YOU TO START BEING INDEPENDENT, MAMEZO.
BUT...
YOU'LL SEE ME AGAIN SOON.
SEE YOU.
TAKE CARE OF YOURSELVES, EVERYONE.
GREAT-GRANDPA, LET'S GO BACK TOGETHER...
IT'S ONLY GOING TO MAKE IT HARDER FOR US TO PART IF WE STAY TOGETHER ANY LONGER.

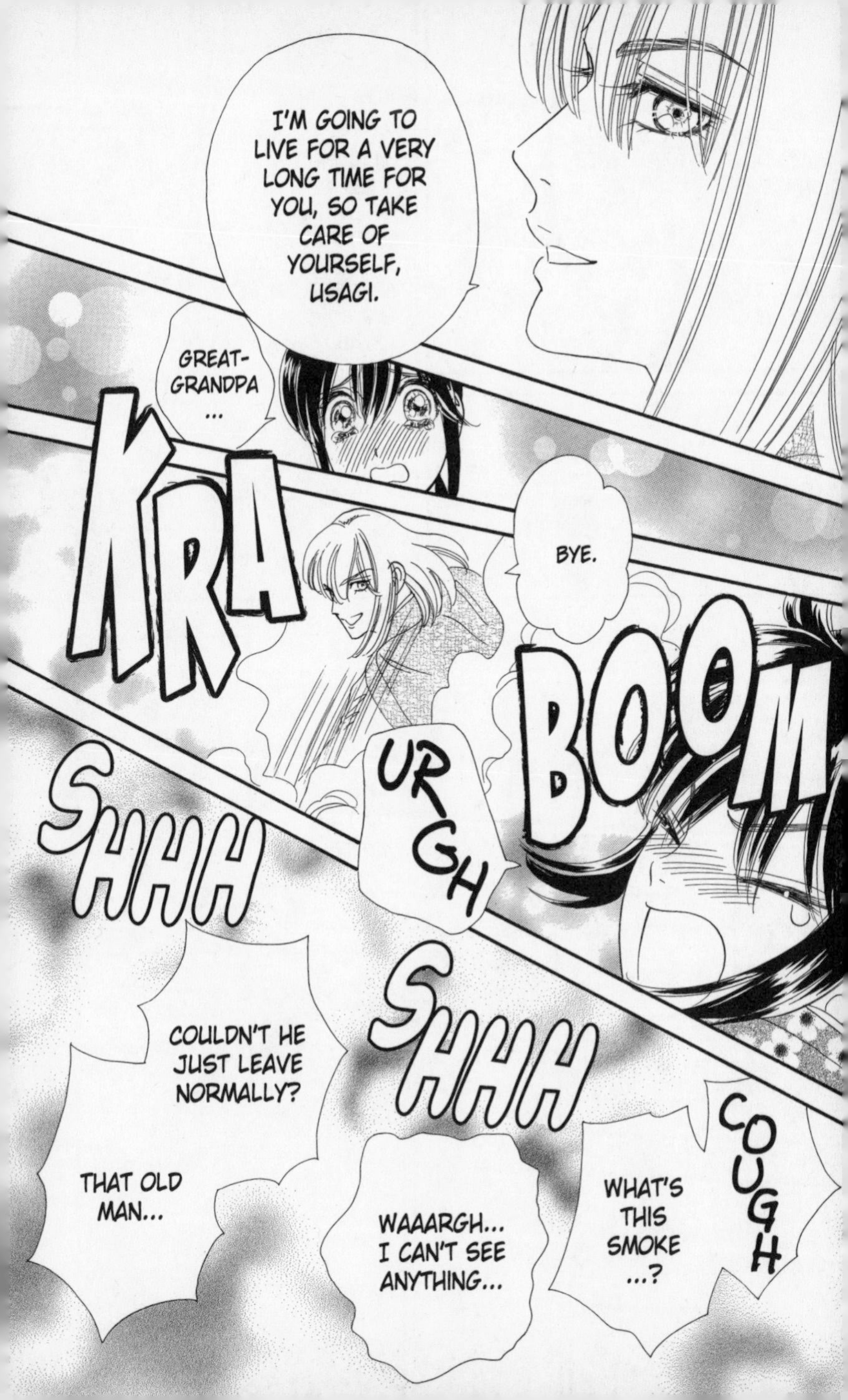

I'M GOING TO LIVE FOR A VERY LONG TIME FOR YOU, SO TAKE CARE OF YOURSELF, USAGI.
GREAT-GRANDPA...
BYE.
KRA
BOOM
URGH
COUGH
WHAT'S THIS SMOKE...?
WAAARGH... I CAN'T SEE ANYTHING...
SHHH
SHHH
COULDN'T HE JUST LEAVE NORMALLY?
THAT OLD MAN...

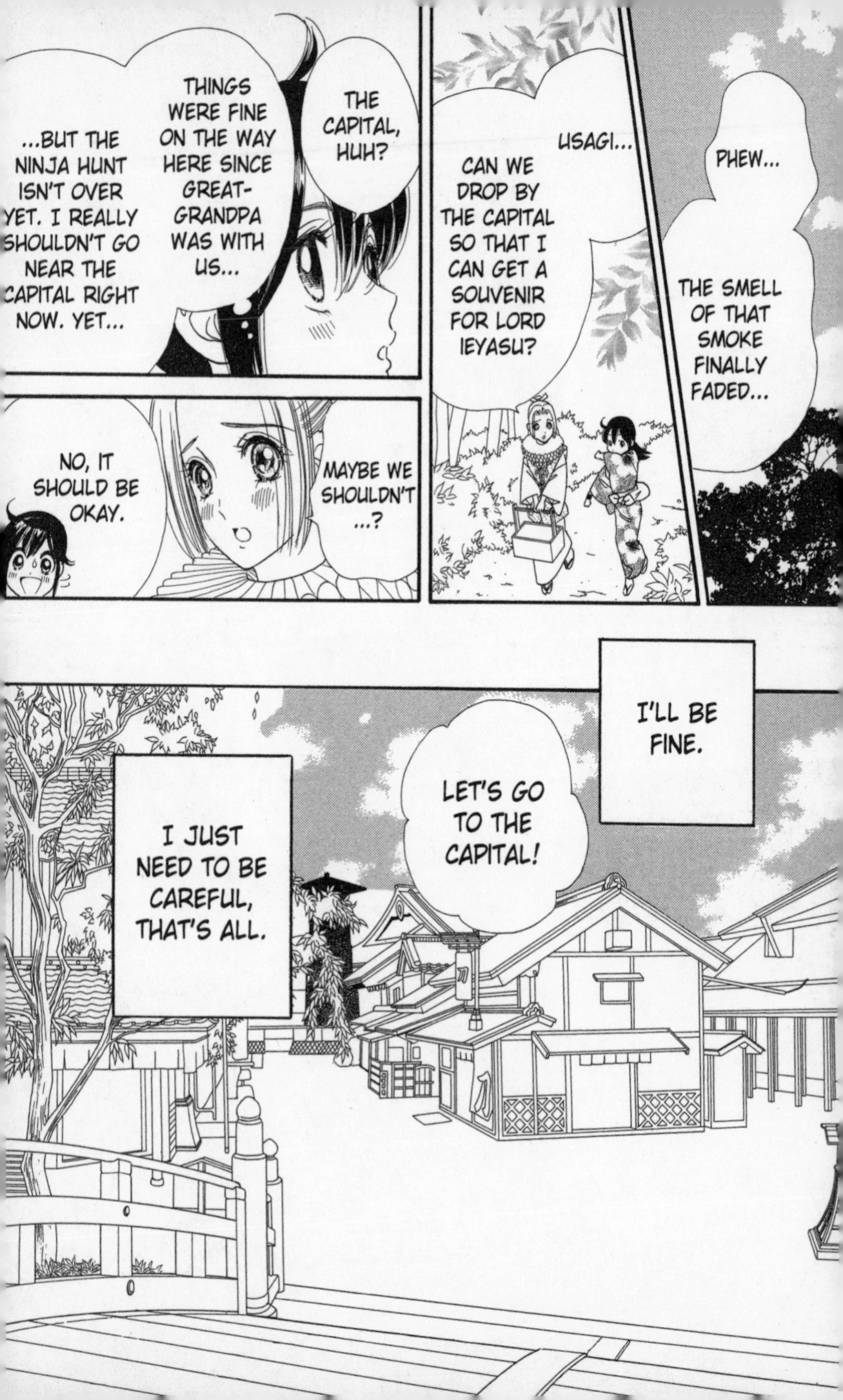
PHEW...
THE SMELL OF THAT SMOKE FINALLY FADED...
USAGI...
CAN WE DROP BY THE CAPITAL SO THAT I CAN GET A SOUVENIR FOR LORD IEYASU?
THE CAPITAL, HUH?
THINGS WERE FINE ON THE WAY HERE SINCE GREAT-GRANDPA WAS WITH US...
...BUT THE NINJA HUNT ISN'T OVER YET. I REALLY SHOULDN'T GO NEAR THE CAPITAL RIGHT NOW. YET...
MAYBE WE SHOULDN'T ...?
NO, IT SHOULD BE OKAY.
I'LL BE FINE.
LET'S GO TO THE CAPITAL!
I JUST NEED TO BE CAREFUL, THAT'S ALL.

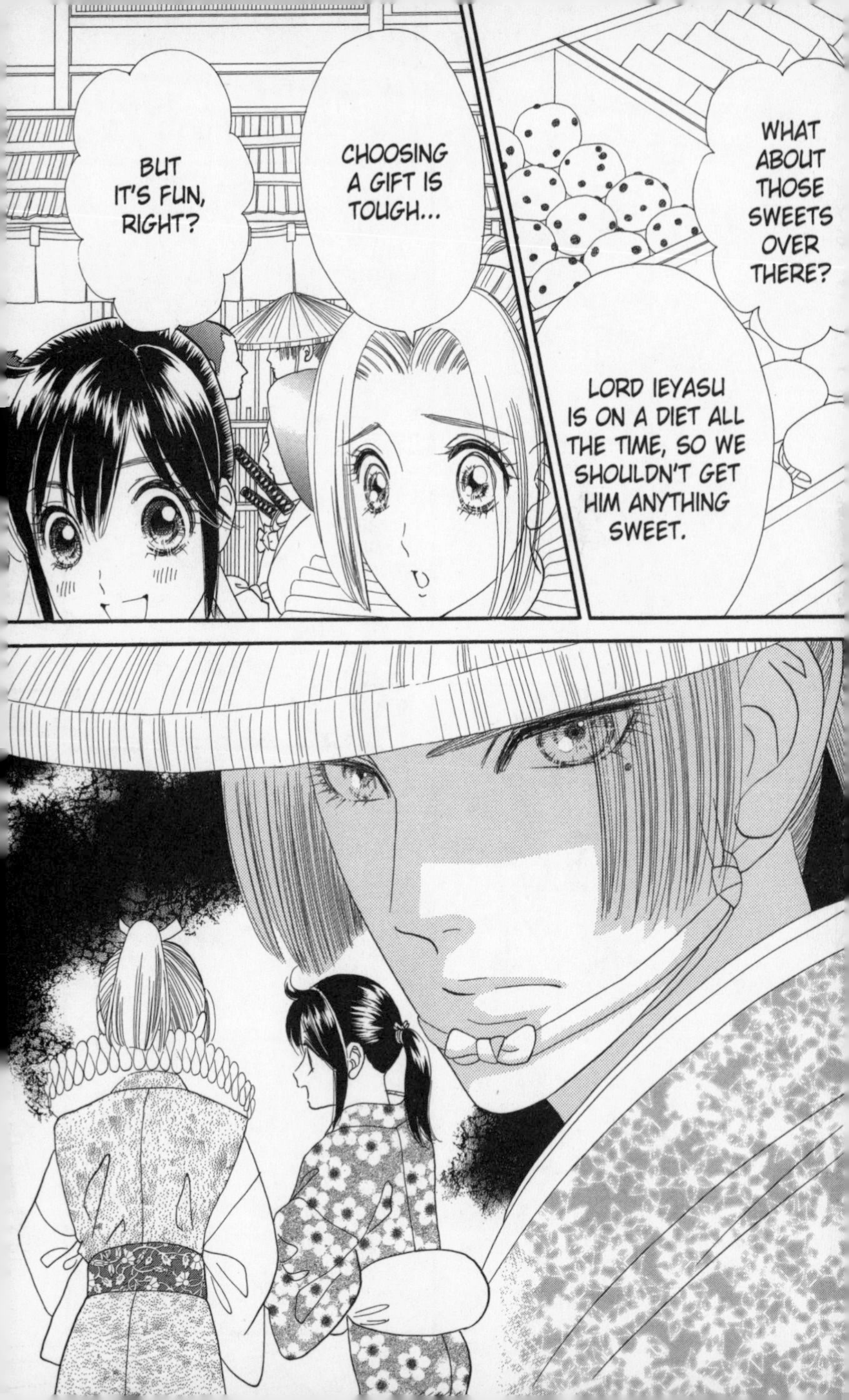
WHAT ABOUT THOSE SWEETS OVER THERE?
LORD IEYASU IS ON A DIET ALL THE TIME, SO WE SHOULDN'T GET HIM ANYTHING SWEET.
CHOOSING A GIFT IS TOUGH...
BUT IT'S FUN, RIGHT?

LET'S GO!

LITTLE HANZO

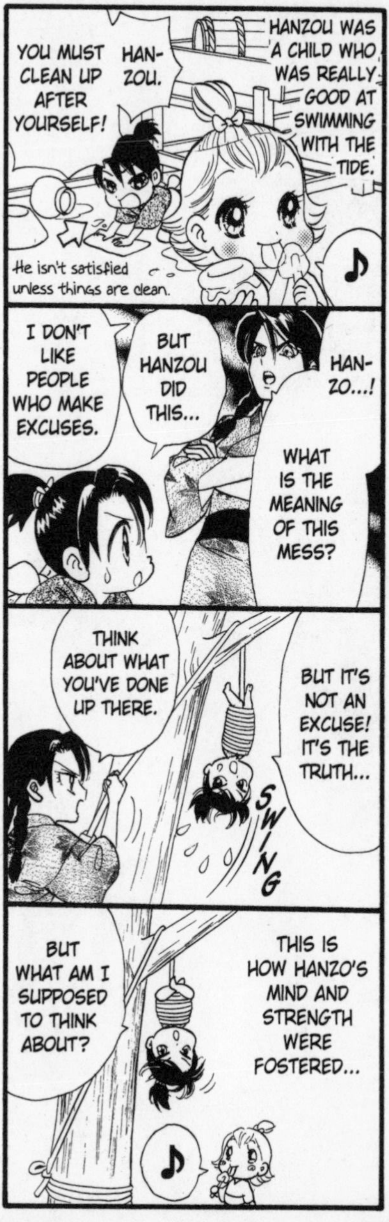
HANZOU WAS A CHILD WHO WAS REALLY GOOD AT SWIMMING WITH THE TIDE.
♪
HAN-ZOU.
YOU MUST CLEAN UP AFTER YOURSELF!
He isn't satisfied unless things are clean.
HAN-ZO...!
WHAT IS THE MEANING OF THIS MESS?
BUT HANZOU DID THIS...
I DON'T LIKE PEOPLE WHO MAKE EXCUSES.
BUT IT'S NOT AN EXCUSE! IT'S THE TRUTH...
SWING
THINK ABOUT WHAT YOU'VE DONE UP THERE.
THIS IS HOW HANZO'S MIND AND STRENGTH WERE FOSTERED...
BUT WHAT AM I SUPPOSED TO THINK ABOUT?
♪

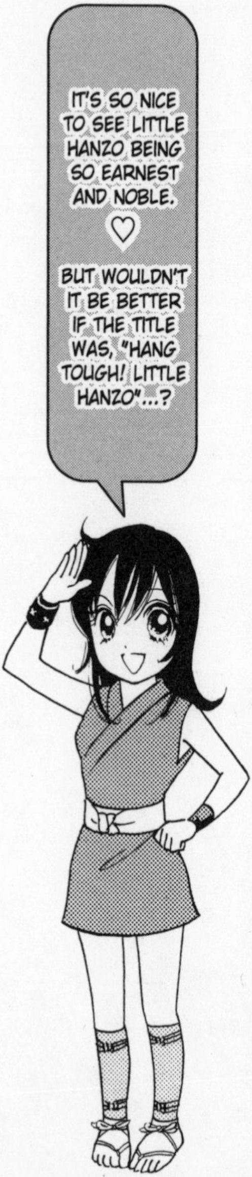
IT'S SO NICE TO SEE LITTLE HANZO BEING SO EARNEST AND NOBLE. ♡
BUT WOULDN'T IT BE BETTER IF THE TITLE WAS, "HANG TOUGH! LITTLE HANZO"...?

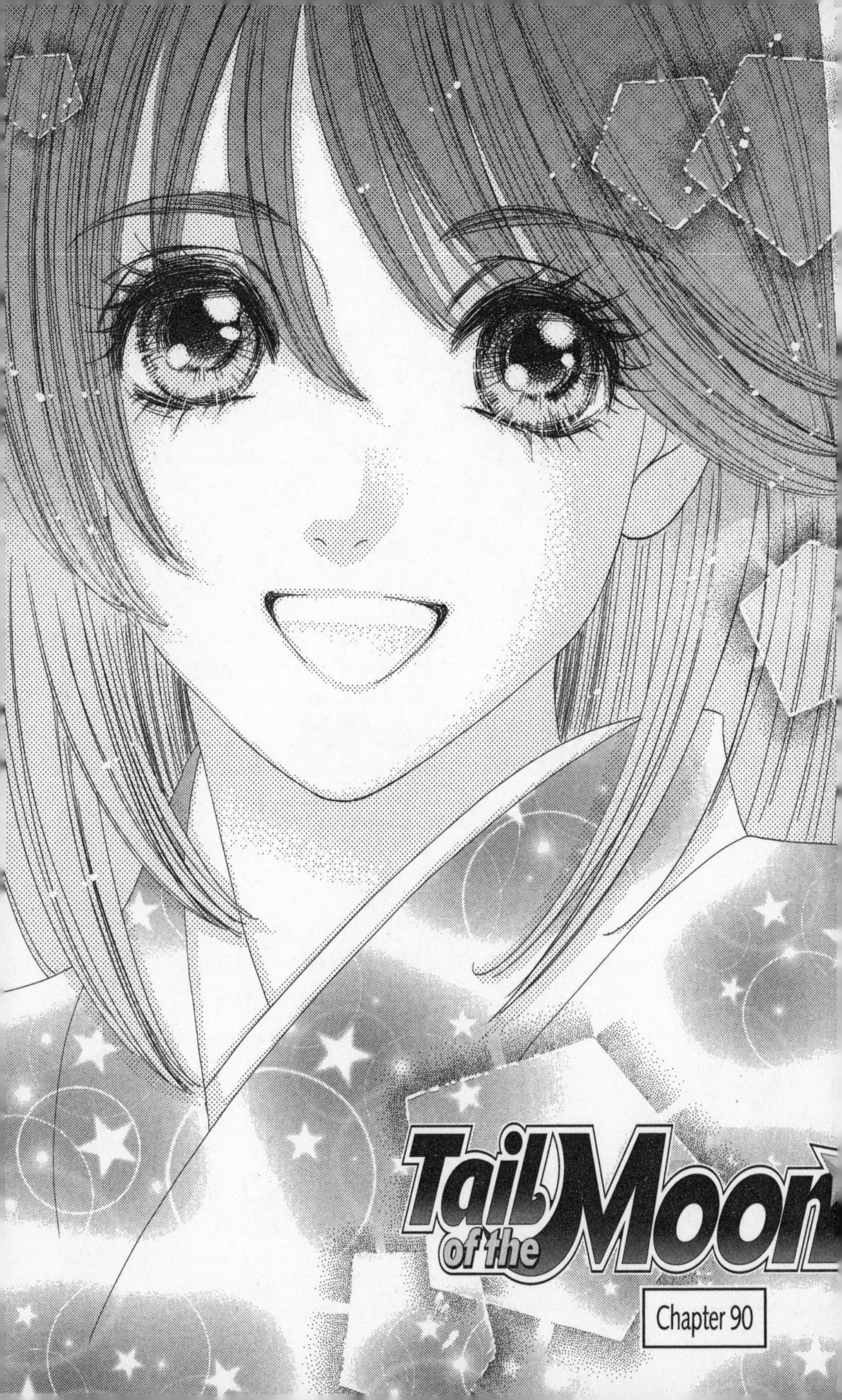
Tail of the Moon
Chapter 90

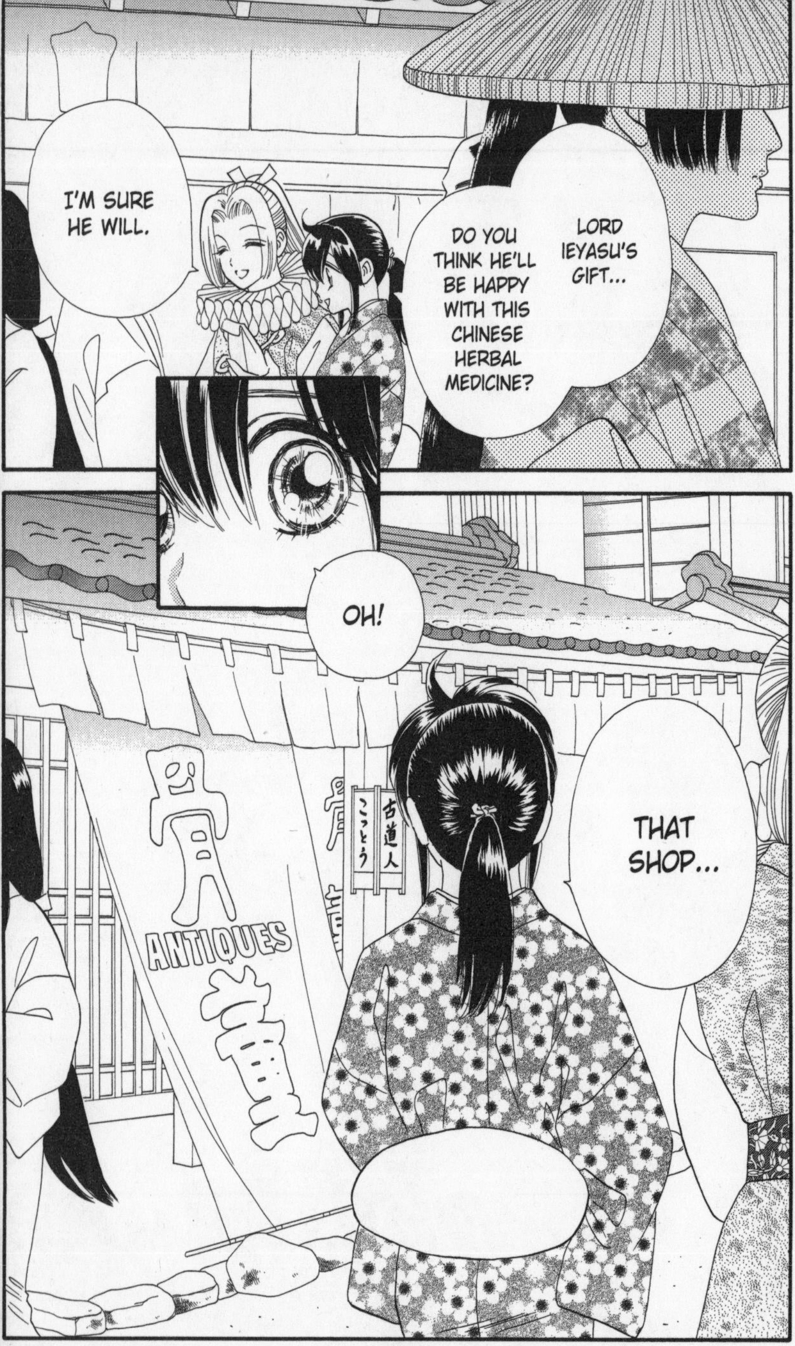
LORD IEYASU'S GIFT...
DO YOU THINK HE'LL BE HAPPY WITH THIS CHINESE HERBAL MEDICINE?
I'M SURE HE WILL.
OH!
THAT SHOP...
ANTIQUES

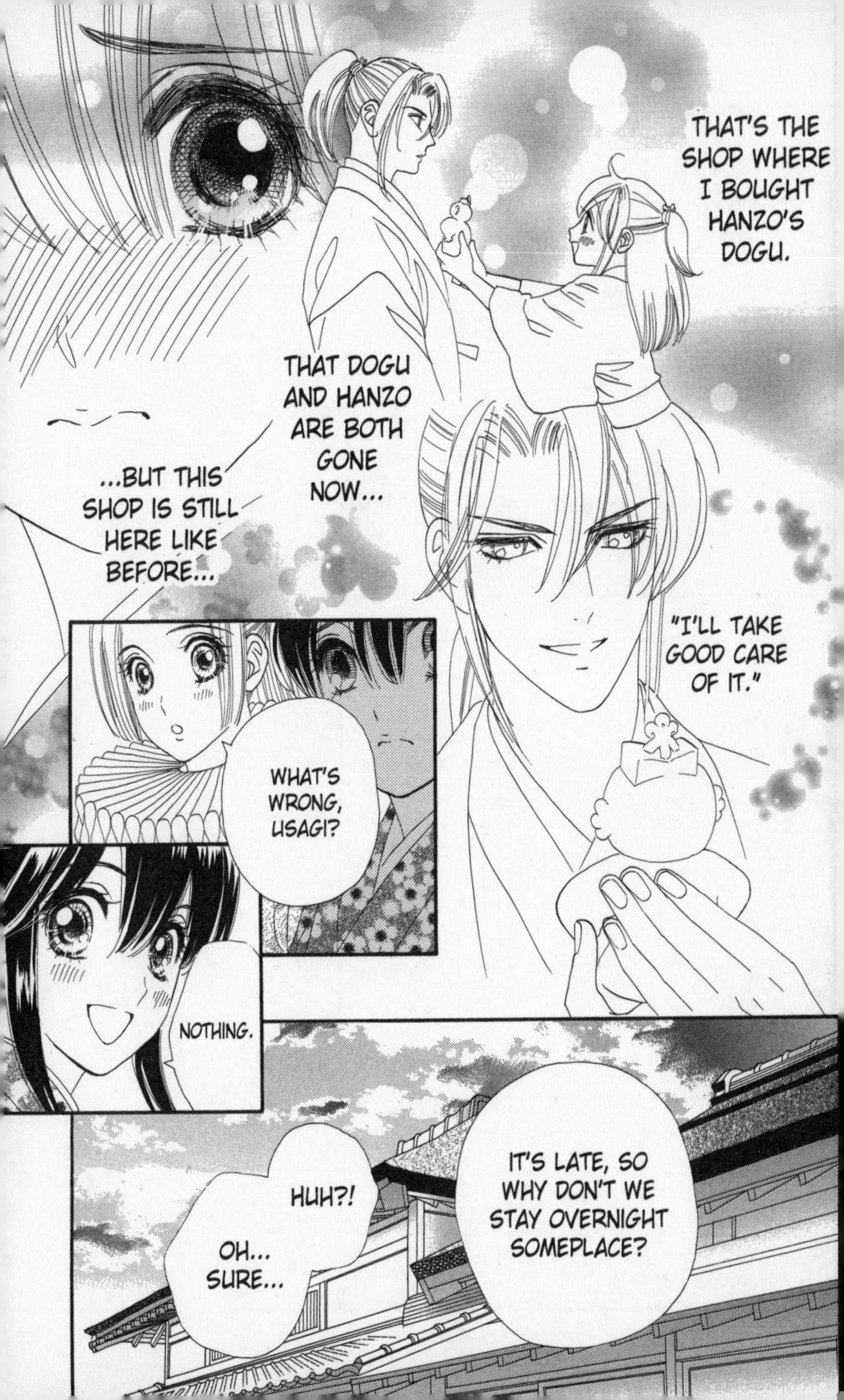
THAT'S THE SHOP WHERE I BOUGHT HANZO'S DOGU.
"I'LL TAKE GOOD CARE OF IT."
THAT DOGU AND HANZO ARE BOTH GONE NOW...
...BUT THIS SHOP IS STILL HERE LIKE BEFORE...
WHAT'S WRONG, USAGI?
NOTHING.
IT'S LATE, SO WHY DON'T WE STAY OVERNIGHT SOMEPLACE?
HUH?!
OH... SURE...

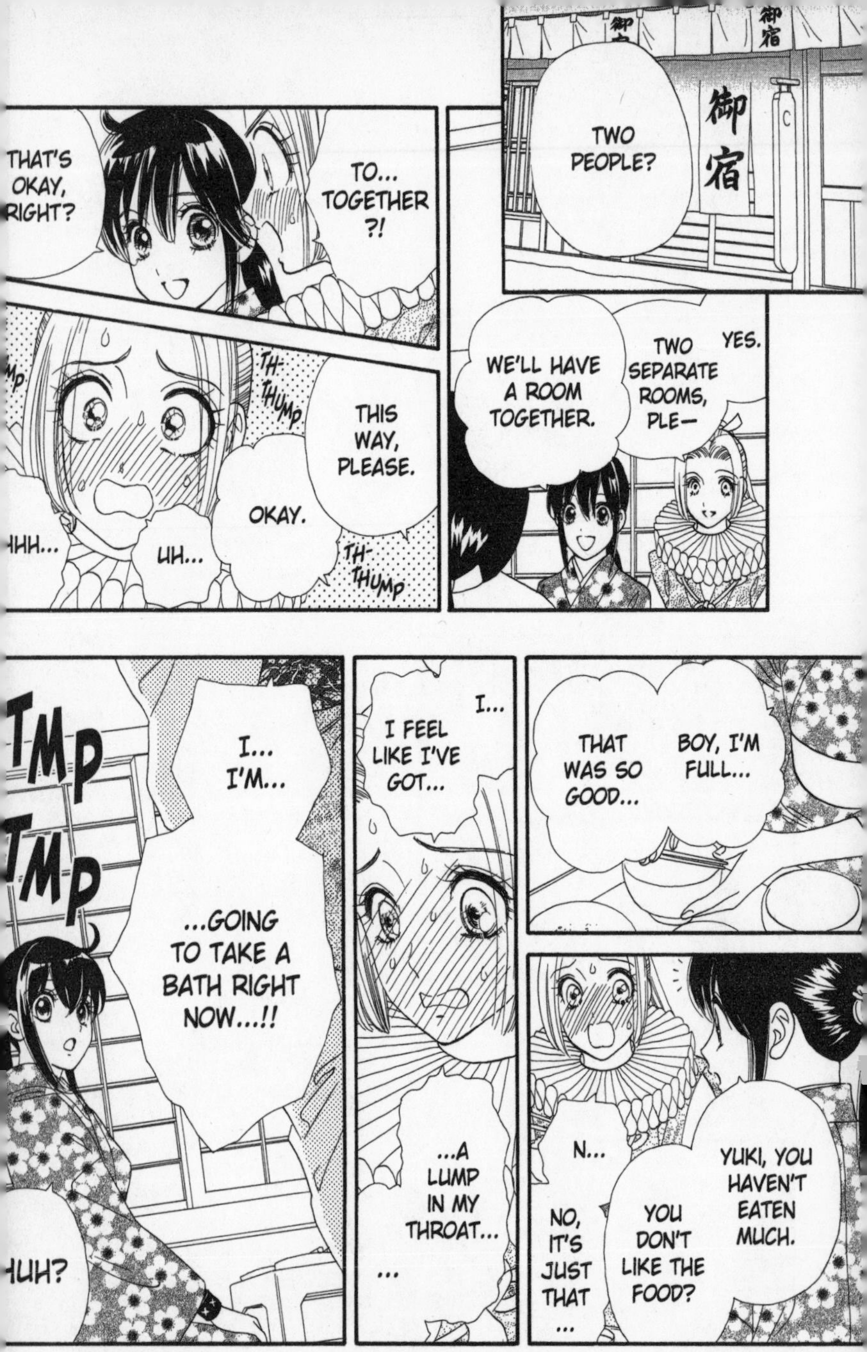
TWO PEOPLE?
YES.
TWO SEPARATE ROOMS, PLE—
WE'LL HAVE A ROOM TOGETHER.
TO... TOGETHER?!
THAT'S OKAY, RIGHT?
TH-THUMP
THIS WAY, PLEASE.
TH-THUMP
OKAY.
UH...
HHH...
BOY, I'M FULL...
THAT WAS SO GOOD...
YUKI, YOU HAVEN'T EATEN MUCH.
YOU DON'T LIKE THE FOOD?
N...
NO, IT'S JUST THAT ...
I...
I FEEL LIKE I'VE GOT...
...A LUMP IN MY THROAT...
...
I... I'M...
...GOING TO TAKE A BATH RIGHT NOW...!!
TMP
TMP
HUH?

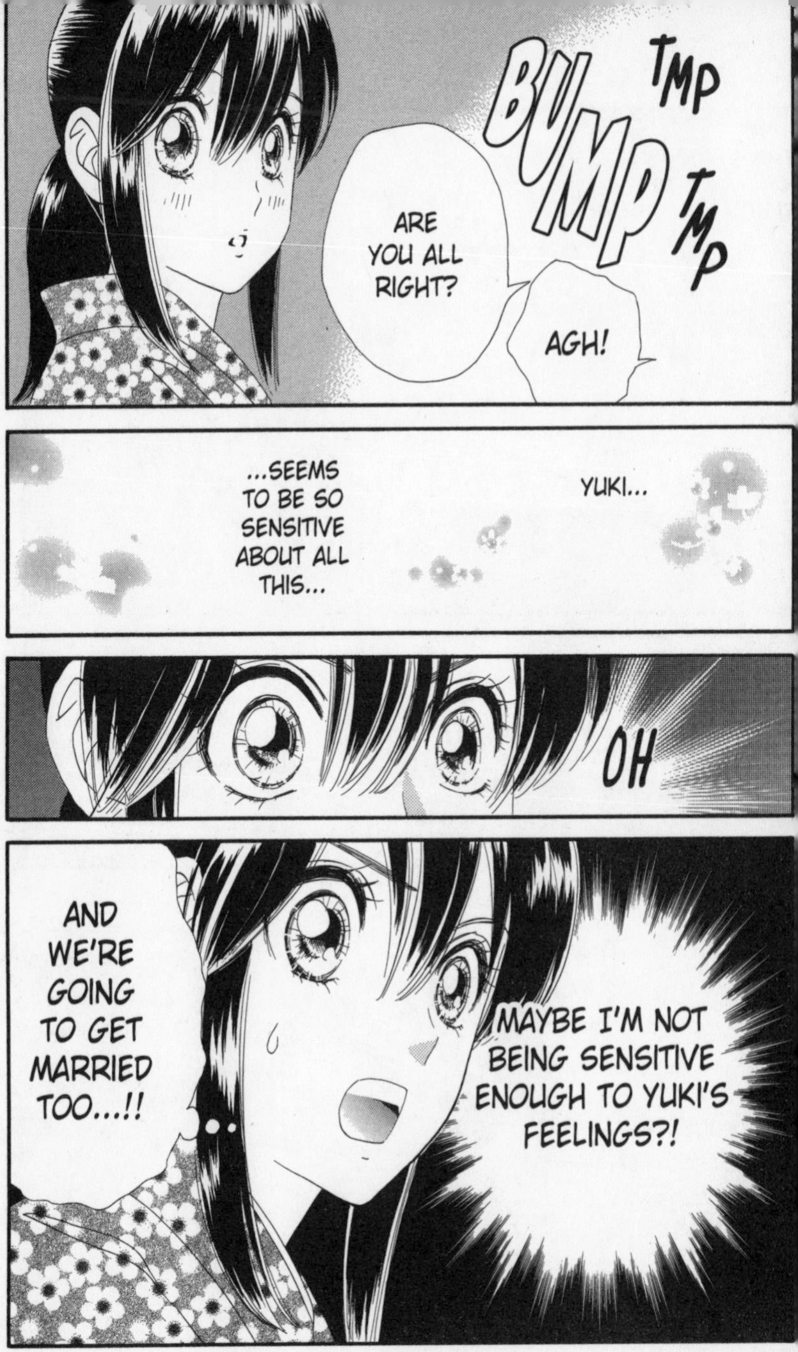
BUMP TMP TMP
AGH!
ARE YOU ALL RIGHT?
YUKI...
...SEEMS TO BE SO SENSITIVE ABOUT ALL THIS...
OH
MAYBE I'M NOT BEING SENSITIVE ENOUGH TO YUKI'S FEELINGS?!
AND WE'RE GOING TO GET MARRIED TOO...!!

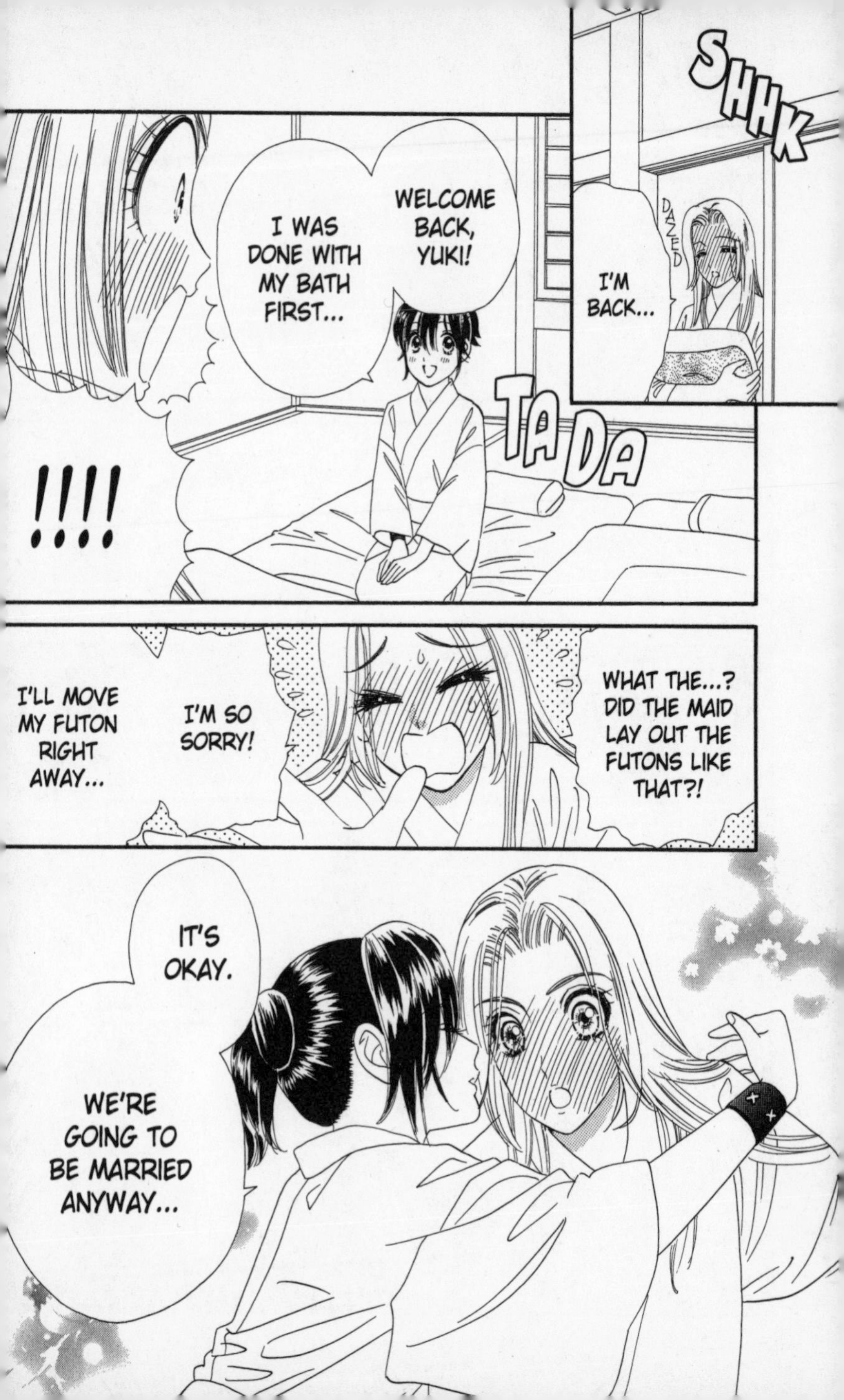
SHHK
DAZED
I'M BACK...
WELCOME BACK, YUKI!
I WAS DONE WITH MY BATH FIRST...
TA DA
!!!!
WHAT THE...? DID THE MAID LAY OUT THE FUTONS LIKE THAT?!
I'M SO SORRY!
I'LL MOVE MY FUTON RIGHT AWAY...
IT'S OKAY.
WE'RE GOING TO BE MARRIED ANYWAY...

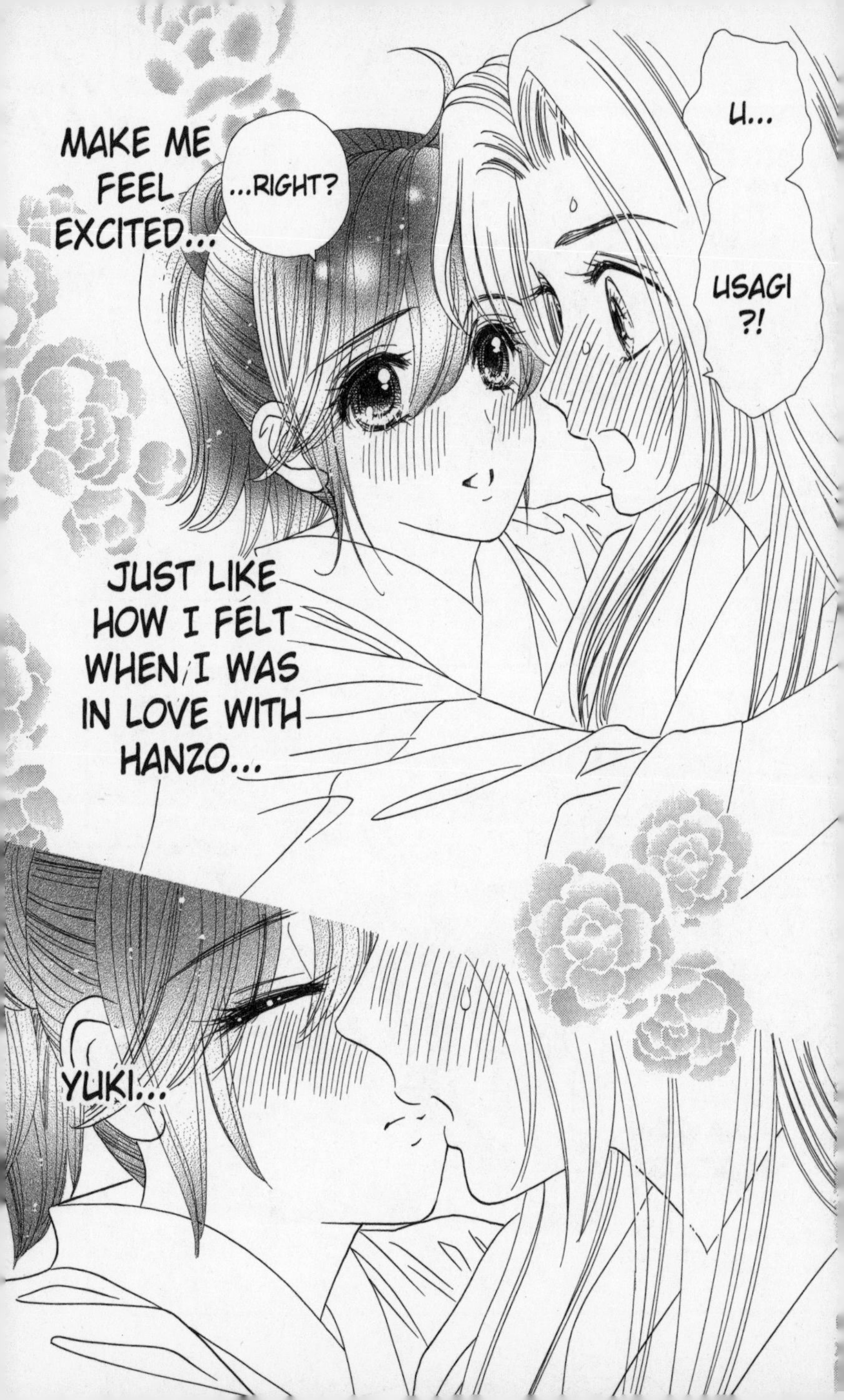
U... USAGI?!
MAKE ME FEEL EXCITED...
...RIGHT?
JUST LIKE HOW I FELT WHEN I WAS IN LOVE WITH HANZO...
YUKI...

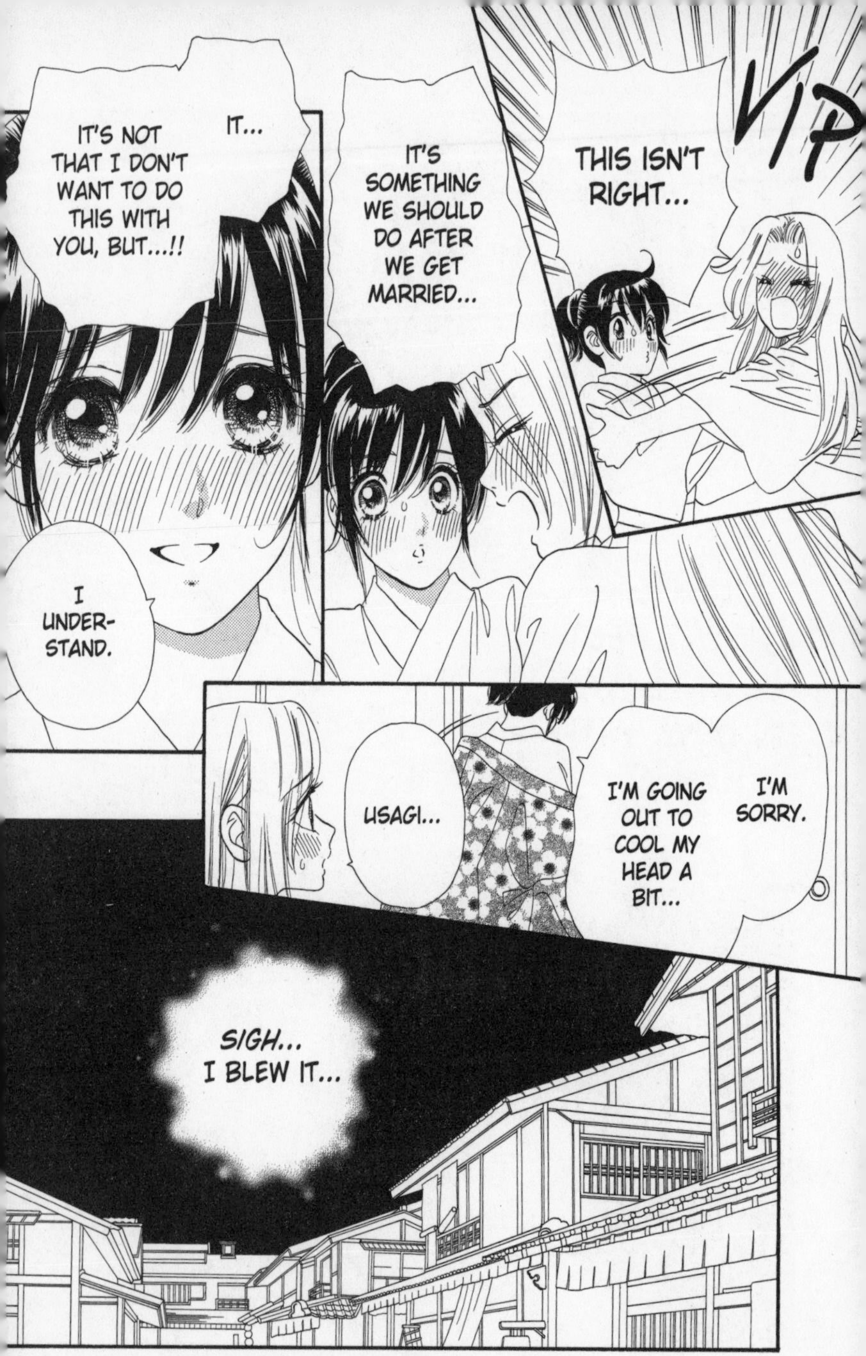
VIP
THIS ISN'T RIGHT...
IT'S NOT THAT I DON'T WANT TO DO THIS WITH YOU, BUT...!!
IT...
IT'S SOMETHING WE SHOULD DO AFTER WE GET MARRIED...
I UNDER-STAND.
I'M SORRY.
I'M GOING OUT TO COOL MY HEAD A BIT...
USAGI...
SIGH... I BLEW IT...

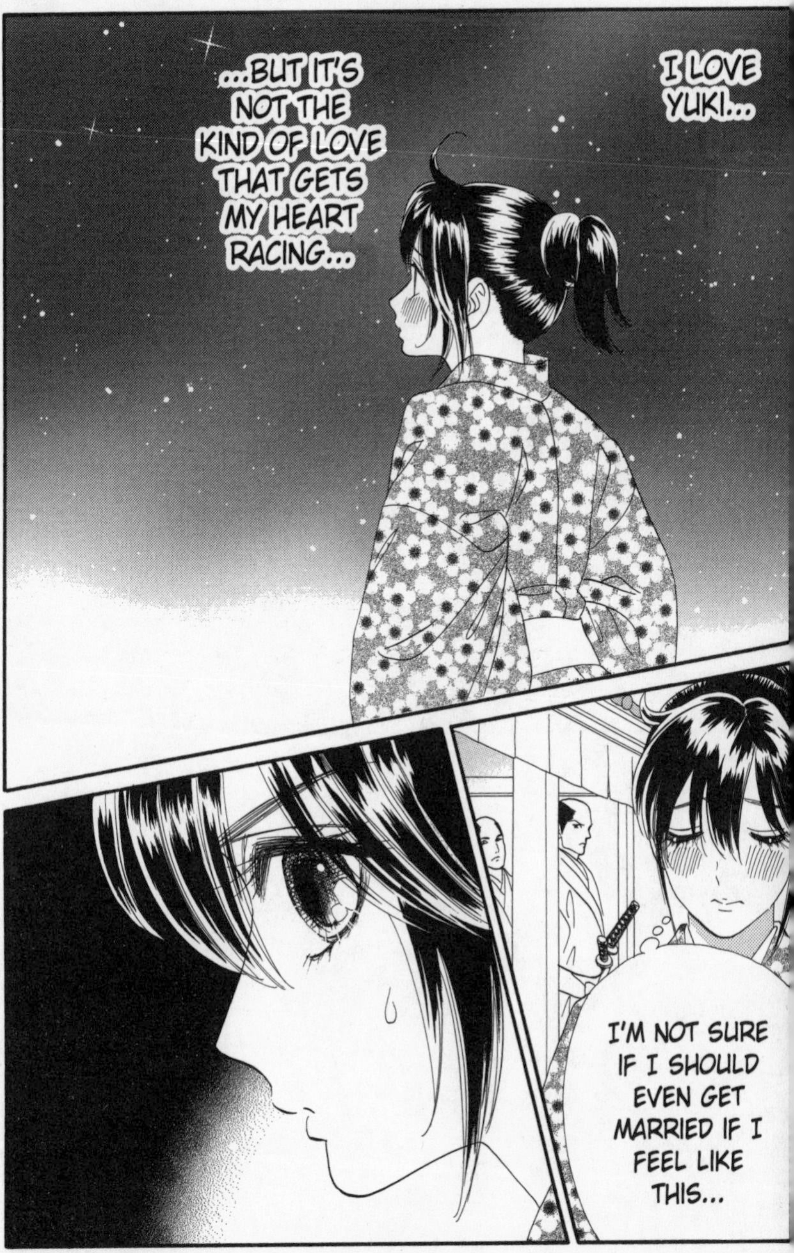
I LOVE YUKI...
...BUT IT'S NOT THE KIND OF LOVE THAT GETS MY HEART RACING...
I'M NOT SURE IF I SHOULD EVEN GET MARRIED IF I FEEL LIKE THIS...

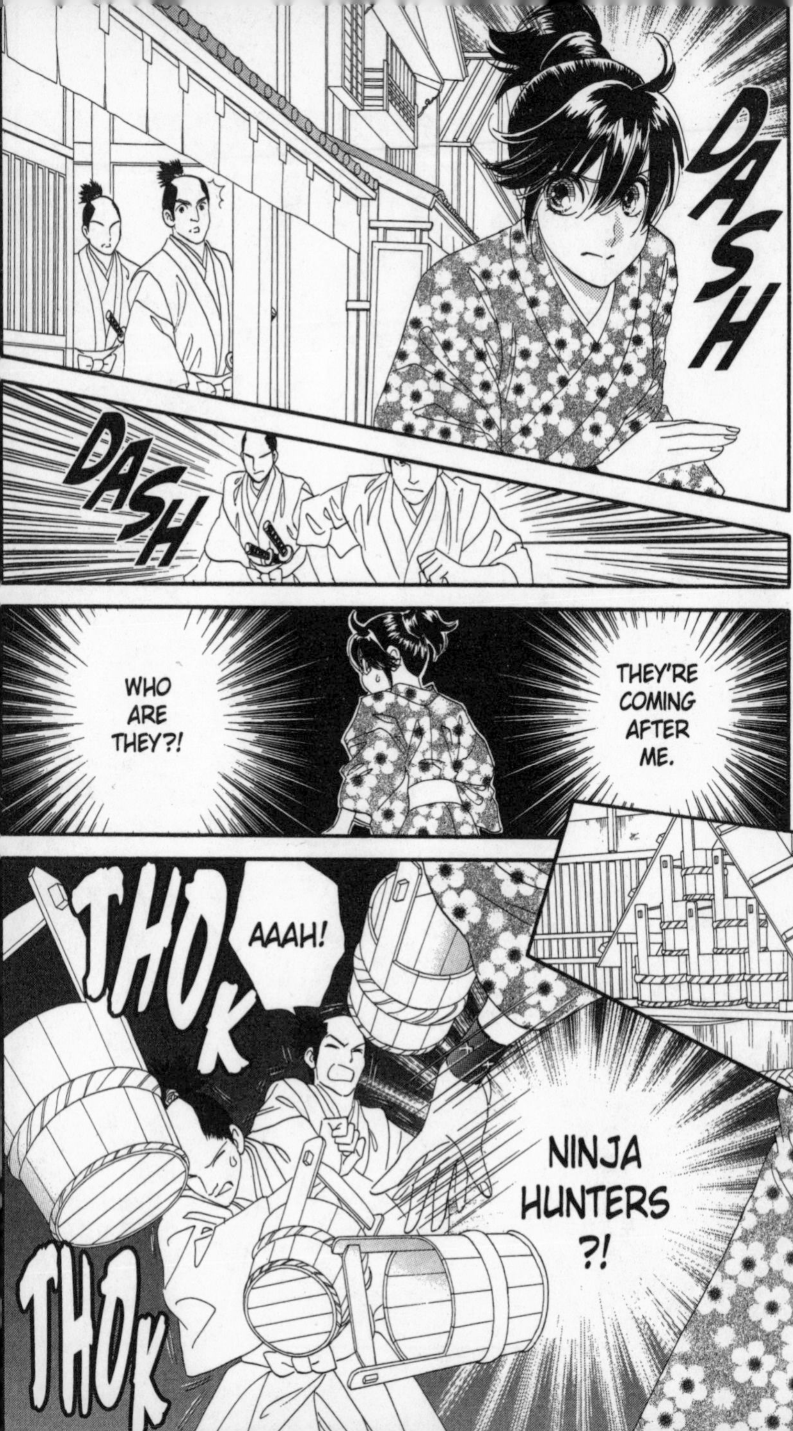
DASH
DASH
THEY'RE COMING AFTER ME.
WHO ARE THEY?!
NINJA HUNTERS ?!
AAAH!
THOK
THOK

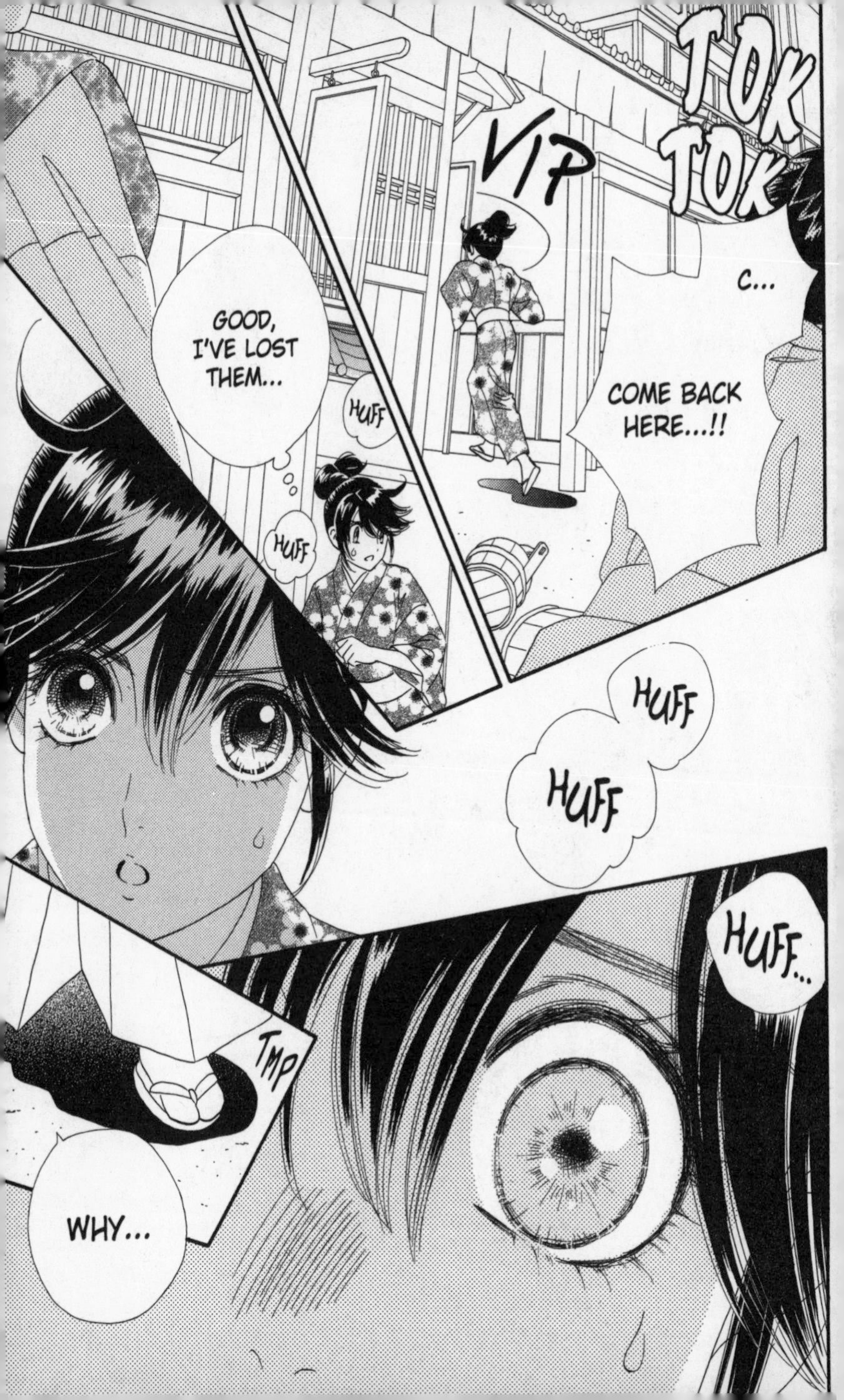
TOK TOK
C...
COME BACK HERE...!!
VIP
GOOD, I'VE LOST THEM...
HUFF
HUFF
HUFF
HUFF
HUFF...
TMP
WHY...

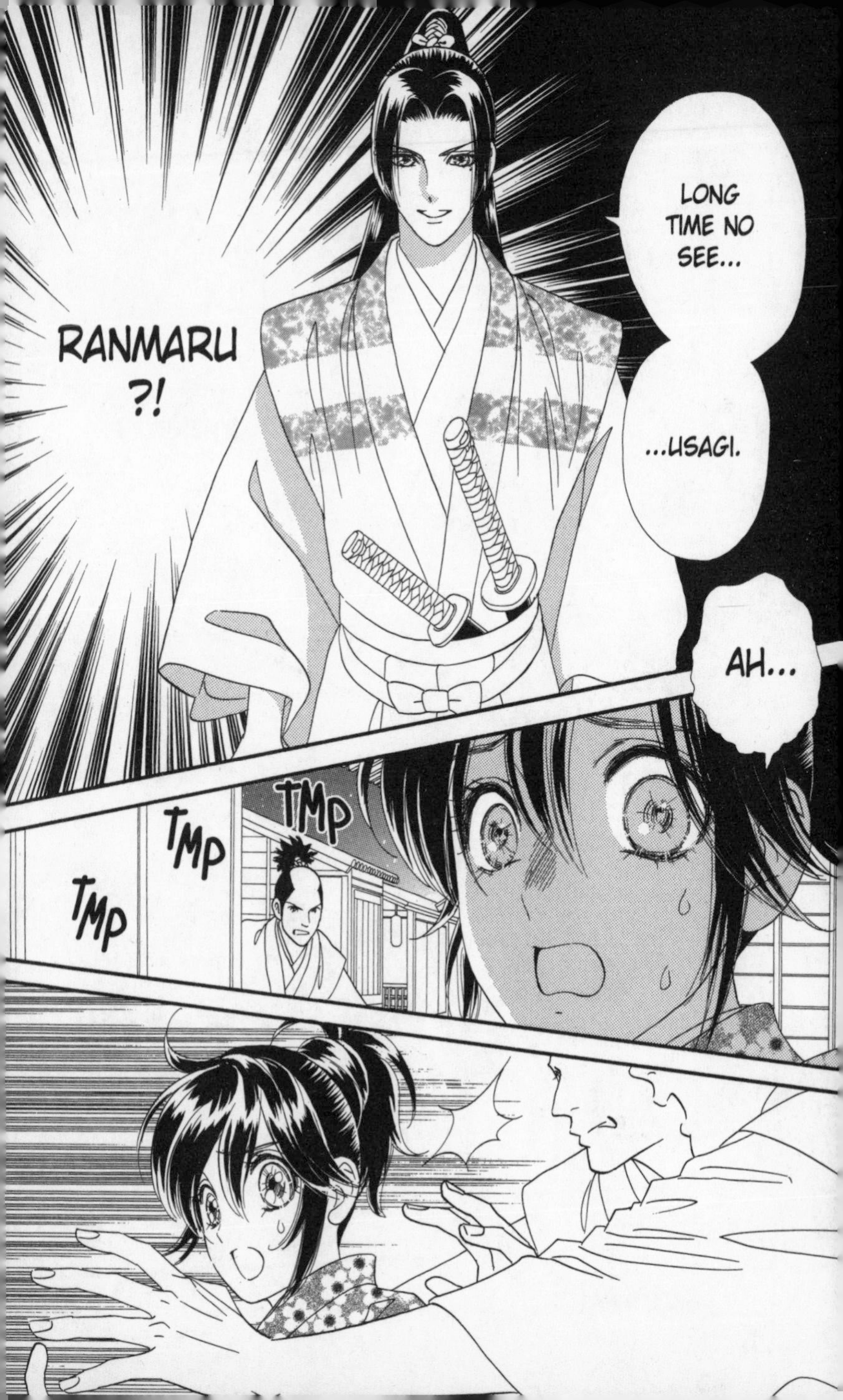
LONG TIME NO SEE...
...USAGI.
RANMARU ?!
AH...
TMP
TMP
TMP

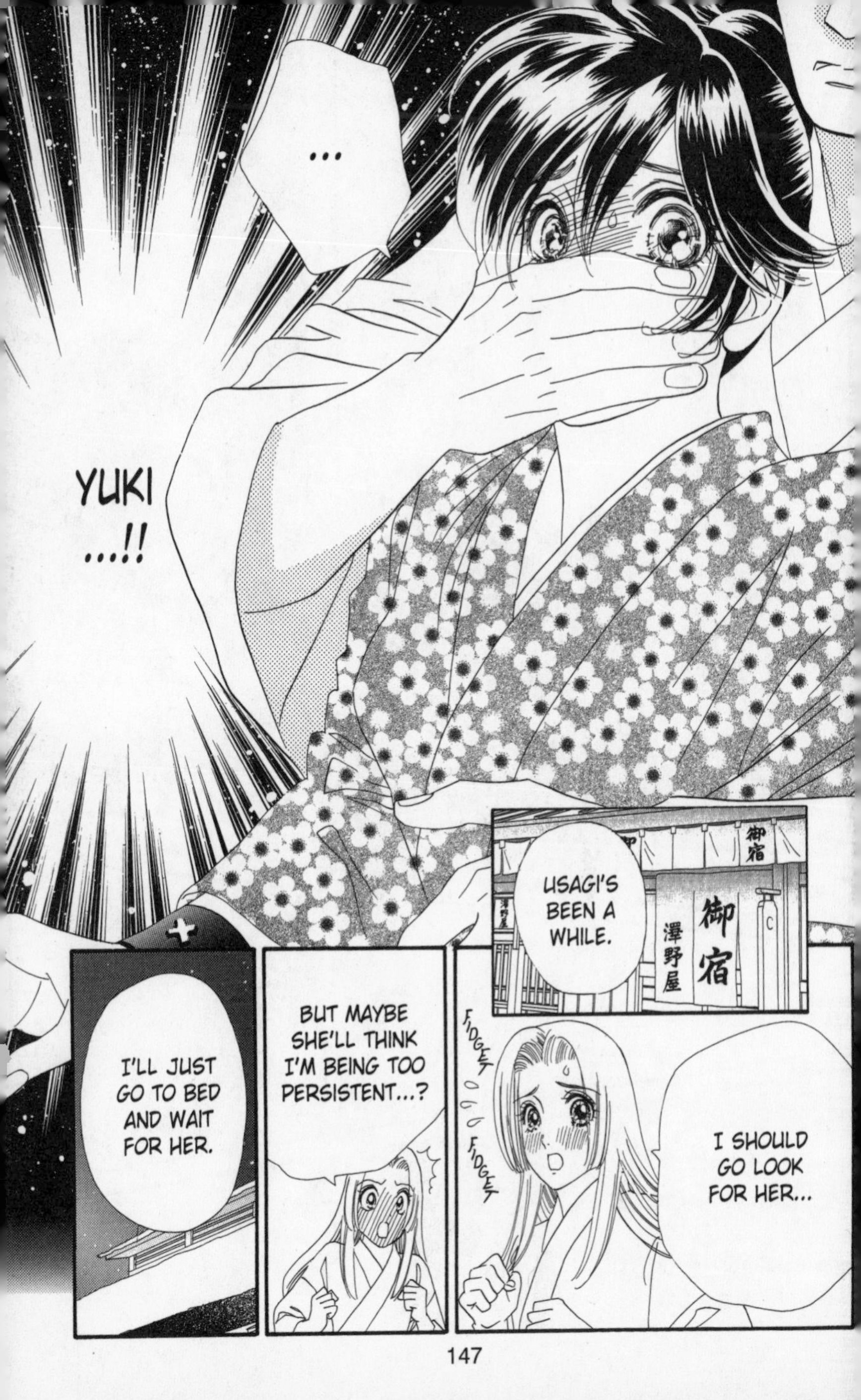
...
YUKI ...!!
御宿
USAGI'S BEEN A WHILE.
御宿
澤野屋
I SHOULD GO LOOK FOR HER...
FIDGET FIDGET
BUT MAYBE SHE'LL THINK I'M BEING TOO PERSISTENT...?
I'LL JUST GO TO BED AND WAIT FOR HER.

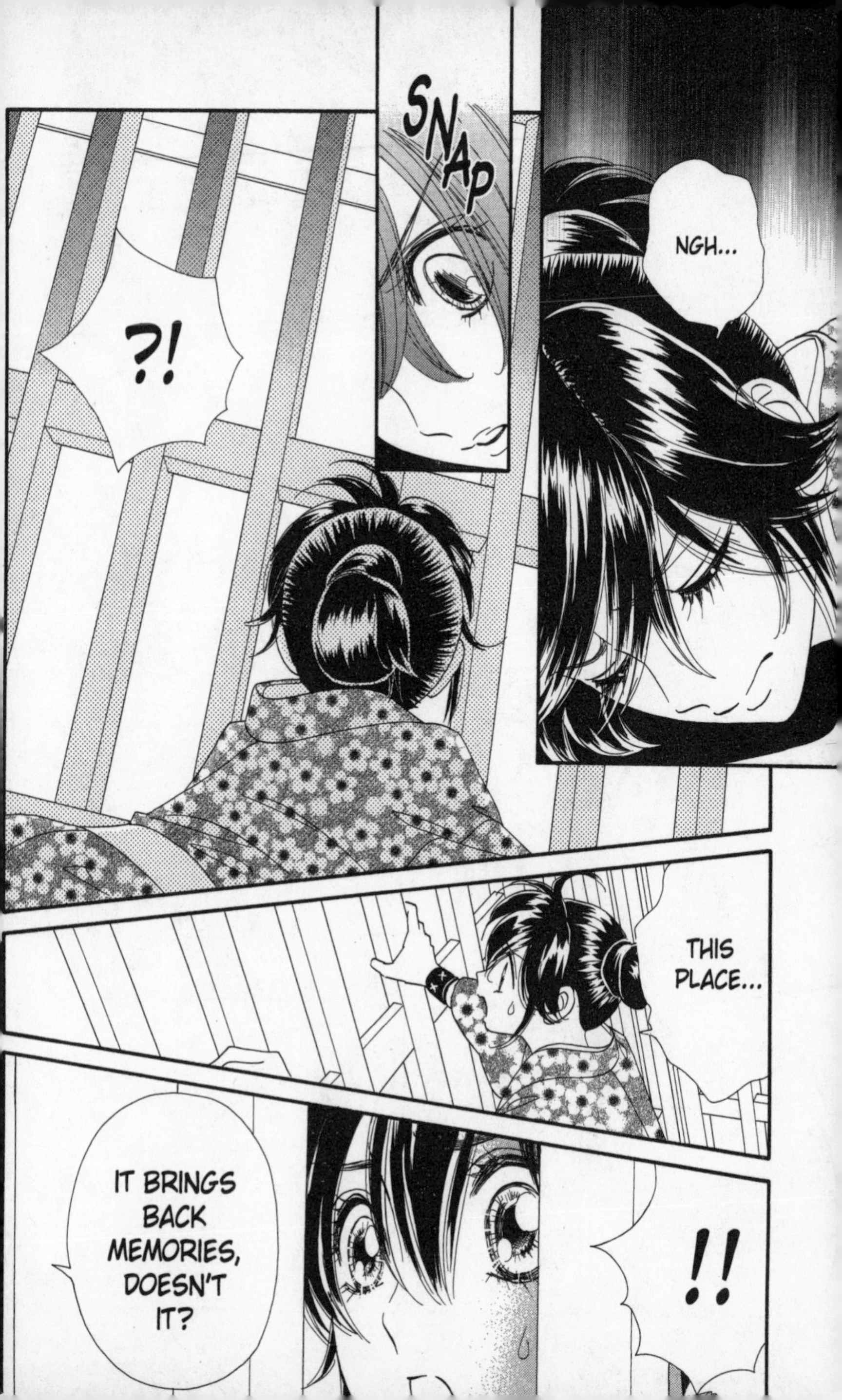
NGH...
SNAP
?!
THIS PLACE...
!!
IT BRINGS BACK MEMORIES, DOESN'T IT?

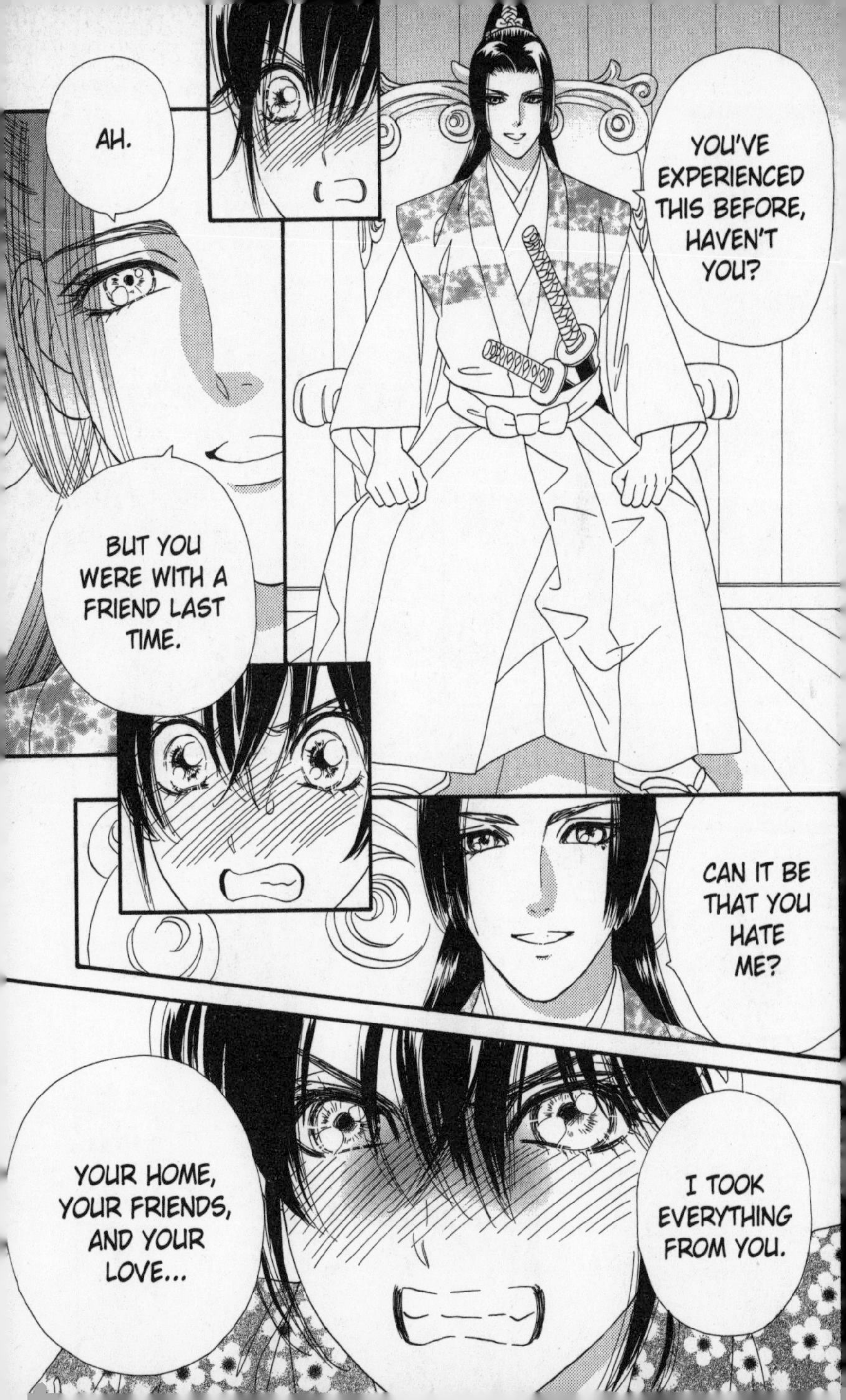
YOU'VE EXPERIENCED THIS BEFORE, HAVEN'T YOU?
AH.
BUT YOU WERE WITH A FRIEND LAST TIME.
CAN IT BE THAT YOU HATE ME?
I TOOK EVERYTHING FROM YOU.
YOUR HOME, YOUR FRIENDS, AND YOUR LOVE...

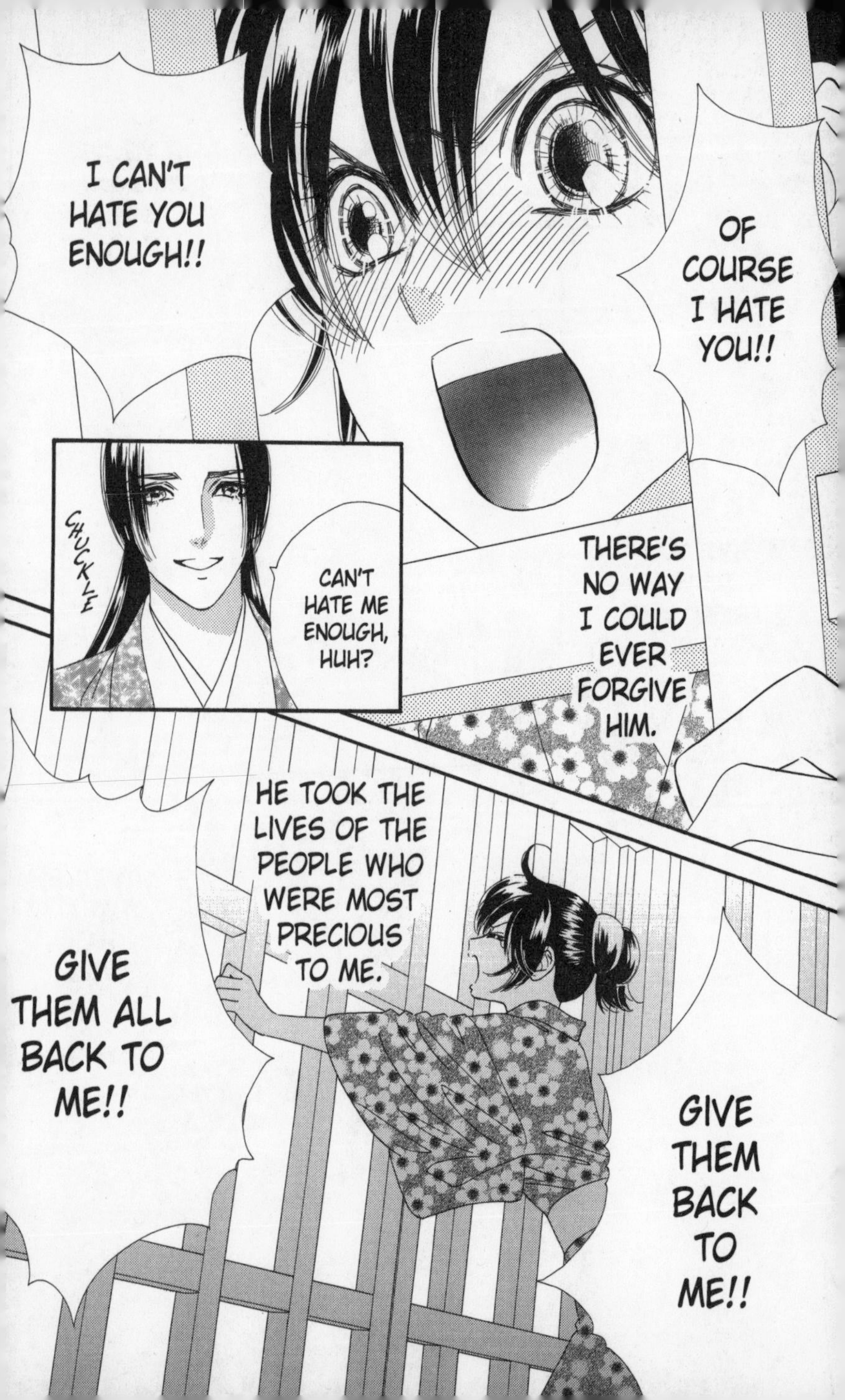
OF COURSE I HATE YOU!!
I CAN'T HATE YOU ENOUGH!!
THERE'S NO WAY I COULD EVER FORGIVE HIM.
CHUCKLE
CAN'T HATE ME ENOUGH, HUH?
HE TOOK THE LIVES OF THE PEOPLE WHO WERE MOST PRECIOUS TO ME.
GIVE THEM BACK TO ME!!
GIVE THEM ALL BACK TO ME!!

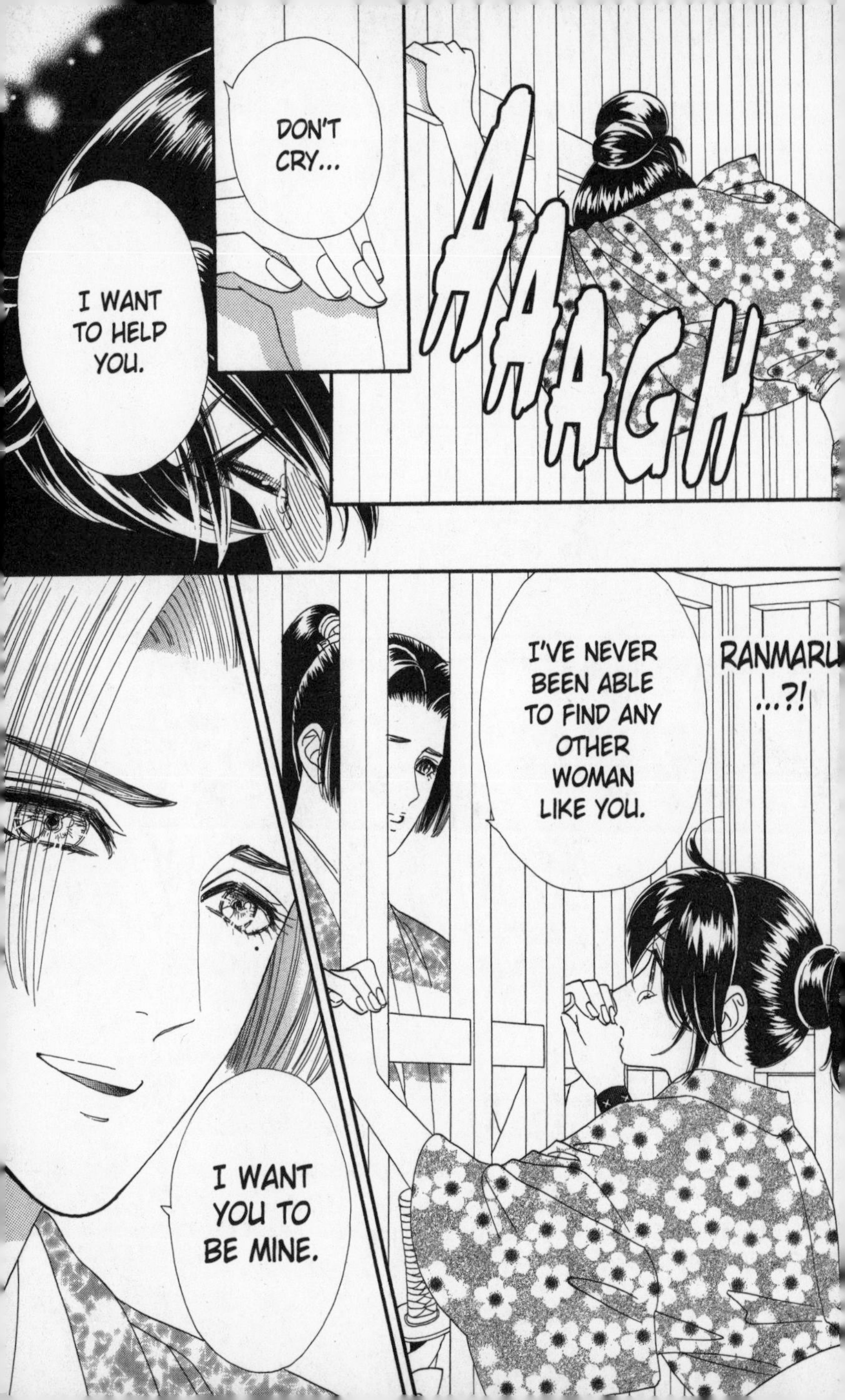
AAAGH
DON'T CRY...
I WANT TO HELP YOU.
RANMARU ...?!
I'VE NEVER BEEN ABLE TO FIND ANY OTHER WOMAN LIKE YOU.
I WANT YOU TO BE MINE.

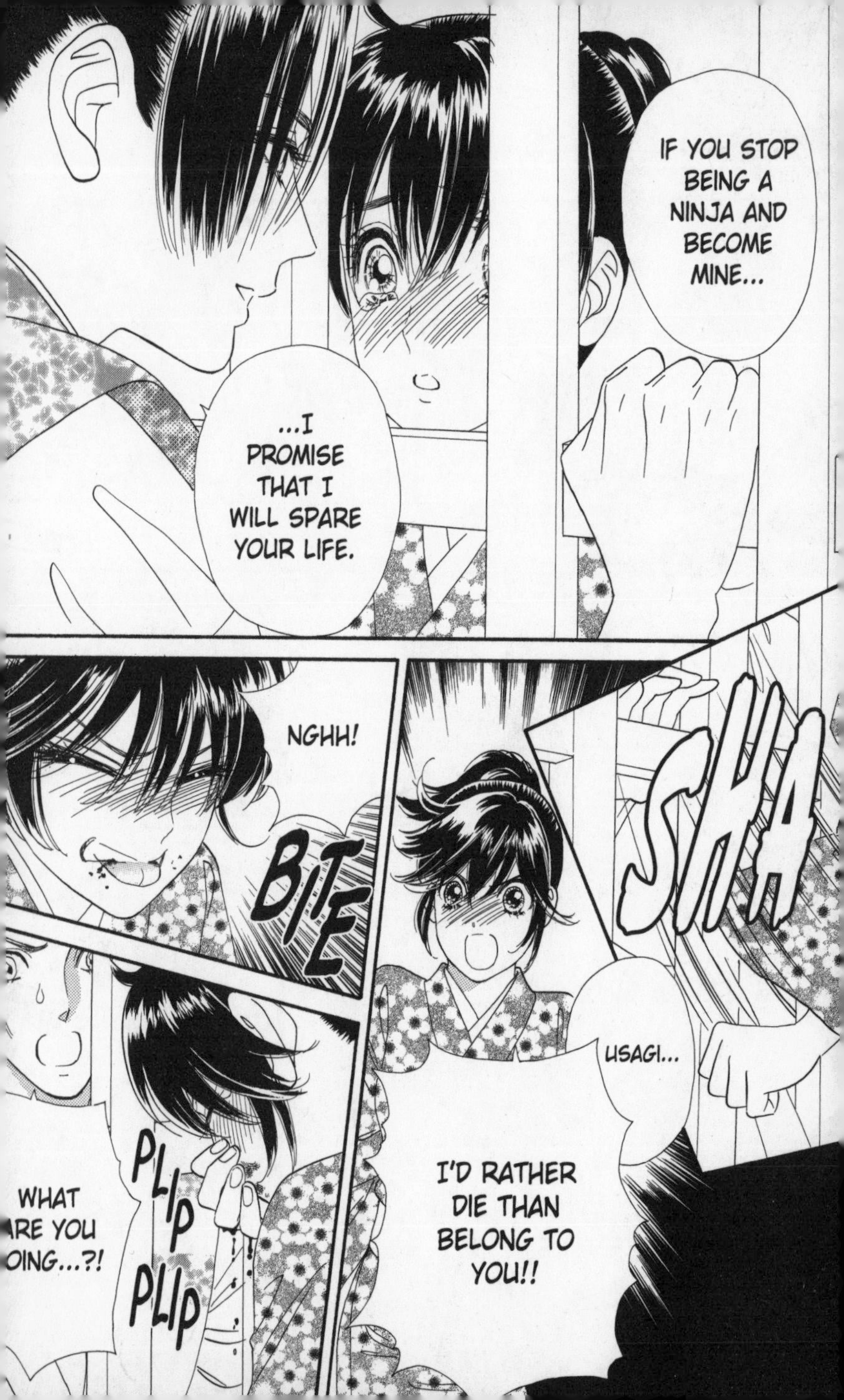
IF YOU STOP BEING A NINJA AND BECOME MINE...
...I PROMISE THAT I WILL SPARE YOUR LIFE.
SHA
USAGI...
I'D RATHER DIE THAN BELONG TO YOU!!
NGHH!
BITE
PLIP PLIP
WHAT ARE YOU OING...?!

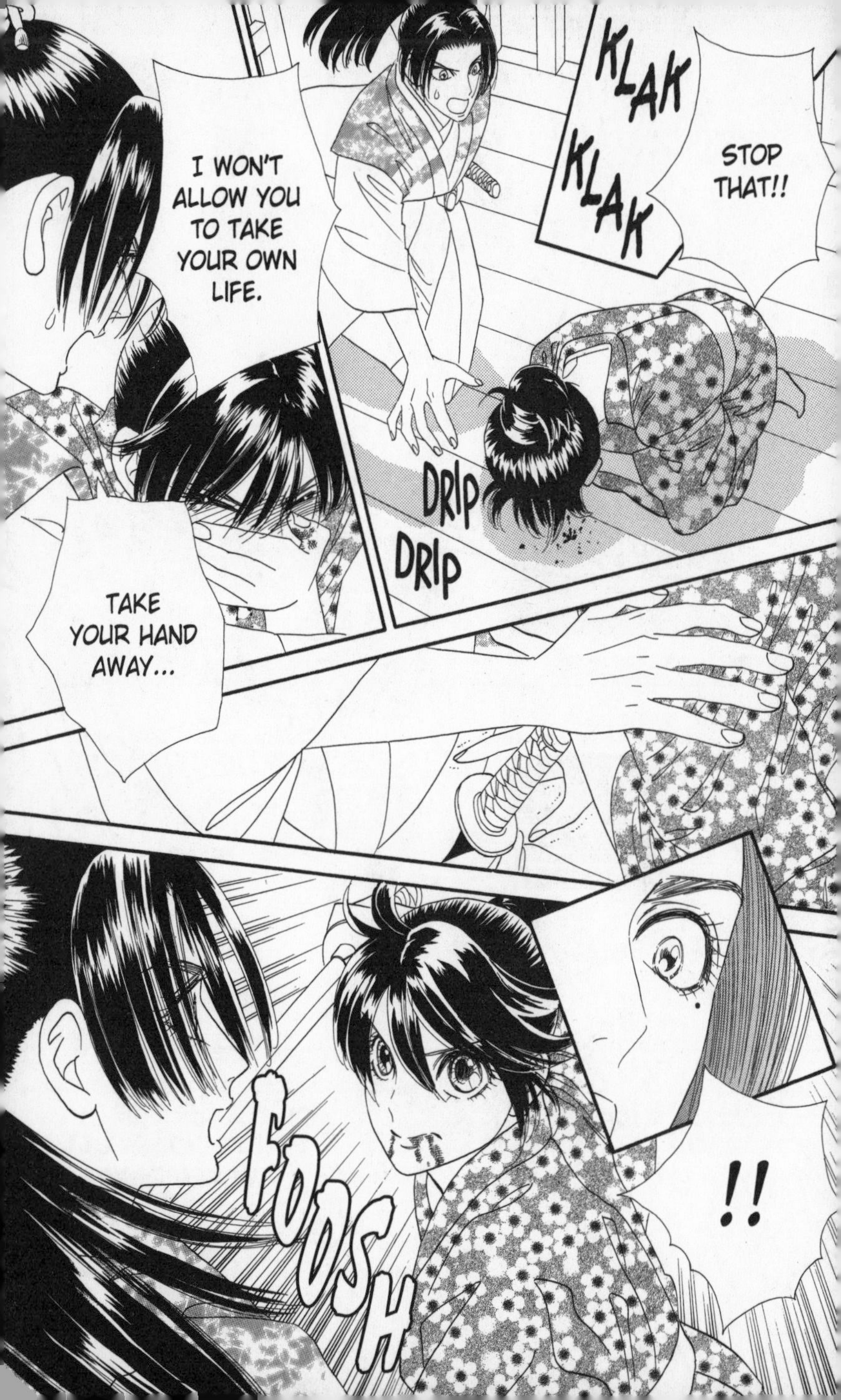

KLAK KLAK
STOP THAT!!
DRIP DRIP
I WON'T ALLOW YOU TO TAKE YOUR OWN LIFE.
TAKE YOUR HAND AWAY...
!!
FOOSH

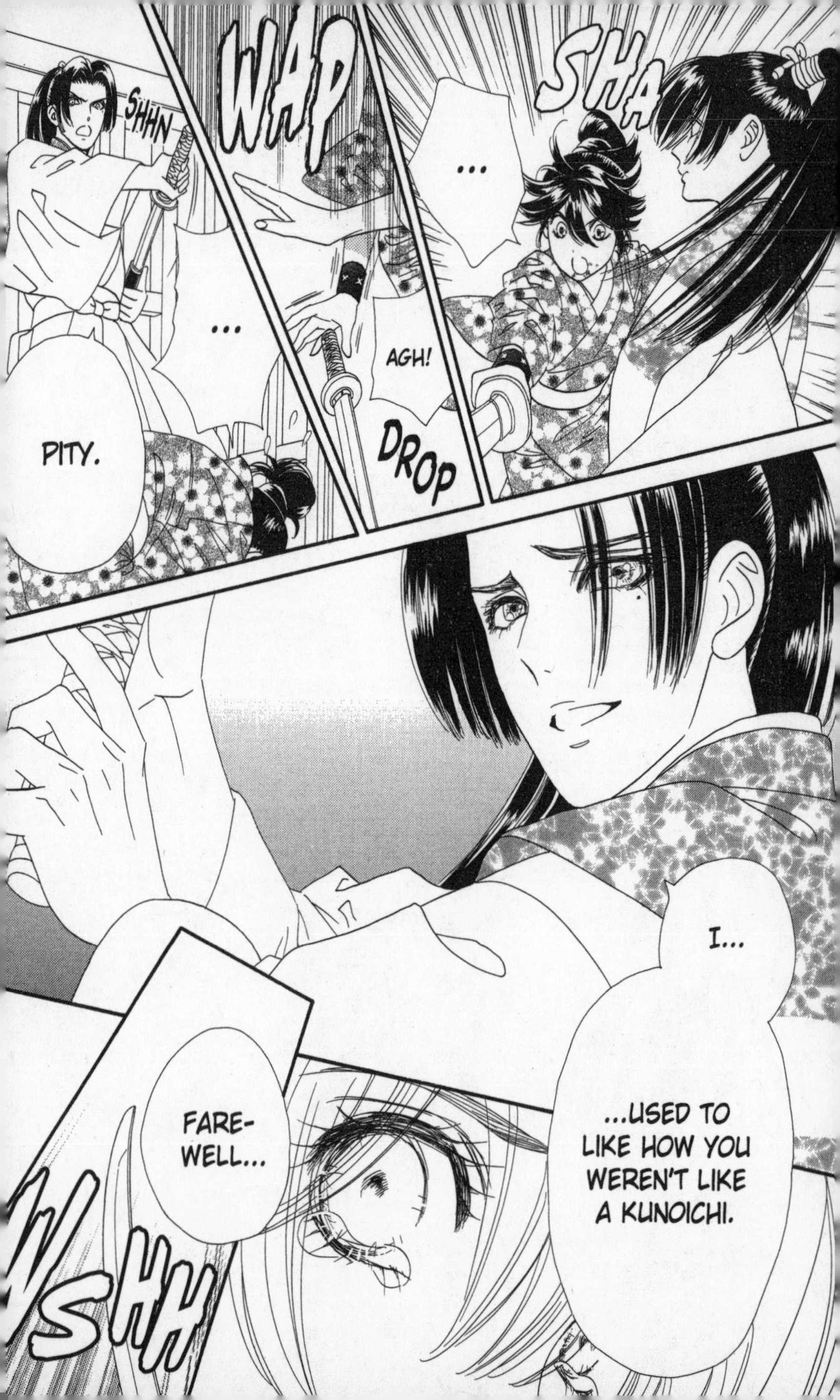

SHA
...
WAP
AGH!
DROP
SHHN
...
PITY.
I...
...USED TO LIKE HOW YOU WEREN'T LIKE A KUNOICHI.
FARE-WELL...
WSHH

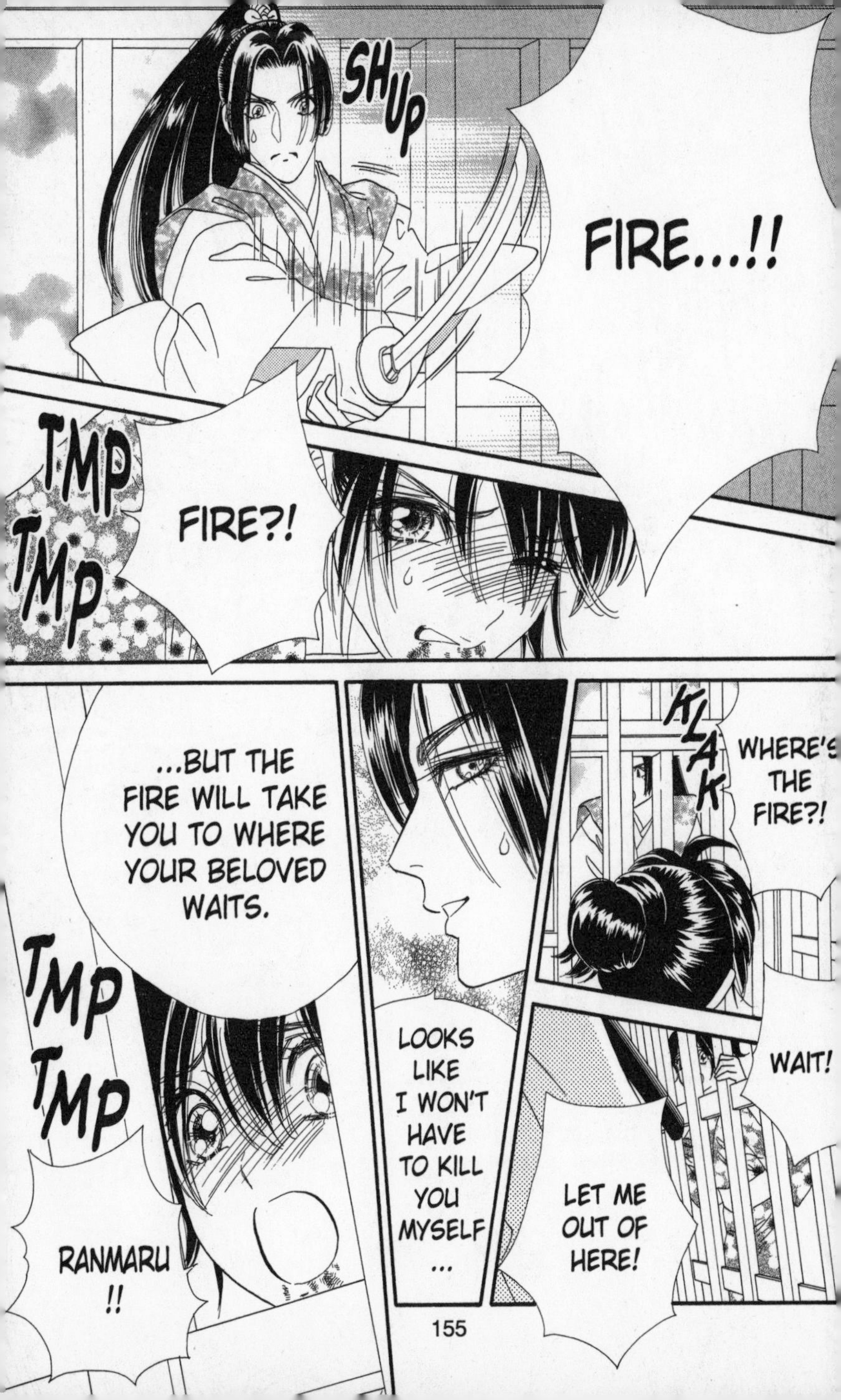
FIRE...!!
SHUP
FIRE?!
TMP TMP
KLAK
WHERE'S THE FIRE?!
WAIT!
LET ME OUT OF HERE!
LOOKS LIKE I WON'T HAVE TO KILL YOU MYSELF ...
...BUT THE FIRE WILL TAKE YOU TO WHERE YOUR BELOVED WAITS.
TMP TMP
RANMARU !!

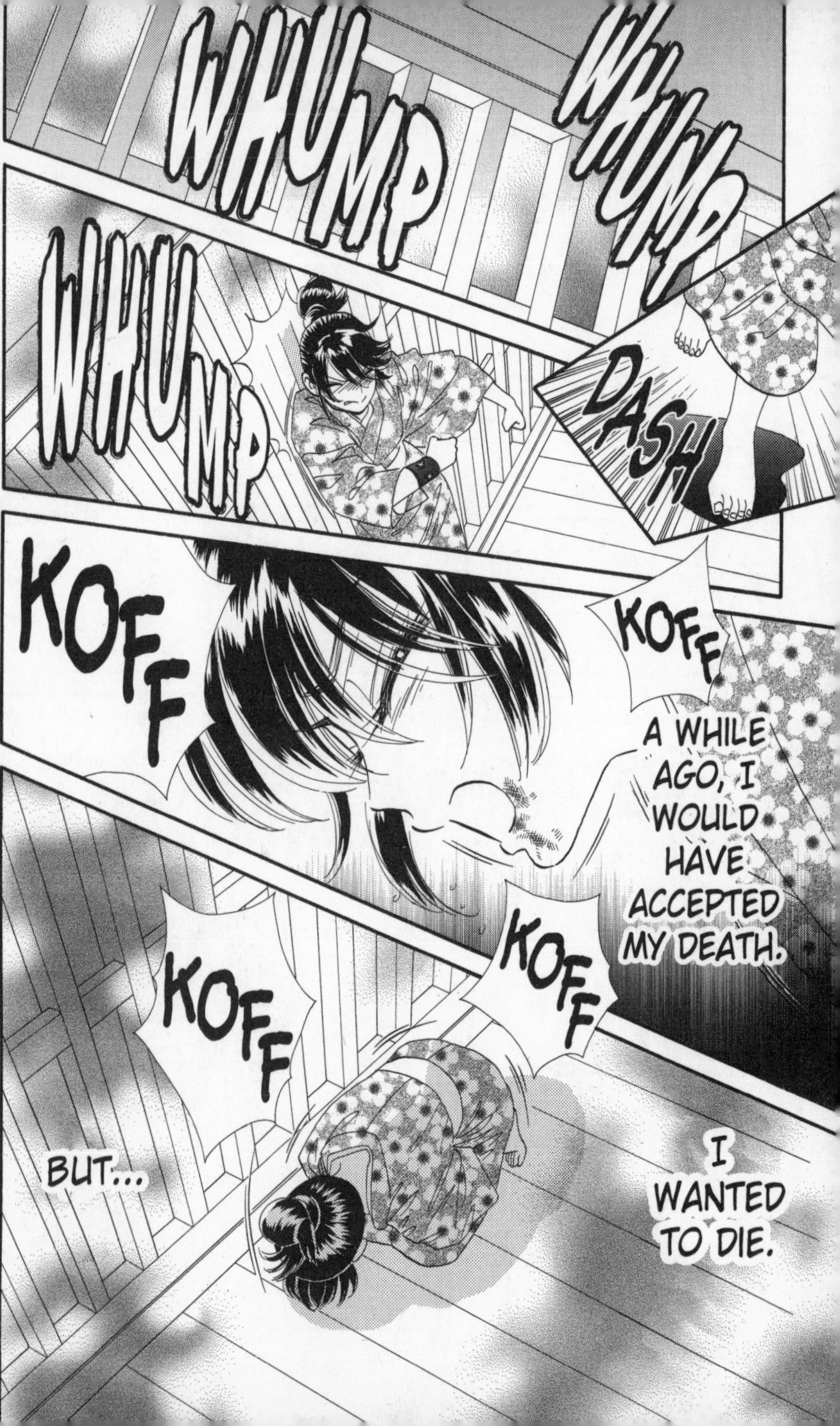
WHUMP
WHUMP
DASH
WHUMP
KOFF
KOFF
A WHILE AGO, I WOULD HAVE ACCEPTED MY DEATH.
KOFF
KOFF
I WANTED TO DIE.
BUT...

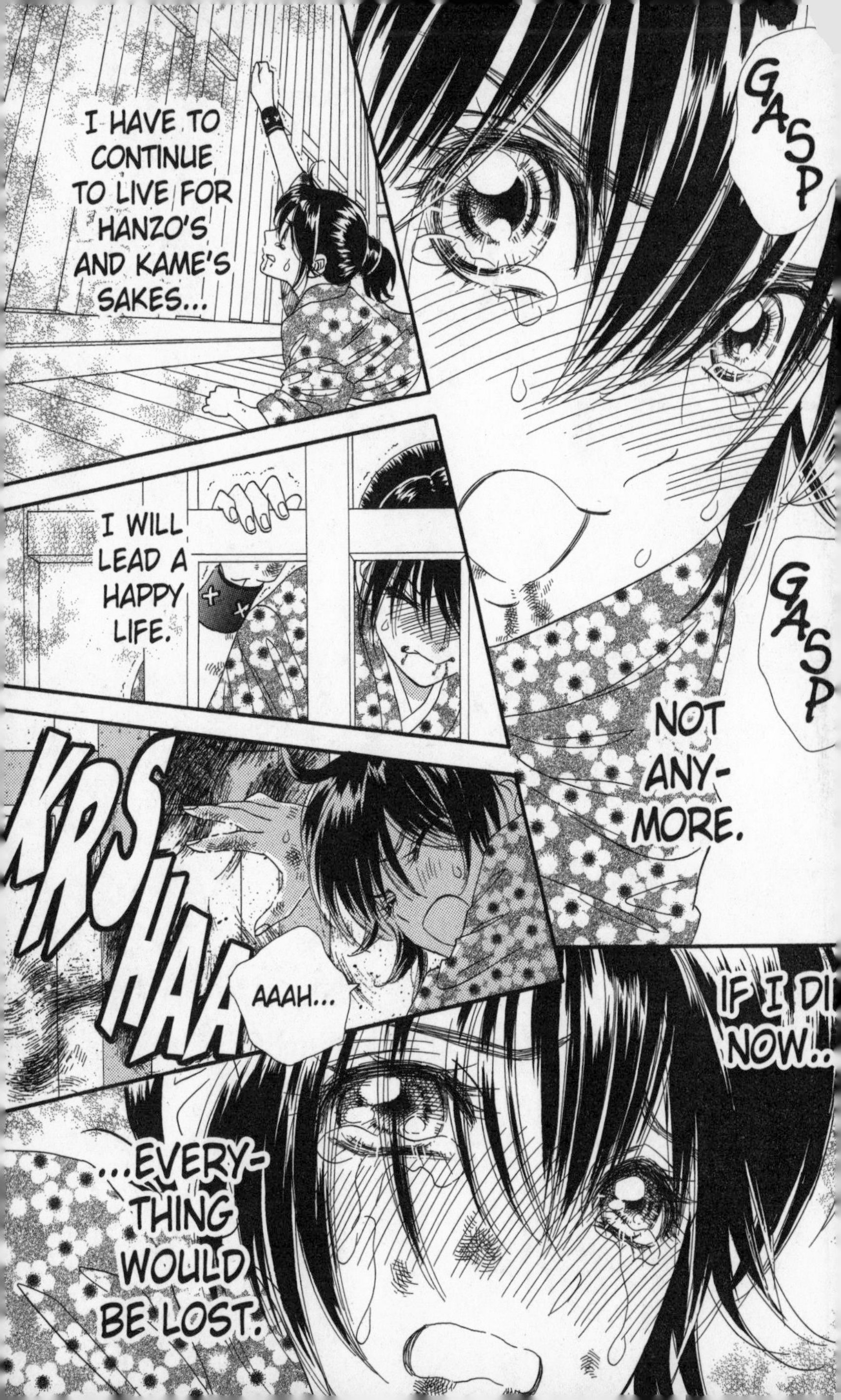
GASP
GASP
NOT ANY-MORE.
I HAVE TO CONTINUE TO LIVE FOR HANZO'S AND KAME'S SAKES...
I WILL LEAD A HAPPY LIFE.
KRSHAA
AAAH...
IF I DI NOW...
...EVERY-THING WOULD BE LOST.

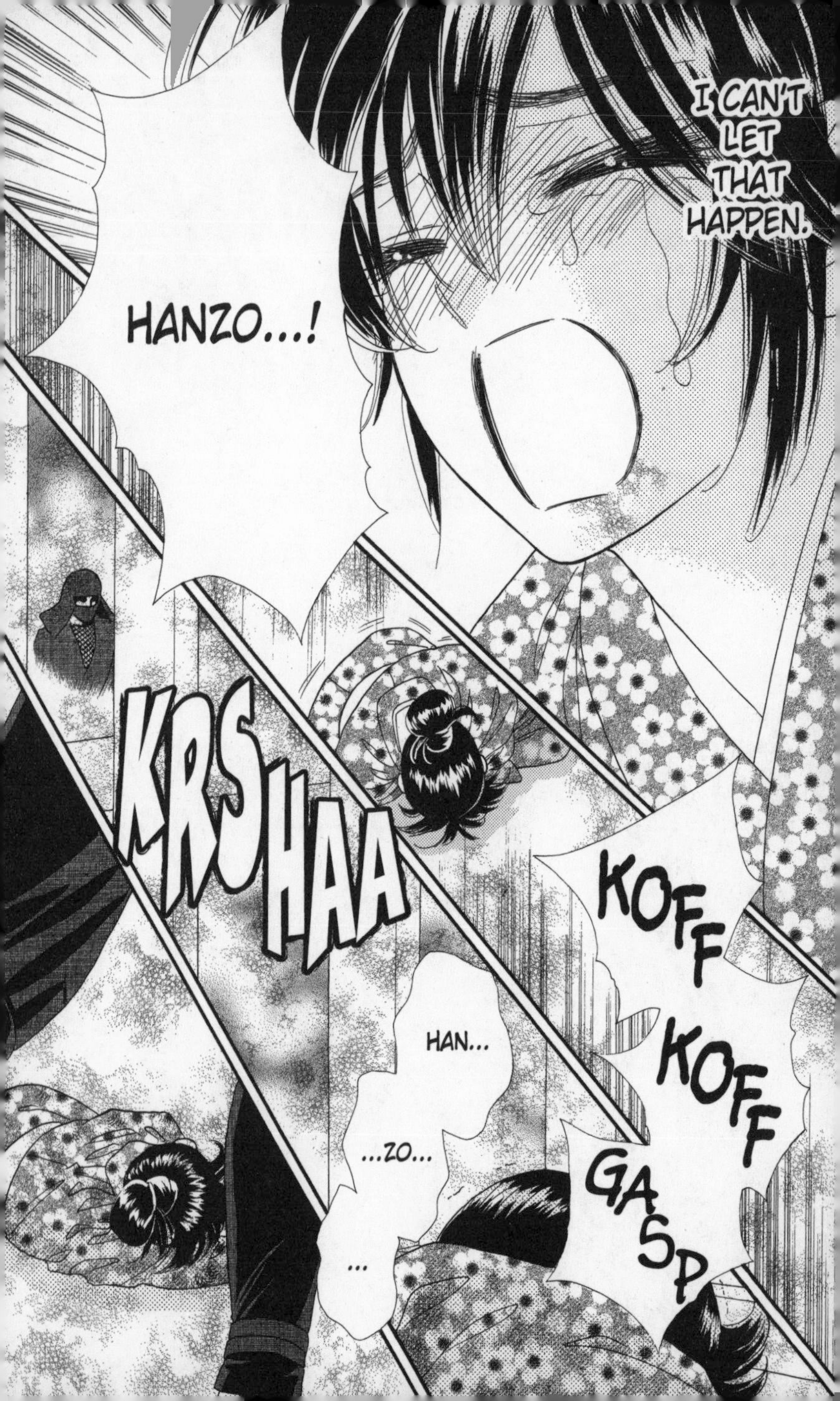
I CAN'T LET THAT HAPPEN.
HANZO...!
KRSHAA
KOFF KOFF GASP
HAN...
...ZO...
...

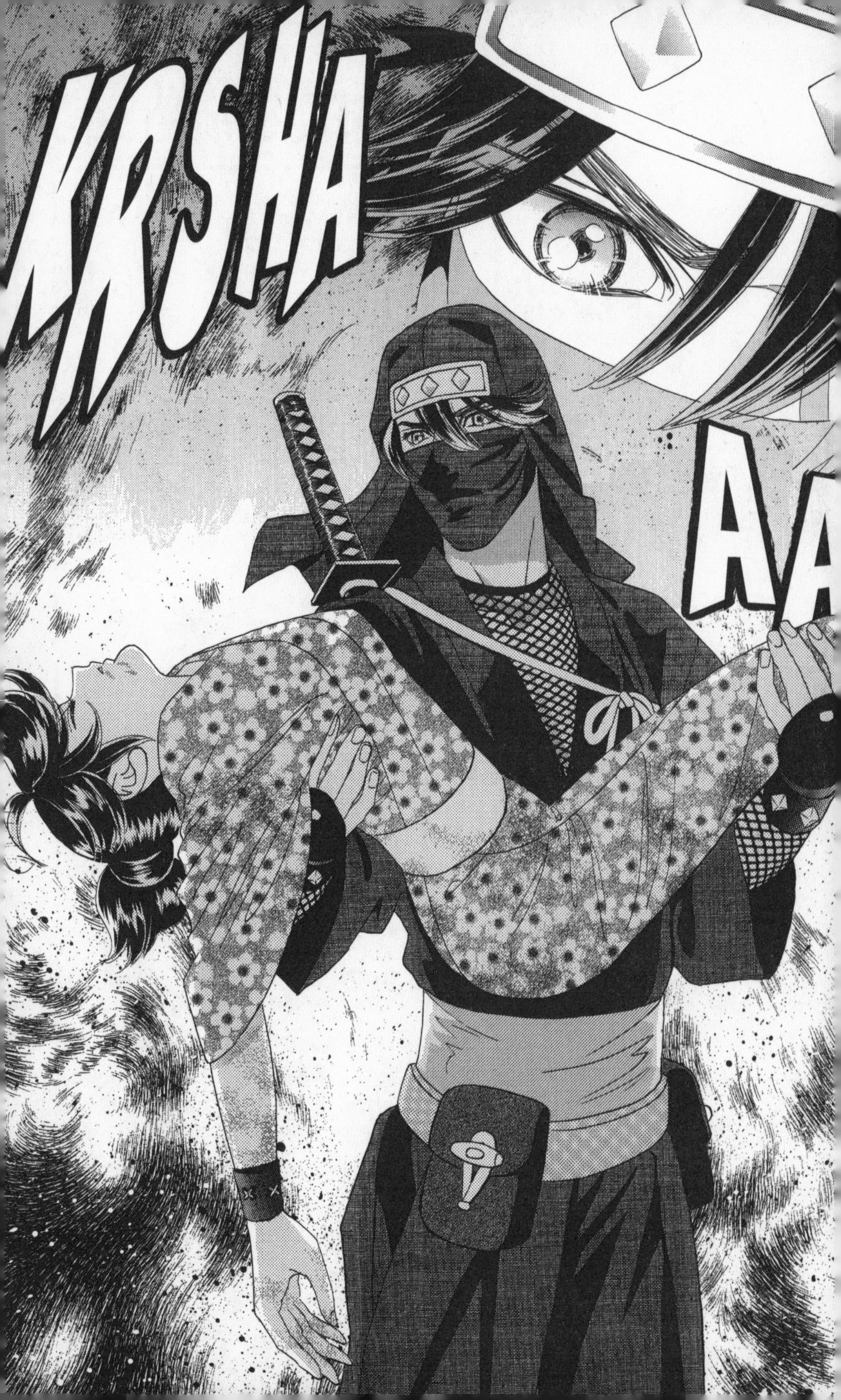
KRSHA
AA

LET'S GO! LITTLE HANZO

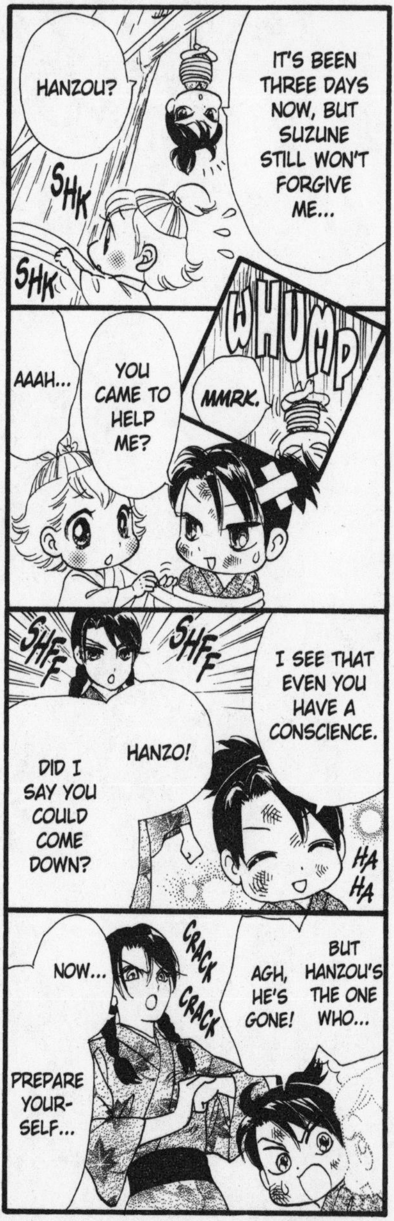
IT'S BEEN THREE DAYS NOW, BUT SUZUNE STILL WON'T FORGIVE ME...
HANZOU?
SHK
SHK
WHUMP
MMRK.
YOU CAME TO HELP ME?
AAAH...
SHFF
SHFF
I SEE THAT EVEN YOU HAVE A CONSCIENCE.
HANZO!
DID I SAY YOU COULD COME DOWN?
HA HA
BUT HANZOU'S THE ONE WHO...
AGH, HE'S GONE!
CRACK CRACK
NOW...
PREPARE YOUR-SELF...

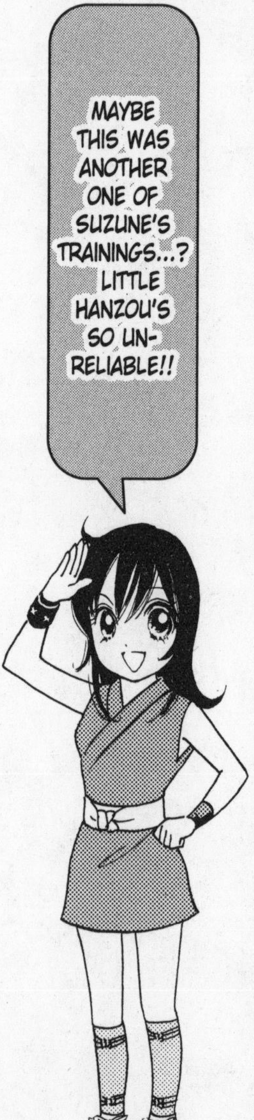
MAYBE THIS WAS ANOTHER ONE OF SUZUNE'S TRAININGS...? LITTLE HANZOU'S SO UN-RELIABLE!!

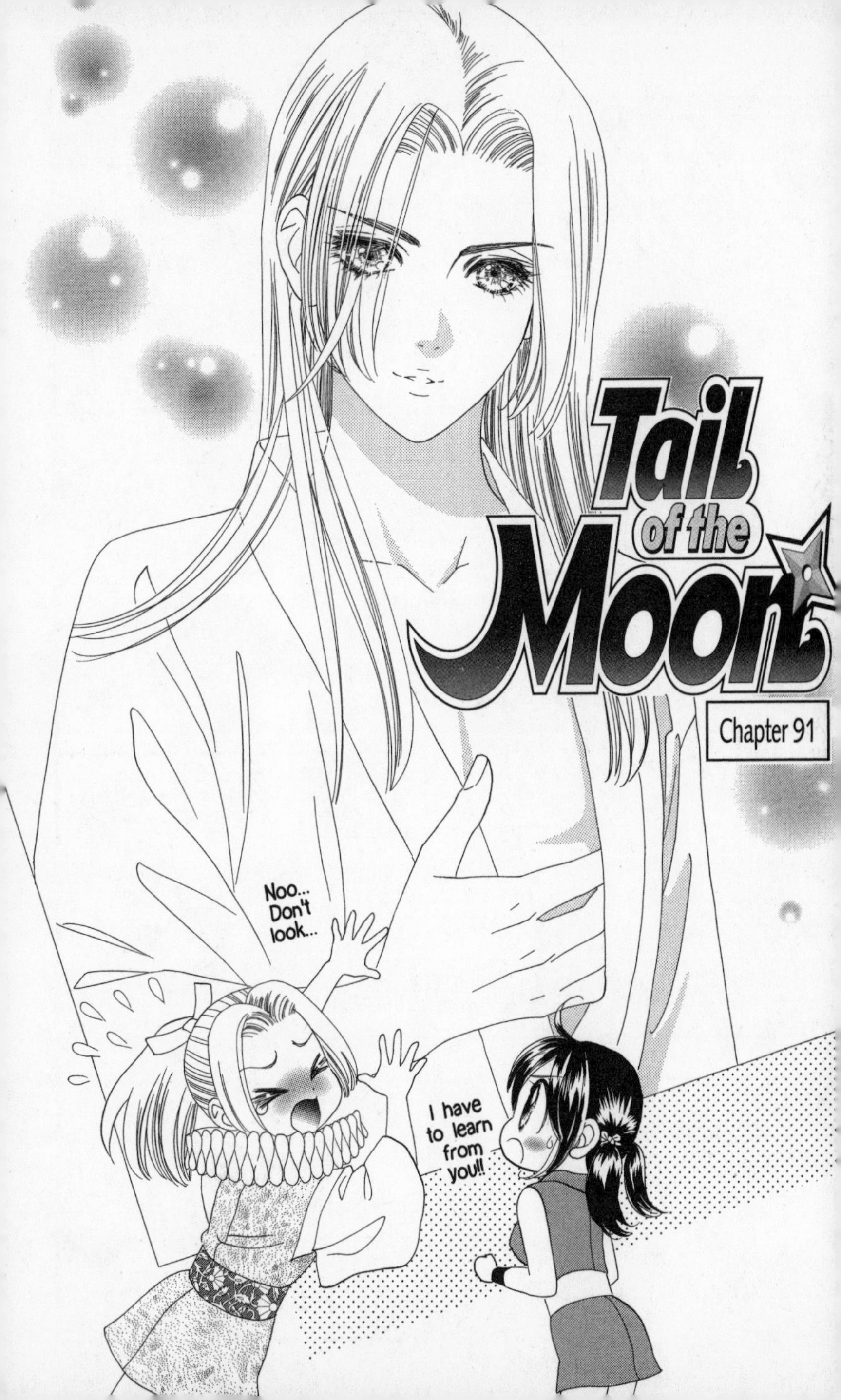
Tail of the Moon
Chapter 91
Noo... Don't look...
I have to learn from you!!

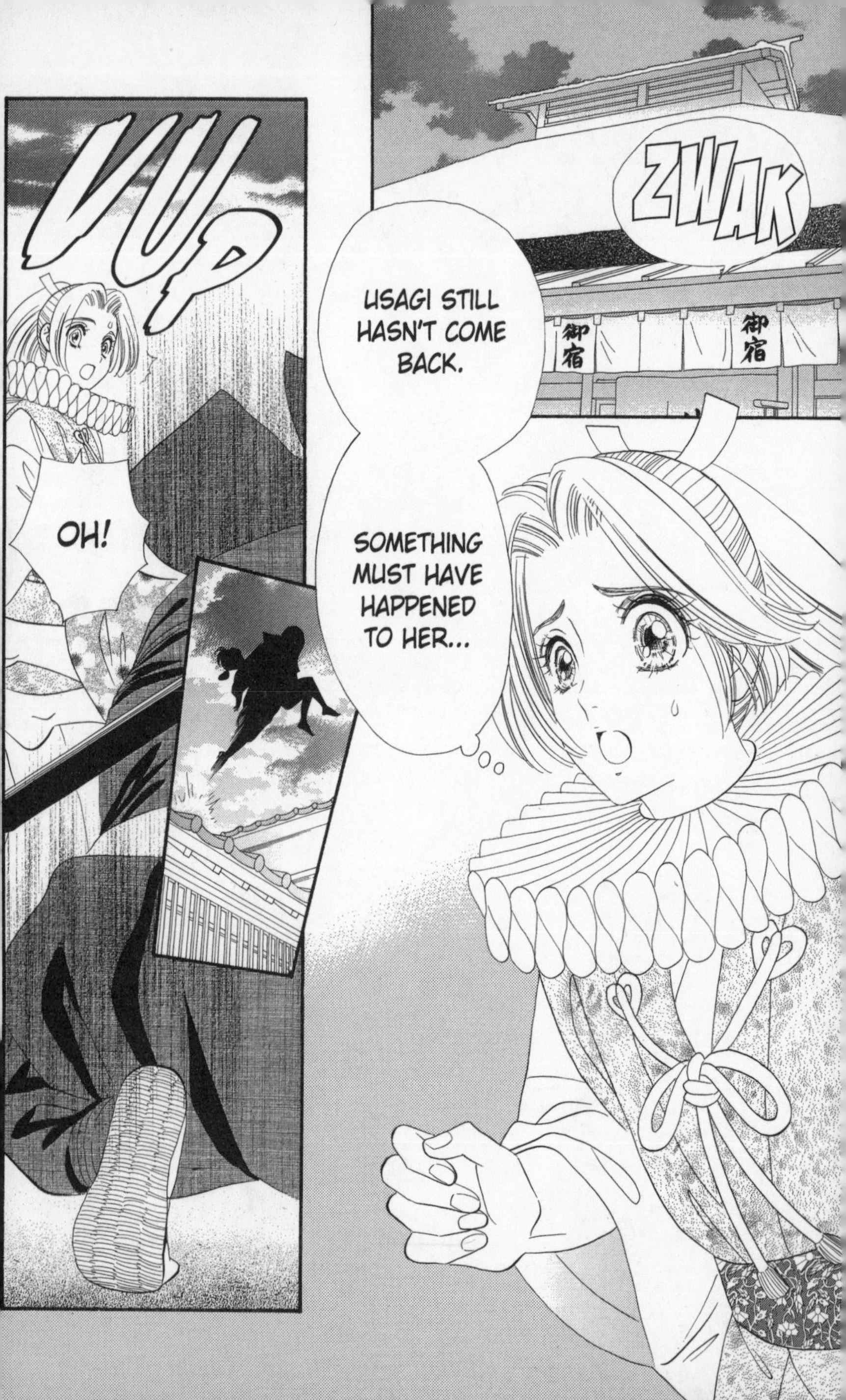
ZWAK
御宿
御宿
USAGI STILL HASN'T COME BACK.
SOMETHING MUST HAVE HAPPENED TO HER...
VUP
OH!

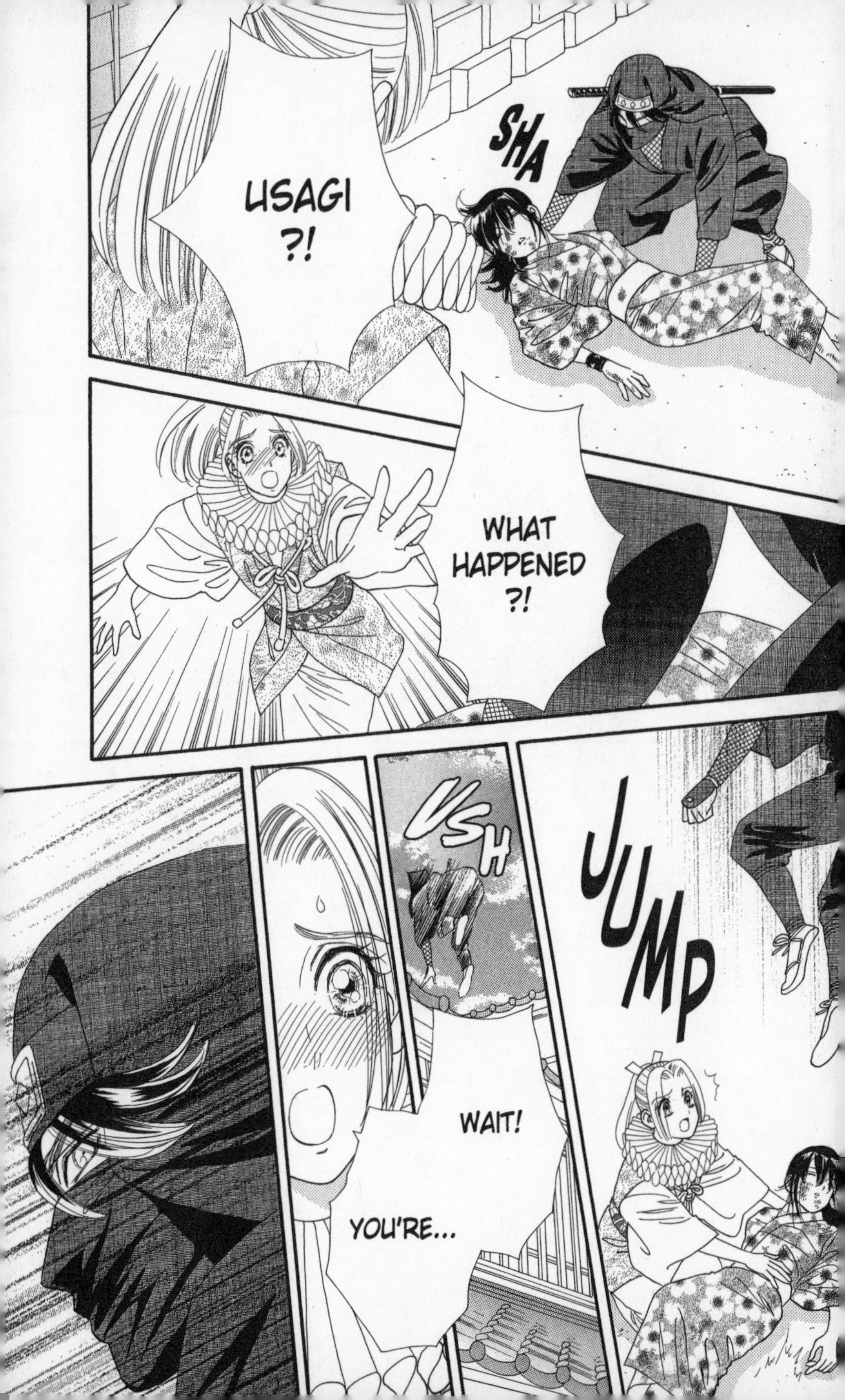
SHA
USAGI ?!
WHAT HAPPENED ?!
JUUMP
VSH
WAIT!
YOU'RE...

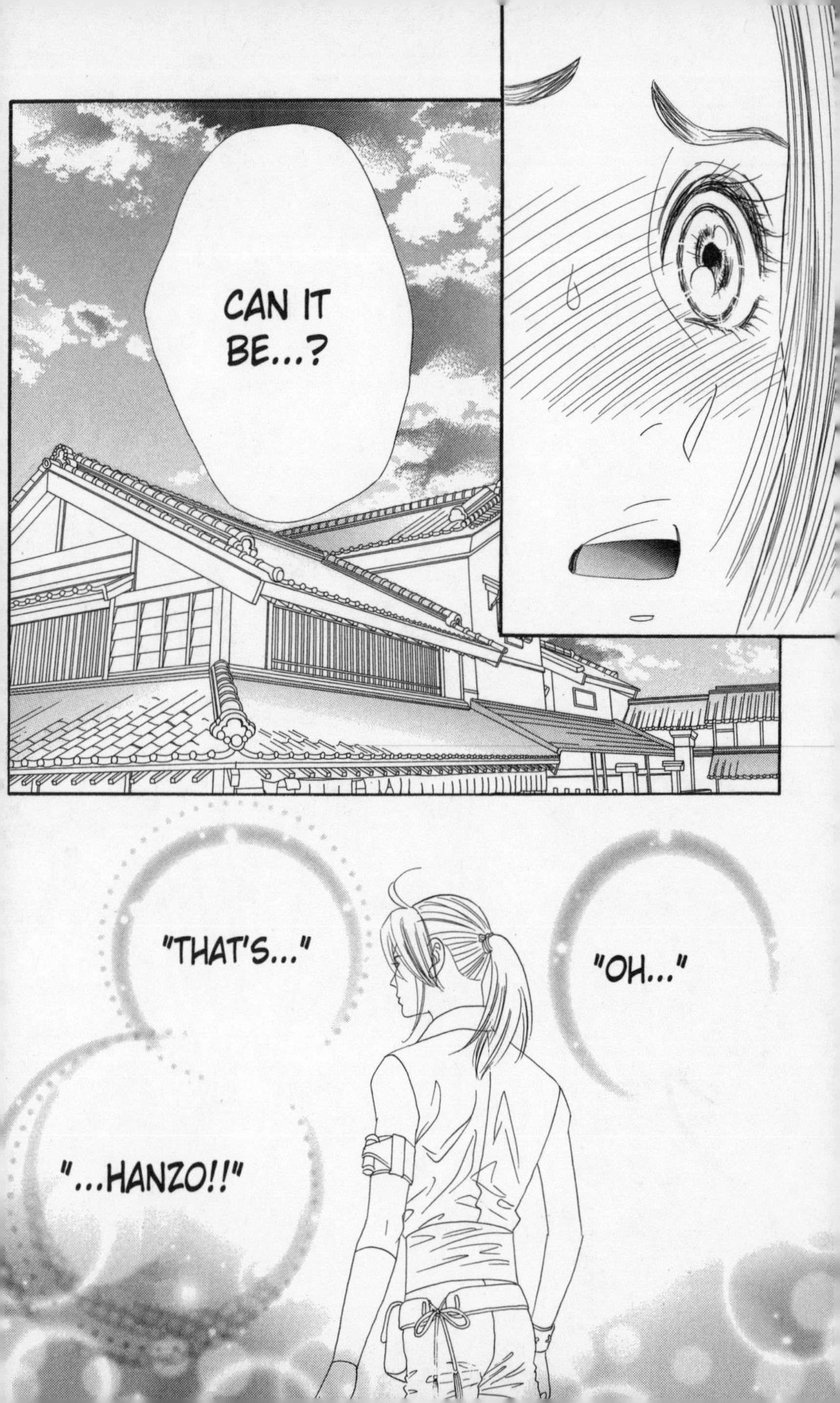
CAN IT BE...?
"OH..."
"THAT'S..."
"...HANZO!!"

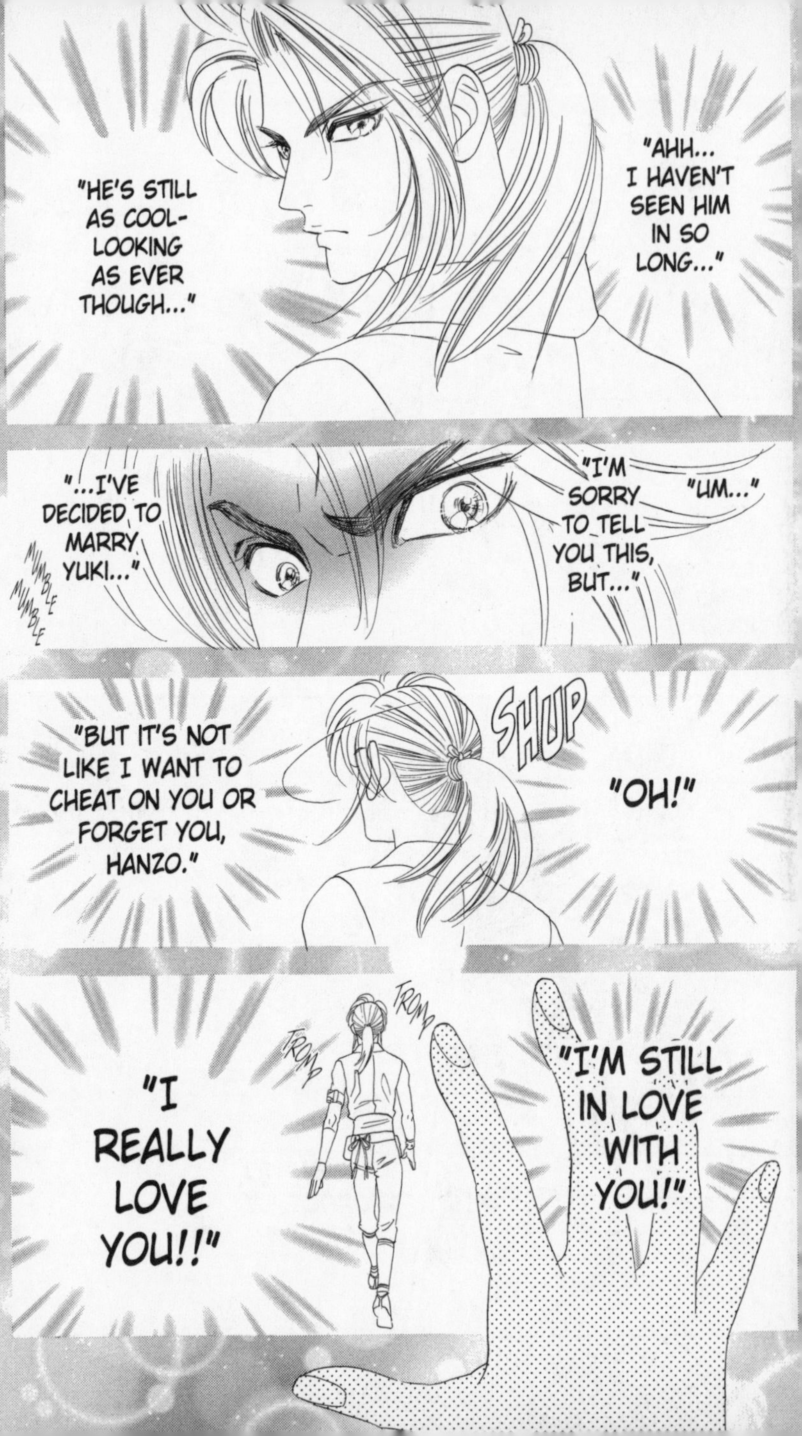
"AHH... I HAVEN'T SEEN HIM IN SO LONG..."
"HE'S STILL AS COOL-LOOKING AS EVER THOUGH..."
"UM..."
"I'M SORRY TO TELL YOU THIS, BUT..."
"...I'VE DECIDED TO MARRY YUKI..."
MUMBLE MUMBLE
SHUP
"OH!"
"BUT IT'S NOT LIKE I WANT TO CHEAT ON YOU OR FORGET YOU, HANZO."
"I'M STILL IN LOVE WITH YOU!"
TROMP
TROMP
"I REALLY LOVE YOU!!"

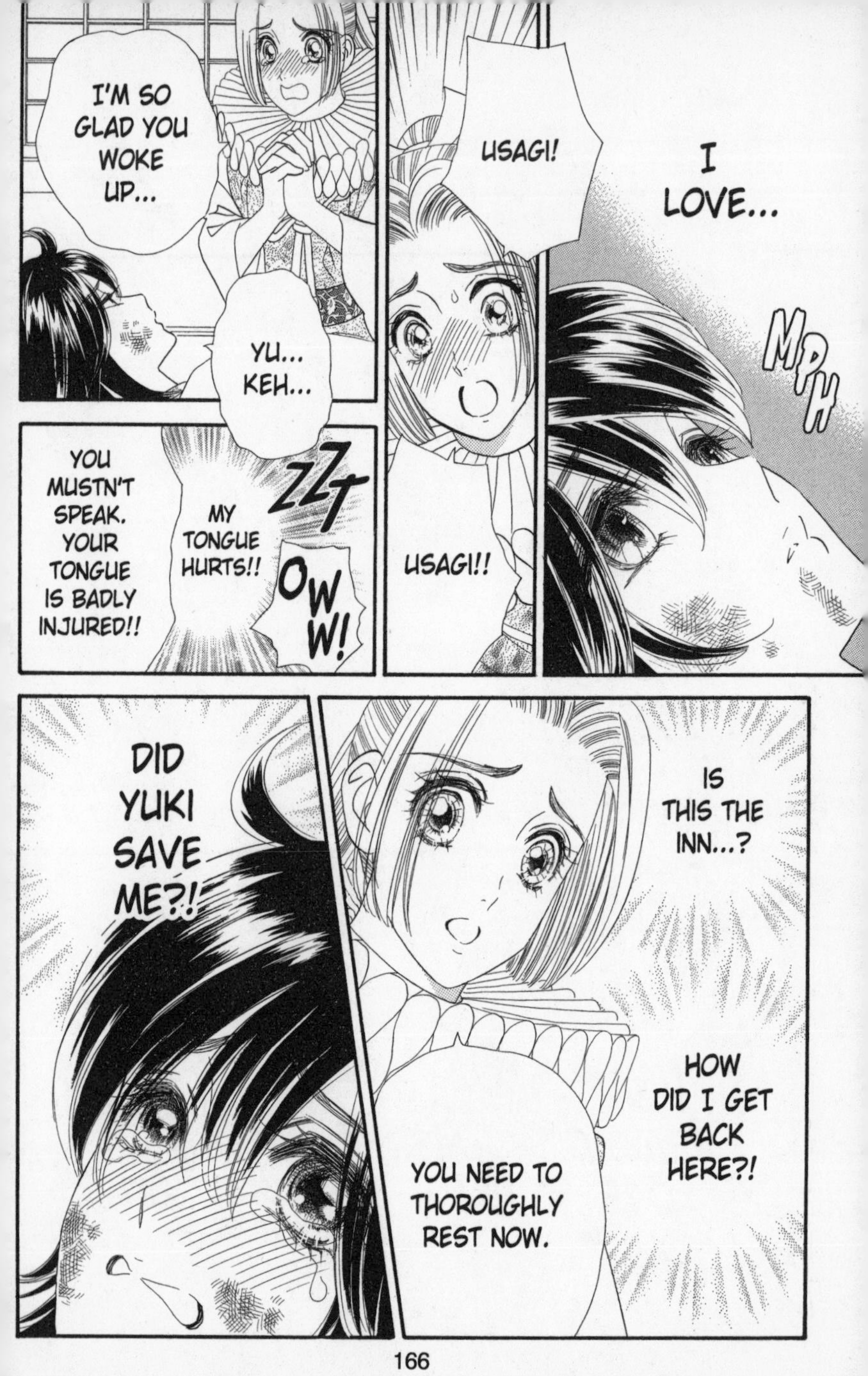
I LOVE...
MPH
USAGI!
USAGI!!
I'M SO GLAD YOU WOKE UP...
YU... KEH...
ZZT
OWW!
MY TONGUE HURTS!!
YOU MUSTN'T SPEAK. YOUR TONGUE IS BADLY INJURED!!
IS THIS THE INN...?
HOW DID I GET BACK HERE?!
YOU NEED TO THOROUGHLY REST NOW.
DID YUKI SAVE ME?!

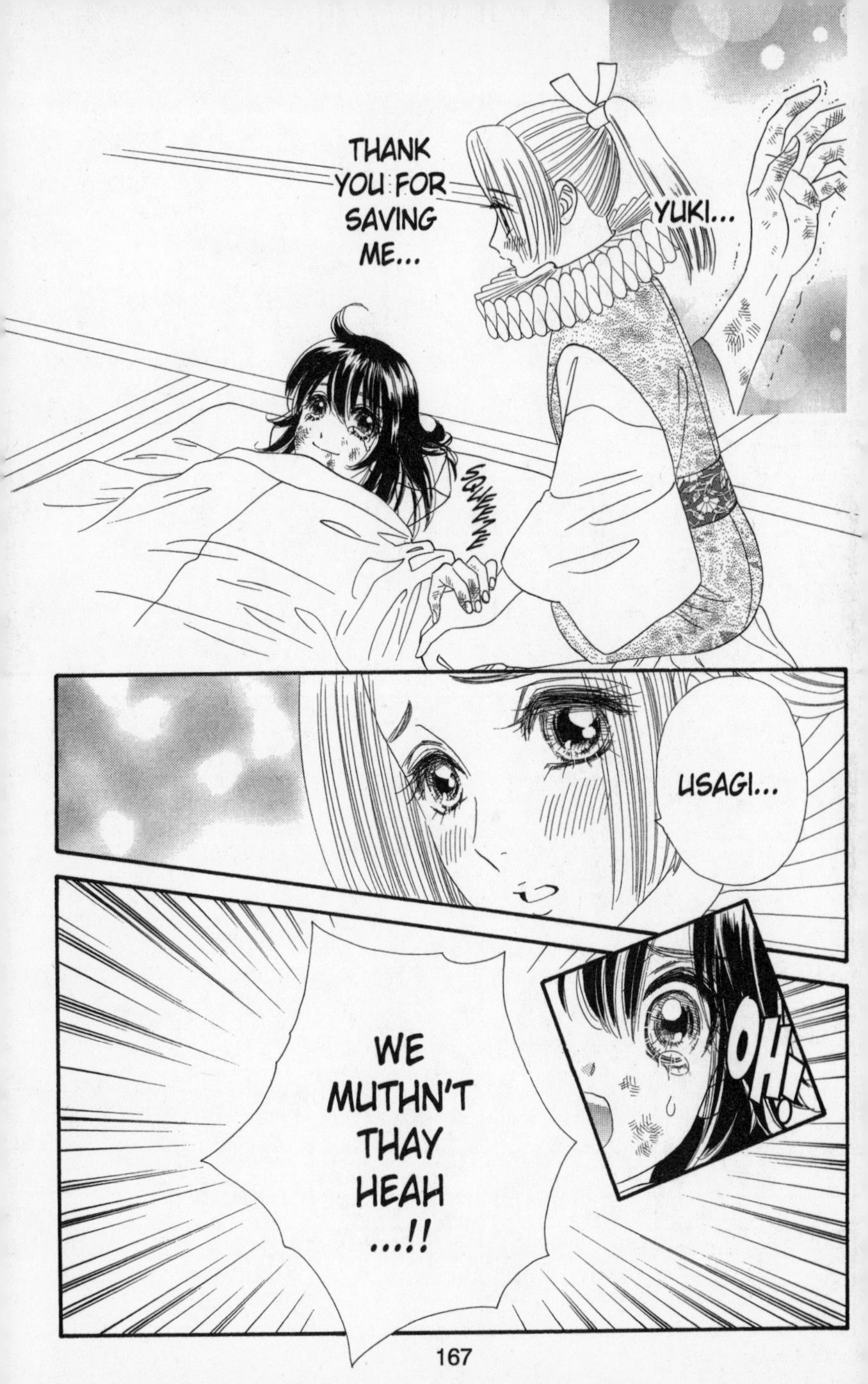
YUKI...
THANK YOU FOR SAVING ME...
SQUEEZE
USAGI...
OH!
WE MUTHN'T THAY HEAH ...!!

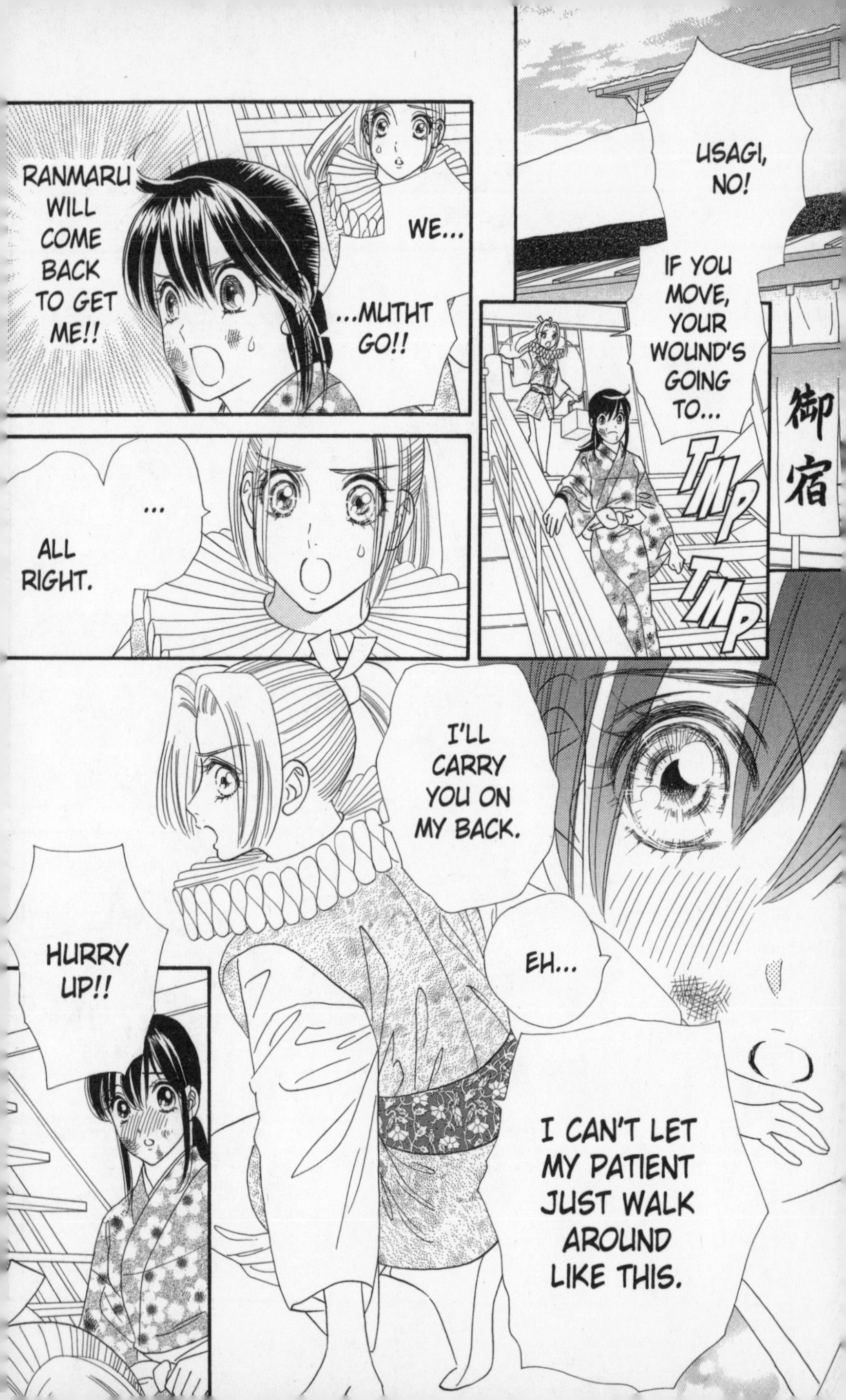
USAGI, NO!
IF YOU MOVE, YOUR WOUND'S GOING TO...
御宿
TMP
TMP
RANMARU WILL COME BACK TO GET ME!!
WE...
...MUTHT GO!!
...
ALL RIGHT.
I'LL CARRY YOU ON MY BACK.
EH...
I CAN'T LET MY PATIENT JUST WALK AROUND LIKE THIS.
HURRY UP!!

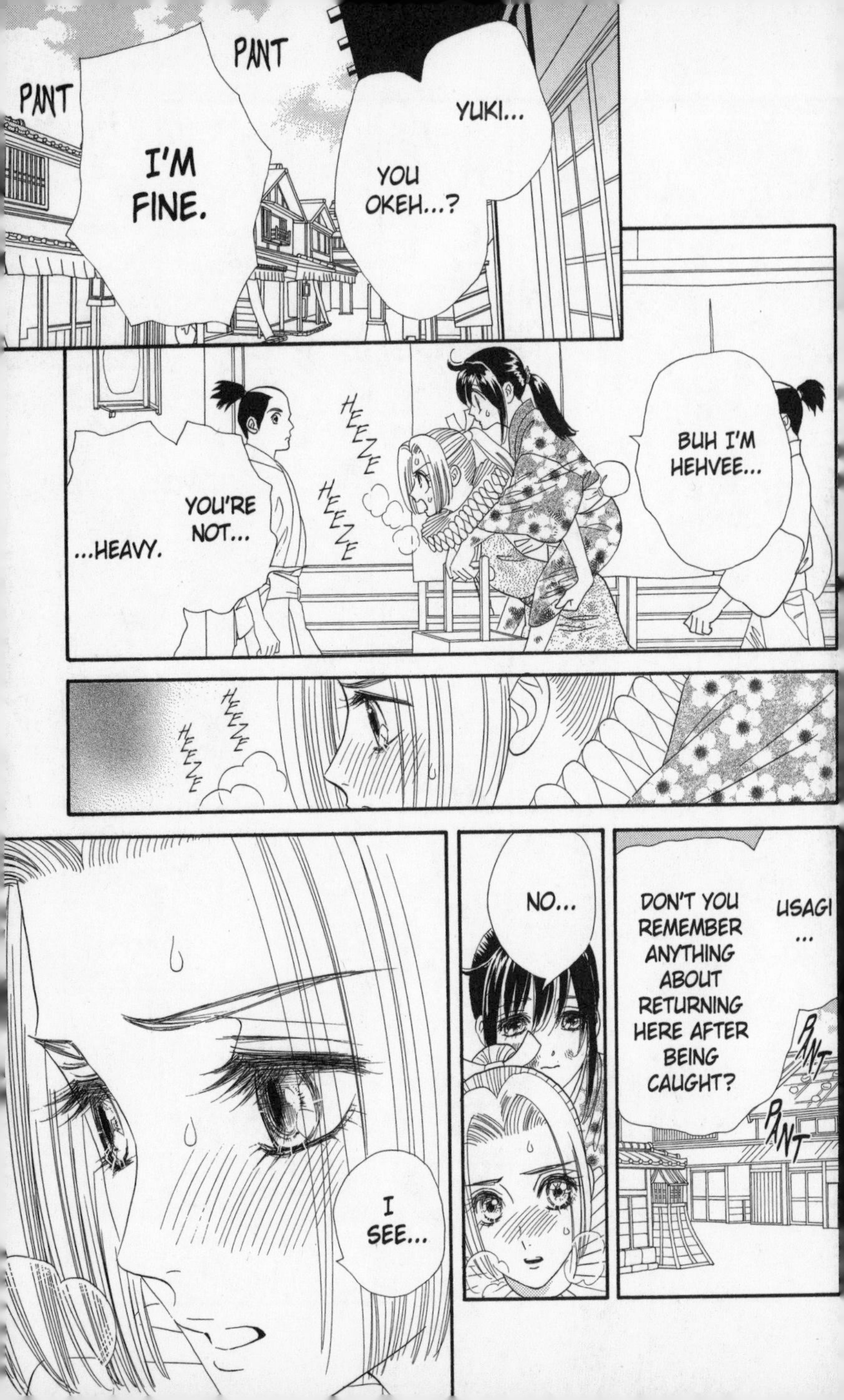
YUKI... YOU OKEH...?
PANT
PANT
I'M FINE.
BUH I'M HEHVEE...
HEEZE
HEEZE
YOU'RE NOT...
...HEAVY.
HEEZE
HEEZE
USAGI ...
PANT
PANT
DON'T YOU REMEMBER ANYTHING ABOUT RETURNING HERE AFTER BEING CAUGHT?
NO...
I SEE...

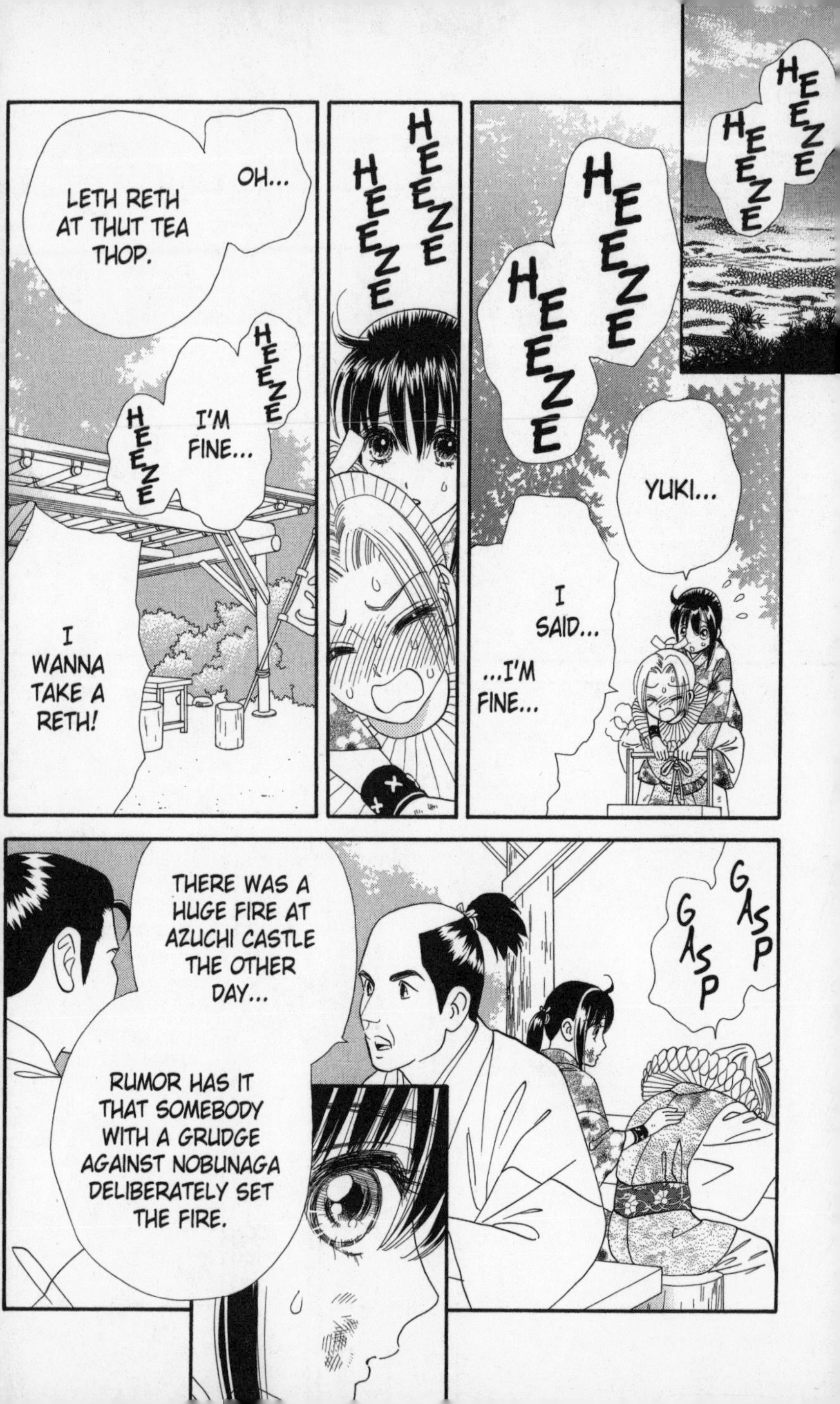
HEEZE HEEZE
HEEZE HEEZE
YUKI...
I SAID...
...I'M FINE...
HEEZE HEEZE
OH...
LETH RETH AT THUT TEA THOP.
HEEZE HEEZE
I'M FINE...
I WANNA TAKE A RETH!
GASP GASP
THERE WAS A HUGE FIRE AT AZUCHI CASTLE THE OTHER DAY...
RUMOR HAS IT THAT SOMEBODY WITH A GRUDGE AGAINST NOBUNAGA DELIBERATELY SET THE FIRE.

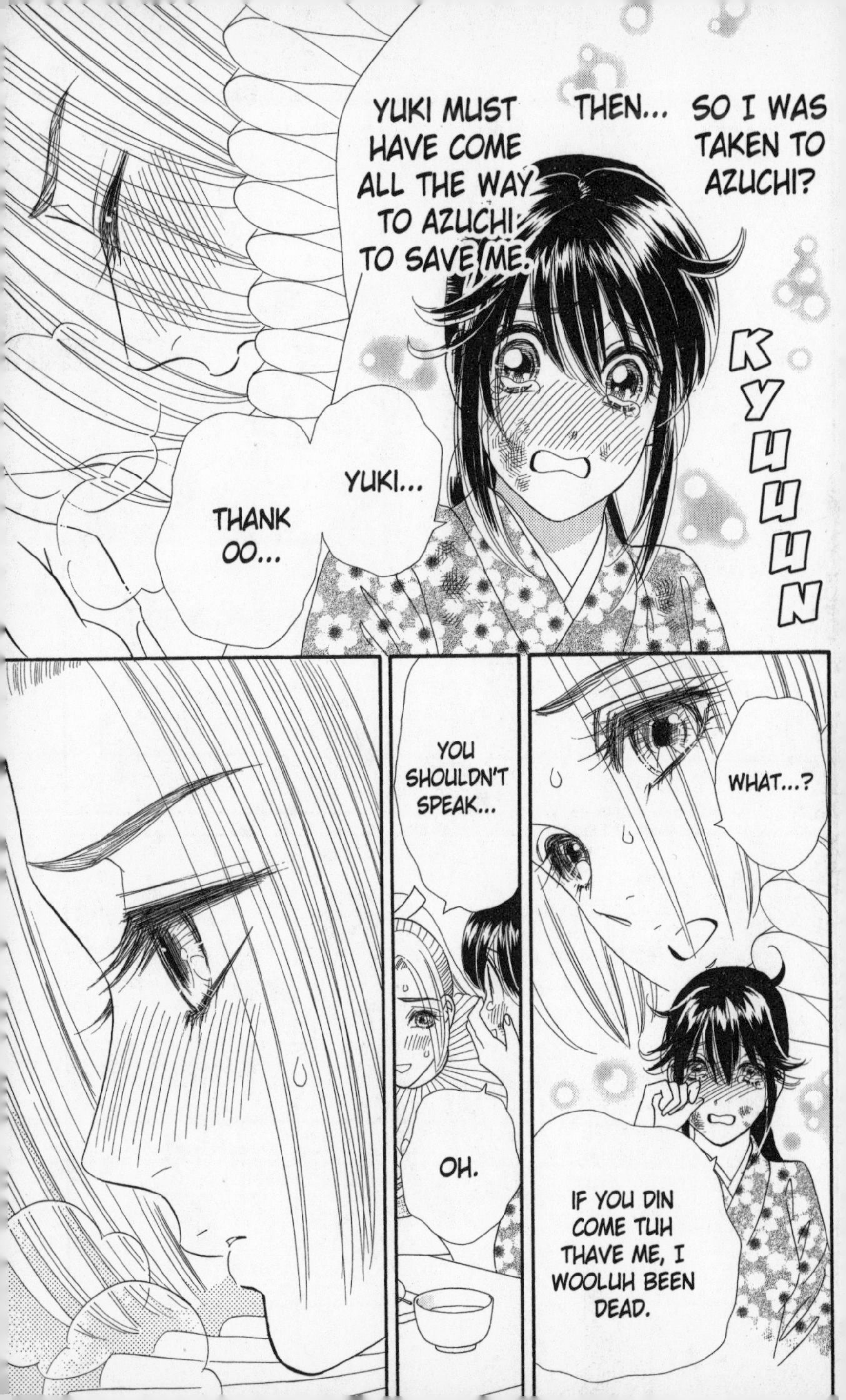
SO I WAS TAKEN TO AZUCHI?
THEN...
YUKI MUST HAVE COME ALL THE WAY TO AZUCHI TO SAVE ME.
KYUUUUN
YUKI...
THANK OO...
WHAT...?
IF YOU DIN COME TUH THAVE ME, I WOOLUH BEEN DEAD.
YOU SHOULDN'T SPEAK...
OH.

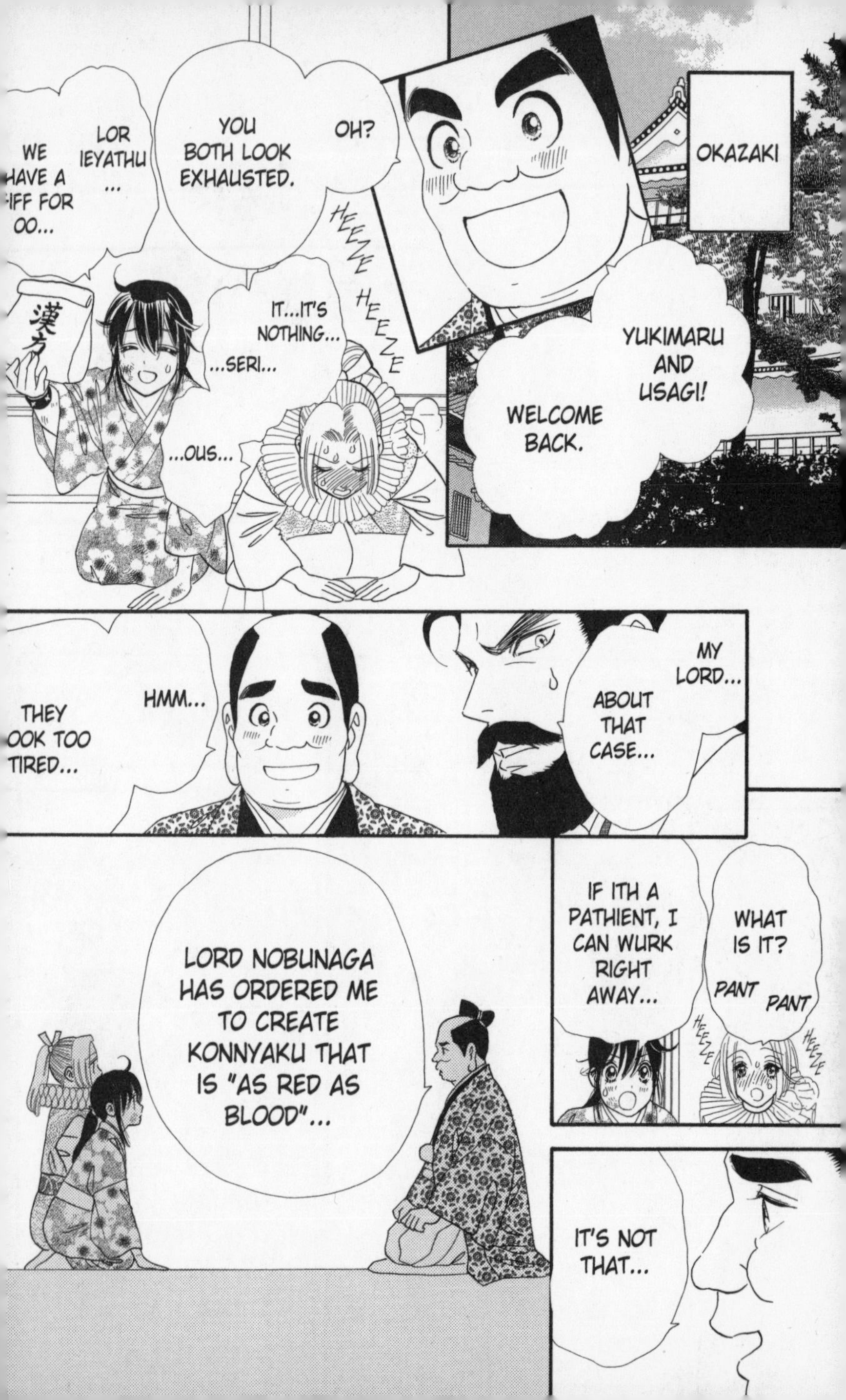
OKAZAKI
YUKIMARU AND USAGI!
WELCOME BACK.
OH?
YOU BOTH LOOK EXHAUSTED.
HEEZE HEEZE
LOR IEYATHU ...
WE HAVE A IFF FOR OO...
漢方
IT...IT'S NOTHING...
...SERI...
...OUS...
MY LORD...
ABOUT THAT CASE...
HMM...
THEY OOK TOO TIRED...
WHAT IS IT?
PANT PANT
HEEZE
HEEZE
IF ITH A PATHIENT, I CAN WURK RIGHT AWAY...
IT'S NOT THAT...
LORD NOBUNAGA HAS ORDERED ME TO CREATE KONNYAKU THAT IS "AS RED AS BLOOD"...

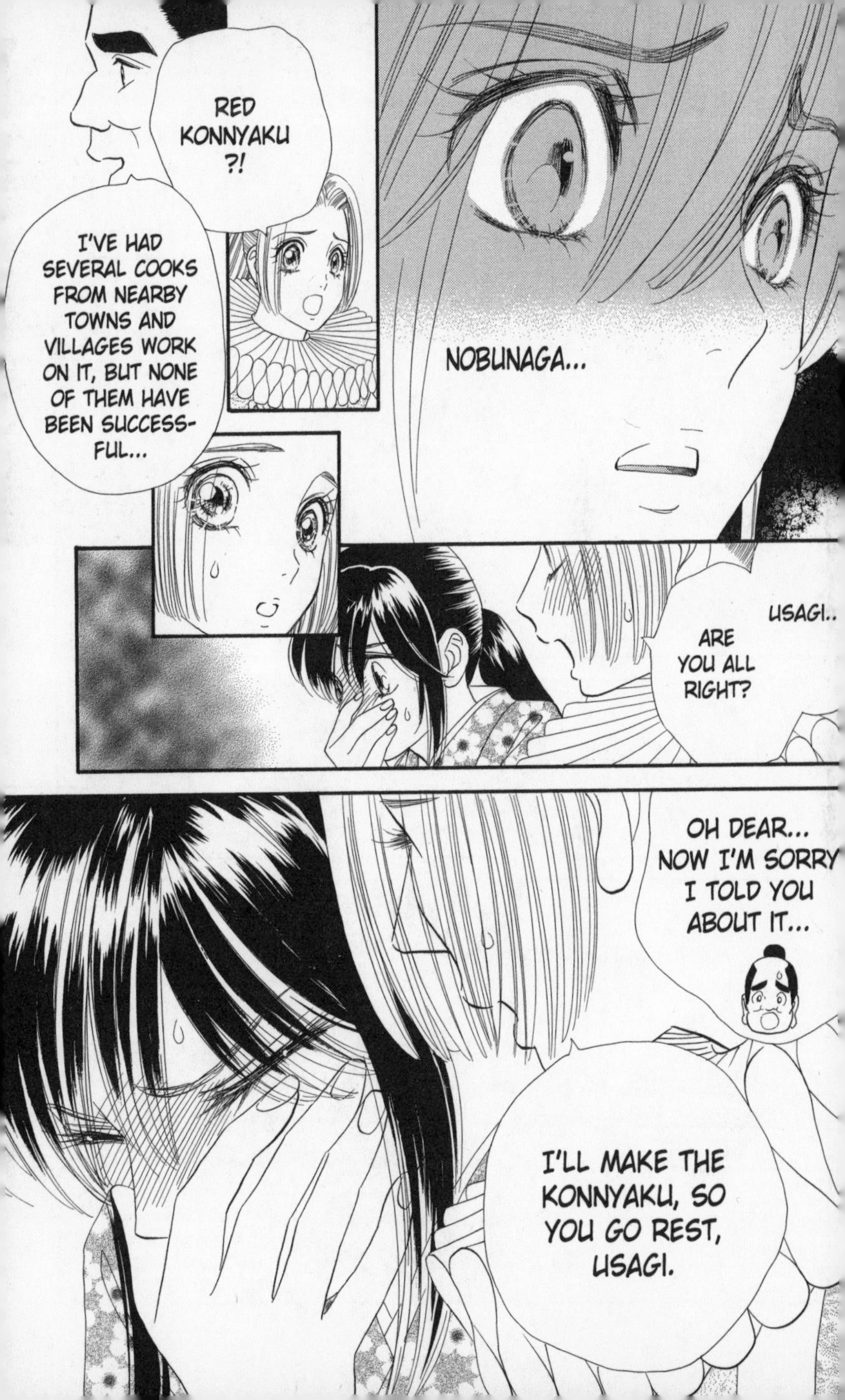
NOBUNAGA...
RED KONNYAKU ?!
I'VE HAD SEVERAL COOKS FROM NEARBY TOWNS AND VILLAGES WORK ON IT, BUT NONE OF THEM HAVE BEEN SUCCESS-FUL...
USAGI..
ARE YOU ALL RIGHT?
OH DEAR... NOW I'M SORRY I TOLD YOU ABOUT IT...
I'LL MAKE THE KONNYAKU, SO YOU GO REST, USAGI.

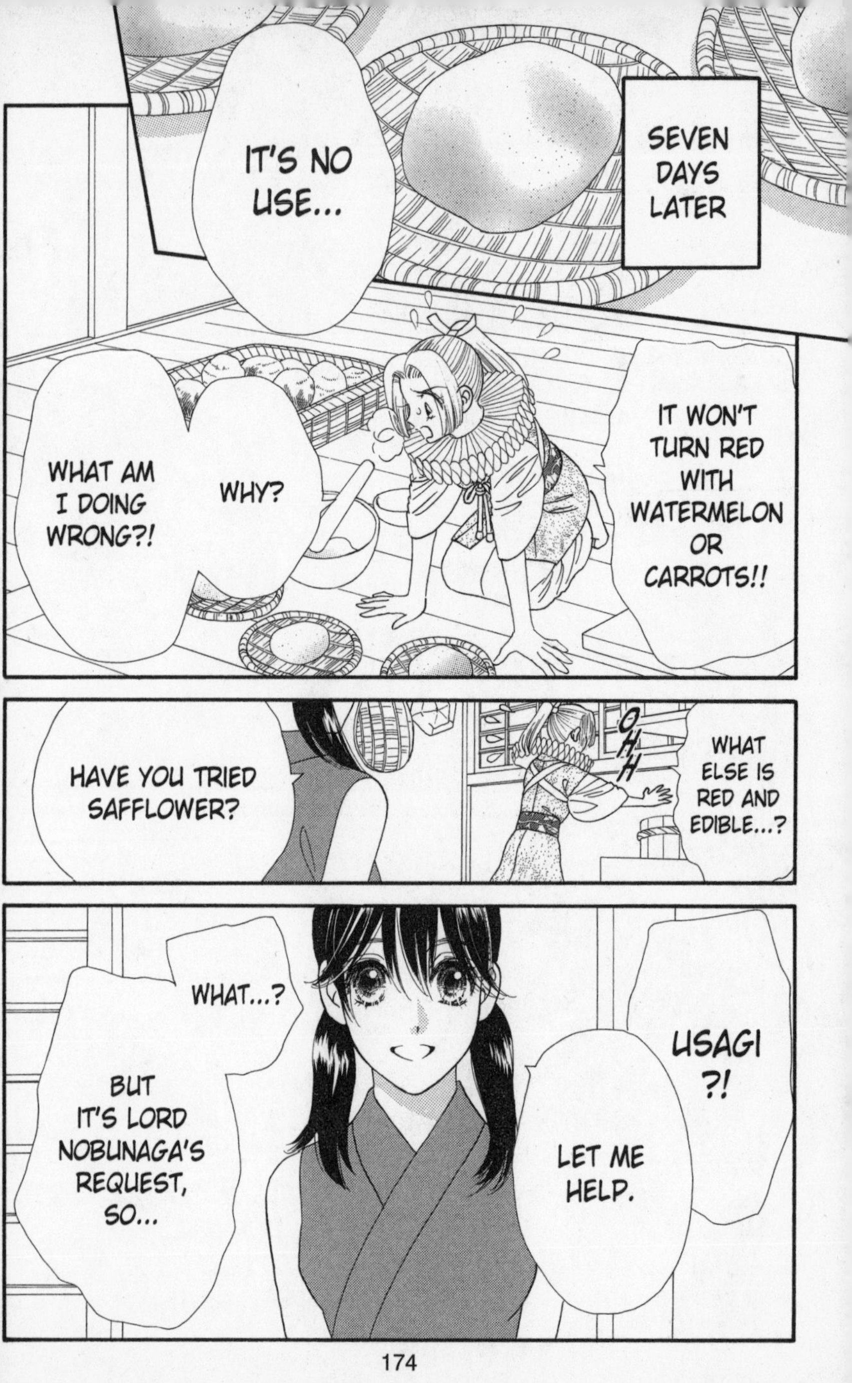
SEVEN DAYS LATER
IT'S NO USE...
IT WON'T TURN RED WITH WATERMELON OR CARROTS!!
WHY?
WHAT AM I DOING WRONG?!
WHAT ELSE IS RED AND EDIBLE...?
OHH
HAVE YOU TRIED SAFFLOWER?
USAGI ?!
LET ME HELP.
WHAT...?
BUT IT'S LORD NOBUNAGA'S REQUEST, SO...

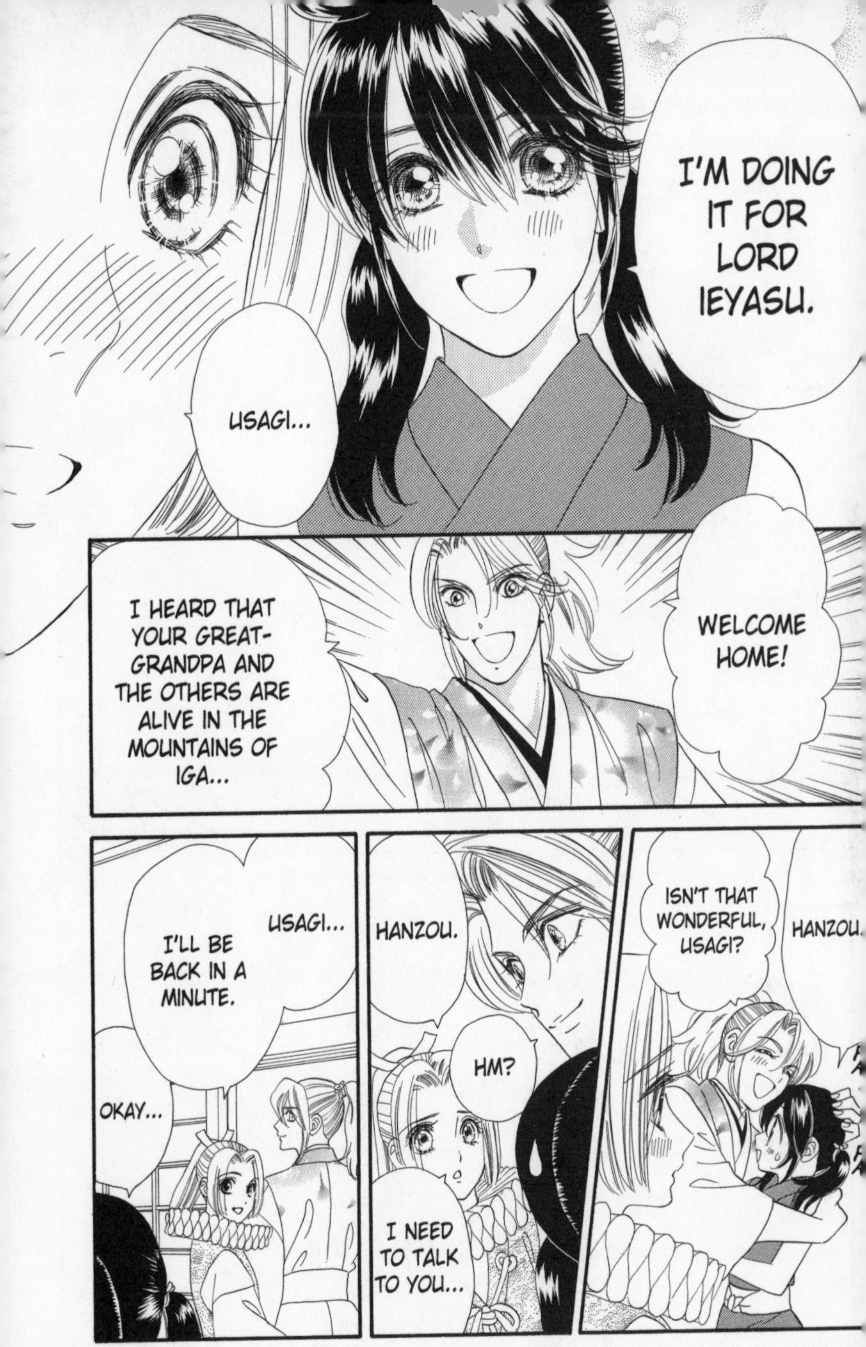
I'M DOING IT FOR LORD IEYASU.
USAGI...
WELCOME HOME!
I HEARD THAT YOUR GREAT-GRANDPA AND THE OTHERS ARE ALIVE IN THE MOUNTAINS OF IGA...
HANZOU.
ISN'T THAT WONDERFUL, USAGI?
HANZOU.
HM?
I NEED TO TALK TO YOU...
USAGI...
I'LL BE BACK IN A MINUTE.
OKAY...

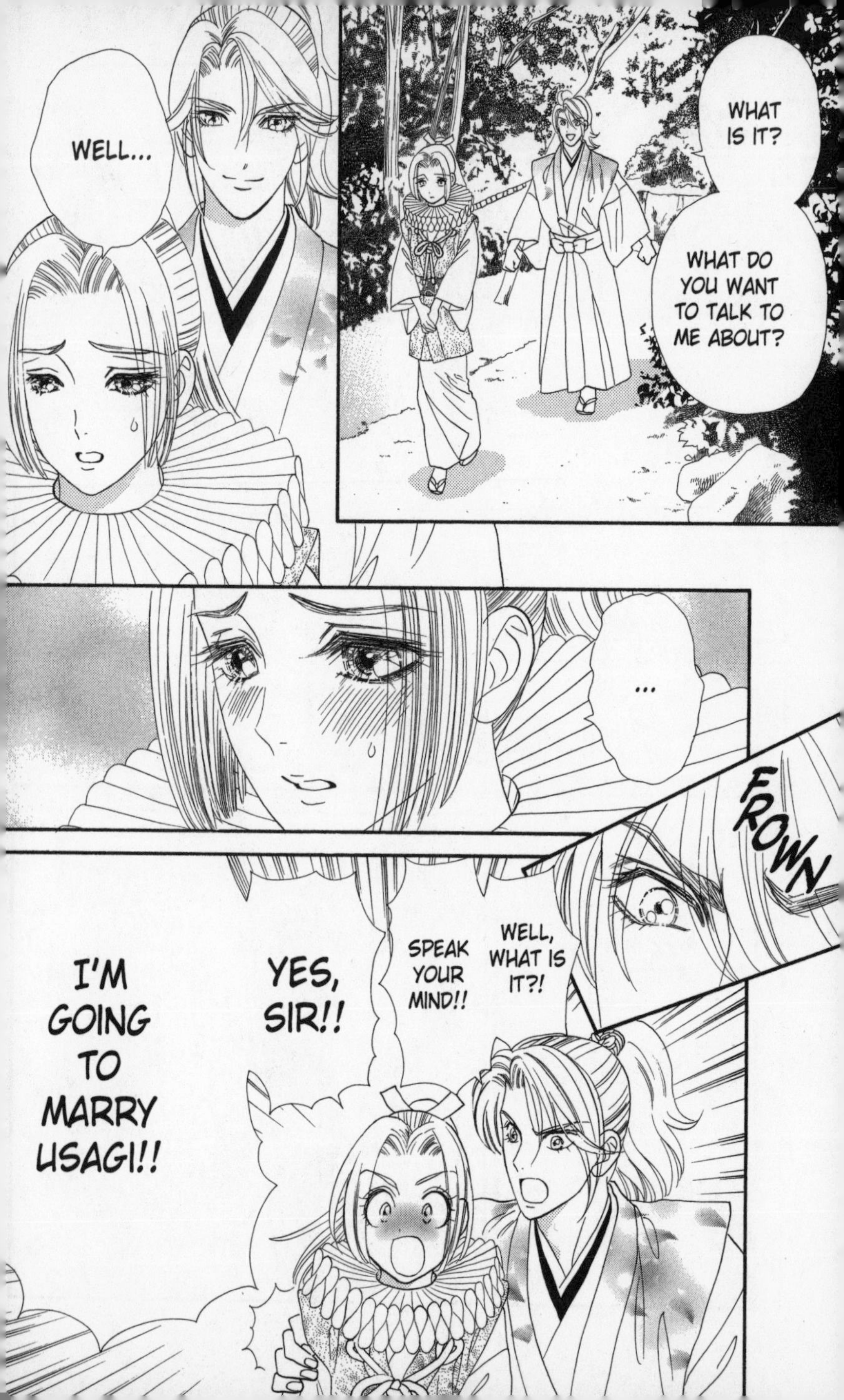
WHAT IS IT?
WHAT DO YOU WANT TO TALK TO ME ABOUT?
WELL...
...
FROWN
WELL, WHAT IS IT?!
SPEAK YOUR MIND!!
YES, SIR!!
I'M GOING TO MARRY USAGI!!

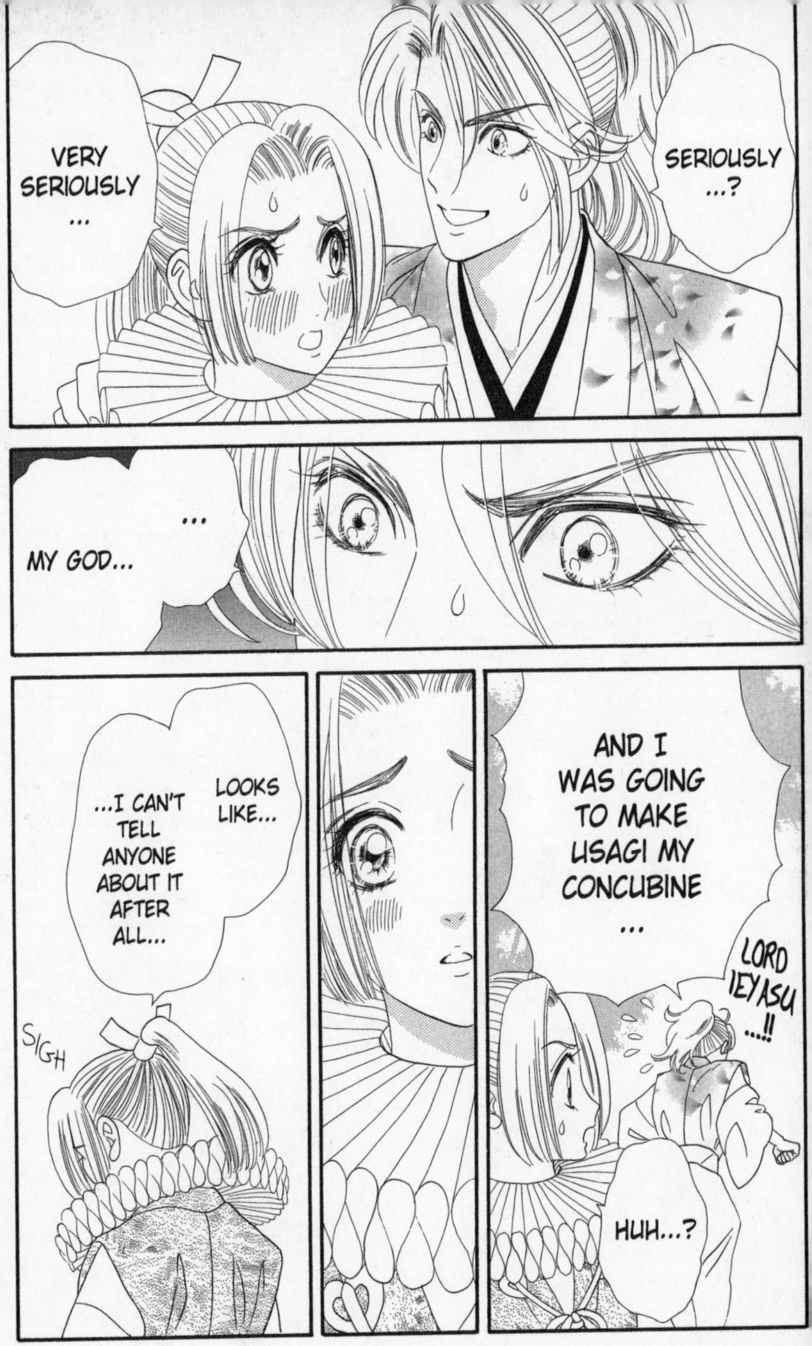
SERIOUSLY ...?
VERY SERIOUSLY ...
... MY GOD...
AND I WAS GOING TO MAKE USAGI MY CONCUBINE ...
LORD IEYASU ...!!
HUH...?
LOOKS LIKE...
...I CAN'T TELL ANYONE ABOUT IT AFTER ALL...
SIGH

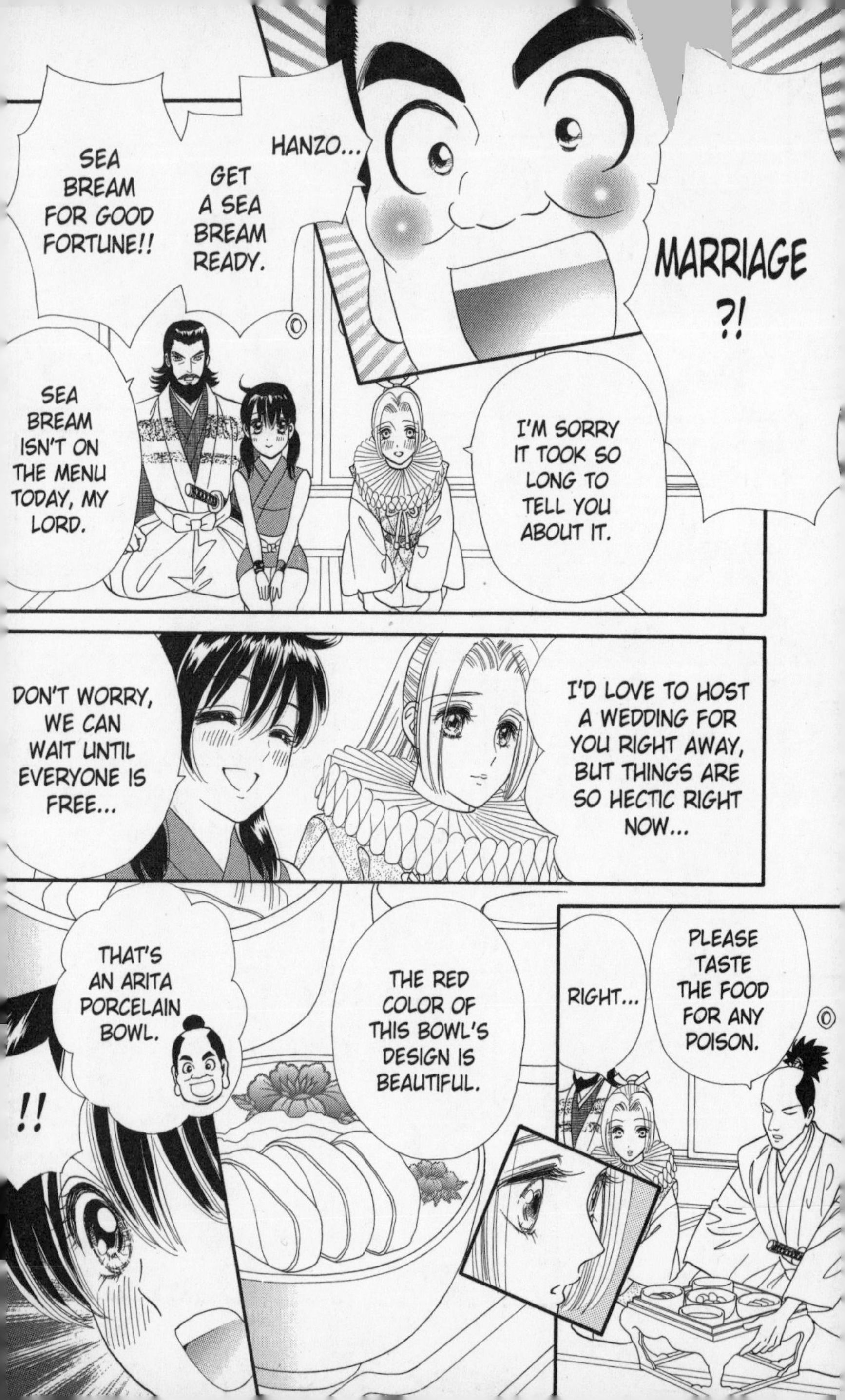
MARRIAGE ?!
HANZO...
GET A SEA BREAM READY.
SEA BREAM FOR GOOD FORTUNE!!
I'M SORRY IT TOOK SO LONG TO TELL YOU ABOUT IT.
SEA BREAM ISN'T ON THE MENU TODAY, MY LORD.
I'D LOVE TO HOST A WEDDING FOR YOU RIGHT AWAY, BUT THINGS ARE SO HECTIC RIGHT NOW...
DON'T WORRY, WE CAN WAIT UNTIL EVERYONE IS FREE...
PLEASE TASTE THE FOOD FOR ANY POISON.
RIGHT...
THE RED COLOR OF THIS BOWL'S DESIGN IS BEAUTIFUL.
THAT'S AN ARITA PORCELAIN BOWL.
!!

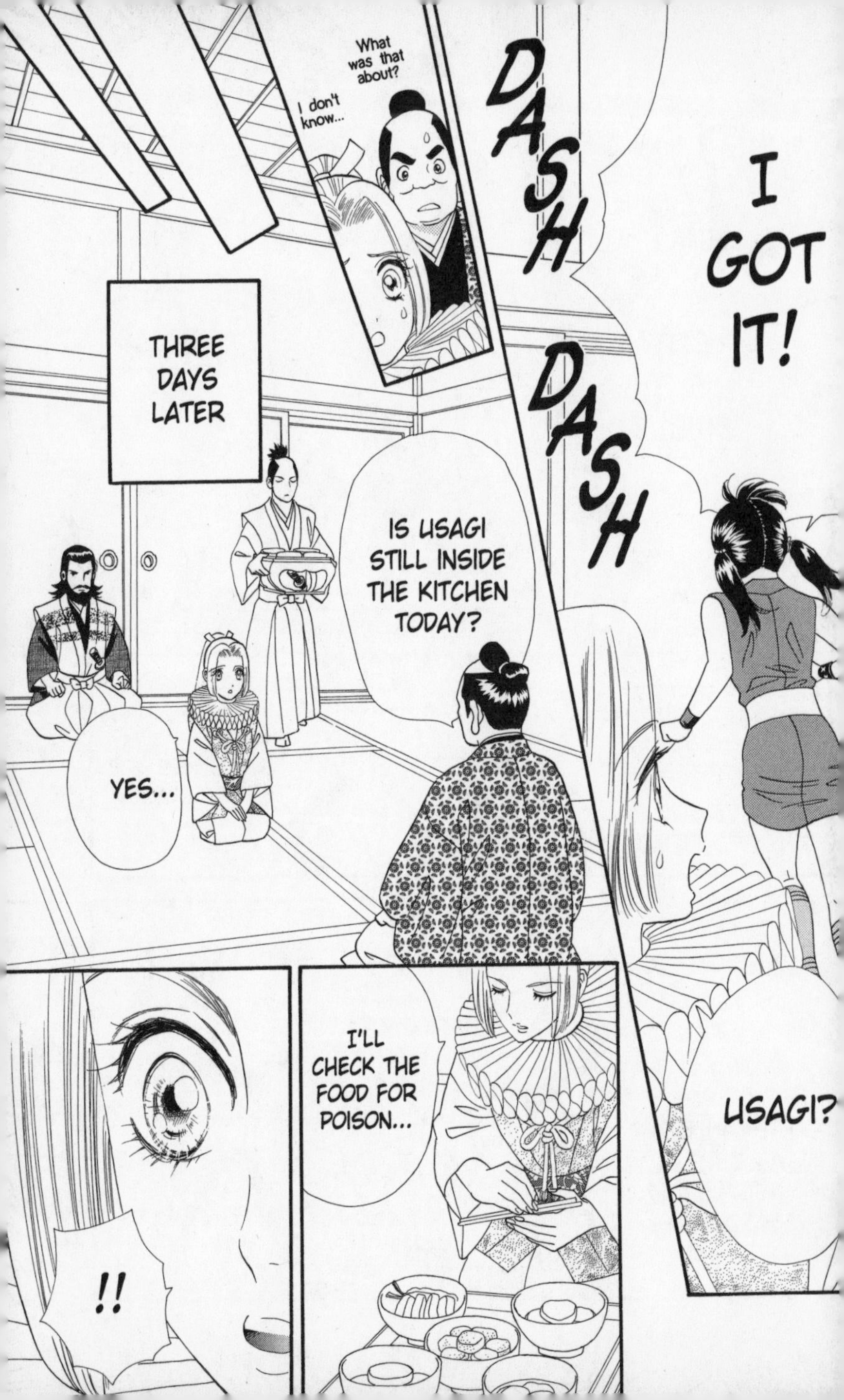

I GOT IT!
DASH DASH
USAGI?
What was that about?
I don't know...
THREE DAYS LATER
IS USAGI STILL INSIDE THE KITCHEN TODAY?
YES...
I'LL CHECK THE FOOD FOR POISON...
!!

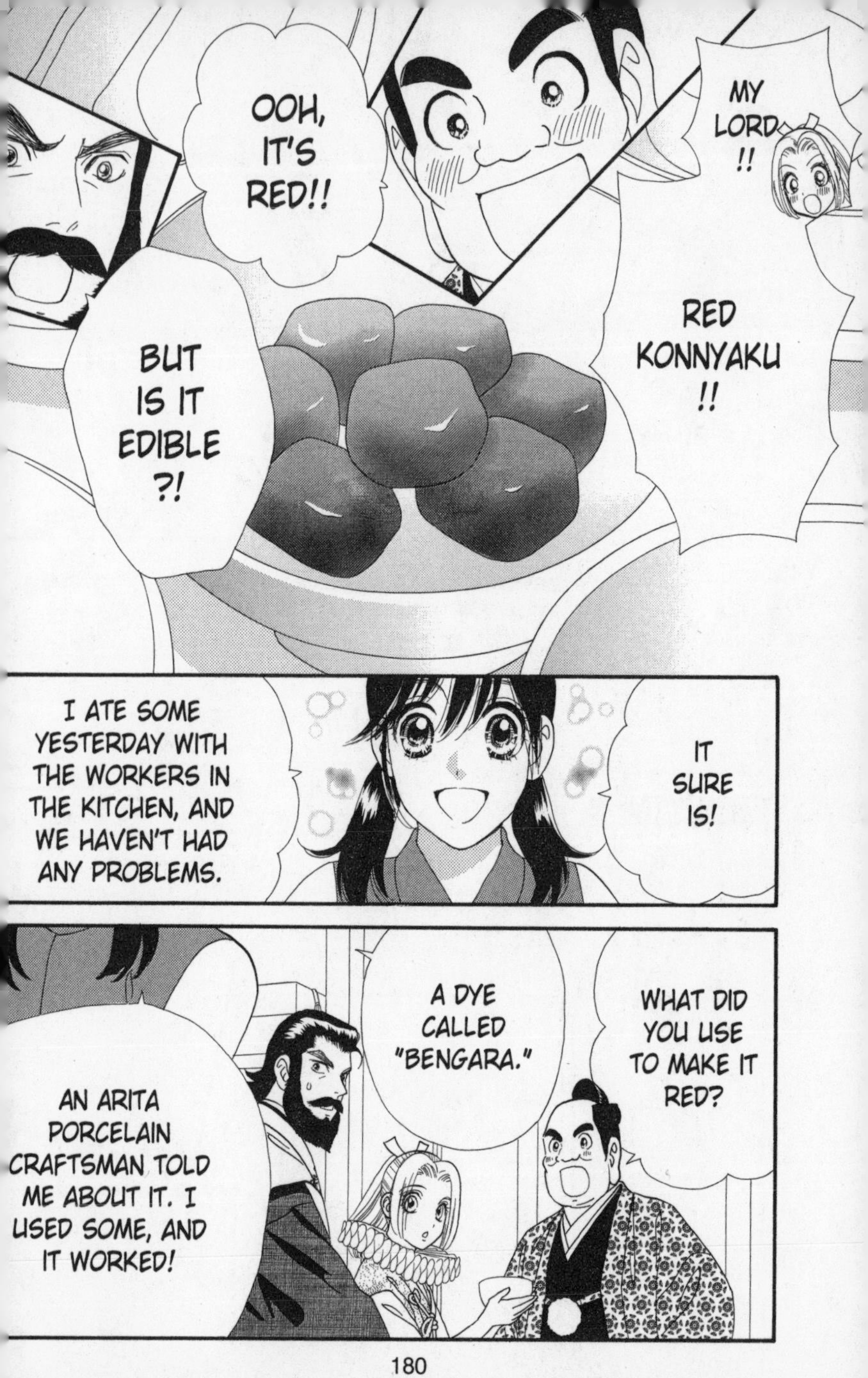
MY LORD!!
OOH, IT'S RED!!
RED KONNYAKU!!
BUT IS IT EDIBLE?!
IT SURE IS!
I ATE SOME YESTERDAY WITH THE WORKERS IN THE KITCHEN, AND WE HAVEN'T HAD ANY PROBLEMS.
WHAT DID YOU USE TO MAKE IT RED?
A DYE CALLED "BENGARA."
AN ARITA PORCELAIN CRAFTSMAN TOLD ME ABOUT IT. I USED SOME, AND IT WORKED!

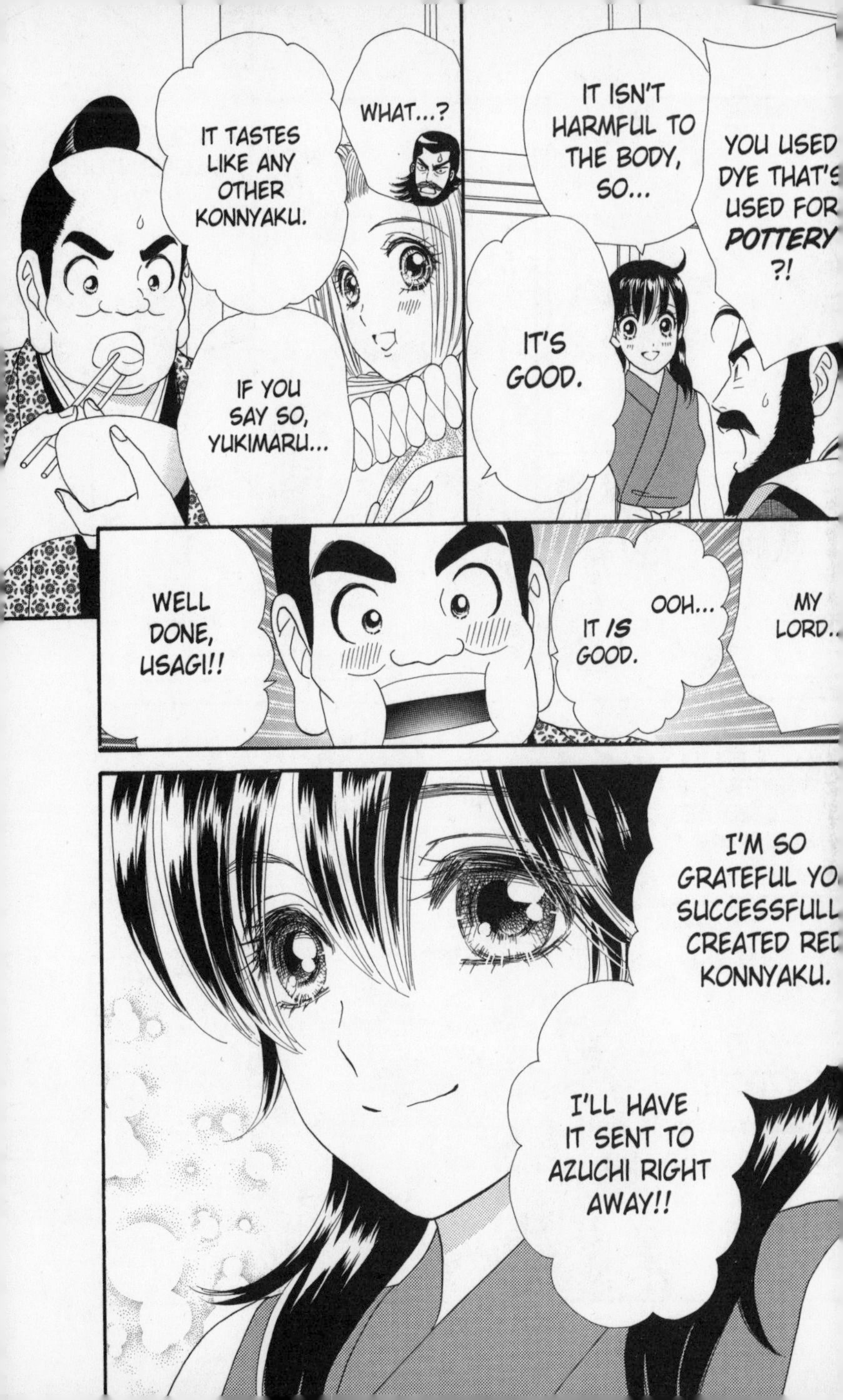
YOU USED DYE THAT'S USED FOR *POTTERY* ?!
IT ISN'T HARMFUL TO THE BODY, SO...
IT'S GOOD.
WHAT...?
IT TASTES LIKE ANY OTHER KONNYAKU.
IF YOU SAY SO, YUKIMARU...
MY LORD..
OOH...
IT *IS* GOOD.
WELL DONE, USAGI!!
I'M SO GRATEFUL YO SUCCESSFULL CREATED RE KONNYAKU.
I'LL HAVE IT SENT TO AZUCHI RIGHT AWAY!!

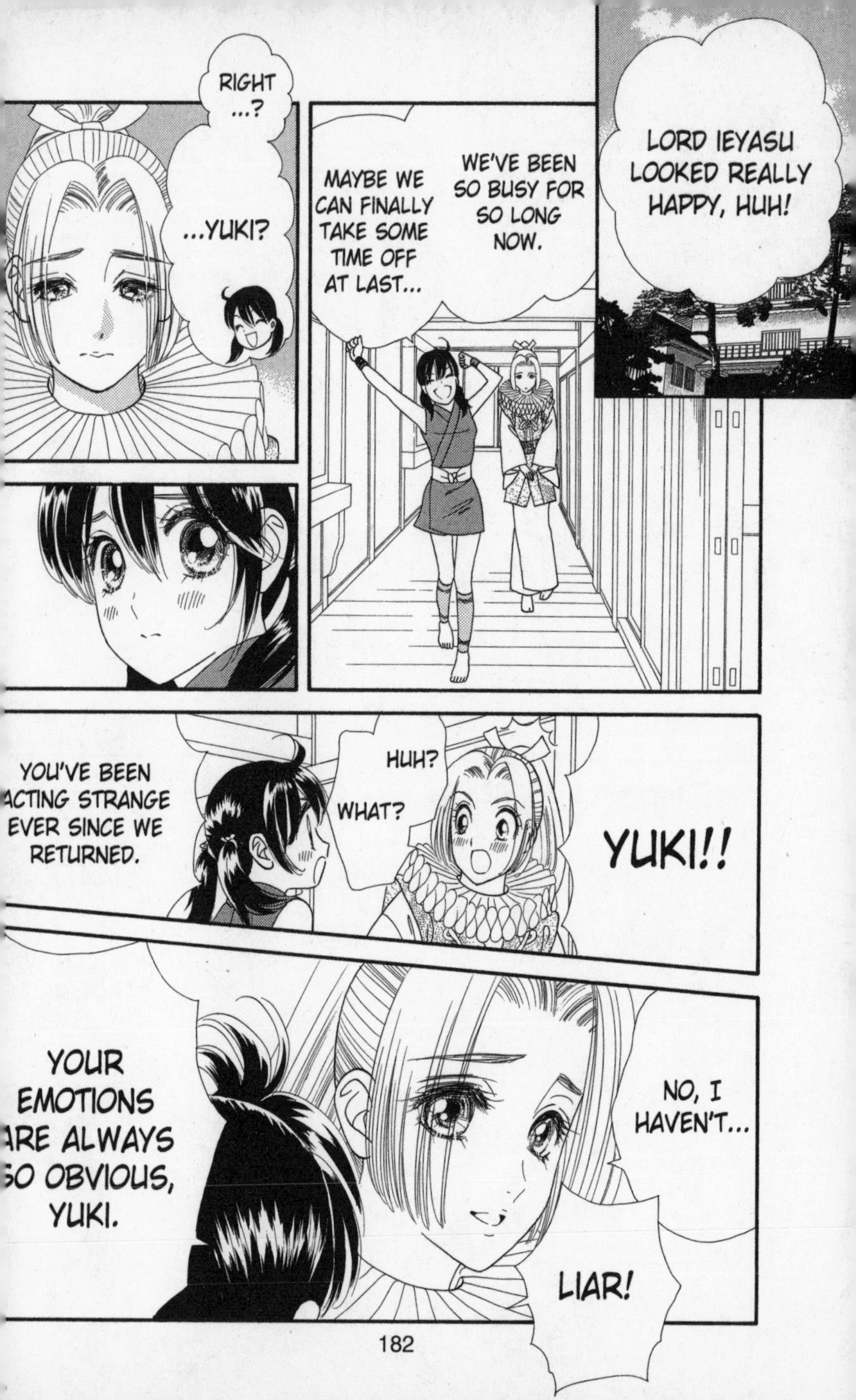
LORD IEYASU LOOKED REALLY HAPPY, HUH!
WE'VE BEEN SO BUSY FOR SO LONG NOW.
MAYBE WE CAN FINALLY TAKE SOME TIME OFF AT LAST...
RIGHT ...?
...YUKI?
YUKI!!
HUH?
WHAT?
YOU'VE BEEN ACTING STRANGE EVER SINCE WE RETURNED.
NO, I HAVEN'T...
LIAR!
YOUR EMOTIONS ARE ALWAYS SO OBVIOUS, YUKI.

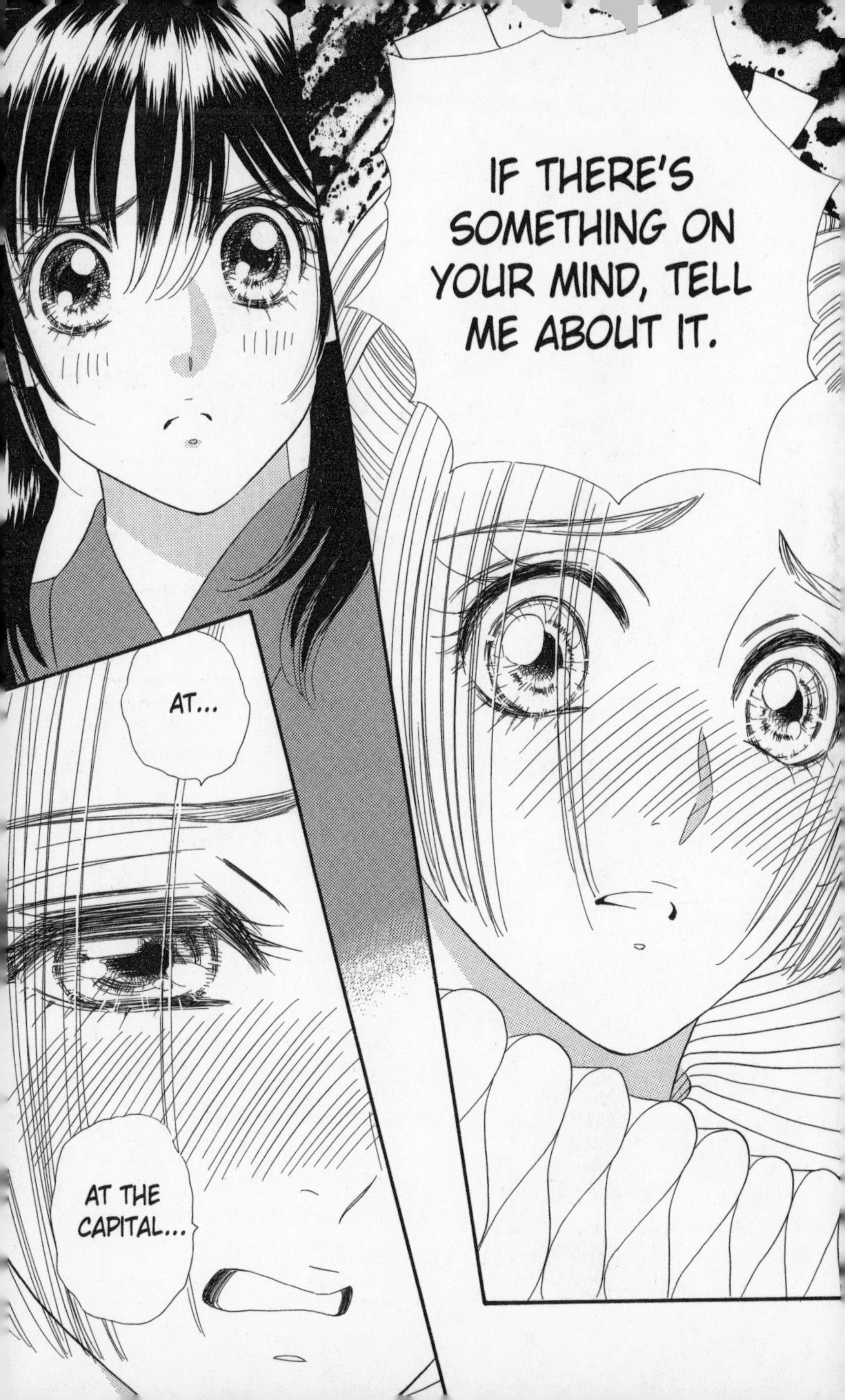
IF THERE'S SOMETHING ON YOUR MIND, TELL ME ABOUT IT.
AT...
AT THE CAPITAL...

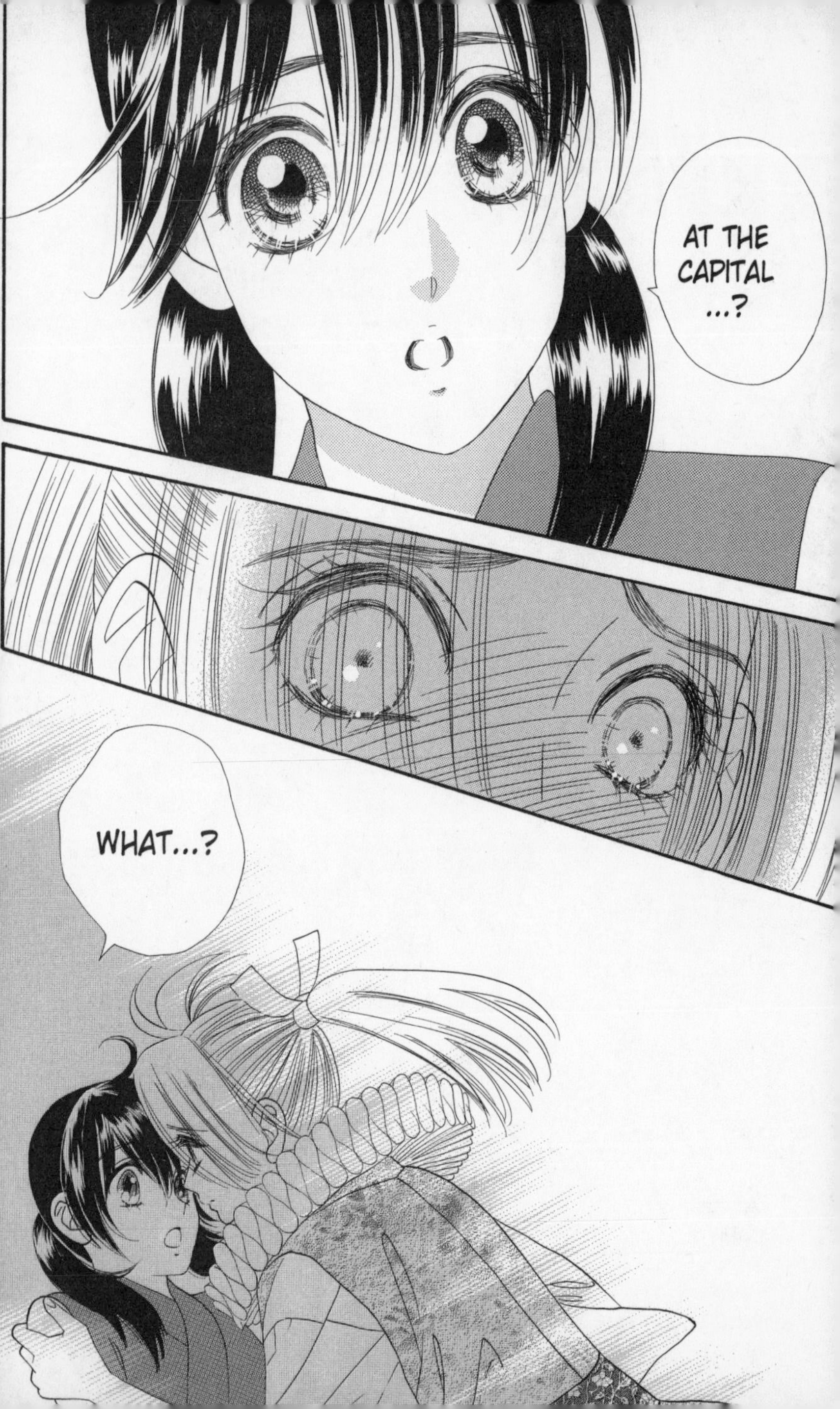
AT THE CAPITAL ...?
WHAT...?

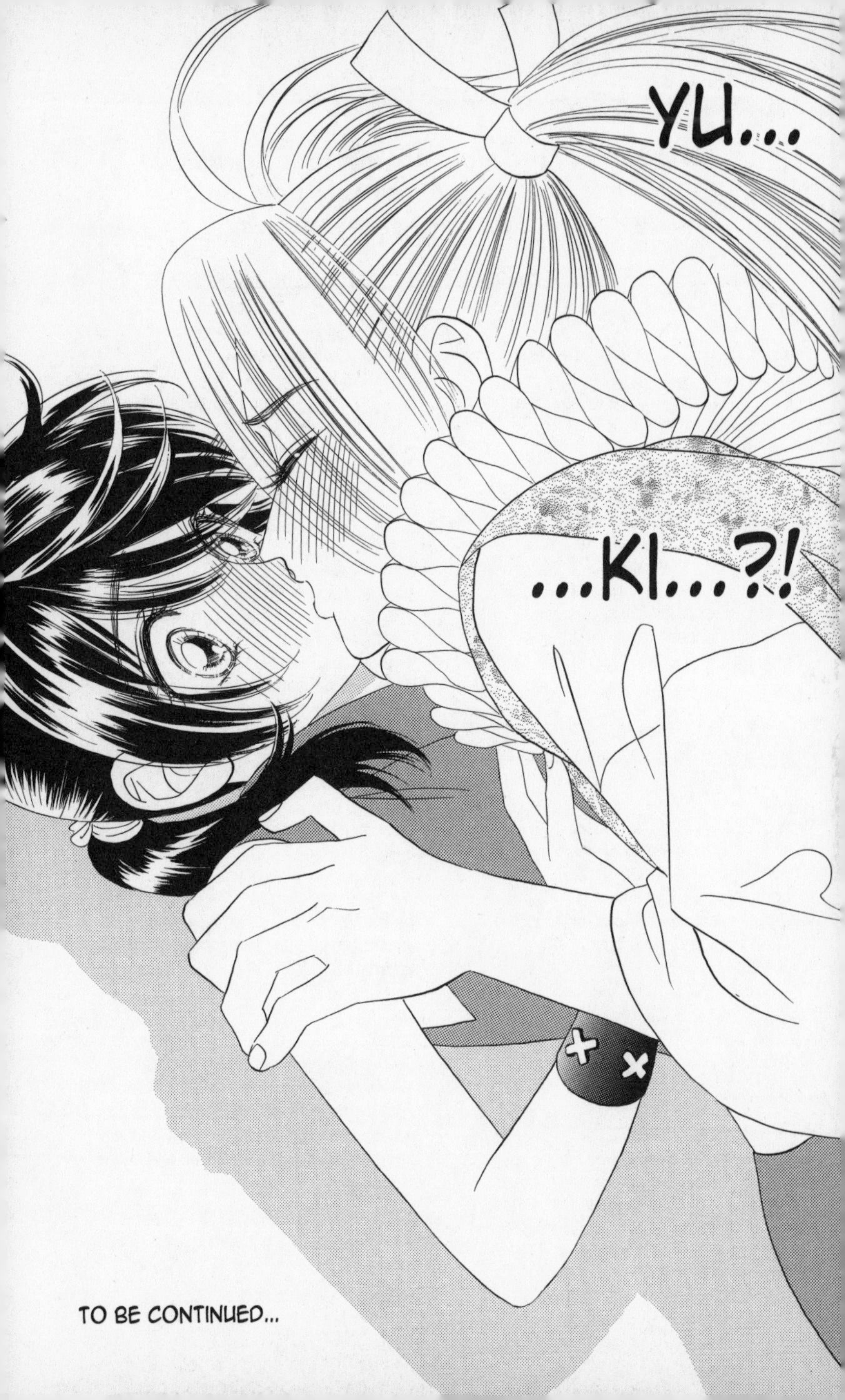
YU...
...KI...?!
TO BE CONTINUED...

> *The ways of the ninja are mysterious indeed, so here is a glossary of terms to help you navigate the intricacies of their world.*

Page 16, panel 3: Okazaki Castle
Okazaki Castle is in the city of Okazaki in Aichi prefecture. This castle was home to various leaders throughout history, including Tokugawa Ieyasu. Though demolished in 1873, the castle was reconstructed in 1959.

Page 23, panel 3: Kunoichi
A term often used for female ninja. The word is spelled くノ一, and when combined, the letters form the kanji for woman, 女。

Page 25, panel 2: Ninjutsu
Ninjutsu means the skill or ability of a ninja.

Page 35, panel 5: Sakai
Sakai is a city in Osaka prefecture that is one of the largest and most important seaports in Japan. Once known for samurai swords, Sakai is now famous for quality kitchen knives and other cutlery.

Page 118, panel 2: Dotera
A thickly padded overcoat worn in the winter.

Page 137, panel 1: Dogu
Dogu are clay figurines that were made during the Jomon period of ancient Japan. Their purpose remains unclear, but they were most likely used as effigies to which people could transfer illnesses and then destroy, clearing that person of the illness or misfortune.

Page 2: Oda Nobunaga
Oda Nobunaga lived from 1534 to 1582, and came close to unifying Japan. He is probably one of the most famous Japanese warlords. He was the first warlord to successfully incorporate the gun in battle and is notorious for his ruthlessness.

Page 2: Iga
Iga is a region on the island of Honshu and also the name of the famous ninja clan that originated there. Another area famous for its ninja is Kouga, in the Shiga prefecture on Honshu. Many books claim that these two ninja clans were mortal enemies, but in reality inter-ninja relations were not as bad as stories might suggest.

Page 2: Tokugawa Ieyasu
Tokugawa Ieyasu (1543-1616) was the first Shogun of the Tokugawa Shogunate. He made a small fishing village named Edo the center of his activities. Edo thrived and became a huge town, and was later renamed Tokyo, the present capital.

Page 6, panel 4: Odawara Castle
Odawara Castle was the stronghold of various rulers in Japanese history because of its strong defenses and strategic location. The original castle was eventually destroyed by the Meiji government, but it was rebuilt in 1960.

Page 146, panel 1: Ranmaru Mori
Ranmaru Mori was one of Oda Nobunaga's most famous vassals. He became Nobunaga' attendant at a young age and was recognize for his talent and loyalty.

Page 170, panel 5: Azuchi Castle
Azuchi Castle was one of Oda Nobunaga's main castles. It is located on the shores of Lake Biwa in Shiga prefecture. The castle's strategic location enabled Nobunaga to manage his foes more easily, namely the Uesugi clan to the north and the Mouri clan to the west.

Page 172, panel 7: Konnyaku
Konnyaku is a traditional Japanese jelly-like health food made from the starch of the "devil's tongue" plant (a relative of the sweet potato).

Page 178, panel 2: Sea Bream
In Japan, *tai* (sea bream) is often eaten during celebrations because the name is a wordplay on *medetai*, which means "happy occasion."

Page 178, panel 7: Arita Porcelain
A type of Japanese porcelain first made in 1616, Arita porcelain often has dragons, flowers, and sometimes bamboo as part of its design.

Page 180, panel 5: Bengara
Bengara is the Japanese term for the red-ocher dye imported from Bengal, India.

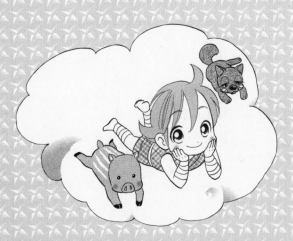

I started drawing the "Little Hanzo" mini manga since Mamezo is all grown up now. I wanted to draw little children, but it's really hard…!! I always take my time when I think of how to develop the story for the main manga. It's extremely difficult for the mini manga though, since I need to be more selective with the phrases and information to include in them. But although it's difficult, I do find it to be very worthwhile.

–Rinko Ueda

Rinko Ueda is from Nara prefecture. She enjoys listening to the radio, drama CDs, and Rakugo comedy performances. Her works include *Ryo*, a series based on the legend of Gojo Bridge; *Home*, a story about love crossing national boundaries; and *Tail of the Moon (Tsuki no Shippo)*, a romantic ninja comedy.

TAIL OF THE MOON
Vol. 13
The Shojo Beat Manga Edition

STORY & ART BY
RINKO UEDA

Translation & Adaptation/Tetsuichiro Miyaki
Touch-up Art & Lettering/Mark McMurray
Design/Izumi Hirayama
Editor/Amy Yu

Editor in Chief, Books/Alvin Lu
Editor in Chief, Magazines/Marc Weidenbaum
VP of Publishing Licensing/Rika Inouye
VP of Sales/Gonzalo Ferreyra
Sr. VP of Marketing/Liza Coppola
Publisher/Hyoe Narita

Printed in Canada

Published by VIZ Media, LLC
P.O. Box 77064
San Francisco, CA 94107

Shojo Beat Manga Edition
10 9 8 7 6 5 4 3 2 1
First printing, October 2008

www.viz.com   store.viz.com

Tell us what you think about Shojo Beat Manga!

Our survey is now available online. Go to:

shojobeat.com/mangasurvey

Help us make our product offerings better!